INTERACTIVE MULTIMEDIA

Edited by **Ioannis Deliyannis**

Interactive Multimedia
Edited by Ioannis Deliyannis

Published by InTech
Janeza Trdine 9, 51000 Rijeka, Croatia

Publishing Process Manager Daria Nahtigal

Technical Editor Teodora Smiljanic

Cover Designer InTech Design Team

Additional hard copies can be obtained from orders@intechopen.com

Interactive Multimedia, Edited by Ioannis Deliyannis
p. cm.
ISBN 978-953-51-0224-3

For EU product safety concerns:
IN TECH d.o.o., Prolaz Marije Krucifikse Kozulić 3, 51000 Rijeka, Croatia,
info@intechopen.com or visit our website at intechopen.com.

Meet the editor

Dr Ioannis Deliyannis holds a Computer Science Degree (1997) and a Ph.D in the field of Interactive Multimedia (2002) from the University of Wales. Today he is an appointed lecturer at the Department of Audio and Visual Arts, Ionian University, Corfu, Greece in the field of Interactive Multimedia and Digital Technology. His research interests include the development of User-Oriented Multimedia Technologies for Information Society, while he designs and implements experimental interactive multimedia systems for Interactive TV, Computer Games and New-Media Art applications. He is the Editor-in-Chief of the International Journal of Interactive Multimedia and the author of a series of research publications in the above fields, followed by books that target the experimental and creative aspects of the technologies involved. In his free time he enjoys competing at international sailing regattas all around the Mediterranean as the captain of the Ionian University Sailing Team and his Sigma 33.

Contents

Preface

The extended use of networking and the availability of multimedia processing and sharing applications have clearly gained momentum in the informationised society where Interactive Multimedia theories, technologies, applications and systems stage the principal role, as they furnish users with the necessary communication tools. In that respect, multimedia-enabled devices and tablet computers support fully featured interactive multimedia applications and cover wide-ranging interaction requirements from communication and business to games and interactive art. Although the interdisciplinary nature of interactive multimedia renders the field extremely rich in terms of the number of applications, it also presents great difficulties to those who wish to identify the interactive multimedia novelty under each, as they are published in disparate fields.

This book offers a unique insight on the research aspects of interactive multimedia, as it organises and presents novel scientific work, proven methodologies and interdisciplinary case studies that exhibit important advances under the areas of Interfaces and Interaction, Interactive Multimedia Learning, Teaching and Competence Diagnosis Systems, Interactive TV, Film and Multimedia Production and Video Processing. In that respect, interaction is identified as the common ingredient across these domains, offering the reader the ability to identify, isolate and utilise interdisciplinary solutions into the development of new interactive systems.

Dr Ioannis Deliyannis
Ionian University,
Department of Audio and Visual Arts,
Plateia Tsirigoti, Corfu,
Greece

Part 1

Interdisciplinary Issues of Interactive Multimedia

1

From Interactive to Experimental Multimedia

Ioannis Deliyannis
Department of Audio and Visual Arts,
Ionian University, Corfu,
Greece

1. Introduction

Perhaps the most dramatic Information Society development witnessed today is the wide availability of social networking capabilities for the users, orchestrated through the wide variety of virtual multimedia communication tools. Mobile and networked interactive multimedia applications are employed to promptly capture or create user-centered content that after being processed and enriched with the appropriate context is relayed back to the community. Tools destined to serve various purposes emerge in various fields including entertainment, marketing, education, engineering, scientific research, medicine, business, art and communication (Jain et al., 2011). In the literature, their popularity is attributed to social multimedia dynamics (Naaman, 2010), combined with the wide accessibility of networking and networked devices (Castells, 2011). Other important factors that allow interactive access to multimedia content include the availability of virtual multimedia-data storage technologies, streaming and content-discovery repositories, simplified URL-based information linking across social software applications, cloud infrastructures and reduced wireless internet-access cost.

Naturally, the extensive use of multimedia introduces a high content volume produced and shared today, which is commonly referred to as "Big Data" (Manovich, 2011, Boyd and Crawford, 2011). Its management requires advanced indexing, tracking (Pino and Di Salvo, 2011) and retrieval techniques to be applied (Pino and Di Salvo, 2011, Lu et al., 2011, Lew et al., 2006). Currently, leading social software systems employ multimedia metadata standards and methods that permit direct content categorisation and effortless indexing through storage of temporal, geographical or context-based information alongside the submitted content (Schallauer et al., 2011). In some instances, partial metadata information may be added directly; for instance when a photograph or a video is captured, a GPS-enabled camera presents the user with the option to add a timestamp and location-coordinates. Additional information may be embedded by the user during the process of content-submission, as a result of social interaction where other users identify themselves in the audio-visual content, or via post-processing of image, audio and video analysis algorithms for landmark, voice and facial recognition (Wang, 2012, Mahapatra et al., 2011). Context exploitation poses practical challenges (Riek and Robinson, 2011), as it requires analysis on the situational context, identification of the social roles of individuals, the cultural context and the social norms that are in effect at that time (Hanjalic, 2012). Most algorithmic content-context analysis approaches suffer from various inefficiencies, particularly when they are employed to assess and decide on the social context captured in the content. Studies that relate the functionality of interactive multimedia systems to their content complexity have identified multiple areas that need to be addressed during design time in order to achieve a high-quality end-system. These include technical aspects, process engineering, content and context complexity issues (Webb and Gallagher, 2009).

Increased system complexity is also introduced when socially-sourced multimedia data are examined temporally (Baecker, 2011). Designing interactive multimedia applications that adapt to short-term and long-term user-needs is clearly an intricate process. Today leading social software developers have identified the significance of chronological user-driven information, as temporal data analysis can be employed to identify user trends, preferences, social context and other valuable information that may be employed to furnish systems with additional functionality. Take for example the physical and mental changes that occur during the second decade of a humans' life, alongside the surrounding cultural and social changes. Typical issues that need to be resolved by the designer of such an application include the construction of an adaptive user interface which should offer expressive flexibility to the user, provide the necessary age restrictions and parental controls, cover age-based usability issues while it adapts according to the wider cultural and personal aesthetic issues. In that respect, a developer needs to monitor particular user characteristics including the users' cognitive load and adjust the content appropriately (Kalyuga et al., 2011), while at the same time external social conditions and exploration of temporal changes can help identify correlation between user taxonomies (Cagliero, 2011, Nardelli, 2010).

1.1 Chapter aims

The interdisciplinary nature of interactive multimedia systems requires the combination of various scientific, research and creative fields. This introduces research and developmental complexities as multiple factors have an impact on the interaction process: stochastic processes, content demands cultural factors and the user senses. Selecting the appropriate underlying developmental methodology that suits best the end-user and system demands is the requirement here. This is not an easy task, as these methodologies are not categorised comprehensively under a single field. State-of-the-art scientific developments, theories and methodologies are referenced across multiple research fields, rendering hard the task to identify the most appropriate for the task in hand. To state an example, one may refer to recent educational research results that demonstrate how the development of interactive templates may support course evaluation, while the use of re-programming for each course is reduced (Koong and Wu, 2011). The presented concept and technology are not new, as similar ideas and their applicability have been tested approximately a decade ago, in fields of engineering science where a similar system was developed for the presentation of educational and research data (Deliyannis, 2002), and their commercial availability (INNFM, 2002). The proposed methodology allows course-oriented content-ontologies to be stored in appropriate multimedia templates, generate automatically their interaction structure based on content and destined use and allow students and scientists to use varying interaction modes in order to navigate through the data enabling learning and content-exploratory scenarios to be realised effortlessly. The same underlying system principles were later utilised with the use of the appropriate learning framework for students with learning disabilities (Deliyannis et al., 2008, Deliyannis and Simpsiri, 2008, Deliyannis, 2007), proving the flexibility of the methodology to adapt and evolve.

The wider need for interactive multimedia frameworks, methodologies and applications, and the effect that these present to society combined with the creative and communication aspects introduced by these technologies should clearly receive greater attention. It is imperative therefore to capture and organise comprehensively the underlying philosophy, emerging theories, novel research, technology and all the necessary building components that can furnish interactive multimedia research with the essential planning, design and development tools. This work may be considered as a starting point that touches upon a number of issues that need to be resolved. Chapter 2 discusses and proposes a contemporary definition for interactive multimedia. In chapter 3 the field of experimental multimedia is introduced, where novelty in technology and content are combined for the development of innovative systems, while chapter 4 discusses the creative and communication aspects introduced. Chapter 5 concludes this work that proposes possible future developments and directions for the field of interactive multimedia.

2. Interactive multimedia definition

According to New Oxford American Dictionary, the term "**Multimedia**" when it refers to computer applications, they are meant to "*incorporate audio and video, especially interactively*", while when multimedia refers to art or education systems then it is implied that they are "*using more than one medium of expression or communication*". Interpretation of the word "Expression" and "Communication" used in the definition, signifies implicitly the existence of interactive processes. Communication in that respect may be considered as an interactive process between two parties that exchange information and evolve or change as a result. Today, multimedia is used to define an extremely wide area that includes the fields of informatics, telecommunications, the audio-visual production sector, cinema and digital media. In that respect, the term "**interactive multimedia**" is used to describe a scientific and creative research field within "**multimedia**" that supports expression or communication through multiple media with the ability to influence and alter their content and context.

The same dictionary states that when the term "**Interactive**" is used in conjunction to two people or things, it means they have an effect or influence each other. To extend the interactive definition further, this effect may be identified in the physical world, i.e. an action that may trigger a reaction, or a change of the user's mental state and condition. Both conditions may also co-exist, particularly when the process is temporally examined. Take for example a painter who in order to create a painting interacts both mentally and physically when using the canvas, palette of colour and the appropriate tools. Although these processes stop for the artist when the painting is completed, the medium itself continues to instigate interaction when another person is influenced, inspired or moved by that painting. This in turn may result into a physical reaction expressed by the urge to capture the image or purchase a copy or the actual artwork, which may then be user as the starting point for new interactive behavior. Similarly, in New Media Arts this interactive process often involves multiple media.

The term "**Interactive Multimedia**" may be used to describe a physical or digital system where multiple media or people have an effect on each other through their interactive behavior. When "**Interactive Multimedia**" is used in fields such as art or education it implies the use of multiple media used for expression or communication and the existence of a dynamic user-state or content-altering capability.

2.1 Interactive media, the foundation of interactive multimedia

In his 2002 book, Manovich refers to "interactive media" and the varying interaction levels involved: "When we use the concept of "interactive media" exclusively in relation to computer-based media, there is danger that we interpret "interaction" literally, equating it with physical interaction between a user and a media object (pressing a button, choosing a link, moving the body), at the sake of psychological interaction". (Manovich, 2002). The hidden meaning of this statement beyond the danger to reduce the meaning of "interaction" to human "action-reaction" response is that computer-based media have the potential to become interactive, provided that they are used in a manner that enables interaction. Storing a movie on a computer does not make it interactive. Displaying the movie on a screen through a counter responsive system may trigger the user to interact, thus it may in that context be considered interactive. In order to clarify this argument, let us reverse the example. We can safely assume that if an analog media object such as a film enables psychological interaction, it will continue to do so when it is digitised, stored and reproduced by the computer, as the new presentation medium allows the user to comprehend the content using the psychological processes of filling-in, hypothesis forming, recall and identification.

One may call on a different example to clarify things further. Can we characterise as interactive the "Newspaper" exhibit displayed in the year 1979 at the Museum of Science and Industry in Chicago that used laserdiscs to allow visitors to search for past issues of the front page of the Chicago Tribune newspaper? What if we stapled together the same newspaper covers in printed format and we provided an installation next to the "Newspaper" exhibit enabling users to "interact" with? That new system would still be an analog analogy of the digital system that allows user-system interaction through multiple-media (image and text). The significance of the above examples is identified in the fact that the system provides the potential for interaction, not the computerisation of the content. In that respect, the answer to the above questions is that these systems may be characterised interactive. The example stated above identifies clearly the need to utilise an appropriate taxonomy in order to classify interactive multimedia systems and applications. This categorisation may serve multiple purposes, depending on the factors used for system-classification.

2.2 Activity theory, interactivity and system taxonomy

Interactive multimedia systems incorporate a number of important characteristics (Bryant et al., 2005) enabling them to be perceived as a socio-technical systems where humans the leading role within their "social situatedness" (Lindblom and Ziemke, 2002): they support object-oriented actions, a notion that under this context refers towards the objective of the actions, not the computer science term; humans are actors engaged in activities; they are influenced by the community and the current state; they use the tools that are available to them which in most cases were created by others and are influenced by the culture and social knowledge; creation is a shared process between acting members and there are rules that regulate the activities in the system. The activity theory model seems to describe the interactive multimedia design and development process more accurately than traditional cognitive science approaches as it may be used to explain the underlying process used under "consciousness". At the system level, most contemporary computer-based interactive multimedia applications and tools demonstrate typical data-processing behavior based on a point-and-click interface that triggers the underlying processes.

In contrast to many purely cognitive approaches, the psychological model termed "activity theory" that Lev Vygotsky, Alexander Luria and Alexei Leont'ev started developing in the 1920's and 1930's is today used to describe interaction between humans and interactive multimedia systems. A temporal perspective is employed where humans are born and start their personal development in a created environment which is already shaped by the needs and tools of others (Bertelsen and Bødker, 2003). A person is influenced and in turn influences the environment and others as human mind and human activities are linked under the model. As a result, the changes that a person introduces to the environment influence humans that are born within this environment. These principles may apply to both narrow and wide human-computer interaction contexts (Nardi, 1996).

Interestingly, some of the most informative examples of interactive multimedia system taxonomies were developed with multimedia art systems in mind as they pose complex and novel interaction requirements (Nardelli, 2010, Edmonds et al., 2004, Hannington and Reed, 2002, Sommerer and Mignonneau, 1999). This categorisation may be attributed to the fact that interactive new media art systems utilise technology in an experimental manner. This non-conventional use of technology that aims to fulfil the artists' presentation requirements often results into the expansion of the technical limits through innovation. In other words, it is common for artists to experiment with issues such as multisensory inputs, parallel projections, immersion, interaction, virtual worlds, audio-visual effects and other sense-enhancing technologies in a non-conventional manner, a process that furnishes their new media art creations with interactive multimedia capabilities in an attempt to communicate with their audience. We refer to this type of interactive multimedia systems with the term "Experimental Multimedia" first used in 2009 by Dr Ioannis Deliyannis to name a new course taught at the department of Audio and Visual Arts, Corfu, Greece. In this course student-artists were guided to envision, design and create interactive multimedia systems that combine technological and artistic innovation. Typical examples of such systems include original interactive multimedia installation art systems produced as a result of a Ph.D degree within Interactive New Media Arts, or other systems that fulfil the above requirements (Karydis et al., 2011, Deliyannis and Karydis, 2011, Deliyannis and Pandis, 2009). Under activity theory, one may categorise interactive-art and experimental multimedia systems as experimentation tools, which may be used to influence and advance further the technological and social proficiency. It is informative to examine these taxonomies and assess whether they may be used to describe Interactive Multimedia Systems according to their functional characteristics.

3. Experimental multimedia

Artists often extend system capabilities as they deliver their message through multimedia communication processes and systems designed to use the maximum potential of the underlying interactive multimedia technologies. This is certainly a task that requires the combination and coordination of interdisciplinary research fields in order to fulfil the artist's requirements and aesthetic result (Trifonova et al., 2009, Trifonova et al., 2008). In order to describe their functionality in terms of complexity, scientists have proposed various taxonomical methods (Pino and Di Salvo, 2011, Nardelli, 2010, Edmonds et al., 2004, Hannington and Reed, 2002). Interestingly, these taxonomies may be applied to non-artistic interactive multimedia systems and they describe the degrees of freedom supported by the end-system.

"**Experimental multimedia**" is a term used to describe the interdisciplinary field where novel interactive works are implemented through the use of customised interactive multimedia systems and applications designed to cater for their specific content presentation-demands and advanced interaction-requirements. This implies that the originality of the work is traced both at content and system levels. Typical examples of such systems include pioneering interactive artwork, research-based works, and the end products of doctoral and postdoctoral research in the field of interactive multimedia and new media arts.

Those who are familiar with the term multimedia may argue that there is no need for experimental multimedia, as multimedia itself may be used to describe the above works. A typical definition used to support such an argument may be found at the New Oxford American Dictionary: "*using more than one medium of expression or communication: a multimedia art form that is a mélange of film, ballet, drama, mime, acrobatics, and stage effects*". We argue that this is true: all experimental multimedia instances may be categorised under the generalised multimedia definition. The word experimental is used in this context as an adjective in order to express explicitly their combined innovative attributes and characteristics introduced within their technological and artistic forefronts. Similarly, various categorisations are often introduced under the classical Multimedia definition, classifying further the main focus: analog, digital, linear, non-linear, interactive, adaptive etc.

3.1 Artists and engineers: Combining creativity with innovation

Researchers and philosophers have examined from various standpoints the issues that arise when art and technology are combined in order to create an expressive tool, in a process that combines culture, history, theory and technology (Turner, 2007, Popper, 2005, Hansen, 2004, Lister, 2003). The fundamental objective of an experimental multimedia system under an art-bases scenario is communication between the artist and the audience, where technology assumes an active role as the medium that materialises the artists' ideas. Many have studied the inner-workings and have proposed system-development methodologies employed within multidisciplinary teams (Trifonova et al., 2008, Jaccheri and Sindre, 2007, Biswas and Singh, 2006).

Interactivity is a key factor, as it furnishes experimental multimedia systems with communication capabilities (Stromer-Galley, 2004). In that respect it is used beyond the typical point-and-click setting of a computer-based application, providing interactive experimental functionality able to trigger the human senses through multiple communication channels, thus providing multi-sensory communication. The use of technology as a rich interactive method of expression clearly offers increased artistic flexibility.

3.2 Invisible places – Immense white

A typical interactive video installation that may be categorised as an experimental multimedia instance is the work by the Greek video-artist Marianne Strapatsakis entitled "Invisible places - immense white" (Strapatsakis, 2008). Here, biometric activity is utilised to detect what state the user is in: relaxed or stressed. The collected data are then used for the adjustment of the audio-visual environment, and direct interaction with the artwork via interactive drawing of a coloured line directly on the video, based on the user's mental state and its alterations. The installation consists of five synchronized screens that project a continuous and dynamically adjusting/rendering video sequence in an attempt to affect the user's stress levels, under a cinematic audio-visual scenario. A corridor where each wall is a reverse-projection display, leads to a cyclic projection comprising of three arc-shaped screens. An appropriately edited video is displayed across the five screens, while on the left corridor wall the user's stress level is drawn dynamically. Sensors measuring brain wave activity, complete with batteries and a Bluetooth wireless network were appropriately fitted originally into wearable items of clothing in order users to be able to move freely within the installation. User-system interaction under the currently examined project extended beyond the development of a simple action-response system to a fuzzy decision process that temporally tracks, senses and plots directly in the artwork the state of multiple users that experience the environment.

4. Creative and communication aspects of interactive multimedia

The term interactive multimedia is used to describe the combination of technology and multimedia content for the development of interdisciplinary systems employed in a wide array of applications including research, education and interactive art. The plethora of creative and communication aspects offered by interactive multimedia, present multifaceted complexities, particularly as the development of real-life applications is viewed from multiple user-perspectives. Some believe that developments are driven by the dynamics of information (Dezsö et al., 2006), others that innovation precedes technology (Nonaka and Takeuchi, 1995), or simply that it is a matter of sensation and perception (Mather, 2011). It is informative therefore to examine diverse perspectives, in order to identify the aspects of communication and creativity of importance to each group.

Active users in social networks perceive interactive multimedia applications as a tool that allows them to be informed virtually about the developments within their social circle, where direct one-to-one or mass-communication is permitted. In fact, what social networking technology offers to users is the ability to adjust their social interaction timeframe by exchanging digitised multimedia content and experiences within their social circle at their own pace and location (Camarillo and Garcia-Martin, 2011). When social networking systems are used in passive mode they may be contrasted to non-interactive media such as television where the user can sit back and observe what others do. Even so, multimedia content displayed in a live-mode triggers the user to react introducing an action-reaction response that is channelled through the system in an iterative multimedia cycle.

From the developers' perspective, building interactive multimedia applications in the past was an expensive production task that required a team of experts, industrial-level equipment and access to marketing routes. The availability of open-source software, libraries and tutorials has enabled non-professional developers to design, implement and provide new tools, applications and services. These offer innovative data access and manipulation capabilities through intuitive interfaces, deal with technological issues that often arise in rich-media applications such a quality of service (QoS) issues and they are able to compete with industrial-level competitors (Holzer and Ondrus, 2011). Software developers believe that the principal factors that support the growth of the Interactive Multimedia sector include the increased user-researcher interest, the oversized market demand and the availability of open access programming-development tools. As a result, the software development process today is simplified, as a personal computer with the appropriate software may be utilised to create high-level multimedia applications featuring interactive scenarios (Garrand, 2010), that may then be distributed through proprietary web-based application stores (Sans and Diaz, 2011). Multimodal user-input is also supported at the technological level, as portable devices offer advanced processing and multimedia delivery capabilities, while they support a wide range of sensor-based inputs. It is common for a handheld communications device to feature internet access, built-in and wireless microphones, camera-based video tracking capabilities, multi-touch screen, support for GPS, compass, altimeter, movement and other multi-sensory information (Ghinea et al., 2011).

5. Conclusion

The field of interactive multimedia has matured as it provides the underlying tools that are required in order to design and develop new sense-enabling communication media. Recent developments in popular fields such as mass communication media (Deliyannis et al., 2011b) and computer games (Deliyannis et al., 2011a), have shown that these systems have the ability to shape the society as they clearly extend the virtual communication capabilities offered today. The developments are so rapid that they even introduce new legislation issues that need to be resolved (Deliyannis et al., 2011b).

This work touched upon the issues of definition clarification, taxonomies and applications that trigger further research in multiple forefronts under interactive multimedia, a field that clearly requires further analysis. Finally, the introduction of experimental multimedia as an interdisciplinary field that introduces a high volume of innovation is considered necessary, as it enables clear identification of the level of proficiency offered by interactive systems today.

6. References

Baecker, D. 2011. Why Complex Systems Are Also Social and Temporal.

Bertelsen, O. W. & Bødker, S. 2003. Activity theory. *HCI models, theories, and frameworks: Toward a multidisciplinary science*, 291-324.

Biswas, A. & Singh, J. 2006. Software Engineering Challenges in New Media Applications. *Software Engineering Applications SEA 2006.* Dallas, TX, USA.

Boyd, D. & Crawford, K. 2011. Six Provocations for Big Data.

Bryant, S. L., Forte, A. & Bruckman, A. Becoming Wikipedian: transformation of participation in a collaborative online encyclopedia. 2005. ACM, 1-10.

Cagliero, L. 2011. Discovering temporal change patterns in the presence of taxonomies. *IEEE Transactions on Knowledge and Data Engineering*.

Camarillo, G. & Garcia-Martin, M. A. 2011. *The 3G IP multimedia subsystem (IMS): merging the Internet and the cellular worlds*, John Wiley & Sons.

Castells, M. 2011. *The Rise of the Network Society: The Information Age: Economy, Society, and Culture Volume I*, Wiley-Blackwell.

Deliyannis, I. 2002. *Interactive Multimedia Systems for Science and Rheology*. Ph.D, Ph.D Thesis, University of Wales.

Deliyannis, I. 2007. Exploratory Learning using Social Software. *Cognition and Exploratory Learning in the Digital Age (CELDA)*. Algarve, Portugal.

Deliyannis, I. & Karydis, I. 2011. Producing and Broadcasting Non-Linear Art-Based Content Through Open Source Interactive Internet-TV. *ACM EuroITV*. Lisbon, Portugal.

Deliyannis, I., Karydis, I. & Anagnostou, K. 2011a. Enabling Social Software-Based Musical Content for Computer Games and Virtual Worlds. *4th International Conference on Internet Technologies and Applications (ITA2011).* Wrexham, North Wales, UK.

Deliyannis, I., Karydis, I. & Karydi, D. 2011b. iMediaTV: Open and Interactive Access for Live Performances and Installation Art. *4th International Conference on Information Law (ICIL2011).* Thessaloniki, Greece.

Deliyannis, I. & Pandis, P. An Interactive Multimedia Advertising System for Networked Mobile Devices. 4th Mediterranean Conference on Information Systems (MCIS), 2009 Athens.

Deliyannis, I. & Simpsiri, C. Interactive Multimedia Learning for Children with Communication Difficulties using the Makaton Method. International Conference on Information Communication Technologies in Education, 10-12 July 2008 Corfu, Greece.

Deliyannis, I., Vlamos, P., Floros, A. & Simpsiri, C. Teaching Basic Number Theory to Students with Speech and Communication Disabilities Using Multimedia. International Conference on Information Communication Technologies in Education, 10-12 July 2008 Corfu, Greece.

Dezsö, Z., Almaas, E., Lukács, A., Rácz, B., Szakadát, I. & Barabási, A. L. 2006. Dynamics of information access on the web. *Physical Review E,* 73, 066132.

Edmonds, E., Turner, G. & Candy, L. Approaches to interactive art systems. 2004. ACM, 113-117.

Garrand, T. 2010. Interactive Multimedia Narrative and Linear Narrative. *Write Your Way Into Animation and Games: Create a Writing Career in Animation and Games.*

Ghinea, G., Andres, F. & Gulliver, S. 2011. Multiple Sensorial Media Advances and Applications: New Developments in MulSeMedia. Information Science Reference.

Hanjalic, A. 2012. A New Gap to Bridge: Where to Go Next in Social Media Retrieval? *Advances in Multimedia Modeling,* 1-1.

Hannington, A. & Reed, K. Towards a taxonomy for guiding multimedia application development. 2002. IEEE, 97-106.

Hansen, M. B. N. 2004. *New Philosophy for New Media,* MIT Press.

Holzer, A. & Ondrus, J. 2011. Mobile application market: A developer's perspective. *Telematics and Informatics,* 28, 22-31.

INNFM. 2002. *Rheology Films* [Online]. Institute for Non-Newtonian Fluid Mechanics. Available: http://www.innfm.org.uk/Films.html 2012].

Jaccheri, L. & Sindre, G. 2007. Software Engineering Students meet Interdisciplinary Project work and Art. *11th International Conference Information Visualization (IV '07).* Zurich, Switzerland.

Jain, R., Del Bimbo, A., Chua, T. S. & Furht, B. 2011. Survey papers in multimedia-guest editorial. *Multimedia Tools and Applications,* 1-4.

Kalyuga, S., Ayres, P. & Sweller, J. 2011. *Cognitive Load Theory,* Springer.

Karydis, I., Deliyannis, I. & Floros, A. 2011. Augmenting Virtual-Reality Environments with Social-Signal Based Music Content. *17th International Conference on Digital Signal Processing (DSP2011).* Corfu, Greece.

Koong, C. S. & Wu, C. Y. 2011. The applicability of interactive item templates in varied knowledge types. *Computers & Education,* 56, 781-801.

Lew, M. S., Sebe, N., Djeraba, C. & JAIN, R. 2006. Content-based multimedia information retrieval: State of the art and challenges. *ACM Trans. Multimedia Comput. Commun. Appl.,* 2, 1-19.

Lindblom, J. & Ziemke, T. 2002. Social situatedness: Vygotsky and beyond.
Lister, M. 2003. *New Media: A Critical Introduction*, Routledge.
Lu, Y., Sebe, N., Hytnen, R. & Tian, Q. 2011. Personalization in multimedia retrieval: A survey. *Multimedia Tools and Applications*, 1-31.
Mahapatra, A., Wan, X., Tian, Y. & Srivastava, J. 2011. Augmenting image processing with social tag mining for landmark recognition. *Advances in Multimedia Modeling*, 273-283.
Manovich, L. 2002. *The Language of New Media*, MIT Press.
Manovich, L. 2011. Trending: The Promises and the Challenges of Big Social Data. *Debates in the Digital Humanities, ed MK Gold. The University of Minnesota Press, Minneapolis, MN.[15 July 2011].*
Mather, G. 2011. *Sensation and Perception*, Taylor & Francis.
Naaman, M. 2010. Social multimedia: highlighting opportunities for search and mining of multimedia data in social media applications. *Multimed. Tools Appl.(in press), doi,* 10.
Nardelli, E. A classification framework for interactive digital artworks. International ICST Conference on User Centric Media, 2010 Palma, Mallorca.
Nardi, B. A. 1996. *Context and consciousness: activity theory and human-computer interaction*, The MIT Press.
Nonaka, I. & Takeuchi, H. 1995. *The knowledge-creating company: How Japanese companies create the dynamics of innovation*, Oxford University Press, USA.
Pino, C. & Di Salvo, R. A survey of semantic multimedia retrieval systems. 2011. World Scientific and Engineering Academy and Society (WSEAS), 353-358.
Popper, F. 2005. *From Technological to Virtual Art*, MIT Press Ltd.
Riek, L. D. & Robinson, P. 2011. Challenges and opportunities in building socially intelligent machines. *IEEE Signal Processing*.
Sans, V. & Diaz, J. Implementing a multimedia application on iPhone: a case study. 2011. IEEE, 233-238.
Schallauer, P., Bailer, W., Troncy, R. & Kaiser, F. 2011. Multimedia Metadata Standards. *Multimedia Semantics*, 129-144.
Sommerer, C. & Mignonneau, L. 1999. Art as a living system: interactive computer artworks. *Leonardo*, 32, 165-173.
Strapatsakis, M. 2008. Interactive art-installation: Invisible places - immense white. Strasbourg November 2008.
Stromer-Galley, J. 2004. Interactivity-as-Product and Interactivity-as-Process. *The Information Society Journal*, 20, 391-394.
Trifonova, A., Ahmed, S. U. & Jaccheri, L. 2009. SArt: Towards Innovation at the Intersection of Software Engineering and Art
Information Systems Development. *In:* Barry, C., Lang, M., Wojtkowski, W., Conboy, K. & Wojtkowski, G. (eds.). Springer US.
Trifonova, A., Jaccheri, L. & Bergaust, K. 2008. Software engineering issues in interactive installation art. *Int. J. Arts and Technology*, 1, 43-65.
Turner, G. 2007. *Supportive methodology and technology for creating interactive art.* PhD, University of Technology.
Wang, F. C. 2012. A Novel Approach to Mine Knowledge from Social Images. *Advanced Materials Research*, 430, 1068-1071.
Webb, B. & Gallagher, S. 2009. Action in context and context in action: Modelling complexity in multimedia systems development. *Journal of Information Technology*, 24, 126-138.

Part 2

Interactive Multimedia Learning, Teaching and Competence Diagnosis Systems

2

Educational Digital Recycling: Design of Videogame Based on "Inca Abacus"

Jorge Montalvo
University of Lima, Scientific Research Institute -IDIC
Peru

1. Introduction

The use of multimedia applications in schools is quite common. However, according to Alfonso Gutiérrez (2003: 42), these are often attributed educational advantages, which perhaps they do not have and just like that, it is assumed it favors learning. From a creative design perspective, how can we make educational multimedia resources really contribute to an effective teaching-learning process? We believe a key aspect has to do with the possibility of digitally recreating or recycling some traditional teaching materials that have proven to be effective teaching tools. Among them, we find the so-called "Inca abacus" known in Peru and other countries of the region as "*yupana*".

Fig. 1. Drawing made by chronicler Felipe Guamán Poma

On the lower left corner of a 16th century drawing (figure 1), made by chronicler Felipe Guamán Poma, there is a sketch of a *yupana* next to the *quipu*; therefore, it is believed they were complementary calculation tools. The term *yupana* comes from the Quechua word "*yupay*" that means "to count". Originally, it consisted of a clay or stone tablet with several columns and boxes with small grooves for placing corn kernels. Researchers have not reached an agreement on how it was used in the olden days; however, for its use in schools, the interpretation made by the engineer William Burns has been chosen, which is based on the decimal system (Bousany, 2008: 18). The tablet has been turned into a horizontal position, where each column has the value of a multiple of ten and each circle has the value of one multiplied by the value in its column. The upper boxes are used as a memory or for exchange and underneath, there are ten circles, grouped in two, three and five units to facilitate counting (figure 2).

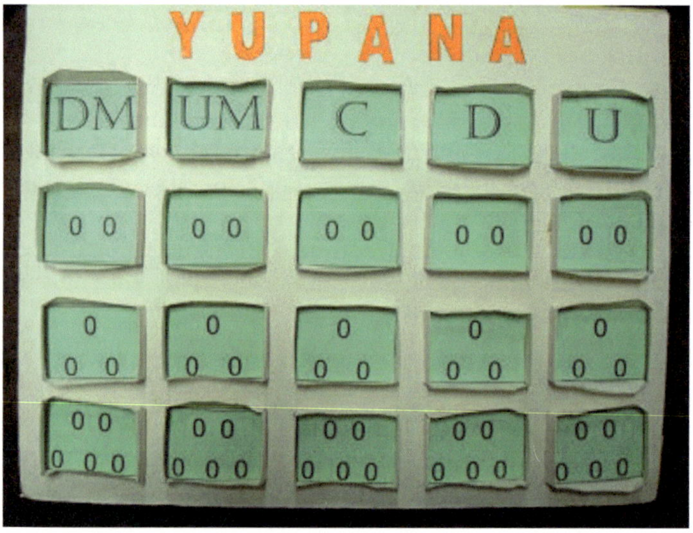

Fig. 2. Representation of the decimal system in the *yupana*

In the eighties, the *yupana* was promoted as a teaching aid for the first elementary grades by the Peruvian teacher Martha Villavicencio; since then, some schools make use of traditional *yupanas* made from wood, cardboard or Styrofoam and numbers are represented with buttons or seeds (figure 3).

There are research and testimonies certifying the educational capacity of the *yupana* in facilitating the understanding of the positional value of numbers in the decimal system and the execution of immediate arithmetic calculations (Vargas & López, 2000: 75). It is stated this is an educational and historic tool "[...] that helps students understand certain mathematical algorithms that are many times applied in a mechanical way without knowing the logical part." (Torres, 2009). Taking into account the importance of mathematics in basic education and the difficulties and resistance generated in its learning, we decided to investigate the feasibility to digitally recycle the *yupana* with the purpose of strengthening its qualities and make it more attractive for digital natives. For this interdisciplinary work, we counted with the advisory services of a specialist in mathematics education, David Palomino, and of a multimedia application designer, David Chura.

Fig. 3. Use of the traditional *yupana* in school

2. Educational digital recycling

2.1 Traditional learning and digital recycling

The origin and sense of the term "apprentice" is interesting. Professor Mariano Aral, a specialist in Spanish lexis, explains it in the following way:

The complement of an apprentice is basically the teacher, that is, the traditional teacher (one who masters a trade). [...] What was characteristic of all skills in relation to their respective apprentices was that it made them work (apprentices did not just learn, they learned by doing). [...] When passing from a traditional society to an industrial one, it was discovered that the industry was not the best place for apprentices, they went straight to production and they had to know already and take a productive space in the company. Therefore, learning had to be achieved in school and not in the industry. [...] It was a total revolution. Instead of masters they gave them teachers. Instead of providing them with machines, tools and working material, they gave them paper and pencils, and books and blackboards. Instead of practice, they were given explanations and more explanations and instead of turning them into apprentices, they remained as students. (Aral, 1999).

This interesting text from Mariano Aral expresses certain nostalgia for traditional education based on practical learning with specific materials. Other authors go beyond and link traditional culture with the digital era. Juan Freire -in agreement with the expert in innovation Charles Leadbeater- believes that the industrial society was an anomaly and that the digital era is not a revolution but the recovery of ways to work, participate and share that we believed had been forgotten. The industrial revolution meant an increase in efficiency in detriment of the pleasure of learning by doing, of talking with those around us and of making collective decisions without external authorities. With the arrival of the digital era, Freire once again says, "[...] spectators become digital artisans, the profane knowledge is reappraised, and knowledge is shared once more, it is copied and remixed in a creative virtuous cycle." (Freire, 2006). A way of conceptually explaining this phenomenon is through McLuhan's laws on the media. According to Piscitelli's review (2005: 121-122), these laws state that each technology expands or amplifies a skill, by doing so, it outdates an older means and at the same time, it recovers something that was previously obsolete; and if it expands too much, it turns into something new. As we can see, the fact that a new technology rescues previous forms or means is a central part of the proposal.

We can define educational digital recycling as a way of recovering and transforming traditional learning materials to introduce them into a new life cycle more in tune with the new generations. Here, the sense of transformation involved in this process is worth pointing out. Today, there are virtual educational resources but many of them are limited to copying or simulating materials from the real world. In order to analyze this point, I would like to tell you a personal anecdote.

When my oldest son was three years old, he used to play with a Disney multimedia to learn to paint. The interactive design of the interface showed a brush, drawings for coloring, paint jars with basic colors and a pallet for mixing colors. The task or challenge consisted in painting the drawings with the same colors as in some reference pictures. My son always had a hard time obtaining green by mixing the yellow and blue paints and if he did, it was just by chance. One day, we were walking down the street and he needed to go to the bathroom. So, we went into a public restroom where they had just finished cleaning and the toilet water was blue from the disinfectant. When he started urinating, my son was surprised to see how the blue water changed color. I took the opportunity to explain that by mixing yellow with blue you get green and he never forgot this lesson. Moreover, he was capable of transferring what he had learned. Once he poured a yellow-colored soft drink into a blue glass and when he saw the glass turn green, he immediately remembered the restroom experience.

Some experiential learning processes are impossible to reproduce virtually. Therefore, the first condition for educational digital recycling is to start from a resource or material that can be subject to transformation and be enriched with digital technology. On the other hand, if we compare the Disney multimedia with the bathroom experience, we can discover several differences. The multimedia interface shows an environment that simulates an artistic surrounding, appropriate for someone who is getting ready to paint with a set of colors. On the other hand, a public restroom is an unusual and rather inappropriate place for learning to paint. But maybe, just because of that, it is capable of generating greater surprise and interest. Neuroscience has shown that emotion favors learning. According to John Medina (2010: 94-95), when the brain detects an event with an emotional content, it releases dopamine, a neurotransmitter that aids memory and information processing. It is like if the brain placed a chemical post-it note with the statement: "¡Remember this!" so the information can be processed more thoroughly. Another basic difference between multimedia and the restroom experience is in relation to the way the green color appeared. In the Disney material, when the brush dipped in the blue paint touches the yellow paint in the palette, the green color appears automatically, as if by magic. In the toilet bowl, the effect is in real time, progressive, which fixes the attention on the mixture of colors and increases curiosity.

As we said before, many educational virtual resources simulate materials from the real world. For example, there are several digital applications of the Chinese abacus on the web (figure 4) that reproduce its physical characteristics with some interactive functions.

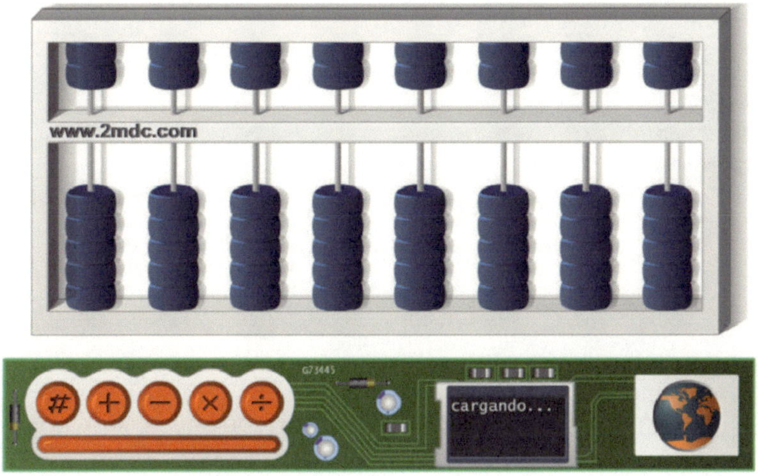

Fig. 4. Digital version of the Chinese abacus

On the other hand, there are recent projects in Bolivia (Murillo, 2010) and Colombia (I.E. Once de Noviembre, 2010) of digital or virtual *yupanas* (figure 5). In all of these cases, they are multimedia resources that use digital technology but not the digital "culture"; that is, they are applications that do not take advantage of communication formats or styles that have developed around the new mediums.

Fig. 5. Examples of virtual *yupanas*

In our case, we decided to creatively transform the *yupana* into a space videogame, which we called "Yupi 10" (figure 6). We only included four columns in the prototype (up to thousands) and we aligned all the circles vertically with the purpose of simplifying the design and facilitating its use, not only in PCs, but in mobile phones and tablets as well. The game was developed with Adobe Flash. In the case of platforms or devices that do not support Adobe Flash Player, we would have to develop versions of the game with other tools, such as Objective-C, Java or HTML5.

Fig. 6. Main screen of the Yupi 10 videogame

2.2 Yupi 10 basic rules

Educational videogames can be included in a category called "serious games." This concept usually includes games that have a purpose other than simple entertainment and whose application field is quite varied: ranging from military training to education in health and going through business training or artistic education. (Susi et al., 2007).

In relation to the educational potential of electronic games, it has been criticized (Buckingham, 2008: 173) that a large part of these packages are focused on the practice of out-of-context skills or factual contents of subjects, where the user just has to answer questions choosing from various options; more than teaching, the intention seems to be that of assessing skills or pre-acquired knowledge. Tejeiro & Pelegrina (2008: 135) quote studies, which alert of the possibility that educational videogames favor experiential cognition, based on reactions to successive events, but not reflexive cognition, which would enable applying what has been learned to other areas. It is stated that the context of the game causes higher motivation levels; however, this seems to interfere with reflexive cognition, so students are able to transfer their understanding of game principles to other games but not to extract the rules on which they are based. It has also been observed that without guidance from a teacher, participants in an educational videogame focus on the competitive nature of the game and not on following up of their own understanding. This has been interpreted in reference to Vygotsky's concept of the zone of proximal development, according to which individuals can pass a learning level when they are helped by a more competent person. Other authors have indicated that videogames can be useful for "[…] teaching external abstractions such as mathematics or physics, but they have limitations when representing introspection or philosophy." (Zagalo, 2010: 65).

In reality, all these observations do not invalidate the use of electronic games in school; they just warn us about the conditions a videogame should meet to really be educational. We believe that the main condition has to do with the basic rules of the game, understood not so much as the playing instructions but rather as structural principles of the creative design. For example, a videogame in the form of a labyrinth would be appropriate to learn notions of laterality and spatial orientation (left / right, up / down). However, there are cases in which the labyrinth is only a recreational pretext to "catch" numbers, letters, animals or any object related to an allegedly educational subject. It would seem that first the format is decided upon and then content is sought for it. But this problem is not exclusive of the digital setting, in the real world there are tabletop games with a board and spaces to move, related to geography, road safety, environment, health, among others.

In the case of Yupi 10, the basic rules of the game correspond to the following tasks. First the user has to choose a mission for the ship. In the prototype, we include nine missions (figure 7), with increasing levels of difficulty that correspond to second grade. All missions have an "audio-problem" form and represent acted out situations in which the captain and lieutenant of the ship take part. For example, there is an emergency and the number of oxygen tanks has to be determined through a subtraction or addition operation.

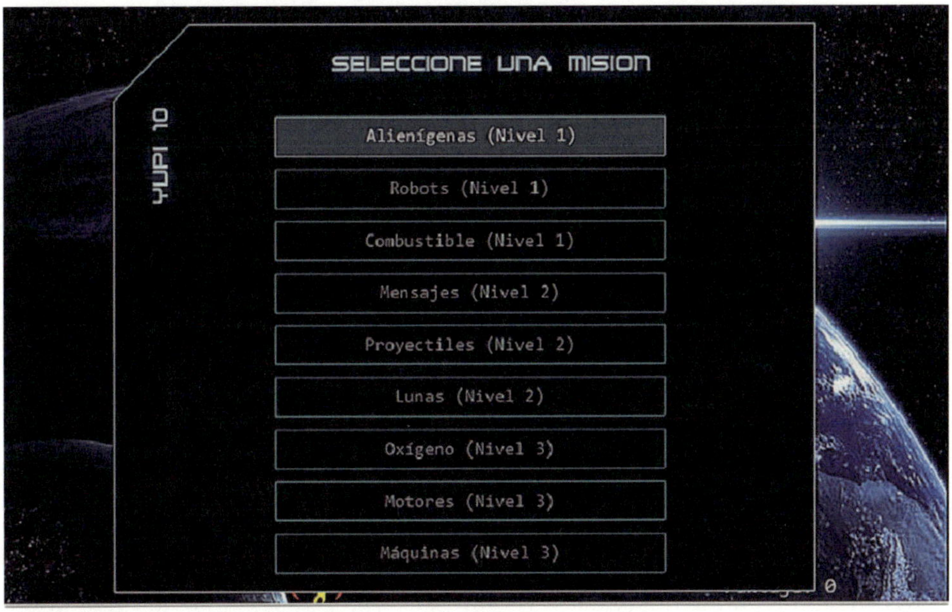

Fig. 7. Missions with increasing levels of difficulty

The next step is to use the ship's color board to graphically represent the problem data (figure 8) and execute the corresponding arithmetic operation. Finally, the result is verified in the option menu in order to go on to the next mission.

Let's see how an addition operation is carried out (figure 9). Let's suppose we have to add 18 + 5. First we represent number eighteen by lighting eight units and one ten (figure 9a). Then we add the five units, but as we only have two available circles (figure 9b), we have to exchange the ten units for a ten. For this purpose, we turn off the entire red column with the upper circle and we light up a circle in the blue column (figure 9c). Then we continue adding the three remaining units and at the end the total appears represented: twenty-three (figure 9d).

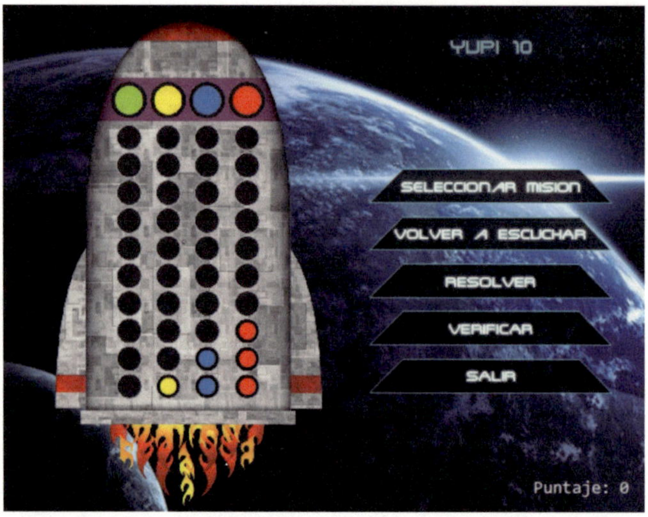

Fig. 8. Color Board with data and option menu

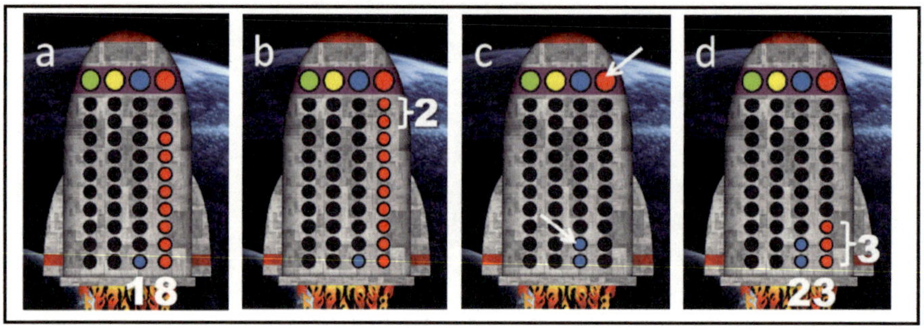

Fig. 9. Addition example (18 + 5 = 23)

In a subtraction operation, the process is the other way around (figure 10). Let's suppose we want to subtract 23 - 5. First we represent number twenty-three (figure 10a). Then we subtract number five, but as there are only three circles available (figure 10b), we have to exchange a ten for ten units. For this purpose, we turn off a blue circle and we light up the entire red column with the upper circle (figure 10c). Then we continue turning off the two remaining red circles and at the end we have the subtraction result: eighteen (figure 10d).

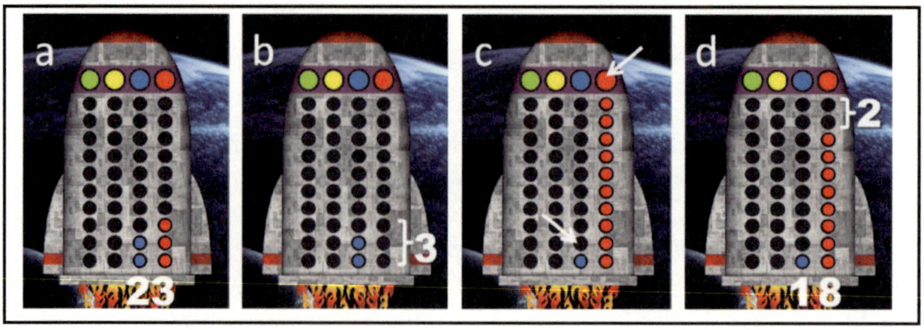

Fig. 10. Subtraction example (23 - 5 = 18)

2.3 Interactivity and sensory elements

In relation to the educational videogame design, some authors state that unlike commercial videogames, to have very limited budgets “[...] has huge consequences in the quality of graphics and the level of interactivity and consequently, in its capacity to attract reluctant students.” (Buckingham, 2008: 155). We believe that educational videogames should not be compared to commercial videogames but to school books, in face of which they are more attractive. In addition, there are studies that warn about the distracting effect of drawings that are too complex or real (Medina, 2010: 279). On the other hand, regarding the symbolic game - which has great influence in developing children’s thoughts - experts affirm that playing materials “[...] the more simple and functional they are [...], results obtained from the symbolic game will be positively better and greater (Licona, 2000). That is why in the case of Yupi 10 we chose a simple interface design to help give context to the game and facilitate interactivity.

Educational digital recycling of traditional material requires the identification of essential actions, which should be kept and which should be eliminated or modified. Lighting and turning off circles in Yupi 10 is an interactive way of putting and taking away seeds in the physical *yupana*. This is a key aspect because they are actions that represent addition and subtraction operations. Another important factor in an interactive application is to decide if certain function should be automatic or manual. For example, in the Yupi 10 exchange process, there is the technical possibility that after completing the ten circles in a column, all “automatically” turn off and one lights up in the following column; but it is preferably for the user to do it “manually” - like in the traditional *yupana* - so the person can assimilate decimal system equivalences better. In the case of the Disney multimedia we mentioned before, if the green color does not appear in an automatic or instant form but rather in a mechanic or progressive way, it would surely result in better learning on the blend of basic colors. Digital technology makes it possible to reproduce or strengthen both automatic processes, typical of the industrial society, as well as the manual systems, inherent to traditional society.

According to neuroscience experts, it is convenient for all educational material to be multi-sensorial: “When the sense of touch is combined with visual information, learning improves in almost thirty percent.” (Medina, 2010: 244). It is also stated that nerve endings on our fingertips generate brain activity that helps in understanding. When you understand what is being taught, several brain areas are activated, whereas when you memorize without sense, the activity in nerve cells is much poorer (Fernández, 2010: 5). Several years ago, in relation to movies, Michel Chion (1993: 10) proposed that there are transensorial influences between what we see and what we hear. According to this author, you do not see the same when you hear and you do not hear the same when you see. At present, with the boom of touch screens and physical recognition systems, transensorial influences in the media and teaching materials will become more frequent and varied.

In relation to Yupi 10, we have mentioned the exclusive audible nature of audioproblems. This decision seems to contradict the convenience for teaching materials to be multi-sensorial. However, we had several reasons to avoid the use of aiding images when presenting the problems. In the first place, several math teaching experts sustain that as of second grade, when children are introduced to arithmetic problems, which they have to read from their textbooks, they begin to lose the ability to listen that they developed in first grade. They also state that in daily life, the majority of arithmetic problems that arise and need to be solved are oral. Therefore, they recommend looking for an adequate balance in school between written and oral problems (Capote, 2005). On the other hand, audio stories require a higher level of attention and concentration, which helps children process and analyze information better. As Shanker (2010) indicates, the calmer, focused and alert a child is, the better will he be able to integrate sensory information received by his brain and assimilate it and organize his or her thoughts and actions.

2.4 Levels of difficulty and reasoning

Another important aspect related to problems was determining the way to write and classify them according to levels of difficulty. Several math teaching specialists indicate that in order to solve a problem effectively, boys and girls should make a global analysis of the text meaning, that is, to understand the problem formulation. In this sense, there is a semantic classification of verbal elemental arithmetic problems into four categories: combination, change, comparison and equating (Puig & Cerdán, 1988). Combination problems are the simplest ones and describe the relationship between two parts and a whole. For example: "There are 35 people at a meeting, 12 are men; how many of them are women?" Here, the unknown factor is one of the parts that make up a whole. Another possibility is for the unknown factor to be the whole: "There are 12 men and 23 women at a meeting; how many people are there in total?"

Change problems have a slightly higher level of difficulty. There is an initial amount, a change amount and the final amount. For example: "Ana had 12 coins, she earns 7 coins; how many coins does she have now?" Here, the unknown factor is the final amount, but it can also be the initial amount: "Ana had some coins, she earns 7 coins, now she has 19 coins; how many coins did she have at the beginning?" Another possibility is for the change amount to be the unknown factor: "Ana had 12 coins, she earns some coins, now she has 19 coins; how many coins did she earn?" These same change problems can be expressed in a decreasing way, replacing the expression "earning coins" for "losing coins."

The degree of difficulty of comparison problems is higher and shows a static relationship between two quantities: the referential one and the compared quantity. For example: "Juan is 8 years old, Ana is 13. How much older is Ana than Juan?" Here the unknown factor is the difference but it can also be the compared quantity: "Juan is 8 years old, Ana is 5 years older than Juan. How old is Ana?" Another possibility is for the unknown factor to be the referential quantity: "Ana is 13 years old and 5 years older than Juan. How old is Juan?" These same problems can be formulated in a negative way by replacing the expression "older than" for "younger than."

Equating problems are usually the most difficult and also imply comparisons between two quantities but using a connector of the type "as much as" or "equal to." For example: "Juan weighs 27 kilos, Ana weighs 18 kilos. How many kilos does Ana have to gain to weigh as much as Juan?" Here, the unknown factor is the difference but it can also be the compared quantity: "Juan weighs 27 kilos, if Ana gains 9 kilos she would weigh as much as Juan. How many kilos does Ana weigh?" Another possibility is that the unknown factor is the referential quantity: "Ana weighs 18 kilos, if she gains 9 kilos she will weigh as much as Juan. How many kilos does Juan weigh?" As in the previous case, these same problems can be expressed in a negative way by replacing "gain kilos" for "lose kilos".

The degrees of difficulty of these four categories are not absolute. There are studies that suggest that some specific forms of an inferior category are more difficult that other specific forms of a higher category. For example, the change form: "Ana had some coins, she loses 7 coins, now she has 19 coins. How many coins did she have at the beginning?", is often more difficult than the comparison form: "Juan is 8 years old, Ana is13. How much older is Ana than Juan?"

This semantic classification of verbal elemental arithmetic problems puts emphasis not so much on children's calculation skills but on their analysis and reasoning ability. Based on these criteria, we drew up the nine missions of the Yupi 10 prototype and we grouped them into three levels of difficulties: initial, intermediate and high.

2.5 Validation of the prototype and results

The challenge of every educational innovation consists in being able to turn knowledge objects into objects of desire. (Ferrés, 2008: 180). In this sense, during the qualitative validation of the prototype with three groups of children between the ages of 7 and 9, we could observe that the videogame awaken interest and curiosity, despite the simplicity of its design and the usual resistance math generates in students. However, we also noticed an inconvenience: some children listened to the audio problems too quickly and decided to do the problem - addition or subtraction - without thinking too much, almost by guessing and when they checked the answer and it said "error detected," they simply carried out the opposite operation and they got "mission accomplished". They noticed that by choosing the operation at random, they had a 50 percent chance of being successful, which encouraged a conduct similar to throwing dice to see what they got. As we mentioned before, audio problems were designed based on a semantic classification that requires analysis and reasoning. Consequently, the children's attitude contradicts the educational purpose of the multimedia. In order to correct this defect, it would be convenient to include in the game instructions a score system: winning points for each right answer and losing points for each mistake. This reward and sanction system is usual in some commercial videogames and we believe it could be useful for Yupi 10, despite the fact it is a behaviorist strategy. During the validation, we tentatively assessed this. When we warned the children: "think well, if you make a mistake, you can lose points," they listened to the audio problems again to analyze them better.

Here we need to ask ourselves about the importance of chance in playing activities. In football for example, chance is a factor that goes beyond players' ability and that in addition to adding interest to the match, it can influence the final result. Would it be appropriate to add the chance component into an educational videogame? We believe that eventually it could be used in aspects not related to those we have called basic rules of the game (unless understanding the notion of "by chance" is the educational objective of the material). Thus, this would increase the participants' interest without affecting the expected learning.

Another inconvenience we noticed during the validation was that some children, instead of using the ship board to show the problem data on a graph and carry out the respective operation, made mental calculations (or used their fingers) and only used the interface to check the result, especially the easiest problems. We got the impression children wanted to find the answer very quickly and thought that using the ship board was too slow. Probably this attitude is influenced by the customary practice of commercial videogames in which the reaction speed is a key factor in success and also by the habit of some teachers to value results of an operation more than the process followed. In any case, it is an attitude that does not contribute to the purpose of incentivizing reflection and reasoning. A way to overcome this inconvenience would be to include in the multimedia the possibility of checking not only the result of the operation but also some of the previous steps: for example, representing the problem date adequately and choosing the addition or subtraction option correctly. Thus, we would be promoting a methodic and progressive attitude in children in order to reach a goal.

Regarding teachers, a notable result of validation has to do with its mediating function between the material and the children. In a previous research on audiovisual riddles (Montalvo, 2011: 130) we maintained that such function consisted in facilitating "clues" or individual aid to students and that this type of personalized tutoring could hardly be assumed by a machine because technology tends to standardize users. The validation of Yupi 10 supports this criterion. The videogame test allowed us to experiment situations in which we had to assume the role of an aiding facilitator suited to each child. In one case, it was necessary to teach how to represent numbers on the ship board. In other cases, we had to put illustrative examples or use graphs or diagrams - made on the spot - to clarify the sense of an audio problem. In general, we verified that there are many differences and gaps in the students' previous knowledge, which implies that the mediating participation of the teacher would be essential if we want to achieve significant learning processes with Yupi 10.

3. Conclusion

In this chapter, we have systemized the experience of designing a multimedia application in the form of an educational videogame based on a traditional material of proven educational effectiveness. The study of the Yupi 10 case allows us to affirm that educational videogames are really educational when the basic rules of the game (structural principles of creative design) fully agree with the material's learning objectives. Otherwise, they only incentivize the review of previously acquired knowledge and correspond to a multimedia application category that conceive the educational process more as the transmission of information rather than the building principles of learning. On the other hand, it is worth highlighting the way math problems are formulated in Yupi 10, which seeks to privilege reasoning over calculation skills. We believe it is a very appropriate approach for current times because in a society where there is an abundance of accessible data, knowing how to reason is one of the competencies needed to analyze information and turn it into knowledge. Finally, in relation to interactivity, we must point out the educational value of manipulative actions, which are usually minimized as opposed to multimedia visual and audio aspects. Therefore, maybe we should rather call educational videogames "videotoys" so we can always keep in mind their multisensory nature.

Regarding the educational digital recycling, we believe this is a timely strategy for this transitional era, in which we can foresee the future without losing sight of the past. In order to appreciate the creative flexibility of the digital society, we have to imagine it as an inclusive culture capable of taking in and strengthening the best educational resources, both from traditional society as well as from the industrial society. Could it be that maybe we are so fascinated with new technologies that we forget about the good educational practices of the past? How many valuable traditional resources created by anonymous teachers in small schools could be digitally recycled to increase their benefits and launch them to the world? Digital culture knows no time or space boundaries. The Inca *yupana* was created more than 600 years ago in a long-gone society and was rescued as educational material at the end of the last century. Today, by digitally recycling it as Yupi 10, maybe it will have the opportunity of starting a new life cycle.

4. References

Aral, M. (1999). Aprendizaje. (Access: 11 February 2011) Available from: <http://www.elalmanaque.com/julio/21-7-eti.htm>.

Bousany, Y. (2008). Yupanchis. La matemática inca y su incorporación a la clase. ISP Collection. Paper 1. (Access: 20February 2010) Available from: <http://digitalcollections.sit.edu/isp_collection/1>.

Buckingham, D. (2008). *Más allá de la tecnología. Aprendizaje infantil en la era de la cultura digital.* Manantial, ISBN 978-978-500-112-1, Buenos Aires, Argentina.

Capote, M. (2005). *Planteamiento de un problema aritmético con texto en la escuela primaria.* (Access: 8 October 2010) Availablefrom: <www.ucp.pr.rimed.cu/sitios/revistamendive/nanteriores/Num8/pdf/3.pdf>.

Chion, M. (1993). La audiovisión. Introducción a un análisis conjunto de la imagen y el sonido. Paidós. Retrieved from: <www.lapizdigital.com.ar/.../la%20audiovisión%20-%20michel%20chion.pdf>, Barcelona, Spain.

Fernández, J. A. (2010). Neurociencias y enseñanza de la matemática. Prólogo de algunos retos educativos. In: *Revista Iberoamericana de Educación*, nº 51, OEI. (Access: 22 August 2010) Available from: <http://fernandezbravo.ning.com/profiles/blogs/algunos-articulos-y-documentos>.

Freire, J. (2006). La era industrial fue una anomalía. In: *Nómada* [blog]. (Access: 12 February 2011) Available from: <http://nomada.blogs.com/jfreire/2006/12/la_era_industri.html>.

Ferrés, J. (2008). *La educación como industria del deseo. Un nuevo estilo comunicativo.* Gedisa. ISBN: 978-84-9784-288-4,Barcelona, Spain.

Gutiérrez, A. (2002). *Alfabetización digital. Algo más que ratones y teclas.* Gedisa. ISBN: 84-7432-877-2, Barcelona, Spain.

I.E. Once de Noviembre (2010). Proyectos pedagógicos. In: *Institución Educativa Inem Once de noviembre* [blog]. (Access: 20 March 2011) Available from: <http://inemoncedenoviembre.blogspot.com/>.

Licona, A. (2000). La importancia de los recursos materiales en el juego simbólico. *Revista Pixel-Bit*, n°14. (Access: 10February 2011) Available from: <http://www.sav.us.es/pixelbit/pixelbit/articulos/n14/n14art/art142.htm>.

Medina, J. (2010). *Los 12 principios del cerebro. Una explicación sencilla de cómo funciona para obtener el máximo desempeño.*Norma. ISBN: 978-958-45-2897-1, Bogotá, Colombia.

Montalvo, J. (2011). Adivinanzas audiovisuales para ejercitar el pensamiento creativo infantil. In: *Comunicar*, nº 36,(March, 2011), pp. 123-130, Grupo Comunicar, ISSN: 1134-3478, Andalucía, Spain.

Murillo, J. (2010). Yupana digital. Available from: <http://es.scribd.com/doc/36501843/Yupana- Digital>.

Piscitelli, A. (2005). *Internet, la imprenta del siglo XXI.* Gedisa. ISBN: 84-9784-060-7, Barcelona, Spain.

Puig, L. & Cerdán, F. (1988). *Problemas aritméticos escolares.* Síntesis. (Access: 8 October 2010) Retrieved from:<http://www.uv.es/puigl/lpae3.pdf>. Madrid, Spain.

Shanker, S. (2010). Self-regulation: calm, alert and learning. *Education Canada,* vol. 50. (Access: 22 August 2010) Available from: <http://www.cea-ace.ca/education-canada/article/self-regulation-calm-alert-and-learning>.

Susi, T.; Johannesson, M. & Backlund, P. (2007). Serious games-*an overview.* University of Skövde, Suecia. Available from: <http://74.125.155.132/scholar?q=cache:ttMLMX_9wRUJ:scholar.google.com/+serious+games&hl=es&as_ sdt =2000>.

Tejeiro, R. & Pelegrina, M. (2008). *La psicología de los videojuegos. Un modelo de investigación.* Aljibe. ISBN: 978-84-9700-440-4, Málaga, Spain.

Torres, I. (2009). Proyecto interdisciplinario la yupana para aprender matemática en el marco de la enseñanza para lacomprensión. Colegio Abraham Lincoln. Available from <http://cibem6.ulagos.cl/ponencias/ cibemPresentGimnasio/ Presentacion%20de%20la%20conferencia%20puerto%20montt%202009.ppt>.

Vargas de Avella, M. & López de Castilla, M. (2000). *Materiales educativos. Relato de una experiencia en Bolivia, Ecuador y Perú.* Convenio Andrés Bello, Bogotá, Colombia.

Zagalo, N. (2010). Alfabetización creativa en los videojuegos: comunicación interactiva y alfabetización cinematográfica.
In: *Comunicar,* nº 35, (October, 2010), pp. 61-68, Grupo Comunicar, ISSN: 1134-3478, Andalucía, Spain.

3

Interactive Multimedia Module with Pedagogical Agent in Electrochemistry

Kamisah Osman and Tien Tien Lee
The National University of Malaysia & Sultan Idris Education University, Malaysia

1. Introduction

Members of the young generation who are literate in science and technology play a vital role in developing countries like Malaysia. The education system in Malaysia therefore puts greater emphasis on science and mathematics. In consonance with the National Education Philosophy, science education in Malaysia nurtures a science and technology culture by focusing on the development of individuals who are competitive, dynamic, robust and resilient and able to master scientific knowledge and demonstrate technological competencies. It is hoped that this young generation can help the country achieve Vision 2020 as an advanced industrial country in the world.

1.1 Chemistry curriculum in Malaysia

Like other countries once colonized by the British, science as a subject was introduced by the British to Malaysia. Practices in science education are therefore similar to British science education, and both syllabus and rubrics are borrowed from the British to make modifications based on local conditions. In Malaysia, the Science subject was introduced by colonialists in the early 1970s (Lewin, 1975) in secondary schools. Formal science education was started in primary schools for Year Five students. Science as a subject was introduced on a trial basis in selected schools in 1993 and introduced in all schools in 1995 (Khalijah, 1999). Science for primary school curriculum consisted of five main themes: (1) The Living System, (2) The Physical System, (3)The World of Matter, (4) The Earth, and (5) Technology. Teaching methods included directed investigation, discovery learning, group projects, experimenting, simulation and role play to encourage discussions among students and application of rules in decision-making. integrated science, modern physics, modern chemistry, modern biology and modern science were gradually introduced in secondary schools throughout the country. The Table 1 shows the history of science as a subject in Malaysia.

Chemistry as a subject is taught at upper secondary level for science stream students. The themes for the chemistry syllabus are: (1) Introducing Chemistry, (2) Matter Around Us, (3) Interaction between Chemicals, and (4) production and Introduction and Management of Manufactured Chemicals. The chemistry curriculum has been designed not only to provide opportunities for students to acquire scientific knowledge and skills, develop thinking skills and thinking strategies, and apply the knowledge and skills in everyday life, but also to

Subject	Stage	Basis	Year introduced
Integrated Science	Form 1 - 3	Scottish Integrated Science	1969
Modern Physics, Modern Chemistry, Modern Biology	Form 4 -5 (Science stream)	Nuffield Physics / Chemistry / Biology 'O' Level	1972
Modern Science	Form 4 - 5 (Art stream)	Nuffield Secondary Science	1974

Table 1. History of science education in Malaysia

inculcate in them noble values and the spirit of patriotism (Mahzan, 2005). Chemistry is the science of matter concerned with the composition of substances, structure, properties and interactions between them. Chemistry should be taught in three representation levels, macroscopic, microscopic and symbolic (Johnstone, 1993). Macroscopically, the chemical process can be observed and sensed by our sensory motors. The arrangement and movement of particles and the interactions among them can be explained in the microscopic level. All the chemical processes involved can be represented by symbols, numbers, formulae and equations symbolically.

1.2 Study of electrochemistry

Electrochemistry is a study of inter-conversion of chemical energy and electrical energy occurs in electrolysis and voltaic cell (Tan et al., 2007). Previous studies (Bojczuk, 1982; Lee & Kamisah, 2010; Lin et al., 2002; Roziah, 2005) showed that the topic is difficult to learn because the concepts are abstract. Students often encounter misconceptions in the learning of this topic (Garnett & Hackling 1993; Garnett & Treagust 1992; Garnett et al. 1995; Lee & Mohammad Yusof 2009; Lee 2008; Lin et al. 2002; Sanger & Greenbowe 1997a; Sanger & Greenbowe 1997b). Macroscopically, students need to study the concepts of electrolytes and non-electrolytes, the electrolysis process and voltaic cells. Microscopically, they need to understand the movement of ions and electrons during the electrolysis process. Besides that, they also need to transform the process into chemical formulae and equations symbolically. Students face difficulties in understanding the abstract chemical processes especially on microscopic and symbolic levels (Garnett & Hackling 1993; Garnett & Treagust 1992; Garnett et al. 1995; Lee & Mohammad Yusof 2009; Lee 2008; Lin et al. 2002; Sanger & Greenbowe 1997a; Sanger & Greenbowe 1997b). Generally, some common misconceptions or problems faced by students in learning Electrochemistry are: (1) students are always confused between the flow of current in the conductors and in the electrolytes; (2) they cannot identify the anode and cathode/positive and negative terminal in the cell; (3) they cannot describe and explain the process happening at the anode and cathode; (4) they mix up the oxidation and reduction process at the electrodes; and (5) they are unclear about the concept of electrolyte (Lee & Mohamad Yusof, 2009; Lee, 2008).

Students' major problem in learning abstract chemistry topics is the ability to visualize the concepts, that is, to form a mental image or picture in the mind (Lerman, 2001). Chemistry is a visual science (Wu & Shah, 2004). In educational practice, visualization is applicable to one of the following situations: (a) the experiment is too long or too short; (b) the dimensions of the examined object are too small or too large; (c) the environment of the experiment is not accessible; (d) the parameters of the experiment or its effects are not directly available to the observer's senses; (e) there is a need for multiple revisions of the experiment; (f) the experiment is difficult to arrange or revise effectively; (g) the experiment is dangerous; and (h) the experiment is too expensive (Burewicz & Miranowicz, 2002). In the context of Electrochemistry, the dimension of the examined objects (movement of particles) is too small and the parameters of the experiment are not directly available to the observer's senses in which the changes of the process are at the microscopic level. Hence, the teaching and learning of Electrochemistry should be aided with the use of a multimedia module. This enables the students to visualize the abstract chemical processes by using the application of multimedia elements in the module.

1.3 The use of ICT in teaching and learning

The use of Information and Communication Technology (ICT) is aiding understanding and explanations of concepts, especially visualizing abstract concepts and processes (using models, simulations, games, digital video and multimedia adventures) (Oldham, 2003). Hence, designing instructions using multimedia becomes a trend in this ICT era. Application of multimedia in education through World Wide Web, CD-ROMs, DVD and virtual reality can help students visualize the abstract concepts especially in the learning of chemistry. The use of multimedia creates the environment where students can visual the abstract chemical processes via animation and video in macroscopic, microscopic and symbolic levels (Bowen, 1998; Burke et al. 1998; Rodrigues et al. 2001; Russell et al. 1997). Studies (Doymus, 2010; Gois & Giordan, 2009; Lerman & Morton, 2009) have been carried out and results showed that animation and simulation using ICT can help students to visualize and hence enhance students' understanding in learning abstract chemistry topics.

The use of ICT especially the multimedia modules is able to assist students in visualizing the abstract concepts; however, the rate of using multimedia modules in the schools is still very low (Lee & Kamisah, 2010). Teachers are not interested in using the modules available in the market in the learning process because they find that these modules are too formal, not interesting and do not follow the syllabus (Norsiati, 2008; Roziah, 2005). Following the Teaching and Learning of Science and Mathematics using English implemented by the government since 2003, the government delivered related teaching multimedia modules to the schools. Some of the teachers used the module provided by the government to teach Electrochemistry. But, there were a lot of problems faced by the teachers in using the module. Some of them complained that the buttons in the module were not functioning, the videos were stuck when playing, the teachers do not have enough time to set up the projector and laptop in the laboratory etc. Hence, the rate of using multimedia module in the teaching of Electrochemistry was low among the Chemistry teachers (Lee & Kamisah, 2010). Furthermore, students lack of sufficient metacognitive awareness and comprehension monitoring skills in order to make effective choices (Hill & Hannafin, 2001; Land, 2000). They lack the skills to find, process and use information and ideas. Students as novice learners do not always make connections with prior knowledge or everyday experiences in ways that are productive for learning (Land, 2000). As a result, Pedagogical Agents (PAs) are designed to facilitate learning in computer-mediated learning environments (Chou et al., 2003; Craig et al., 2002; Johnson et al., 2000; Moundridou & Virvou, 2002; Predinger et al., n.d., Slater, 2000). The use of PAs in the interactive multimedia module in this study makes the module different from the modules already available in the market.

1.4 Pedagogical agents in interactive multimedia module

Pedagogical agents are animated life-like characters designed to facilitate learning in computer-mediated learning environments. They show human characteristics in terms of appearance such as changes in facial expressions, gestures and body movements when interacting with the users. Users can communicate with the agent via speech or on-screen text. The appearance of PAs is varied in terms of gender (male or female), realism (cartoon and realistic) and ethnicity (African-American and Caucasian) (Baylor, 2005). Normally, PAs are designed as experts (Baylor, 2005; Baylor & Kim, 2004; Chou et al., 2003; Hayes-Roth et al., 2002; Kim et al., 2006; Kizilkaya & Askar, 2008; Moreno et al., 2000; Moreno & Mayer, 2005) who are knowledgeable in specific areas in order to provide guidance to students. However, there are also PAs which act as co-learners (Chou et al., 2003; Kim et al., 2006; Maldonado & Hayes-Roth, 2004; Maldonado et al., 2005; Xiao et al., 2004) or motivators (Baylor, 2005; Baylor & Kim, 2004; Kizilkaya & Askar, 2008). The co-learners or motivators accompany the students, encourage and motivate them to be involved in the learning process.

PAs in a multimedia module serve to enhance students' metacognitive awareness of what they know and what they should know for the topic being studied. One strategy for providing metacognitive guidance involves embedding support, or scaffolds for procedural, strategic, or metacognitive control (Land, 2000). This guidance or support is provided by the PAs in the module. PAs could make learners aware of the opportunities presented to them, provide advice for the learners on the tools to be used, and explain the functionalities of the tools in an open learning environment (Clarebout & Elen, 2007).

Studies abroad were carried out by several research groups using PAs in multimedia software for a variety of subjects such as environmental sciences (Moreno & Mayer, 2000), language (Maldonado et al., 2005; Predinger et al., n.d.), ecosystem (Biswas et al., 2004), art (Hayes-Roth et al., 2002), ecology (Clarebout & Elen, 2007), mathematics (Kim et al. 2006; Atkinson, 2002), space (Kizilkaya & Askar, 2008). In Malaysia, studies related to pedagogical agents have been done in Islamic Education (Mohd Feham, 2006) and Physics Education (Farah et al., 2008; Nabila Akbal et al., 2008). Studies conducted by Kirk (2008) and Baylor (2005) give students the freedom to choose their preferred PAs to assist them in the learning process. However, these agents are designed to differ only in terms of appearance (the image of an anthropomorphic pig, a green alien, and a robot), gender (male and female), ethnicity (African-American and Caucasian) and realism (real or cartoon), but were similar in terms of role. Studies on electrochemistry and the freedom to choose different roles of PAs still cannot be found. Hence, an interactive multimedia module with pedagogical agents (IMMPA) with different roles of PAs, named EC Lab was developed in order to assist students in the learning of Electrochemistry.

1.5 Objective of the study

The objectives of the study are listed below:

a. Identify the effectiveness of IMMPA EC Lab in improving students' achievement levels in the learning of Electrochemistry topic.

b. Identify the effectiveness of IMMPA EC Lab in improving students' motivation level in the learning of an Electrochemistry topic.

2. Methodology

2.1 Research design

The study is a quasi experiment non equivalent pretest/post-test control group design (Campbell & Stanley, 1963). Normally a school will arrange the classes according to students' achievements and subjects selected. Hence, it was impossible to run the study using true experimental designs. There are two groups of samples: a treatment group and a control group. Samples in the treatment group will learn an Electrochemistry topic using IMMPA EC Lab developed by the researcher. On the other hand, Electrochemistry will be taught by a Chemistry teacher using the traditional method for the students in the control group.

2.2 Sample

The selection of samples was based on some criteria. For instance, overall students' achievement in Lower Secondary Examination (Peperiksaan Menengah Rendah, PMR); the ratio of female and male students; the experience of a Chemistry teacher who taught the classes and the number of computers in the computer laboratory. Finally, 127 (50 males and 77 females) Form Four students (16 years old) from two secondary schools were involved in the study. The students were From Four classes, with two classes randomly selected as control groups and two classes as treatment groups. There were 24 males and 39 females in the control group, 26 males and 38 females in the treatment group. Each school has one treatment group and one control group taught by the same chemistry teacher. Both teachers had more than 20 years of experience in teaching chemistry.

2.3 Materials

2.3.1 Achievement test and specific entry test

Materials utilized in the study are the pretest/post-test, specific entry test, motivation questionnaire and the IMMPA titled EC Lab. There are two structured questions in the achievement test. The questions test knowledge on Electrolytic Cell and Voltaic Cell concepts at the macroscopic, microscopic and symbolic levels. Macroscopically, the students need to identify the anode and cathode in the cell and describe the observations at both electrodes during the electrolysis process. Microscopically, they need to draw the ions that exist in the electrolyte and the direction of the flow of the electrons in the circuit. Symbolically, they have to represent the oxidation and reduction process at the electrodes by writing the half-equations. Questions in the pretest and the post-test are similar in terms of the difficulty level and the concepts tested. The only difference is the types of electrodes and electrolyte used in the cells. A reliability analysis was carried out and the KR20 is 0.65 for the pretest and 0.71 for post-test. The specific entry test consists of ten multiple-choice questions testing on some basic skills that will be applied in the Electrochemistry learning process.

2.3.2 Motivation questionnaire

The motivation questionnaire is a Likert scale questionnaire. There are three sub dimensions involved, namely Adhered Value, Expectancy Components and Affective Components.

Adhered Value consists of three subscales, namely intrinsic goal orientation, extrinsic goal orientation and task value. On the other hand, Expectancy consist of control of learning belief and self-efficacy for learning and performance. Affective involve test anxiety. There are 28 items in the questionnaire with Likert scale provided, where 1 - Strongly Disagree, 2 -Disagree, 3 - Not Sure, 4 - Agree, and 5 - Strongly Agree. Items in the questionnaire have been taken from the study of Sadiah and colleagues (2009) which were translated from the original instrument by Pintrich and DeGroot (1990). In this study, the researcher used the motivation section only and changed the scale from seven points to five points. The Cronbach Alpha reliability coefficient for the motivation questionnaire is 0.87.

2.3.3 EC Lab

EC Lab was developed by the researcher by using the combination of two instructional design models: the Kemp Model and Gerlach and Ely Model. The reasons for using the combination of these two models are that they are classroom-oriented models (Gustafson & Branch, 1997) with their own strengths. The Kemp Model describes elements, not 'step, stage, level or sequential item' in an instructional design (Kemp et al., 2004). The oval shape of the model indicates the independency of the elements in the model. It is a non-linear model with no starting and ending point. All the processes of designing, developing, implementing and evaluating can be done concurrently and continuously. The Gerlach and Ely Model is suitable for the novice instructional designers who have knowledge and expertise in a specific context (Qureshi, 2001, 2003, 2004). This model is classroom-oriented and is suitable for teachers at secondary schools and higher education institutions. The Gerlach and Ely Model focuses more on the instructional materials and resources without identifying the instructional problems. Hence, the researchers combined the two models as the instructional design model to develop the EC Lab. The conceptual framework of the combination of these two models used in the study is presented in Figure 1 below.

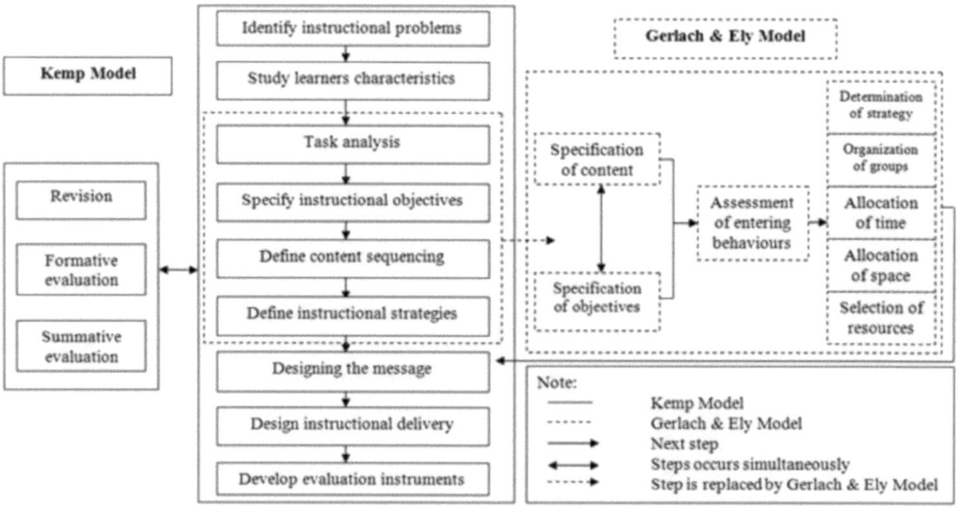

Fig. 1. Conceptual framework of combination of two instructional design models

There are two PAs in the EC Lab, namely Professor T and Lisa. Professor T is a sixty year-old male PA who acts as an expert in Electrochemistry. He gives accurate information and explains new concepts to the students. Professor T speaks slowly in a formal way with little body gestures and facial expressions. On the other hand, Lisa is a fifteen-year old female youth who speaks with an energetic voice. She is a learning companion in the EC Lab. She learns together with the students, gives motivation and encouragement to the students to complete the tasks and exercises in the module. Students are free to choose the PA they want to accompany them in the learning of Electrochemistry after they key in their name in the module. The interface for the choosing of PAs is shown in the Figure 2.

Fig. 2. Interface for PAs selection

The main menu for the EC Lab consists of tutorial, experiment, exercise, quiz, memo and game. There are five sub units in the EC Lab: (1) Electrolytes and Non-Electrolytes, (2) Electrolysis of Molten Compounds, (3) Electrolysis of Aqueous Solutions, (4) Voltaic Cells and (5) Types of Voltaic Cells. All the information delivery for the sub units is presented in the tutorial session. The experiment session consists of five experiments in Electrochemistry. The first experiment about the concept of electrolyte and non-electrolyte is done through the simulation. Another three experiments investigating the factors that determine the ions to be discharged at the electrodes and experiment for simple voltaic cell are hands on investigation. The students were guided by the PAs to carry out the experiments in the chemistry laboratory and they need to apply scientific process skills and manipulative skills during the investigations. There is a session named 'Micro-World' (Figure 3) in the module. When students click on magnifying glass button, they will be shown the moving of electrons and ions in microscopic level. This 'Micro-World' session describe the detail process happened in the cell during the electrolysis process. After the information delivery process, students will do some exercises to enhance their understanding on the concepts learnt. Quiz will be given at the end of every sub unit. Each quiz is divided into three levels. The first level is to let the students do some reflections on what they have learnt in the sub unit. The students then need to compare their prior idea with the new idea to review whether the conceptual change has occurred. The second level of the quiz consists of five simple multiple-choice questions and some elementary structured questions. Students need to click the answers for the multiple-choice questions and write down the answer for the structure

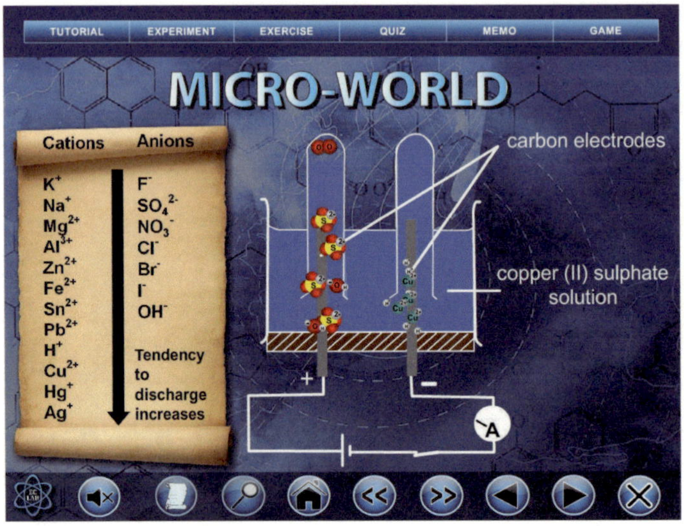

Fig. 3. Micro-World shows the process happened in the cell in microscopic level

questions. The third level of the quiz is more challenging, with some difficult structured questions and essays. Students can check their answers by clicking on the SOS button. A memo is created to give some hints or tips on learning of some of the Electrochemistry concepts. For instance, mnemonics (Figure 4) are given to help the students in memorizing the list of anions and cations in the Electrochemical Series. There are four games in the game session to let the students relax their mind after the learning process. The games are applications of Electrochemistry concepts; for instance, one of the games asks the students to set up an electrolytic cell and a voltaic cell with the apparatus given.

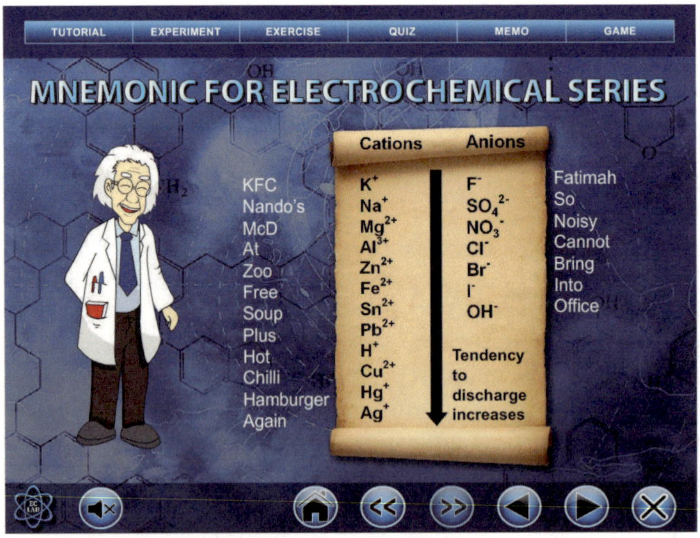

Fig. 4. Mnemonics in the memo to help students memorize the list of Electrochemical Series

The complete flow of each sub unit follows the five phases in the learning process created by Needham (1987). The five phases are orientation, elicitation of ideas, restructuring of ideas, application of ideas and review. In the EC Lab, the *Think about it* session (Figure 5) is the orientation phase. The students will be shown some pictures that are familiar to them. Those pictures are related to the concepts to be learnt in every sub unit. Then, in the *Do you still remember* session, the students will be reminded of some concepts that they have learnt before. Those concepts are related to the new concepts to be learnt in the sub unit. Next, in the *Give me your ideas* session (Figure 6), the students are given the chance to give their ideas regarding some activities that are related to the concepts to be learnt. Students need to type, click or drag the pictures to give their ideas regarding the concepts being tested. Students can then check their answers to evaluate themselves based on the feedback given by the PAs. Then, in the *Are you sure* session, the students need to give some ideas, make some guesses or predictions on some outcomes of the situations. In order to examine their ideas, guesses and predictions, the students need to carry out some investigations in *Let's do it* or watch related videos in *Show time* sessions. In these two sessions, the students will be exposed to the conflict situations if their ideas, guesses or predictions are different from what is being shown in the experiments or videos. Hence, conceptual change should happen here and the students need to modify, extend or replace their existing ideas. Then, reinforcement of the constructed ideas will be done in the *Practice makes perfect* session. The students will apply the concepts learnt in new situations and examples. Students need to do exercises related to the concepts learnt in each sub unit. Lastly, *Before and after* session is created to enable the students to reflect upon the extent to which their ideas have changed. The students need to answer certain activity questions again and compare their prior answers to the new answers. *Testing yourself* and *Challenge yourself* sessions contain multiple-choice questions, structured questions and essay questions to let the students evaluate themselves on the concepts learnt.

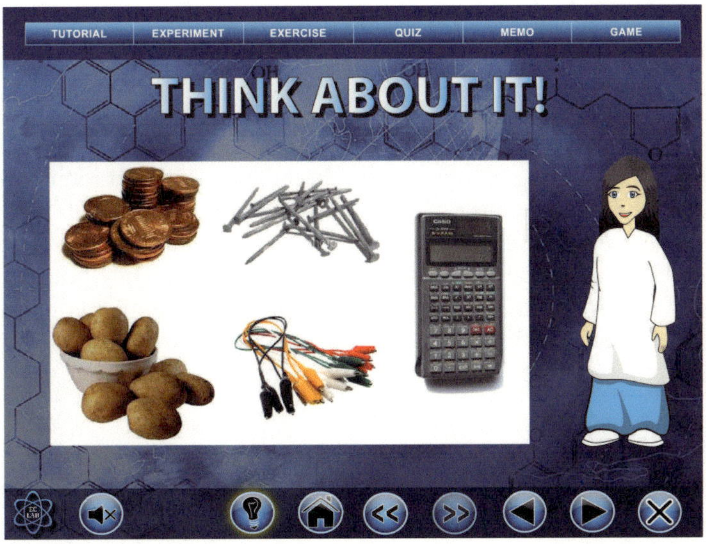

Fig. 5. Pictures shown in *Think about it* session in Sub Unit 4

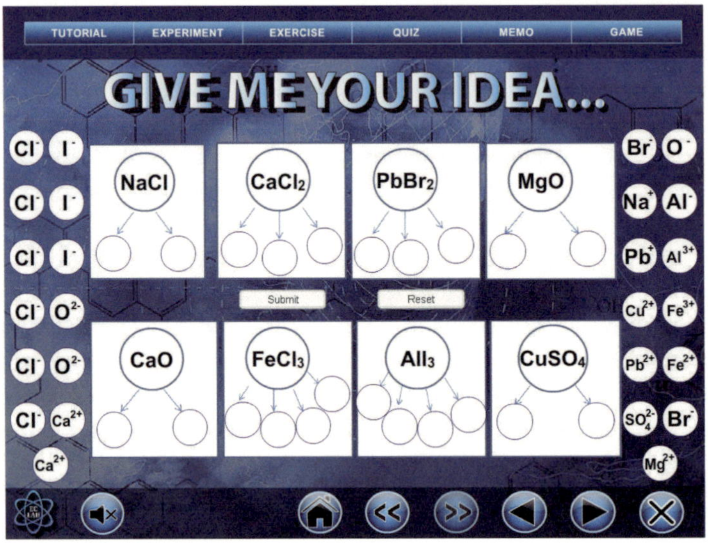

Fig. 6. Students need to drag the answers to the correct spaces

3. Procedure

The study was carried out in the schools using chemistry periods during the normal school hours. Two chemistry teachers were involved in the study. The same chemistry teacher handles both the treatment and control groups in one school. The teacher used the traditional 'chalk and talk' method to teach the control group and EC Lab module to teach the treatment group during the teaching and learning process of Electrochemistry. The procedure of the study is shown at the flow chart.

Samples in both treatment and control groups were given one hour to answer the pretest. After that, they need to answer the specific entry test and motivation questionnaire in about 15 minutes respectively. The students who had poor results for the specific entry test were given some revision notes. They were told to study the revision notes before the treatment sessions. In the next meeting, students in the treatment group went to the computer lab to study the Electrochemistry topic using the EC Lab. The user manual was given to the students, followed by a briefing on how to use the EC Lab. Then, students were told the sub unit to be learnt on that day to ensure every student learn the same sub unit. Then, students were free to explore the first sub unit in 80 minutes. Since the number of computers in the school is limited, each computer was shared by two students. They put on the earphone to listen to the script delivered by the PAs. On the other hand, students in the control group were taught by their teacher using the traditional method. Each meeting is about 80 minutes (two periods) and students learned one sub unit in each meeting either with their teacher or with EC Lab.

Students learnt the second sub unit in the next meeting. The teaching and learning process for a treatment group was carried out in computer laboratory while for the control group, they used the chemistry laboratory to study Electrochemistry. Sub unit three consists of three experiments in studying the factors that determine the ions discharged at the electrodes. Students therefore need to attend three meetings to complete sub unit three in

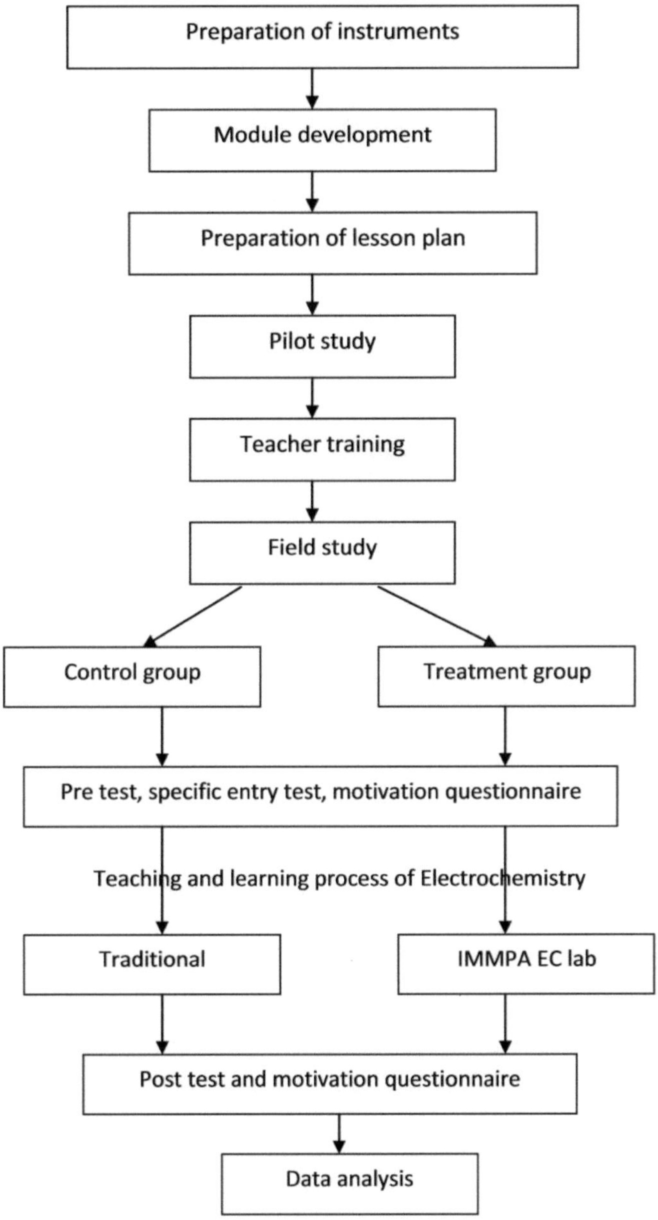

Fig. 7. Flow chart of the procedure

EC Lab. As a result, the third, fourth and fifth meetings were conducted at the chemistry laboratory. Students need to carry out the experiments to investigate the three factors that determine the ions to be discharged at the electrodes. Students learnt sub unit four in the sixth meeting. There was an experiment regarding simple voltaic cell in the unit. Hence, students conducted the experiment in the chemistry laboratory. For the seventh meeting, students explored sub unit five in EC Lab about types of voltaic cell. Students in the control group were given notes and lecture for the same sub unit.

After completing the sub units in the Electrochemistry topic, students need to answer the post-test and motivation questionnaire in the next meeting. As usual, students in both control and treatment groups were given 60 minutes to answer the post-test and 15 minutes to answer the motivation questionnaire. All the pretest, post-test, specific entry test and questionnaire were collected and analyzed. The pretest and post-test were used to analyze students' achievement level while the motivation questionnaire was used to analyze students' motivation level in the learning of Electrochemistry. The results were compared between treatment and control groups to identify the effectiveness of EC Lab in increasing students' knowledge and motivation in the learning of Electrochemistry.

4. Results and discussion

4.1 Specific entry test

Specific entry competencies are prerequisite knowledge, skills and attitudes that learners must possess to benefit from the training (Morrison et al., 2007). Students' specific entry competencies were identified through the specific entry test. Students were given this test in order to assess their prior knowledge regarding concepts that will be applied in the learning of Electrochemistry. Concepts being tested were related to proton number, nucleon number, arrangement of electrons, chemical formulae and chemical equation. Students need to have the skills to write chemical formulae and chemical equations in describing the process that takes place in the electrolytic cells. The test consisted of ten multiple-choice questions. Each question was followed by four alternative answers. Each correct answer was given one point and no point was given for the wrong answer. Both control and treatment groups have the same questions in the test.

Table 2 shows the t-test table to compare the specific entry test result for treatment and control group. There was no significant difference in scores for treatment ($M = 61.25$, $SD = 23.40$) and control group [$M = 58.57$, $SD = 23.82$; $t(125) = 0.64$, $p = 0.05$]. The magnitude of the differences in the means was very small (eta squared = 0.003). These show that students in both groups have similar level of prior knowledge before they learn Electrochemistry. The students' results ranged from 10% to 100%. The results showed that the students were still weak in the concept of proton number (Item 7, only 39.4% of the students answered correctly). Students who scored less than 50% ($n = 39$) of the specific entry test were given remedial help before they started with the treatment sessions. They were given some revision notes for Chapter Two: The Structure of Atom and Chapter Three: Chemical Formulae. Students were reminded to do revisions before they started the lesson for Electrochemistry.

Group	N	Mean	Std. Deviation	t value	Sig (2-tailed)
Treatment	64	61.25	23.40	0.639	0.524
Control	63	58.57	23.82		

Table 2. t-test table for specific entry test between control group and treatment group

4.2 Achievement test

A series of paired-sample t-test was conducted to evaluate the impact of the interventions on the students' scores in the achievement test. There was a statistically significant increase in test scores from pretest ($M = 4.46$, $SD = 3.52$) to post-test [$M = 35.9$, $SD = 18.44$, $t(62) = 12.57$, $p < 0.05$] for the control group. On the other hand, students' achievement in the treatment group also showed statistically significant increase in test scores from pretest ($M = 7.11$, $SD = 4.00$) to post-test [$M = 46.01$, $SD = 29.94$, $t(63) = 11.03$, $p < 0.05$]. The eta squared statistic (.50) for both groups indicated a large effect size. Although the overall results for the post-test were better compared to the pretest for both groups, 52.4% and 43.75% of them from control group and treatment group respectively still failed the post-test. The results for the post-test ranged from 4.26% to 61.70% for the control group and 2.13% to 93.62% for the treatment group. Both groups showed significant increase results for the achievement test from pretest to post-test indicating that students' knowledge in Electrochemistry was increased after they gone through the interventions. However, the results for the post-test for treatment group were higher than control group. Table 3 shows the mean scores for post- test between control group and treatment group.

Group	N	Mean	Std. Deviation	t value	Sig (2-tailed)
Treatment	64	46.01	29.94	2.295	0.024**
Control	63	35.90	18.44		

Table 3. t-test table for post-test between control group and treatment group

An independent-samples t-test was conducted to compare the post-test result for treatment and control group. There was a statistically significant difference in scores for treatment ($M = 46.01$, $SD = 29.94$) and control group [$M = 35.90$, $SD = 18.44$; $t(105.06) = 2.30$, $p = 0.05$]. The magnitude of the differences in the means was small (eta squared = 0.04). Questions in the test consisted of items testing Electrochemistry concepts in macroscopic, microscopic and symbolic levels. Students need to understand the whole process happens during the electrolysis at both electrodes. Comparatively, students from treatment groups were more able to give reasons and explanations to their answers especially in microscopic level. For instance, when copper (II) nitrate solution was changed to concentrated copper (II) chloride solution in electrolytic cell (Item 11), some students from both groups were able to give the correct observations at both electrodes at macroscopic level. However, students from treatment group (e.g. ET 22 & ET33) can explain the reasons to the observations in microscopic level describing the movements of ions and processes happened at both electrodes. On the other hand, students from control group (e.g. KL29) tended to give conclusion as reason for the observation given.

> *Since the Cl^- ion is more concentrated than OH^-, Cl^- ion is chosen for discharging to form chlorine gas (ET22).*
>
> *Cl^- ions are selectively discharged as it is more concentrated even though it is placed higher at the electrochemical series (ET33).*
>
> *The chlorine gas is produced (KL29).*

Micro-World in some of the sub units shows the movements of ions in the electrolyte during the electrolysis process. Students can watch the process of gaining of electrons at cathode and releasing of electrons at anode microscopically. Students can visualize (Lerman, 2001) the whole process through the animations in Micro-World. IMMPA EC Lab makes the abstract concepts 'concrete' because students can watch the whole process visually at three representation levels (Bowen 1998; Burke et al. 1998; Rodrigues et al. 2001; Russell et al.

1997). Hence, students learning Electrochemistry with animations and simulations in multimedia module will gain higher achievements compared to traditional method (Hasnira, 2005; Sanges & Greenbowe, 2000).

4.3 Motivation

The motivation questionnaire was used to assess the students' goals and value beliefs for chemistry (especially Electrochemistry), their beliefs about their ability to succeed in the subject and their anxiety toward the test and examination on Electrochemistry. Both groups answer the similar motivation questionnaire before and after the interventions. The paired sample t-test was unable to show any significant difference between pre-motivation and post-motivation mean scores for the both groups. Mean score for control group decreased from pre motivation (M = 3.64, SD = 0.48) to post motivation [M = 3.59, SD = 0.38; t(62) = -0.98, $p < 0.05$]. On the other hand, mean score for treatment group increased from pre-questionnaire (M = 3.64, SD = 0.39) to post-questionnaire [M = 3.68, SD = 0.39, t(63) = 1.10, $p < 0.05$]. The eta squared statistic (.50) indicated a small effect size for the both groups. Although the post-motivation mean score for treatment group is slightly higher than control group, but the t-test was unable to show significant difference between the groups.

Group	N	Mean	Std. Deviation	t value	Sig (2-tailed)
Treatment	64	3.68	0.39	1.429	0.156
Control	63	3.59	0.38		

Table 4. t-test table for post-motivation mean score between control and treatment group

Independent samples t-test result in Table 4 above show that there was no significant difference in post- motivation mean scores for treatment (M = 3.68, SD = 0.39) and control group [M = 3.59, SD = 0.38; t(125) = 1.43, p = 0.05]. The magnitude of the differences in the means was small (eta squared = 0.02). Items in the motivation questionnaire consists of six subscales, namely intrinsic goal orientation, extrinsic goal orientation, task value, control of learning belief, self-efficacy for learning and performance and test anxiety. Students showed the highest mean score in extrinsic goal orientation (treatment group: M = 4.16, SD = 0.61; control group: M = 4.04, SD = 0.63) among all the subscales, indicating that they were trying to show to others that they can perform well in Chemistry. They expected to get reward and praise from the parents and teachers if they got good grades in the subject. The examination oriented education system in the country (Anthony, 2006; Keeman, 2007) causes the students to learn to get good grades in the examinations. For instance item six 'Getting a good grade in this class is the most satisfying thing for me right now' had a high mean score of 4.31 (SD = 0.72) with majority of them agree (39.4%) and strongly agree (45.7%) with the statement. Results also showed that students were more extrinsically motivated than intrinsically motivated (Chang, 2005). Students were more concerned with the rewards and grades rather than enjoy and learn the Electrochemistry.

Control of learning belief obtained second high mean scores for the control and treatment groups with 4.01 (SD = 0.58) and 4.07 (SD = 0.59) respectively. With high control beliefs, students are confident in employing learning strategies to manage their learning and believe that this will bring about the desired results. As such, they may self-regulate more when their control beliefs are improved (Melissa Ng & Kamariah, 2006). Students believed that if they tried their best (Item 15, M = 4.24, SD = 0.70), and studied in an appropriate way (Item 2, M = 4.17, SD = 0.71), they will be able to learn and can understand the subject well.

Anxiety subscale measures students' nervous and worried feelings towards examination. Students with high anxiety level are not confident and are always worried about their academic results. Students who are not well prepared or who expect to fail are more likely to have higher anxiety than those students who are well prepared and expect to succeed (Shores & Shannon, 2007). Previous research showed that test anxiety is related to high extrinsic goal orientation (Kivinen, 2003) and the control of learning belief (Melissa Ng & Kamariah, 2006) and it was proven in this study. Extrinsic goal orientation and test anxiety for treatment group were found to be positively related to each other ($r = .5$, $p < .01$). On the other hand, test anxiety was found to be positively related to the control of learning belief ($r = .3$, $p < .01$). Students are more likely to worry about examinations if they believe that the attainment of the desired grades is not within their control (Melissa Ng & Kamariah, 2006).

5. Conclusion

The result from the study showed that the IMMPA EC Lab was able to increase the students' score in the achievement test in the learning of Electrochemistry. This is parallel with studies abroad (Kizilkaya & Askar, 2008; Moreno et al., 2000) where students were found to achieve higher performance when learning with a tutorial supported by PAs. However, IMMPA EC Lab was not able to increase students' motivation level compared to students learning Electrochemistry with traditional methods. Further investigation, such as interviewing the students from treatment group should be carried out in order to assess the weakness of the IMMPA EC Lab in terms of motivating students in the learning of Electrochemistry. Study regarding PAs is still new among researchers in East-Asia. Studies associated with PAs should therefore be increased in order to involve various fields and should be applied in various stages of education so as to benefit students from diverse backgrounds.

6. References

Anthony, C. (2006). Exam Oriented Education System, 13.10.2011, Available from *http://drca.wordpress.com/2006/04/01/exam-oriented-education-system/*

Atkinson, R.K. (2002). Optimizing Learning From Examples Using Animated Pedagogical Agents. *Journal of Educational Psychology*, Vol.94, No.2, pp. 416-427.

Baylor, A.L. & Kim, Y. (2004). Pedagogical Agent Design: The Impact of Agent Realism, Gender, Ethnicity and Instructional Role. In: International Conference on Intelligent Tutoring Systems. Maceio, Brazil, 2004.

Baylor, A.L. (2005). The Impact of Pedagogical Agent Image on Affective Outcomes. *Proceedings of Workshop on Affective Interactions: Computers in the Affective Loop, International Conference on Intelligent User Interfaces*, San Diego, CA, 2005.

Biswas, G., Leelawong, K., Belynne, K., Viswanath, K., Vye, N., Schwartz, D., Davis, J. (2004) Incorporating Self-Regulated Learning Techniques into Learning by Teaching Environments, 16.7.09, Available from http://www.cogsci.northwestern.edu/cogsci2004/papers/paper365.pdf

Bowen, C.W. (1998). Item Design Considerations for Computer-Based Testing of Student Learning in Chemistry. *Journal of Chemical Education*,Vol.75, No.9, pp. 1172-1175.

Burewicz, A.& Miranowicz, N. (2002). Categorization of visualization tools in aspects of chemical research and education. *International Journal of Quantum Chemistry,*Vol.*88*, pp. 549-563.

Burke, K.A., Greenbowe, T.J. & Windschitl, M.A. (1998). Developing and Using Conceptual Computer Animations for Chemistry Instruction. *Journal of Chemical Education,*Vol.5, No.12, pp. 1658-1661.

Bojczuk, M. (1982). Topic Difficulties in O- and A-Level Chemistry. *School Science Review,*Vol.64,pp. 545–551.

Campbell, D.T. & Stanley, J.C. (1963). *Experimental and Quasi-Experimental Designs for Research.*Rand Mcnally College Publishing Company, Chicago.

Chang, H.H. (2005). The relationship between extrinsic/intrinsic motivation and language learning strategies among college students of English in Taiwan. Master Thesis, Ming Chuan University.

Chou, C.Y., Chan, T.W. & Lin, C.J. (2003). Redefining the learning companion: the past, present and future of educational agents. *Computers & Education,*Vol.40,pp. 255-269.

Clarebout, G. & Elen, J. (2007). In Search of Pedagogical Agents' Modality and Dialogue Effects in Open Learning Environments. 23.7.2009, Available from http://www.ascilite.org.au/ajet/e-jist/docs/vol10_no1/papers/full_papers/clarebout_elen.pdf

Craig, S.D., Gholson, B. & Driscoll, D.M. (2002). Animated Pedagogical Agents in Multimedia Educational Environments: Effects of Agent Properties, Picture Features and Redundancy. *Journal of Educational Psychology,*Vol.94, No.2,pp. 428-434.

Doymus, K., Karacop, A. &Simsek, U. (2010). Effects of jigsaw and animation techniques on students' understanding of concepts and subjects in electrochemistry. *Education Tech Research Dev,*Vol.58, pp. 671-691.

Farah Mohamad Zain, Hanafi Atan, Noorizdayantie Samar, Omar Majid & Zuraidah Abd Rahman. (2008). Kesan Maklum Balas Yang Berbeza oleh Agen Pedagogi Terhadap Pencapaian Pelajar yang Berbeza Lokus Kawalan. Paper presented at*2ndInternational Malaysian Educational Technoloy Convention,* 4-7 November, Kuantan, Pahang.

Garnett, P.J. & Hackling, M.W. (1993). Chemistry Misconceptions at the Secondary-Tertiary Interface. *Chemistry in Australia,*Vol.60, No.3,pp. 117–119.

Garnett, P.J. & Treagust, D.F. (1992). Conceptual Difficulties Experienced by Senior High School Students of Electrochemistry: Electrochemical (Galvanic) and Electrolytic Cells. *Journal of Research in Science Teaching,* Vol.29, No.10,pp. 1079–1099.

Garnett, P.J., Garnett, P.J. & Hackling, M.W. (1995). Students' Alternative Conceptions in Chemistry: A Review of Research and Implications for Teaching and Learning. *Studies in Science Education,*Vol.25, pp. 69–95.

Gois, J. Y. &Giordan, M. (2009). Evolution of virtual learning environments in chemistry education. In *Enseñanza de lasCiencias,* Número Extra VIII Congreso Internacionalsobre Investigación en Didáctica de lasCiencias, Barcelona, pp. 2864-2867.

Gustafson, K.L. & Branch, R.M. (1997). *Survey of Instructional Development Model*(3rd ed.), ERIC Clearinghouse on Information Technology,NY.

Hasnira Embong. (2005). Pembinaan dan Keberkesanan Penggunaan Perisian Multimedia Elektrokimia Dalam Pengajaran dan Pembelajaran Kimia Tingkatan 4.Master Thesis, Universiti Pendidikan Sultan Idris.

Hayes-Roth, B., Maldonado, H., & Moraes, M. (2002). Designing for diversity: Multi cultural characters for a multi-cultural world. 15.7.2009, Available from http://www.stanford.edu/~kiky/Design4Diversity.pdf

Hill, J.R. & Hannafin, M.J. (2001). Teaching and Learning in Digital Environments: The Resurgence of Resourse-Based Learning. *ETR&D*,Vol.49, No.3, pp. 37-52.

Johnson, W.L., Rickel, J.W. & Lester, J.C. (2000). Animated pedagogical agents: face-to-face interaction in interactive learning environments. *International Journal of Artificial Intelligence in Education*,Vol.11, pp. 47-78.

Johnstone, A. H. (1993). The Development of Chemistry Teaching: A Changing Response to Changing Demand. *Journal of Chemical Education*,Vol.70,No.9, pp. 701–705.

Keeman. (2007). Malaysia - Exam-Oriented Nation? 13.10.2011, Available from http://keemanxp.com/blog/2007/malaysia-exam-oriented-nation.html

Kemp, J.E., Morrison, G.R. & Ross, S.V. (2004). *Design Effective Instruction*(4th ed.), John Wiley & Sons, New York.

KhalijahMohd. Salleh. (1999). Malaysia, In:*Popularising Science and Technology: Some Asian Case Studies*, SankaranRamanathan, (Ed.),55-65, ISBN 9971905736, Singapore.

Kim, Y., Baylor, A.L. & PALS Group. (2006). Pedagogical Agents as Learning Companions: The Role of Agent Competency and Type of Interaction. *ETR&D*,Vol.54, No.3, pp. 223-243.

Kirk, K. (2008). Performance, Perception and Choice of Animated Pedagogical Agent. Ph.D Thesis, University of Nevada, Las Vegas.

Kivinen, K. (2003). Assessing Motivation and the Use of Learning Strategies by Secondary School Students in Three International Schools. PhD Thesis. University of Tampere, Finland. 6.4.2010, Available from http://acta.uta.fi/pdf/951-44-5556-8.pdf

Kizilkaya, G. & Askar, P. (2008). The effect of an embedded pedagogical agent on the students' science achievement. *Interactive Technology and Smart Education,Vol.*5, No.4, pp. 208-216.

Land, S.M. (2000). Cognitive Requirements for Learning with Open-Ended Learning Environments. *ETR&D*, Vol.48, No.3, pp. 61-78.

Lee, T.T. & Kamisah Osman. (2010). Pembinaan Modul Multimedia Interaktif dengan Agen Pedagogi (IMMPA) dalam Pembelajaran Elektrokimia: Analisis Keperluan. *Proceedings of Kolokium Kebangsaan Pasca Siswazah Sains & Matematik 2010*, pp. 25, Universiti Pendidikan Sultan Idris, December 22, 2010.

Lee, T.T. & Mohammad Yusof Arshad. (2009). Miskonsepsi Pelajar Tingkatan Empat Mengenai Elektrokimia. *Jurnal Sains dan Matematik UPSI*, Vol.1, No.2, pp. 52-64.

Lee, T.T. (2008). Kefahaman Pelajar Tingkatan Empat Mengenai Elektrokimia. Master thesis. Universiti Teknologi Malaysia.

Lerman, Z. M. (2001). Visualizing the Chemical Bond. *Chemical Education International*, Vol.2, (August 2001), pp. 6-13. 21.4.2011, Available from http://old.iupac.org/publications/cei/vol2/0201x0006.html

Lerman, Z.M. & Morton, D. (2009). Using the Arts and Computer Animation to Make Chemistry Accessible to All in the Twenty-First Century. In:*Chemistry Education in the ICT Age*, M. Gupta-Bhowan, S. Jhaumeer-Laulloo, H. Li KamWah, & P.

Ramasami, (Eds.), pp. 31-40, Springer Science + Business Media B.V, ISBN 978-1-4020-9731-7, Mauritius.

Lewin, K. (1975). *Science Education in Malaysia and Sri Lanka.* IDS Discussion Paper No. 74.

Lin, H.S., Yang T.C., Chiu, H.L. & Chou, C.Y. (2002). Students' Difficulties in Learning Electrochemistry. *Proc. Natl. Sci. Counc. ROC(D),Vol.*12, No.3,pp. 100–105.

Mahzan Bakar. (2005). *Curriculum Specifications: Chemistry Form 4,* Ministry of Education Malaysia, Putrajaya, Malaysia.

Maldonado, H. & Hayes-Roth, B. (2004). Toward Cross-Cultural Believability in Character Design. 15.7.2009, Available from http://hci.stanford.edu/publications/2004/CrossCultBelievability0304/CrossCultBelievability0304.pdf

Maldonado, H., Roselyn Lee, J. E., Brave, S., Nass, C., Nakajima, H., Yamada, R., Iwamura, K., Morishima, Y. (2005). We Learn Better Together: Enhancing eLearning with Emotional Characters. In:*Computer Supported Collaborative Learning: The Next 10 Years!*T. Koschmann, D. Suthers, & T.W. Chan, (Ed.),408-417, Lawrence Erlbaum Associates, Mahwah, NJ.

Melissa Ng, L.Y.A. & Kamariah Abu Bakar. (2006) *Motivational Belief and Self-Regulated Learning A Study On Malaysian Students.* In: Eras 2006 Conference. Singapore, 29-31 May 206. 7.4.2010, Available from http://eprints.usm.my/4891/1/Motivational_Belief_And_Self-Regulated_Learning_A_Study_On_Malaysian_Students.pdf

Mohd Feham Md. Ghalib. (2006). Design, Development & Evaluation of a Web Courseware with a Pedagogical Agent. Ph.D. Thesis, Universiti Sains Malaysia.

Moreno, R. & Mayer, R.E. (2000). Pedagogical agents in constructivist multimedia environments: The role of image and language in the instructional communication. 15.7.2009, Available from http://www.unm.edu/~moreno/PDFS/Roundtble.pdf

Moreno, R. & Mayer, R.E. (2005). Role of Guidance, Reflection, and Interactivity in an Agent-Based Multimedia Game. *Journal of Educational Psychology,*Vol.97, No.1, pp. 117-128.

Moreno, R., Mayer, R.E. & Lester, J.C. (2000). Life-Like Pedagogical Agents in Constructivist Multimedia Environments: Cognitive Consequences of their Interaction. 16.7.2009, Available fromhttp://www.unm.edu/~moreno/PDFS/ED-MEDIA-DAP.pdf

Morrison, G.R., Ross, S.M. & Kemp, J.E. (2007). *Designing Effective Instruction*(5th ed.), John Wiley & Sons, Inc., NJ.

Moundridou, M. & Virvou, M. (2002). Evaluating the Persona Effect of an Interface Agent in an Intelligent Tutoring System. *Journal of Computer Assisted Learning,*Vol.18, No.2, 26.8.2009, Available from http://thalis.cs.unipi.gr/~mariam/JCAL.pdf

Nabila Akbal Noorul Kamar, Omar Majid, Zuraidah Abd. Rahman & Hanafi Atan. (2008). Kesan Agen Pedagogi Terhadap Pencapaian dan Motivasi Pelajar dalam Pembelajaran Fizik: Dapatan Kajian Rintis. Paper presented at*2ndInternational Malaysian Educational Technoloy Convention,* 4-7 November, Kuantan, Pahang.

Needham, R. (1987). *CLIS in the Classroom: Teaching Strategies for Developing Understanding in Science* University of Leeds, Leeds.

Norsiati Mohd Ghazali. (2008). Pembangunan Dan Penilaian Perisian Kursus Pengajaran Dan Pembelajaran Multimedia Interaktif "Analisis Kualitatif Garam" Dalam Subjek Kimia. Master Thesis, UniversitiKebangsaan Malaysia.

Oldham, V. (2003). Effective use of ICT in secondary science: guidelines and case studies. *School Science Review*, Vol.84, No.309, pp. 53-60.

Pintrich, R.R., &DeGroot, E.V. (1990). Motivational and self-regulated learning components of classroom academic performance. *Journal of Educational Psychology*,Vol.82, pp.33-40.

Predinger, H., Saeyor, S. & Ishizuka, M. n.d. Animated Agents for Language Conversation Training, 15.7.2009, Available from http://www.miv.t.u-tokyo.ac.jp/papers/helmut-edmedia01.pdf

Qureshi, E. (2001, 2004), Instructional Design Models. 24.9.2009, Available afrom http://web2.uwindsor.ca/courses/edfac/morton/instructional_design.htm

Qureshi, E. (2003). Instructional Design Models. 24.9.2009, Available from http://home.comcast.net/~elenaqureshi/IDModels.htm

Rodrigues, S., Smith, A. & Ainley, M. (2001). Video clips and animation in chemistry CD-ROMS: Student interest and Preference. *Australian Science Teachers Journal*, Vol.47, No.2, pp. 9-15.

Roziah Abdullah. (2005). Pembangunan dan Keberkesanan Pakej Multimedia Kemahiran Berfikir bagi Mata Pelajaran Kimia. PhD. Thesis. Universiti Kebangsaan Malaysia.

Russell, J.W., Kozma, R.B., Jones, T., Wykoff, J., Marx, N. & Davis, J. (1997). Use of Simultaneous-Synchronized Macroscopic, Microscopic, and symbolic Representations to Enhance the Teaching and Learning of Chemical Concepts. *Journal of Chemical Education*, Vol.74, No.3, pp. 330-334.

Sadiah Baharom., Ong, E.T., Marzita Putih., Sopia Mad Yassin., Nurul Huda Abd. Rahman. &MuhamadIkhwan Mat. Saad. (2009). The Validation and adaptation of MLSQ aimed to assess student use of self-regulated learning. Paper presented at *1st International Conference on Educational Research and Practice Enhancing Human Capital through Teacher Education*, 10-11 June, Faculty of Educational Studies, UPM, Serdang.

Sanger, M.J. & Greenbowe, T.J. (1997a).Common Student Misconceptions in Electrochemistry: Galvanic, Electrolytic, and Concentration Cells. *Journal of Research inScience Teaching*,Vol.34, No.4,pp. 377-398.

Sanger, M.J. & Greenbowe, T.J. (1997b). Students' Misconceptions in Electrochemistry: Current Flow in Electrolyte Solutions and the Salt Bridge. *Journal of ChemicalEducation*, Vol.74, pp. 819-823.

Sanger, M.J.& Greenbowe, T.J. (2000). Addressing Student Misconceptions Concerning Electron Flow in Aqueous Solutions with Instruction Iincluding Computer Animations and Conceptual Change Strategies. *International Journal of Science Education*, Vol.22,No.5,pp. 521–537.

Shores, M.L. & Shannon, D.M. (2007). The effects of self-regulation, motivation, anxiety, and attributions on mathematics achievement for fifth and sixth grade students. *School Science and Mathematics*, Vol.107, No.6, pp. 225. ISSN 0036-6803. 6.4.2010, Available from http://www.thefreelibrary.com/The+effects+of+self-regulation%2c+motivation%2c+anxiety%2c+and+attributions+...-a0171211906

Slater, D. (2000). Interactive Animated Pedagogical Agents Mixing the Best of Human and Computer-Based Tutors. Master Thesis, Stanford University.

Tan, Y.T., Loh, W.L. & Tan, O.T. (2007). *Success Chemistry SPM,*Oxford Fajar Sdn. Bhd, ISBN, 978-967-65-9384-9, Shah Alam.

Wu H.K. & Shah, P. (2004). Exploring Visuospatial Thinking in Chemistry Learning. *Science Education,*Vol.*88*, pp. 465-492.

Xiao, J., Stasko, J., & Catrambone, R. (2004). *An empirical study of the effect of agent competence on user performance and perception.* Paper presented at the Autonomous Agents and Multiagent Systems (AAMAS 2004), New York City, 24.11.2009, Available fromhttp://www.cc.gatech.edu/~john.stasko/papers/aamas04.pdf

4

Fostering the Diagnostic Competence of Teachers with Multimedia Training – A Promising Approach?

Christina Barth and Michael Henninger
University of Education Weingarten
Germany

1. Introduction

Multimedia as a learning tool offers new opportunities in supporting learning processes. At the same time, it also plays a role in teacher education through e-learning platforms, which provide online resources for learning or computer- or web-based training, which facilitate the acquisition of specialized knowledge. Soft skills (e.g., communicative or diagnostic skills) can also be trained in a multimedia-based learning environment. In this chapter, fostering the diagnostic competence of pre-service teachers through a multimedia-based learning environment is discussed.

Diagnostic competence is one of the Main competencies that a teacher should have to be able to deal with the current and future challenges of teaching at a school (Bruehwiler et al., 2004; Schrader, 1997). The concept of "diagnostic competence in teaching situations" is a broad one, which brings together different aspects of teaching competence (Barth, 2010). Some of the components of "diagnostic competence" include automated behavior. Automated behavior needs a different instructional approach compared to learning new things (Henninger & Weingandt, 2003). Multimedia-based learning environments can be effective tools in developing the ability to reflect on and change partly automated behavior, such as communication skills. Different studies examining the effects of a multimedia training tool called CaiManOnline© have shown that this can be done (Barth, Hauck, Hörmann & Henninger, 2007; Henninger & Hörmann, 2007; Henninger & Mandl, 2000; Jaschniok, Barth, Amann & Henninger, 2008). This kind of virtual teacher training focuses on the receptive part of communication, i.e., understanding and interpreting utterances, in which video sequences of teaching behavior are used in a multimedia-based learning environment.

Recognizing the need for teachers, who are especially competent in diagnosing learning prerequisites in class, we first want to present a conceptualization of diagnostic competence in teaching situations that focuses on the trainable aspects. Next, a study is presented, which explains the starting point for a multimedia training approach. Following are recommendations on how to create multimedia applications in the field of automated behavior.

2. The importance of diagnostic competencies for teachers

One of the responsibilities of teachers is to be able to diagnose an extremely wide variety of learning prerequisites on an ongoing basis and determine the opportunities available to their students. This diagnosis is a precondition for adaptive teaching competency, which is defined as "the teacher's ability to adjust instruction to the individual learning processes of pupils in such a way as to create favourable conditions for each student's learning for understanding" (Bruehwiler & Vogt, 2007).

Making a competent diagnosis in teaching situations means that a teacher has to be able to recognize how students indicate their learning requirements within the scope of social interaction. The teacher also has to gather additional specific information relevant to this diagnosis or be able to recall this information in order to utilize it (Barth, 2010).

This means that the teacher has to use different sources of information and knowledge to be able to make a diagnosis, such as:

1. Situation-dependent information: This information is gathered from observable aspects of the teaching situation, like the social interaction in the classroom or the individual student's interaction with the lesson content.
2. Person or class-specific information: This is the information about an individual student or a class that is available to the teacher.
3. Professional and experiential knowledge: Both knowledge types take place at the same time since it is assumed that both are integrated in the individual knowledge structures of the teacher. These individual knowledge structures can be described as subjective theories (Groeben et al., 1988; Steinke, 1998; Wahl, 1997).

To foster diagnostic teacher competencies, it is crucial to know which information or knowledge sources play the most important role during the process of diagnosing students' learning prerequisites. If the teachers or pre-service teachers mainly use prior knowledge (e.g., about a special student or class), then the usefulness of a multimedia learning environment, in which video sequences of a classroom situation are used would be very limited. If teachers refer primarily to situation-dependent information, then such a learning environment could have great potential in fostering diagnostic teacher competencies.

In addressing the question of whether multimedia learning environments are able to foster the ability to make a proper diagnosis of learning prerequisites in teaching situations, two different things need to be considered:

1. The theoretical concept of a competent diagnosis in teaching situations
2. The actual diagnosis of learning prerequisites in classroom situations made by the pre-service teachers

3. Analysis of the theoretical concept of competent diagnosis in teaching situations

The term competent diagnosis in teaching situations refers to the diagnosis of situative learning requirements of students during classroom teaching sessions. Three of the most important learning requirements or key learning prerequisites are motivation, emotion and comprehension.

Barth (2010) identified five different dimensions of diagnostic competence in classroom situations:

- Designing the lesson to serve the diagnosis of situative learning requirements
- Competent perception of the situation (which includes the ability to structure the situation cognitively, the ability to change the focus of attention and the willingness and ability to adopt other perspectives)
- Competent hypothesis generation and hypothesis testing
- Reflecting on one's subjectivity
- Competent receptive and productive communicative behavior

Except for the first dimension, all the other dimensions refer to the teacher's behavior in the classroom situation and all imply interpretation and meaning-making processes. This is the first indication that a learning environment, which enables pre-service teachers to reflect on existing interpretation patterns, generate new ones and consciously deal with them, like the CaiManOnline© learning tool, can foster diagnostic competence in classroom situations.

Typical CaiManOnline© Scenario:

The multimedia training tool, CaiManOnline©[1] (Henninger & Mandl, 2003), considers instructional standards deduced from the cognitive-apprenticeship theory (Collins et al., 1989). Pre-Service-teachers or other learners have to analyze video-based communicative situations with CaiManOnline©. While working on this task, the students are assisted by several elements, which support reflection. The students have to verbalize and explain their analysis of the communication situation presented. To foster reflection processes, expert solutions pertaining to the tasks recommended are available. In addition, depending on the specific implementation, online coaches can provide feedback to the students. Feedback by a coach is regarded as a critical factor, which could either motivate or hinder learning (Hattie & Timperley, 2007).

CaiManOnline© is usually integrated into a training as a virtual self-learning phase of a blended learning communication training to foster receptive communication behavior.

4. Analysis of the actual diagnosis of learning prerequisites in classroom situations made by pre-service teachers

The DIAL study (empirical clarification of the basis for the *dia*gnosis of situative *l*earning requirements of students during classroom sessions) conducted at the University of Education Weingarten examines the kind of information and knowledge that pre-service teachers use to make a diagnosis of comprehension as a situative learning requirement. Comprehension was chosen as a learning prerequisite because it is one of the most important in learning situations.

4.1 Research questions

In order to create an adequate learning environment, we need specific answers related to what is being learned in order to decide which video-based material should be included or which specific instructional design should be used to foster reflection of diagnostic behavior.

[1] CaiMan means "Computer-Aided Management Applications"

Thus, the main research questions of the DIAL project were: What kind of class-specific information (information which is independent of the specific situation) do teachers use to make a diagnosis (e.g., basic information about the class)? What kind of situation-dependent information (verbal, nonverbal and paraverbal signs of the students) do teachers use to make a diagnosis? What kind of professional knowledge and experiential knowledge do teachers use to make a diagnosis? How important are the different categories of information and knowledge for the diagnosis?

4.2 Design of the DIAL study

To answer these research questions, this study used a quasi-experimental design. A total of 36 pre-service teachers (29 female, 7 male) were asked to watch videotaped classroom sessions. Each participant was presented with a school lesson in both a school subject that was part of his/her course of studies and with a school subject that was not familiar to him/her. In total, we examined three school subjects: German, geography und chemistry. Furthermore, the information about the school class (information vs. no information) and modes of classroom interaction[2] (individual work/work in pairs vs. teacher interaction with the whole class) was varied.

4.3 Data collection

An online questionnaire was used for the data collection. After the participants had watched the videotaped classroom session, they were asked to make a diagnosis of the degree of comprehension of different students and to explain what information or knowledge led to this diagnosis. The written responses of the participants regarding the source of their information and knowledge were the textual basis of a qualitative content analysis. The setting is presented in Fig. 1.

Fig. 1. Online Questionnaire

[2] With regard to data privacy, we could not disclose real information about the individual pupils to the teachers. Thus, we created an information situation that was comparable to when a teacher meets a new class for the first time: The teacher knows a little bit about the students from information obtained from colleagues or former teachers, but does not have specific information about the individuals. In our scenario, the teachers know something about the level of proficiency of the class, the variance in performance between the pupils in the class or whether there are "difficult" pupils in the class.

The aim of this qualitative analysis was to determine the categories of the different sources of information and knowledge that were relevant to the diagnoses made by the teachers. In addition, quantitative methods were used to find out how often specific categories were used under the different experimental conditions.

4.4 Results of the DIAL study for multimedia learning

In the first result, the categories of the different sources of information and knowledge identified, which the participants used to make a diagnosis, are presented in Table 1. To develop a set of categories, a qualitative content analysis (Mayring, 2008) was used. The following categories were found by analyzing 9 of the 36 data sets and matching them to the previously mentioned sources of information and knowledge. Afterwards, the 36 data sets were categorized by two raters according to the following categories:

Situation-dependent information - observable	Body language (e.g., viewing direction of the student, facial expression, posture/gesture)
	Interaction between the people (e.g., existing or missing interaction between different students, interaction between students and teacher)
	Actions of the people (e.g., verbal expressions of the students, reactions to external stimuli, behavior of their classmates)
	Participation in class
	Observation of how a student works (e.g., positive or negative assessment of how student works, writing behavior)
Situation-dependent information – non-observable	Interpretation of student's appearance (e.g., positive appearance, negative appearance)
	Interpretation of how a student works (e.g., effective way of working, ineffective way of working)
	Stereotypes of students activated by watching the videotape (e.g., stereotypes about personality traits, skills, etc.)
Class-specific information	This category was used by only one participant
Professional and experiential knowledge	Knowledge with respect to teaching, methods and contents of instruction
	Knowledge with respect to the general behavior of a student
	Knowledge with respect to determining if the answers of the students were adequate or inadequate

Table 1. Categories of information and knowledge sources

One remarkable result was that the participants did not refer to the class-specific information provided. Only one of the 20 participants who received class-specific information made a connection between his judgement and this information. We limited the theoretically based category, "person or class-specific information" to "class-specific information" because only "class-specific" information was available to the participants.

Based on these qualitative results, the first research question can be answered: What kind of class-specific information (information which is independent of the specific situation) do teachers use to make a diagnosis (e.g., basic information about the class)?

The qualitative analysis shows that only one participant explicitly used the situation-independent information that was made available prior to the viewing to make a judgment concerning the degree of comprehension of a student. However, it should be noted that only anonymized descriptions of the class were given to the participants due to data privacy concerns. The participant who used the class-information, made just the one statement following the lesson plan [which included a description of the class], which was that "the class is accustomed to working in pairs and group work." On the basis of this statement alone, a differentiated analysis of the class-specific information was not possible. Nevertheless, this category was kept in the data analysis due to the fact that this category is based on theoretical foundations.

What kind of situation-dependent information (verbal, nonverbal and paraverbal signs of the students) do teachers use to make a diagnosis?

To answer this question, we created two categories: one includes specific observable signs and the other is based on inferences about the situational activities.

The "observable" category: This category includes statements made by the participants about the body language of the students (e.g., "He often turns around"), their facial expressions (e.g., "puzzled look") or the posture or gesture of a student (e.g., "she is sealing herself off from the other students with her hand"). This category also includes statements concerning the interaction between the people (e.g., "the boy is discussing the subject matter with the student next to him") or the actions of the people (e.g., "I heard him saying: 'Eh? What a bullshit'"). Statements concerning class participation (e.g., "she doesn't participate in class;" "he is participating actively in class") or an observation of how they work (e.g., "the student quickly begins to complete the text") are also included in this category.

The "non-observable" category: This category includes statements concerning the student's (positive vs. negative) appearance (e.g., "no interest to complete the task;" "it seems the he is preoccupied with something else"), an interpretation of how the student works (effective vs. ineffective) (e.g., "he is distracted whilst working;" "the student is following the lesson attentively") or statements based on stereotypes of the students that were triggered by watching the videotape (e.g., "I think he is a clever tot;" "I assume he is one of the good students in class").

What kind of professional and experiential knowledge do teachers use in making a diagnosis? With regard to the data, we created three sub-dimensions of these knowledge types: The first covered knowledge about teaching, methods and content of instruction (e.g., the work order was quite clear), knowledge about a student's general behavior (e.g., "I suppose she couldn't complete the worksheet because she wasn't able to deal with the content") and knowledge about whether the students gave adequate answers (e.g., "right example;" "wrong answer").

In the next step, all the data of the 36 participants of the study were matched to these categories by two raters. Cohen's kappa coefficient was used to estimate interraterreliability (Cohen's kappa = .67) and showed that there was good agreement according to Altmann (1990). If only the main categories are considered, Cohen's kappa would be even higher (.73). This could be an indication that it is difficult for raters to distinguish between subcategories. In the following step, an analysis was done on how many of the 36 participants (summary of all judgments made of a student's comprehension[3]) mentioned the different categories. The results are presented in figures 2 to 5. The figures indicate the number and percentage of participants who used or did not use a category.

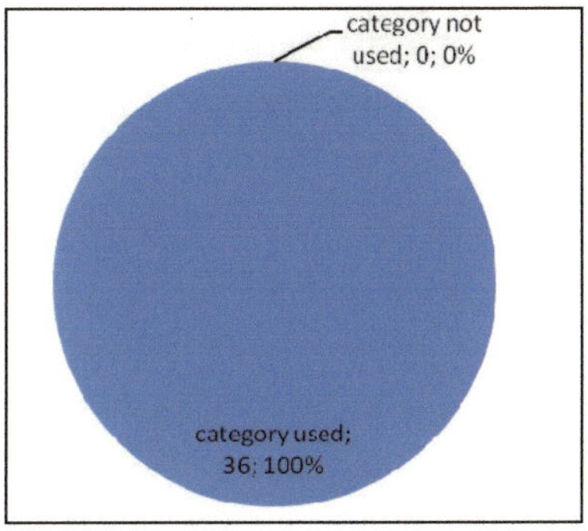

Fig. 2. Situation-dependent information - observable

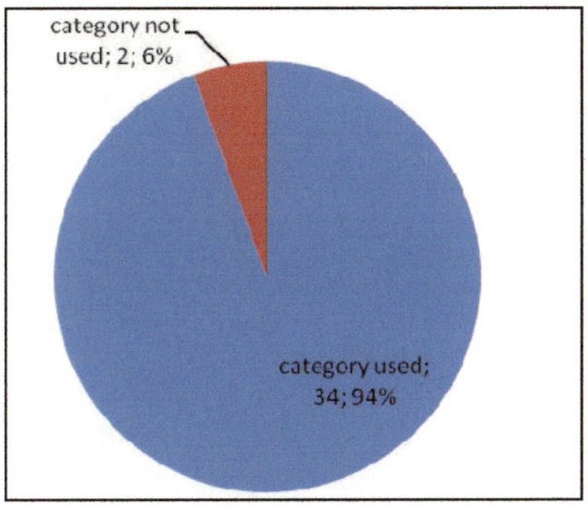

Fig. 3. Situation-dependent information - non-observable

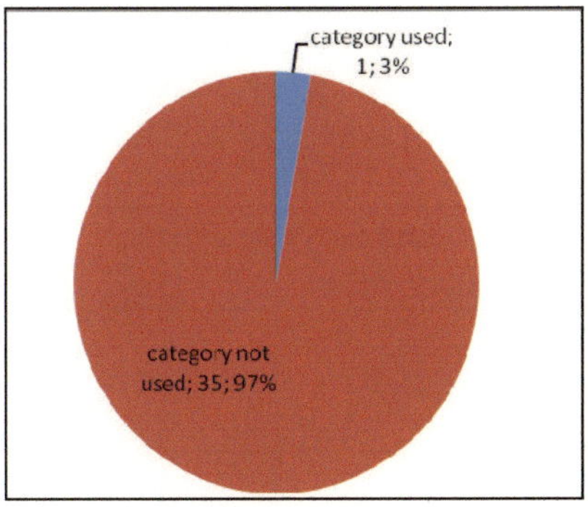

Fig. 4. Class-specific information

[3] In each scene presented (altogether four scenes), the participants were requested to make a diagnosis of at least one student's comprehension after three minutes (a maximum of three diagnostic assessments were possible). Afterwards, the participants were given the opportunity to watch the whole scene again and make another diagnostic assessment of one to three students. The total duration of the different scenes ranged from 4.02 to 10.30 minutes. For reasons of comparability, the results presented in this chapter refer exclusively to the first 3 minutes of each scene.

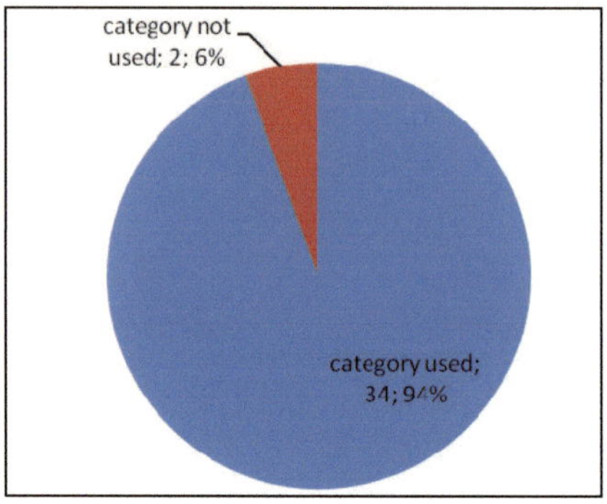

Fig. 5. Professional and experiential knowledge

Based on these diagrams, we can answer the question, "How important are the different category types of information and knowledge for the diagnosis?" The data shows that the overwhelming majority of the participants used situation-specific information, as well as professional and experiential knowledge to make a diagnosis. Just one person explicitly used the class-specific information provided.

To determine if the participants used some of the categories of information and knowledge sources (situation-dependent information - observable, situation-dependent information - non-observable, class-specific information, professional and experiential knowledge) more frequently than others, the data was aggregated. Therefore, the diagnoses of the participants for all four scenes were put together in a way that summarizes the explanatory statements. If a person mentioned the category "professional and experiential knowledge" in three of the four scenes presented, the value 3 was assigned to this person. If a person mentioned this category in only one scene, the value 1 was assigned to this person. In this manner, an ordinal variable was created. With this variable, it was possible to use Friedman's test to examine if a category ranked significantly higher or lower than the others. In fact, the results showed that to be the case ($\chi2$ (3, N=36) = 89.45, p=.000).

	Mean	Standard derivation	Min.	Max.	Percentile		
					25.	50. (Median)	75.
Situation-dependent information - observable	3.83	.378	3	4	4.00	4.00	4.00
Situation-dependent information - non observable	2.50	1.108	0	4	2.00	3.00	3.00
Class-specific information	0.03	.167	0	1	0.00	.00	.00
Professional and experiential knowledge	2.25	1.105	0	4	1.00	2.00	3.00

Table 2. Descriptive statistics (N = 36)

Thereafter, pairwise comparisons were used to identify which categories were used more often. The Bonferroni adjustment was used to calculate the levels of significance ($\alpha = 0.01/6 = 0.002$; $\alpha = 0.05/6 = 0.008$). Statistically, all the differences were highly significant except for the difference between the situation-dependent information - non-observable and professional experiential knowledge categories. The results are presented in tables 2 and 3.

Pairwise comparisons	Mean rank	$\chi 2$	df	Exact significance
Situation-dependent information - observable	1.88	27.00	1	.000
Situation-dependent information (interpretation)	1.13			
Situation-dependent information - non-observable	2.00	36.00	1	.000
Class-specific information	1.00			
Situation-dependent information - observable	1.92	30.00	1	.000
Professional and experiential knowledge	1.08			
Situation-dependent information - non-observable	1.96	33.00	1	.000
Class-specific information	1.04			
Situation-dependent information - non-observable	1.57	1.00	1	.424
Professional and experiential knowledge	1.43			
Professional and experiential knowledge	1.97	34.00	1	.000
Class-specific information	1.03			

Table 3. Pairwise comparisons (N = 36)

According to these results, the category "situation-dependent information - observable" was used most frequently, followed by the category "situation-dependent information - non observable." The difference between the latter category and the category "professional and experiential knowledge" was not statistically significant. As expected, the category "class-specific information was used the least.

Further analyses refer to the influence of the different experimental conditions. To check whether the information about the class, which was given to some of the participants really had no influence on the statements made by them, a Chi^2 test for each of the six classroom scenes presented (German, geography and chemistry - each school subject varied between a situation of individual work/working in pairs or teacher interaction with the whole class) was conducted. The results of the Chi^2 test (see Appendix A) showed that there was no difference in any of the scenes presented. This means that a participant's decision to use or not use a category did not depend on whether the participant received information about the class or not.

However, it should be noted that this test was not based on a random sample of the target population, and that each of the two variables can only take one of two values (class-information vs. no class-information; category used vs. category not used). For the Chi^2 test approximation to be valid, the expected frequency should be at least 5, which was actually not the case in every single Chi^2 test.

These results not only show that the participants who received "class-specific information" did not use the category "class-specific information" more often than participants without this specific information (it was not possible for the participants without class-specific information to use this category), but also that there was no statistically significant difference between both groups of participants in the use of the other categories.

Furthermore, a test was done to see whether a difference between the subjects presented could be determined. Therefore, the aggregate data (sum of all four scenes) was used again. The Wilcoxon test was used to compare how often the different categories were used. The result was that there was no statistically significant difference between the school subjects presented (German, geography, chemistry) in terms of how often the diverse categories are used (situation-dependent information - observable, situation- dependent information - non-observable, class-specific information, professional and experiential knowledge). The results of the different tests are presented in Appendix B.

To compare the classroom scenes showing individual work/work in pairs or an interaction of the teacher with the whole class, the Wilcoxon test was also used. The results showed that there were no statistically significant differences between the different situation types with respect to the categories "situation-dependent information - observable," "situation-dependent information - non-observable" and "class specific" (see Appendix C). This was also not expected because these categories were used by nearly all (category: situation-dependent information) or almost none (category: class-specific) of the participants. A significant difference resulted, however, with the category "professional and experiential knowledge" ($Z= - 2.162$; $p=.031$). In situations where a teacher interacts with the whole class, this category was used more frequently compared to the situations in which the students worked individually or in pairs. This is actually not surprising because in situations where a teacher interacts with the whole class, the participants can hear what the students say and determine whether their statements are correct or incorrect. In situations where the students work individually or in pairs, the participation of the students cannot, by its very nature, be heard or assessed.

More detailed qualitative and quantitative analyses of the DIAL study are still in progress.

4.5 Discussion

In this section, the results of the DIAL study are summarized. The Dial study showed that pre-service teachers mainly used the situation-specific information available to make a diagnosis of a student's comprehension. In doing so, the participants of the DIAL study usually referred to observable information (i.e., their perceptions), but also to non-observable information. This means that the participant interpreted the student's behavior. To outsiders, such as researchers and possibly the pre-service teacher as well, it was not possible to know which perception led to which interpretation. Class-specific information, which was given to only some of the participants, was obviously not used to make a diagnosis.

This result (if confirmed by additional studies) could be an indication that previous knowledge plays less of a role in the process of diagnosing the learning prerequisites of students.

Some of the critical aspects of the DIAL study need to be addressed. Surely one of the most critical aspects is the fact that for reasons of data privacy only anonymized class information was given to the participants instead of situation-independent true information about the different students filmed. In a real classroom situation, it is certainly the exception rather than the rule that a teacher only has previous knowledge about the class instead of previous knowledge about the different students. In the DIAL study, it was therefore not possible to verify the impact of previous knowledge about specific students on the teacher's diagnosis with respect to the learning prerequisites, like comprehension in "real-life" classroom situations.

A further critical aspect of the study is that individual work or work in pairs could not be presented in a realistic way to the participants compared with situations, in which the teacher interacts with the whole class, which were more realistic. This is because of the fact that in a real classroom situation a teacher is able to move about the classroom freely and observe how tasks are processed and solved by the students. Unfortunately, the presentation of a videotaped classroom situation does not provide any interaction. This means that the participant is not able to actively participate in the situation. Therefore, the realistic presentation, especially of the situation with individual work or work in pairs, has to be viewed critically, as well as the transferability of the results concerning these special situations.

5. Conclusions

How can the DIAL study help with respect to developing recommendations for multimedia applications? With regard to a soft skill, like making a diagnosis concerning a student's comprehension, we can draw different conclusions from the findings.

The DIAL study showed that previous knowledge (in this case about the class) plays less of a role compared to the teacher's diagnosis of the student's comprehension. This indicates that a multimedia application could be a worthwhile approach in fostering the teacher competency described. If previous knowledge about the class or individual students does not seem to have a strong influence on the pre-service teacher diagnoses, a learning environment which focuses mainly on situative cues, could be a useful way to foster the ability to make a competent diagnosis in teaching situations. Such a tool, which includes video sequences of classroom sessions and enables students to reflect on existing interpretation patterns and deal with them consciously, could be a promising approach in helping to develop the skills to be able to make a competent diagnosis in teaching situations.

With reference to the DIAL results, a multimedia learning environment could especially support pre-service teachers to become aware of the basis of their own diagnostic behavior. This is possible if a pre-service teacher gets a chance to de-automate his/her automated diagnostic behavior in everyday life (cf. de-automation approach of speech receptive behavior, Henninger & Mandl, 2003). One way to accomplish this is to summon someone to explain the basis of her/his own diagnoses and study how they make the diagnosis. Such a practice was used in the DIAL study, by asking the participants to write down the specific information or knowledge that led to their diagnosis. A similar procedure is also implemented in the CaiManOnline© training tool.

The results of the DIAL study show that it is not easy for pre-service teachers to describe the observations that lead to their diagnoses. Often, they described their interpretations instead, which were not linked to a specific perception. To support pre-service teachers become aware of the perceptions underlying their interpretations, training in a multimedia learning environment could certainly be a viable approach. Additionally, usage of one's own professional an experiential knowledge can be made clear and transparent to the pre-service teachers as learners in a multimedia learning environment, which includes videotaped classroom situations. This can also be done by asking the participants to write down the specific knowledge that led to their diagnosis. In this way, the learners can be supported in developing their professional competence and to be aware of this competence.

All in all, our data suggests that it is useful to create a multimedia-based learning scenario that supports pre-service teachers develop diagnostic competencies. The study shows that teachers could benefit from a reflection of their behavior, thus an instructional design should focus on this aspect.

Therefore, a multimedia learning environment should fulfill the following requirements:

- It should provide a realistic simulation of a classroom situation. This is easy to implement by using a videotaped classroom situation that shows a teacher interacting with the whole class. However, it is barely possible to present a realistic situation of an individual work or a work in pairs. Therefore, the classroom situations presented should be selected carefully.
- Providing a realistic representation implies that a learner does not have to work with classroom scenarios that do not have a context, but rather with scenarios, in which a context is integrated. This can be implemented by giving information about the subject of the lesson and about the scene in the videotaped lesson. In the DIAL study this was realized with a detailed draft for the teaching unit, which was given to the participants. This information could also support pre-service teachers in using their content knowledge, pedagogical content knowledge and generic pedagogical knowledge, which are all part of a teacher's professional knowledge (Shulman, 1986) that enables a teacher to make a hypothesis about a student's comprehension and test it through specific observation, which is one of the dimensions of diagnostic competence in classroom situations (Barth, 2010).
- The diagnosis of learning prerequisites is assumed to be a strongly automated behavior. To change automated behavior, it is necessary to de-automate and become aware of the steps taken and to reflect on them (Antos, 1992; Henninger & Mandl, 2003; Lentiev, 1981; Schooler, Ohlsson & Brooks, 1993). Afterwards, the new behavior can be re-

automated. Therefore, a multimedia learning environment should support a learner in de-automating and reflecting on his/her own diagnostic behavior. This can be realized by asking the pre-service teacher to explain the basis of his/her diagnoses, e.g., in a written text. This not only gives insight into the teacher's diagnoses, such as in the DIAL study, but also gives the teacher insight in understanding why he/she is making a specific diagnosis. This also means that the dimension "reflecting on one's subjectivity" of the diagnostic competence in classroom situations can be developed in a multimedia learning environment (Barth, 2010).

- To become aware of one's own interpretation process, it could also be helpful to the pre-service teachers to have the opportunity to analyze the diagnoses and the basis of the diagnoses of other people, such as expert teachers, or to get an overview of the different sources that can be used to make a diagnosis, like the ones identified in the DIAL study.

The findings of this chapter can be summarized as follows: The potential for fostering the diagnostic competence of teachers with multimedia training exists, even if there are some limitations, like the difficulty in creating a realistic classroom situation in a simulation based on videotaped classroom situations. Although it is not possible to support all dimensions of a competent diagnosis, some of them can be fostered.

This does not mean that practical training, which is an essential part of a teacher's education in Germany, can be replaced because real-life classroom situations cannot be perfectly simulated. However, multimedia teacher training that supports the acquisition of some teaching competencies, especially if they are related to behavioral factors and reflection is necessary to change this behavior pattern, can be helpful.

6. Appendix A

Chi² tests: Information about the class given vs. not given (N = 36)

Category	**Situation**		**Category used**	**Category not used**	**$\chi2$**	**df**	**Exact significance (2-tailed)**
Situation-dependent information – observable	German – interaction with whole class	information given	14	1	.76	1	1.000
		information not given	11	0			
	German – individual work /work in pairs	information given	15	0	test not possible		
		information not given	15	0			
	Geography - interaction with whole class	information given	13	0	test not possible		
		information not given	13	0			
	Geography - individual work /work in pairs	information given	10	4	3.74	1	.105
		information not given	11	0			

Category	Situation		Category used	Category not used	χ2	df	Exact significance (2-tailed)
	Chemistry - interaction with whole class	information given	12	0	2.64	1	.195
		information not given	8	2			
	Chemistry - individual work /work in pairs	information given	12	0	test not possible		
		information not given	10	0			
Situation-dependent Information – non-observable	German -interaction with whole class	information given	9	6	1.41	1	.428
		information not given	4	7			
	German -individual work /work in pairs	information given	13	2	1.90	1	.348
		information not given	7	4			
	Geography - interaction with whole class	information given	9	4	0.08	1	1.000
		information not given	7	4			
	Geography - individual work /work in pairs	information given	9	4	1.39	1	.408
		information not given	5	6			
	Chemistry - interaction with whole class	information given	9	3	.56	1	.384
		information not given	6	4			
	Chemistry - individual work /work in pairs	information given	6	6	.220	1	.691
		information not given	6	4			
Class-specific information	German -interaction with whole class	information given	0	15	test not possible		
		information not given	0	11			
	German - individual work /work in pairs	information given	0	15	test not possible		
		information not given	0	11			
	Geography - interaction with whole class	information given	0	13	test not possible		
		information not given	0	11			
	Geography - individual work /work in pairs	information given	1	12	.88	1	1.000
		information not given	0	11			

Category	Situation		Category used	Category not used	χ2	df	Exact significance (2-tailed)
	Chemistry - interaction with whole class	information given	0	12	test not possible		
		information not given	0	10			
	Chemistry - individual work /work in pairs	information given	0	12	test not possible		
		information not given	0	10			
Professional and experiential knowledge	German -interaction with whole class	information given	7	8	3.31	1	.109
		information not given	9	2			
	German - individual work /work in pairs	information given	6	3	.45	1	.683
		information not given	9	8			
	Geography - interaction with whole class	information given	9	4	.08	1	1.000
		information not given	7	4			
	Geography - individual work /work in pairs	information given	8	5	.01	1	1.000
		information not given	7	4			
	Chemistry - interaction with whole class	information given	9	3	.57	1	.652
		information not given	6	4			
	Geography - individual work /work in pairs	information given	7	5	1.77	1	.231
		information not given	3	7			

Table 4.

7. Appendix B

Wilcoxon tests: School subjects

Category	School subject	N	Mean Rank		Z	Exact significance (2-tailed)
Situation-dependent information – observable	Geography - German	14	Negative Ranks Positive Ranks	1.50 .00	-1.41	.500
	Chemistry- German	12	Negative Ranks Positive Ranks	2.00 2.00	-.58	1.000
	Chemistry - Geography	10	Negative Ranks Positive Ranks	.00 1.00	-1.00	1.000

Category	School subject	N	Mean Rank		Z	Exact significance (2-tailed)
Situation-dependent Information – non-observable	Geography - German	14	Negative Ranks Positive Ranks	3.00 4.00	-.33	1.000
	Chemistry- German	12	Negative Ranks Positive Ranks	4.80 4.00	-.91	.563
	Chemistry - Geography	10	Negative Ranks Positive Ranks	2.50 3.33	-.71	.750
Class-specific information	Geography - German	14	Negative Ranks Positive Ranks	.00 1.00	-1.00	1.000
	Chemistry- German	12	Negative Ranks Positive Ranks	.00 .00	.00	1.000
	Chemistry - Geography	10	Negative Ranks Positive Ranks	.00 .00	.00	1.000
Professional and experiential knowledge	Geography - German	14	Negative Ranks Positive Ranks	5.00 5.00	-1.00	2.54
	Chemistry- German	12	Negative Ranks Positive Ranks	3.00 3.60	-1,67	.094
	Chemistry - Geography	10	Negative Ranks Positive Ranks	4.00 4.00	-1,13	.227

Table 5.

8. Appendix C

Wilcoxon tests: Situations

Category	Situation	N	Mean Rank		Z	Exact significance (2-tailed)
Situation-dependent information – observable	interaction with whole class-individual work /work in pairs	36	Negative Ranks Positive Ranks	3.50 2.50	.00	1.000
Situation-dependent Information – non-observable	interaction with whole class-individual work /work in pairs	36	Negative Ranks Positive Ranks	11.64 12.33	-.32	.806
Class-specific information	interaction with whole class-individual work /work in pairs	36	Negative Ranks Positive Ranks	.00 1.00	-1.00	1.000
Professional and experiential knowledge	interaction with whole class-individual work /work in pairs	36	Negative Ranks Positive Ranks	13.94 11.00	-2.162	.031

Table 6.

9. References

Altman, D.G. (1990) *Practical Statistics for Medical Research*, Chapman and Hall, ISBN 978-0412276309, London, England

Antos, G. (1992). Demosthenes oder: Über die Verbesserung von Kommunikation, In: *Kommunikationsberatung und Kommunikationstrainings, Anwendungsfelder der Diskursforschung*, R. Fiehler & W. Sucharowski (Eds.), 52-66, Westdeutscher Verlag, ISBN 978-3531122441, Opladen, Germany

Barth, C. (03.12.2010). *Kompetentes Diagnostizieren von Lernvoraussetzungen in Unterrichtssituationen: eine theoretische Betrachtung zur Identifikation bedeutsamer Voraussetzungen*. Retrieved from http://opus.bsz-bw.de/hsbwgt/volltexte/2010/70/

Barth, C.; Hauck, G.; Hörmann, C. & Henninger, M. (2007). *Unterrichtsvideos als Ressource für die Diagnostik und Förderung der Unterrichtskompetenz von Lehramtsstudierenden.* Paper presented at the 69th Conference of the AEPF (Arbeitsgruppe für empirische pädagogische Forschung), Wuppertal, Germany, March, 19-21, 2007

Bruehwiler, Ch.; Baer, M.; Beck, E.; Bischoff, S.; Guldimann, T.; Müller, P.; Nidermann, R.; Rogalla, M. & Vogt, F. (2004). *Adaptive Teaching Competency – A New Approach to Teacher Education.* Paper presented at First International Conference of EARLI SIG 11, Stavanger, Norway, August, 11-14, 2010

Brühwiler, C. & Vogt, F. (2007) *Adaptive teaching competency and student learning.* Paper presented at 12th Biennial Conference for Research on Learning and Instruction, Budapest, Hungary, August 28 - September 01, 2007

Collins, A., Brown, J.S. & Newman, S.E. (1989). Cognitive apprenticeship: Teaching the crafts of reading, writing, and mathematics, In: *Knowing, learning, and instruction: Essays in honor of Robert Glaser*, L.B. Resnick (Ed.), 453-494, Erlbaum, ISBN 0-8058-0460-9, Hillsdale, New Jersey, USA

Groeben, N.; Wahl, D.; Schlee, J. & Scheele, B. (1988). *Das Forschungsprogramm Subjektive Theorien. Eine Einführung in die Psychologie des reflexiven Subjekts*, Francke, ISBN 978-3772018213, Tübingen, Germany

Hattie, J. & Timperley, H. (2007). The Power of Feedback. *Review of Educational Research,* Vol. 77, No.1, (March 2007), pp. 81-112, ISSN 0034-6543

Henninger, M. & Weingandt, B. (2003). Training of interpersonal communication with tomorrow's technologies, In: *Educating managers with tomorrow's technologies*, R. DeFillippi & C. Wankel (Eds.), 149-172, Information Age Pub., ISBN 1931576688, Greenwich, Connecticut, USA

Henninger, M. & Mandl, H. (2000). Vom Wissen zum Handeln - ein Ansatz zur Förderung kommunikativen Handelns, In: *Die Kluft zwischen Wissen und Handeln,* H. Mandl & J. Gerstenmaier (Eds.), 197-219, Hogrefe, ISBN 978-3801713386, Göttingen, Germany

Henninger, M. & Mandl, H. (2003). *Zuhören – verstehen – miteinander reden.* Huber , ISBN 3-456-83909-X, Bern, Switzerland

Henninger, M. & Mandl, H. (2006). Fostering reflection in the training of speech-receptive action. In: *Knowledge and Action,* D. Frey; L. v. Rosenstiel & H. Mandl (Eds.), 53-83, Springer, ISBN 978-0889372993, New York, USA

Henninger, M. & Hörmann, C. (2007). The Role of Self Explanations in Fostering Reflection. Multimedia Communication Training for Preservice Teachers, In: *Computers and Advanced Technology in Education,* V. Uskov (Ed.), 272-275, ACTA Press, ISBN 978-0-88986-699-7, Anaheim, California, USA

Jaschniok, M.; Barth, C.; Amann, E. & Henninger, M. (2008). *Lernen für die Praxis oder Lernen in der Praxis? Einfluss von Kontextvariablen auf das Training von Sprachrezeption.* Paper presented at the 71st Conference of the AEPF (Arbeitsgruppe für empirische pädagogische Forschung), Kiel, Germany, August, 25-27, 2008

Leontiev, A. A. (1981). *Psychology and the language learning process,* Pergamon Press, ISBN 978-0080246017, New York, USA

Mayring, P. (2008). *Qualitative Inhaltsanalyse* (8th edition), Beltz, ISBN 978-3407255013, Weinheim, Germany

Schooler, J. W., Ohlsson, S. & Brooks, K. (1993). Thoughts beyond words: When language overshadows insight. *Journal of Experimental Psychology,* Vol. 122, No. 2, (Jun 1993), pp. 166-183, ISSN 19392222

Schrader, F.W. (1997). *Diagnostische Kompetenzen von Lehrern und ihre Bedeutung für die Gestaltung und Effektivität des Unterrichts,* ISBN 978-3631421918, Frankfurt, Germany

Shulman, L.S. (1986). Those who understand: Knowledge growth in teaching. *Educational Researcher* Vol. 15, No. 2, (February 1986), pp. 4-14, ISSN 0013-189X

Steinke, I. (1998). Validierung: Ansprüche und deren Einlösung im Forschungsprogramm Subjektive Theorien, In: *Subjektive Theorien, soziale Repräsentationen, soziale Einstellungen. Beiträge zum 13. Hamburger Symposium der Methodologie der Sozialpsychologie,* E. Witte (Ed.), 120-148, Pabst Science Publishers ISBN 3-933151-20-1, Lengerich, Germany

Wahl, D. (1997). *Handeln unter Druck,* Studien Verlag, ISBN978-3892712497, Weinheim, Germany

5

HigherEd 2.0: Web 2.0 in Higher Education

Edward J. Berger[1] and Charles M. Krousgrill[2]
[1]*Department of Mechanical and Aerospace Engineering, University of Virginia*
[2]*School of Mechanical Engineering, Purdue University*
USA

1. Introduction

The web 2.0 era, which began in the mid-2000's, has ushered in unprecedented opportunities for individuals to author and share content, to amplify their voice, and to generally share information in a rapid and platform-independent way. Throughout the past five years, both blogging and video have become completely mainstream as a result of powerful browser-based platforms such as Wordpress (blogging) and YouTube (video sharing). Bandwidth has become largely ubiquitous, with high-speed wireless connections available in a huge variety of environments. And now, with the surging usage of smartphones and other mobile devices, users can capture video, upload it to YouTube, and share it via a link on their blog or a Twitter update, all from their phone and all within just a few minutes. In the future, the names of the tools may change, but the pervasiveness of powerful authoring and sharing tools will continue to be a primary part of the fabric of communication and social interactions.

The education community has viewed these new tools the way it usually views technology–with much optimism but also with deep skepticism. The history of technology integration in education is replete with strong successes, but also many solutions that failed to achieve widespread adoption or make significant gains in student learning outcomes. The social media tools of the web 2.0 era are often greeted with special skepticism; perhaps this is because of the perception that the user-as-author model for content creation empowers everyone to have a voice, regardless of their authenticity as experts. There is certainly an element of web 2.0 technologies that feeds on a kind of modern narcissism (Grossman, 2006), but it also enables crowdsourcing the energy, ideas, talent, and (often free) labor from a global user community (cf. Wikipedia). And it also challenges the deeply-held beliefs of faculty members and the long-standing traditions of higher education instruction: the instructor is the expert who acts as a knowledge gatekeeper, giving students access to information in a controlled way. Web 2.0 shatters that structure, with learners empowered like never before to access *and create* information, share it with their peers, comment on it, refute it, and generally view it through many different lenses. The expert perspective of the faculty member is no longer the only voice in the classroom.

The HigherEd 2.0 program seeks to harness both the web 2.0 technologies and the energy of the learners in the service of creating a modern learning experience. The program is motivated by the basic recognition that with so many web 2.0 tools to choose from, and so many ways to deploy those tools, educators would be well served by a set of best practices, validated using assessment data, guiding their use of multimedia tools. The consequences of *ad hoc* usage of any tool can be important for learners; tools that are difficult to use, inconvenient, deployed inconsistently/haphazardly, without clear purpose, or that provide no competitive advantage versus other tools can all impose significant cognitive load on the learner and impact his/her learning (see also Section 3). In addition, *ad hoc* usage also undermines widespread adoption, as described in Section 6. The HigherEd 2.0 program is therefore dedicated to deploying web 2.0-based technology interventions in real higher education classrooms, evaluating their usage and effectiveness, and constructing a pedagogical framework that can be used by the education community.

To clearly explain the HigherEd 2.0 paradigm and its implementation, this chapter is organized as follows. In Section 2 we introduce the technologies used in our classrooms, the key elements of which are blogs and videos. In Section 3, we use a cognitive load theory framework (CLT) to connect these multimedia tools to instruction, and explain why carefully-considered usage of these tools makes for sound pedagogy. In Section 4, we discuss our findings on best practices for using web 2.0 tools in higher education. Section 4.1 describes best practices in multimedia production, while Section 4.2 presents more detail about the course blog and its impact as a critical organizing framework for course material, communication, and collaboration. Section 5 introduces the notion of student-generated content (SGC) in which students are empowered to create and share their own educational materials with their peers. Section 6 gives an overview of the evaluation of the HigherEd 2.0 program, including usage data, student survey results, interviews, and connection to learning outcomes. We also introduce a diffusion of innovation framework to understand adoption patterns for HigherEd 2.0 technologies. Finally in Section 7 we summarize our findings and explain the future directions of the research.

2. Multimedia types and uses in engineering education

Multimedia-assisted instruction refers to usage of a combination of media including audio, text, images and video in the delivery of instructional material. The effectiveness of multimedia instruction is supported by the modality principle from educational cognitive theory which, in summary, states that concepts presented *both* visually *and* verbally are remembered better than when stated *either* visually *or* verbally. This principle is employed even in traditional lecture delivery where the student learning can be enhanced by listening to the lecturer present visual materials as compared to reading the same material in the course textbook. Recent web 2.0 technological advances have allowed for the economical production of an expanded base of possible multimedia materials. Critical integration of these multimedia components into course delivery can effectively tap into learning gains from the visual and auditory channels of input.

The philosophy within the HigherEd 2.0 program has been to develop multimedia material using consumer-grade, web 2.0 approaches rather than on the use of enterprise-level synchronous production tools such as Elluminate. Web 2.0 tools were chosen on the basis of ease of use and costs. The tools require little training for the instructors, virtually do-it-yourself in terms of the level of their complexity of use. If used for recording live lecture delivery, the controls are simple enough that the lecturer can comfortably run the recording without the need for additional support personnel. The hardware and software required for production of the multimedia material is typically either available within the academic department or is of sufficiently low cost that they can be easily purchased for use. The portability of the equipment allows for recording at virtually any location, such as in office and/or home environments.

The required web 2.0 multimedia production tools include: tablet input device, inking software and screen/audio capture software. The tablet input device can be either a tablet PC or a drawing/graphics tablet connected to a desktop/laptop computer. Tablet PC's are more common; however, drawing tablets generally provide a larger format for higher quality writing and drawing. There are wide variety of choices of software for inking, with the Microsoft products of Journal and OneNote being the most widely accessible. The recording software must be able to record both the spoken word and handwriting from the screen. Camtasia is a widely-used application available for both Windows and Mac OS computers that allows for a variety of output formats and video compression. A high-quality USB microphone is recommended for capturing the best audio. Basic post-production audio and video editing can be done with applications such as QuickTime Pro; more advanced editing requires applications such as Final Cut Pro. A low-cost, yet high-quality, alternative to the above set of production tools is the smartpen that allows simultaneous recording of speaking and of writing with a digital pen on digital paper. The small size of the pen is considerably more portable than a tablet PC and allows for "anywhere recording" of videos. This approach is, however, more limited in that the recording of handwriting overlaid on prepared notes is not currently possible and the post-production editing of the resulting Flash video can be complicated.

Platform independence of playback is an important consideration in the design of multimedia material. Students should be able to access these learning materials through desktop/laptop computers and mobile computing platforms such as smartphones and tablet devices. Although this chapter does not focus on the deep technical details of the multimedia material, it is important to mention that file format and video compression choices need to be considered. Most HigherEd 2.0 multimedia components have been produced using either H.264 video compression or Flash technologies based on the current omnipresence of such players on the internet. Although smartphones are currently screen size- and resolution-limited, we believe that the delivery of course materials on mobile and/or tablet devices will be less encumbered in years to come.

We acknowledge that production tools such as Elluminate have the advantage of synchronous delivery and, with that, the ability for live interaction with the instructor. However, students often do not take advantage of this interactivity feature, possibly due to a reluctance to interrupt or due to fears that their fellow students will be critical of the questions asked. Within the framework of HigherEd 2.0, the multimedia components are tightly integrated within the course blog; this integration allows for students to ask questions on the blog with the real time of their viewing of the material.

The HigherEd 2.0 program has focused on the development of the following five multimedia components: lecture videos, video solutions, animations, simulations and case studies. The details of these are provided in the following.

2.1 Lecture videos

Generally speaking, a traditional lecture for an engineering course can be divided into three parts: a lecture of fundamental concepts, the working out of solutions for examples related to the lecture topic, and a review discussion. The lecture portion typically covers mathematical details that are relevant to overall conceptual understanding, and provides subtle cues to the students for developing their problem-solving abilities. The opportunity for asynchronous playback of lectures can benefit students across the entire spectrum of academic abilities and time schedules, as well as support different pedagogical styles used by instructors. From a student perspective, even skilled note-takers are often unable to capture all of the relevant points of the lecture. Playback will allow students to "fill in the blanks" on missing sections of their lecture notes. Students unable to attend class due to illness or travel are afforded the opportunity to catch up on a missed class. From a pedagogical perspective, some contemporary ideas on instruction are based on the implementation of a "flip" order of course material presentation (Yale et al., 2009). With this approach, a recorded lecture component is delivered online for viewing by the students prior to the class period. The lecture recording covers the fundamental concepts as well as specific cues to the students that connect to the "live" portion of class, during which directed problem solving sessions and lecture-based quizzes are conducted.

Within HigherEd 2.0 courses, videos of the lecture component ❶[1] of the class are produced, either from a live lecture delivery or from an in-office recording session. The instructor starts either with prepared notes (in PowerPoint or PDF format) or with a blank file on a pen tablet computer. Synchronized voice and screen capture recordings are produced and compressed using appropriate video compression algorithms. When recording live lectures, the instructor is able to easily pause recording on a real time basis to eliminate any segment of the class period not desired on the final recording (such as when addressing administrative course details or example solving portions of the class). For either a live lecture recording or an in-office recording, the lecture module video can be as short as 15-20 minutes and as long as 40-50 minutes, in length. The final lecture recording is then posted for viewing on the course blog.

2.2 Video solutions

During a typical engineering lecture class period, a number of examples related to the class period topic are presented to the students. The instructional goals of these examples are the reinforcement of fundamental course concepts and the direction of students in the development of the problem-solving strategies. Most engineering textbooks contain worked-out example solutions, with the amount of solution detail and number of examples dictated by publishing limitations. Similarly, both the amount of solution detail and number of examples worked out during the lecture period are limited, in this case, by time restrictions.

For courses served by the HigherEd 2.0 program, solution videos ❷ are produced for lecture examples using the voice/screen capture process described above for lecture video recording.

[1] Throughout the text, we use symbols such as ❶ to indicate the presence of a hyperlink to external media; these links and their URLs are summarized in Section 8.

The examples chosen are staged in level of complexity ranging from the simple application of a single concept to multi-concept engineering problems. These solution videos are able to provide deeper insights on problem-solving strategies than that afforded by the space-limited textbook and time-limited in-lecture solutions. The audio component of the recordings allows the instructor to provide significantly more insight on the nuances of the individual examples than is possible otherwise with written words alone. And, of course, asynchronous playback allows students to replay portions of the solutions on difficult concepts on multiple devices.

2.3 Animations

The inability to visualize motion is often a major obstacle to learning in engineering courses, particularly in the area of mechanical sciences. This obstacle manifests itself in two ways. Firstly, if a student is not able to determine how a system moves, he/she will be unable to dissect the system into its relevant components for analysis. Secondly, without well-developed visualization skills, the student will be unable to relate the mathematics of analysis to the physics of the motion (does the final quantitative answer make qualitative sense?). The use of static images in traditional instructional delivery is often insufficient for describing motion since the image presents the geometry of the system at a single snapshot in time.

Computer software such as Working Model (and, in a more limited way, Matlab and Mathematica) can be used for the construction of visually-displayed mathematical models of mechanical systems. These models can be used for showing both the physical motion and the mathematical description of the motion. Through the use of this software, mathematical models for a large number of problems for courses covered in the HigherEd 2.0 program have been developed. Videos are produced for simulations using multiple sets of input parameters. Learning modules ❸ are produced in which these animation videos are integrated with spatially contiguous text directing the students through an examination of the motion displayed. A focus is given to both a discussion of the overall system motion and to the qualitative connection to the mathematics to the motion.

2.4 Simulations

The animation video modules described above represent an application of linear multimedia. The active content of the material progresses without navigational control by the student viewing the video. This presentation and companion textual discussion is limited by the parameters chosen by the designer, and the modules do not allow for nonlinear "what if" investigations by the students. An alternate instructional design could include the replacement of the animations in the modules by direct connections to the Working Model simulation package, where the students would be able to control the system parameters through the package's graphical user interface. An alternative involves the instructor distributing Matlab or Mathematica files that students can then edit and run on their own machines. In either case, software licensing may become an issue, raising both the cost and complexity of solutions like this. These issues certainly speak in favor of browser-based simulations, or even simulations/applications for mobile devices. These solutions generally require a different skillset than most faculty possess, and are therefore uncommon.

2.5 Case studies

The multimedia components described up to this point have been used together in HigherEd 2.0 courses in leading instruction from specific concepts (lecture video) through their application to specific problems (solution videos, animations and simulations). In contrast, case studies are a means for leading a longitudinal study from a specific response back to an understanding its underlying concept. The intended outcome of the study is for the student to gain a sharpened understanding of how the fundamental concept led to the observed response and how this concept can be applied to the understanding of other responses. Case study modules ❹ have been developed for HigherEd 2.0 courses. These modules integrate any number of the above types of multimedia components, including a review of fundamental concepts of a lecture video, example solution videos showing how the concept leads to the observed response, and animations/simulations demonstrating how choices of system parameters lead to this and other types of response.

3. Multimedia pedagogy

The HigherEd 2.0 program employs three main elements that leverage different bodies of literature on student learning: the course blog, video solutions, and student-generated content. The course blog, as an information delivery and communication/collaboration platform, supports students' feeling of inclusiveness and community, both of which are known to support student learning (Halic et al., 2010). Video solutions and other multimedia assets leverage the worked-example effect (Sweller, 2006), which has been repeatedly shown to outperform problem-based learning especially for novices. Student-generated content taps into the scholarship on self-efficacy and constructivism, and cultivates a collaborative learning community among faculty and students. As described in the following sections, the HigherEd 2.0 program and approach is well grounded in the pedagogical literature.

The HigherEd 2.0 program can be grounded in Cognitive Load Theory (CLT) (Sweller et al., 2011), which posits that humans have a finite capacity to process information. In a learning environment, this means that learners are continuously processing new information in *working memory* while simultaneously drawing on their own experiences and prior knowledge from *long-term memory*, in the service of *schema acquisition and automation*. A schema is simply a framework, held in long-term memory, that learners use to understand problems and their solutions–schemas integrate complex information (both new information and a learner's prior knowledge) into a formal approach to cognitive tasks. The ease with which learners acquire or automate schemas (i.e., integrate their new knowledge with their prior knowledge) depends very closely on the cognitive load associated with those tasks and, of course, the complexity of those tasks. CLT breaks cognitive load into three basic categories:

- external cognitive load (ECL): the cognitive load associated with the way information is presented
- intrinsic cognitive load (ICL): the cognitive load related to the inherent complexity of the task or problem
- germane cognitive load (GCL): the cognitive load associated with the acquisition or automation of schemas, i.e., the load associated with actually learning new things

CLT suggests that an individual's cognitive load during learning is simply the sum of ECL, ICL, and GCL. Learning is compromised when this total cognitive load exceeds an individual's cognitive capacity ("cognitive overload"), especially when the elements of the topic to be learned are "interactive" or highly coupled (Sweller, 2010). Moreover, learning is maximized–especially for challenging problems with high ICL–when instructional designers present information clearly with a minimum of extraneous or confusing information (they *minimize* ECL), therefore maximizing the available GCL used to support schema construction. Novice learners spend a great deal of time on schema *acquisition*–learning how to approach problems, which tools and strategies are useful, and which tasks (and in what order) must be executed. Schema acquisition can be very demanding, and therefore instructional approaches must focus on optimizing the learner's cognitive load so that his/her finite cognitive resources can focus on only the most important elements of schema acquisition. On the other hand, more advanced learners spend more time on schema *automation*–the process of making "automatic" the execution of certain solution features. Automation of specific tasks and processes lowers the cognitive load associated with those tasks, and enables learners to focus their cognitive resources on learning other aspects of a problem. Experts tend to have fully automated schemas and therefore solve problems in their domain of expertise with very little cognitive load.

3.1 The course blog and a blended environment

The HigherEd 2.0 paradigm promotes a blended environment, with some instruction taking place in a traditional classroom setting but a great deal of asynchronous interaction using a course blog as well. Controlling the extraneous cognitive load in either environment is obviously critical to fostering learning, and in this section we focus on the course blog as an instructional asset and communication platform. Research on blogging in higher education has largely focused on its comparison to a more traditional course management system (CMS) in terms of performance, functionality (Huang, Huang & Yu, 2011), and ease of use; a key dividing line between CMS and blog platforms is the extent to which they foster *transfer of information* versus *authentic communication* (Hamuy & Galaz, 2009). CMS platforms tend to function as virtual filing cabinets, while blogs can promote conversation and social elements such as tags. In the late 2000's, blogging became completely mainstream in political, social, and other domains, and blog use in higher education is emerging rapidly[2] and changing the course management landscape (as CMS platforms continue to add "social" features such as blogs and threaded discussions).

Scholarship on best practices in blogging has developed over the past 10 years, over which time user comfort levels with blogs have changed dramatically. Controlled trials that evaluate blogging as a learning tool typically take long enough to complete that over the observation period, attitudes about and usage patterns of blogs can change significantly; what we thought was salient about educational blogging in 2004 may no longer be relevant [see (Sim & Hew, 2010) for a review]. Nonetheless, there does seem to be several enduring features of blogging that impact its success as a learning environment, all of which can be recast in a CLT framework. There are specific elements of blogging in the context we present here that either explicitly or implicitly impact ECL:

---

[2] Even five years ago, we had to explain to students what a blog was, why it was being used in our class, and what value it might add. Very little explanation is required today.

- presentation: the presentation, organization, grammar, quality of writing, etc. impact perceptions about usefulness of a blog [Kerawalla et al. (2009), Kim (2008), Lambert et al. (2009), Huang, Huang, Liu & Tsai (2011)]; difficult-to-use blogs or poorly-written blog entries impose a higher ECL on the learner
- connectedness: a sense of isolation/community can inhibit/promote learning, especially for learners in a purely distance (instead of blended) format [Halic et al. (2010), Garrison & Aykol (2009), Kerawalla et al. (2008)]; anxiety about participation in the public forum of a blog, or a lack of feeling of connectedness to the community of learners, induces a higher ECL on the learner
- facilitation: facilitation by an instructor is important to foster focused discussion on the blog [Garrison & Aykol (2009), Hernández-Serrano (2011)]; less-focused discussions make it harder for the learner to identify relevant information, and impose a higher ECL on the learner

The preponderance of the recent scholarship supports the notion that blogging can be a valuable pedagogical tool, and as discussed in Section 4.2, the course blog forms the critical backbone of each HigherEd 2.0 course.

3.2 Fading and the worked-example effect

The HigherEd 2.0 paradigm makes extensive use of video solutions, as well as other multimedia assets, in promoting the learning goals of the course. Indeed, the video solutions form one half of an example-problem doublet, in which students can watch video solutions in preparation for completing homework or practice problems. This doublet arrangement–watching a worked-out example before trying problems on their own–has been repeatedly shown in the CLT literature to promote schema acquisition. Video solutions fall into the category of "example-based learning", in which students study worked-out examples in an effort to learn new problem solving strategies. Homework and other practice problem solving constitute "problem-based learning", in which students actually do problems in order to learn new problem solving strategies. And CLT provides a unifying framework to understand how and why both examples and problems support student learning.

First consider the cognitive load associated with example-based learning using a video solution designed according to the best practices of multimedia production (see also Section 4). While watching the video, students do not need to try to listen and write at the same time (as they do when, for example, taking lecture notes), nor do they have to think about the steps involved in the solution. These two features of the worked-out example (plus its instructional design) reduce the cognitive load associated with presentation of the material (ECL) and with the complexity of the problem (ICL), so that the learner's working memory can focus almost entirely on the germane cognitive load and the acquisition of a problem-solving schema. From this careful and deliberate deconstruction of problem solving into a clear worked-out example, students acquire problem-solving schemas with a minimum of cognitive effort. This is the essence of the *worked-example effect*: students acquire problem-solving schemas by watching experts solve problems. The worked-example effect has been repeatedly shown to be especially potent for novice learners whose prior knowledge is low and whose problem-solving schemas are not at all well formed in long-term memory (Moreno, 2006). The worked-example effect promotes *schema acquisition*.

Problem-based learning takes a different approach, summarized as: students learn how to solve problems by solving problems. But the scholarship on CLT has shown that for novices, solving problems as a means of constructing problem-solving schemas can, paradoxically, inhibit learning. Typically, novices take a problem solving approach that is goal-oriented or "means-ends", meaning that novices consider the current status of their solution, compare it to the goal of the solution, and use an ad-hoc (perhaps even trial-and-error) approach to moving their solution closer to the goal for the problem. This is not uncommon among novices, who have neither the prior knowledge nor the robust problem-solving schemas committed to long-term memory. As such, the means-ends analysis itself imposes a heavy cognitive load (ICL) on the learner, who must think about the problem, the goal, and all the potential steps that would advance their solution toward the goal (Sweller, 1988). Sweller and colleagues have also shown, however, that for more experienced problem solvers, solving problems is more beneficial than worked-out examples (Kalyuga et al., 2001). Sweller contends that solving problems promotes *schema automation*.

Learners undergo a natural transition from novices, when studying worked-out examples promotes schema acquisition, to experienced problem solvers, when actually solving problems promotes schema automation (Renkl & Atkinson, 2003). And HigherEd 2.0 is a program designed for use in actual instructional environments–semester-long courses during which, presumably, novice problem solvers will evolve into experienced problem solvers. A strategy which helps navigate this novice-to-experienced transition using worked examples is called *fading* (Moreno et al., 2006). Fading strategies typically ask students to study a partially-worked-out example, and execute the correct steps to complete the solution. In *backward fading*, learners must complete a solution whose initial steps have been worked out. In *forward fading*, learners must complete the initial steps of a solution whose later stages have been worked out. Fading has reliably proven to be a good novice-to-experienced transition strategy in a variety of specific cognitive tasks, including electrical circuits (Moreno et al., 2006) and financial analysis (Renkl & Atkinson, 2003).

3.3 Student-generated content

The learning impacts of HigherEd 2.0 student-generated content can be understood in a social constructivist framework, mediated by technology. The "social" elements of the theory emphasize student peer-to-peer interactions, peer teaching, and the general role of each student in the co-creation and sharing of knowledge. Rooted in Vygotsky's theories (Vygotsky, 1978) of learning originally developed for elementary school children, social constructivism indicates two basic contributions to learning. The first is that the essence of constructivist learning is student collaboration and sharing, that students can learn from each other, and that the "teacher" often learns more than the "student". Annis (1983) presents an interesting experiment in peer tutoring: three groups of students study material. One group studies in anticipation of taking a test, the second group studies in anticipation of teaching other students the material, and the third group studies in anticipation of teaching other students and then actually teaches others. The "read and teach" group performed better than either of the other groups in learning gains, including on higher-order cognitive tasks. Similar results have been reported by Benware & Deci (1984), Wagner & Gansemer-Topf (2005), Roscoe & Chi (2007), and Gregory et al. (2011). This body of research has recently spawned the notion of *communal constructivism* (Holmes et al., 2001), which stresses the collaborative and intentional construction of knowledge by both teacher and student for the benefit of the community at large. McLoughlin & Lee (2008) provide an extended review of new and emerging enhanced constructivist pedagogies.

The second positive impact of student-generated contact and peer-to-peer collaboration relates to student confidence and self-efficacy, both of which positively correlate to achievement (Multon et al., 1991). Blogs and wikis represent two user-friendly platforms on which students can create and share knowledge and educational resources. The sense of community engendered in such online environments enhances student confidence in addition to their technical skills (Wheeler et al., 2008). The classroom environment becomes collaborative instead of adversarial, and competition among students is supplanted by collective effort in support of learning outcomes (Halic et al., 2010). These and other positive effects of constructivist learning can be stimulated using HigherEd 2.0 strategies, as illustrated in Section 5.

3.4 Multimedia in higher education

Design guidelines for multimedia learning materials are readily available in the literature [e.g. Mayer (2009), Schnotz (2005) and other chapters in the *Cambridge Handbook*], and we refer the reader to those sources for greater depth of coverage. The brief summary we present here focuses on design principles for multimedia learning that serve to optimize cognitive load on the learner. The CLT framework provides rich granularity to the discussion of multimedia authoring, with various "effects" and "principles" serving specific purposes in managing the cognitive load. For example, the *spatial contiguity* principle states that learning is improved when descriptive words are placed spatially closer to related parts of figures. The *modality effect* suggests that descriptions should be presented as narrations rather than as written words. The *coherence effect* directly targets ECL and suggests that extraneous information and material should be removed from multimedia learning materials. These and other effects–temporal contiguity, redundancy, and so on–are well documented and supported by theoretical and empirical research. The HigherEd 2.0 system employs these guidelines as cognitive load reduction strategies [cf. Mayer & Moreno (2003)] in real higher education settings.

4. HigherEd 2.0 best practices

The HigherEd 2.0 program has focused primarily on two types of web 2.0 components for undergraduate engineering education: instructional multimedia and the course blog. The multimedia components include: lecture videos, video solutions, animations, simulations and case studies. The design of these media has been closely aligned with pedagogical principles that foster the best possible student learning. The course blog serves a dual purpose of providing student-to-student interaction through discussion threads and of providing a critical organization framework for the delivery of media and other instructional material. Based upon our extensive experience in deploying web 2.0 technologies in higher education settings, as well as the scholarship about multimedia learning, we have developed the best practices described in the following sections.

4.1 Best practices in the design and production of multimedia

The design and production of multimedia components should fall in the latter stages of the overall instructional design process. The learning objectives of the course topic should shape the overall flow of a multimedia-assisted module. A designer is encouraged to pay attention to the instructional congruence among the learning objective, the instructional method, the media and the learner. Generally speaking, the focus for the module should remain narrow. Attempting to accomplish too much with a single topic can lead to cognitive overload in the learner, sending out an unclear instructional message. Cost and technological complexities should be a consideration in choosing the appropriate media; however, the web 2.0 technologies employed in the HigherEd 2.0 program are generally inexpensive and relatively easy to use. The following provides a description of the connection between the method and media for the media components used in HigherEd 2.0. These descriptions consider the different options on how the related instructional media are developed and produced.

4.1.1 Lecture videos

One of the first considerations in the production of lecture videos is the value of live lecture recording vs. that of an in-office lecture recording. A live lecture environment will be most familiar to the student and will likely be the most engaging when considering the body language, facial expressions and personality of the lecturer. The best live lecture production includes classroom video along with audio and screen capture. The classroom video adds considerable cost and complexity to the production in terms of manpower required for video recording and the post-production process of superimposing the classroom and screen capture videos onto a single frame. Without classroom video, unintended audio irregularities (such as extraneous noises and periods of silence) become distracting to the viewer. The in-office lecture recording model allows for a more polished presentation. Audio quality is more easily controlled. Rehearsing the lecture prior to recording and re-recording segments of the lecture both lead to a better final product. Most screen capture recording software allows for "talking head" video insets of the instructor to be included in the lecture recording. The value of these insets throughout the lecture should be considered [Sorden (2005), Nielsen (2005)]. Do they add communicational value? Is the space on the screen better used by written lecture notes? An alternative is to include a short, full-screen video of the instructor at the beginning and/or end of the lecture when the lecture topics are introduced and/or summarized.

4.1.2 Video solutions

The HigherEd 2.0 program has shown the strength of the worked-example on learning in foundational engineering courses. A solution video and a textbook worked-example share the same pedagogical deconstruction of a problem into its relevant parts and the delineation of problem-solving strategies. The power of the video solution lies in the modality of an audio description with text and graphics. The design and production of solution videos should always remained focused on optimizing the positive impact of this modality. Simply reading what is being written on the screen adds little value. Use the audio component to amplify the problem-solving strategy. Explain nuances and provide context of a problem-solving step to others. Provide considerable detail in the handwritten portion of the video. Although some students may only listen and watch, many will be taking notes; complete written thoughts are important for this group of students. Write legibly. Use color creatively for graphical emphasis, but do so selectively. Rehearsal prior to recording is highly recommended; however, working without a script is good practice in that in leads to a fresher presentation.

4.1.3 Animations and simulations

Animations and simulations allow students to observe the dynamic and visual consequences of mathematical concepts. Animations are motion recordings whose parameters and initial conditions are set by the designer, whereas in simulations the user has control over selected input parameters and initial conditions. Learning objectives totally dictate the design of these components. If the goal is to demonstrate global motion of a system, the animation/simulation should allow visualization of the entire system. Alternately, the learning objective might be focused on a qualitative assessment of analytical results, in which case the visualization needs to focus on graphical representation of those results. Unlike lecture videos and video solutions, animations and simulations are not standalone media components; they require contextual connection to analysis. The best practice is to embed them within a focused learning module. In this module, the problem is concisely described with text and images/videos followed by a summary of analytical results (possibly along with a solution video). The critical component of the module is discussion directed at one aspect of the solution alongside the animation/simulation. Multiple animations (or a single simulation module allowing student interactivity) are required for "what if" discussions. Spatial contiguity principles should be followed in the page layout for the module allowing for students to simultaneously observe related components on the page without scrolling or links to other pages.

4.1.4 Case studies

The instructional method for case studies is based on the illustration of a concept through an example. The case study leads from a specific situation back to the general principle, generally the reverse of the other tools discussed here. The case study is more difficult to design from a pedagogical standpoint. From a media standpoint, its design employs the components described above. The layout of a case study module shares similarities with those used with animations and simulations. The problem is introduced using text and graphics/videos and is connected to relevant lecture and solution videos by textual discussion that lays out the thought process in arriving at the general underlying concept. At the end, the student is allowed to study the relationship of the original example problem to the underlying mathematics through animation and/or simulation components. Spatial contiguity principles dictate the layout the module in the same way as for the animation and simulation modules described earlier.

Table 1 summarizes a set of best practices for multimedia production as learned from the HigherEd 2.0 program.

4.2 Best practices in course blog design

The course blog serves two primary functions. First, the discussion thread of the blog is a social platform that encourages interaction and sharing between students. Second, the

1. *Synchronize all temporal input*: Spoken narration should be synchronized with on-screen action.
2. *Eliminate extraneous information*: Do not include extra information that is not relevant to the problem, because this increases the ECL for the learner.
3. *Keep it short*: Longer videos can contain too much information for students to assimilate. Our experience is that 15 minutes is about right.
4. *Use consistent color schemes, formatting, and overall aesthetics*: Take care to use color and other visual elements consistently both *within and across* videos, so that students can easily recognize the meaning of specific formatting conventions. written descriptions using color ❺; e.g., the red equation accompanies the red annotations and text on a figure.
5. *Keep it current*: Deploy videos when students need them, and make sure students are aware when useful new videos become available.
6. *Don't write a script, but do rehearse*: Use Mayer's personalization principle; use conversational language to describe your approach.
7. *Compress*: Large videos (>100 MB in size) may present problems for students with slow connections at home. Compress your videos using a modern standard, such as H.264. Good-quality videos can be produced at a size of 1 MB/minute for tablet-based videos.
8. *Spend the time and money to polish your hardware and software setup*: Creating your videos on a substandard setup increases the cognitive load on the instructor! Make sure your setup makes it easy for you to produce and distribute your videos.
9. *Distribute video in a format and manner that encourages use*: Use a standard, platform-independent video format, such as Quicktime, so that students can access and play videos on a wide range of devices.
10. *Critique your productions on a regular basis*: Revise (or eliminate) material that has been determined to be ineffective for learning. There is no need to keep media that students do not use.

Table 1. Best practices in video production and distribution.

blog serves as an organizing framework for course material, particularly for the multimedia material for the course. The function and form of each dictates the design and implementation of a successful course blog. This video ❻ describes a typical HigherEd 2.0 course blog, its features, and how it is used and organized.

The discussion threads of the blog should facilitate an uninhibited exchange of ideas among the students leading to cooperative learning. This exchange could mimic that of a small group of students sitting around a table discussing a homework problem for the course. In this small group, the students offer up their opinions without concern of judgement from their peers. Not all opinions are correct; however, after a period of time the group settles on a consensus opinion. The blog discussion can follow this model; however, the blog group includes the entire class, and the participants can remain anonymous via careful choice of their blog username[3]. With the larger group on the blog, the accuracy of the group consensus is improved greatly. The course instructor is able to monitor the discussion but should intervene only when necessary to keep the student bloggers on track. By silently observing the blog discussion, the instructor has gained considerable insight on the depth of the students' understanding. Difficult concepts, as learned from the blog, can become part of a lecture discussion in the next class period.

Issues of learner-control vs. instructor-control need to be considered when maintaining the blog during the course term. We have observed that if the initiation of discussion threads is left up to the students, multiple posts related to the same issue (such as the solution of a homework problem) can appear on the blog. This produces many disconnected threads with few comments per thread. The continuity and interaction of discussion is lost in this way. We recommend that the course instructor add blog posts to initiate discussion threads on anticipated issues of interest to the students (homework problems, exam reviews, etc.). These posts can be used to set the tone and focus of discussion by the blogging students. Students should also be allowed blog permissions to author posts, permitting them to start discussion threads on topics not anticipated by the instructor.

Students are more likely to be engaged in course discussion if the blog is spatially connected with the course multimedia content. To accomplish this, course material is accessed through links to content pages on the blog. With this layout, students do not need to leave the blog as they review course material. Blog comments and posts can be added directly from the course content pages.

Note that blog discussion threads are temporally organized, generally in reverse chronological order. Course material, on the other hand, is best organized topically. This difference in form for the two blog functions should be kept in mind when setting the organizational standards for the blog. One should not insert topical material within the temporally-organized discussion thread. Furthermore, the blog designer should make extensive usage of tags on both discussion threads and content pages to assist the students in locating relevant material.

Table 2 summarizes a set of best practices for blogging as learned from the HigherEd 2.0 program.

5. Student Generated Content (SGC)

The web 2.0 era not only empowers instructors to author multimedia learning materials for their students; it also offer unprecedented empowerment to students to create learning materials for each other. The pedagogical rationale for integrating students into the production and sharing of learning material is simple: in order for students to effectively "teach" their peers, they must develop a high level of expertise in the subject. This peer element of instruction has existed in a variety of forms and with many names essentially since the dawn of time, and it has consistently been shown to add value to learning (Hsiao et al., 2010). But the advent of powerful new tools always injects new excitement and pedagogical opportunities. Web 2.0 tools specialize in authorship and collaboration, two critical elements that empower participants to easily create materials and share them with a large audience.

[3] Of course, the instructor–as blog administrator–will know the user's identity, but other participants on the blog may not.

1. *Don't assume anything*: On the first day of class, (and several times thereafter) discuss the role of the course blog. Students will better understand your expectation throughout the course.
2. *Limit your involvement in discussion threads*: Let students discuss the issues on their own. Your involvement will likely curtail participation.
3. *Reward blog participation*: Giving minimal credit for participation lets the students know that you consider blog participation to be important.
4. *Control who can add to the discussion thread*: Make it easy for students to comments; however, require a login and act as moderator to prevent outside contributors.
5. *Create leads on discussion threads*: You want to keep the students focused on relevant issues. Start out the discussion with a hint.
6. *Learn from discussion threads*: Watch the discussion threads to identify student difficulties or misconceptions that can be addressed in the next class meeting.
7. *Use good organization, and keep it all in one place*: Use tags and categories to help students locate material. Know your 'pages' from your 'posts'. Have all course content on the same blog. A student who leaves the blog to an external link might not return.
8. *Allow user anonymity*: Allow students to choose a user name that protects their identity, if they wish. The instructor should be the blog administrator, and will therefore know users' identities. But allowing anonymity can reduce anxiety associated with participation in a public forum.
9. *Keep it current*: An out-of-date blog signals to the students that you are not interested in them using the blog.
10. *No funny stuff*: Do not post irrelevant material on the blog. Discourage students from doing so.

Table 2. Best practices in blogging.

The HigherEd 2.0 program leverages student creativity and ambition to amplify the voice of the learners. While we have employed a wide range of SGC formats and strategies [including wikis and podcasting assignments (Berger, 2007), (Berger, 2009)], we focus here on the two most productive forms of SGC: blogging and construction of worked examples.

5.1 The course blog and social constructivism

The course blog (the technical details of which were presented in Sec. 4.2) presents a simple, direct avenue for student authoring and sharing. Student participation in blog-based, asynchronous discussion–in a public forum–supports the collective construction of understanding celebrated in *social constructivist* theories of learning. Social constructivism emphasizes that learning is: (i) a process that requires social interactions and is time-evolving; (ii) contextual and reliant on the culture of the learning community; and (iii) personalized, with students influencing the direction and format of the learning. The blog is an inherently social learning tool that encourages discussion, collaboration, and sharing.

In the parlance of CLT, the blog promotes schema acquisition via social means. Students share ideas about how to approach problems, discuss the details and meanings of specific facets of problems, and collectively construct an understanding of how to approach the problems. A typical example of this process is shown in Figure 1, in which students use the nested commenting features of the course blog to asynchronously collaborate on homework solutions. Each individual student brings his/her prior knowledge and schema (under construction) to the discussion, and the outcome can be considered as a transcript of schema construction by these individuals.

(student 1) Reply:
April 20th, 2009 at 10:51 am

I think you must have made a sign error somewhere bc you should end up with (m + (3/2)m) in front of your x_dotdot term. With this I was able to get
omega_n = 15 rad/s
zeta = 0.4
omega_d = 13.74 rad.s (is this correct units?)

(student 2) Reply:
April 20th, 2009 at 2:02 pm
Yes, it has to be radians/s

April 20, 2009 at 10:22 am

(student 3) says:
I got all the same answers as (student 1), also did part (d) and found that the response is x(t) = e^(-15t) * (0.29sin(13.75t))

(student 4) Reply:
April 21st, 2009 at 12:05 am

don't forget that in the exponent of e, zeta is multiplied by w_n

(student 5) Reply:
April 21st, 2009 at 2:52pm

So with zeta = 0.4, the actual answer is x(t) = e^(-6t)*(0.29sin(13.75t))

(student 6) Reply:
April 22nd, 2009 at 12:34pm

I get all the same answer for Part A thru C, but im having a lot of trouble with part D. Im not really sure how to construct my x(t) equation. Any pointers?

April 20th, 2009 at 2:07 pm

(student 7) says:
I got the same answers as (student 1). My EOM was
x_dotdot + (2c/5m)x_dot + (2k/5m)x = 0
and then
x(t) = (e^(-6t)) * [.29 sin(13.75t)]
April 20, 2009 at 2:21 pm

(student 8) says:
I used the sum of the forces in the x-dir of the disk and then sum of the moments about the center of the disk. Solved the moments for friction and then plugged it back in the x-dir equation. I then did sum of the forces in the x-dir of the block and solved for the reaction force at O and plugged it into the x-dir of the disk and simplified for the EOM.
I got
EOM: x_dotdot + (2c/5m)x_dot + (2k/5m)x = 0
wn = 15 rad/s
April 20, 2009 at 2:30 pm

Fig. 1. A sample threaded discussion on the course blog.

5.2 Student worked examples

Another component of student-generated content with HigherEd 2.0 is student creation of worked examples. Throughout the course, students consume instructor-created worked examples as they learn key concepts and problem-solving strategies. Once students have progressed along the novice-to-experienced transition to a sufficient degree, they are in a position to create (video) worked examples for their peers. Video creation is only possible now, with the rise of web 2.0, because the intrinsic cognitive load related to authoring in the video production environment is almost negligible. Students create videos seamlessly, because the authoring tools are so powerful and user friendly that they essentially fade into the background[4]; students are free to focus entirely on the germane cognitive load of constructing worked-out examples for their peers. Throughout their experience in a HigherEd 2.0 course, student have encountered a large number of instructor-generated worked examples, each one a specific example of how to effectively construct multimedia learning materials (Mayer, 2009). Despite their lack of formal training in multimedia pedagogy, students generally create quality solutions consistent with multimedia learning principles, and challenge themselves to truly master the problem solving approach. This example ❼ of a hand-written, student-generated video solution uses a white board, multiple colors, live narration, and a hand-held video.

It might seem counterintuitive that the HigherEd 2.0 approach promotes construction and sharing of worked-out examples by students–students who have already substantially moved beyond the novice phase of problem solving. The worked-example effect is known to be most powerful with novice learners, so why would student-generated content be valuable in this form? The answer lies in the pedagogy; the worked-out solution assignment is not designed to explicitly benefit the learning community (although it certainly can do that by providing solutions to problems with which students might struggle). Rather, students construct these learning materials as an exercise of *schema automation*, therefore accelerating their transition to experts. Indeed, as instructors already know, teaching any material to novices requires a high level of expertise in the subject matter (cf. Section 3.3). Using the familiar Bloom's Taxonomy (Krathwohl, 2002) language, when students create authoritative solutions for problems, they focus on *creation* and *evaluation*, the two highest cognitive domains in the taxonomy. Students build a solution that they perceive to be the "best" solution to a given problem, explain the solution clearly using available tools and techniques, and present it using digital tools so that others can learn from their example.

6. Evaluation methods and results

6.1 Evaluation overview

The HigherEd 2.0 program uses a mixed-methods evaluation that emphasizes both quantitative and qualitative data. Because these strategies are deployed in real higher education courses across an entire semester, the study cannot be conducted in the well-controlled environments characteristic of much of the educational psychology or cognitive science literature. Instead, we have constructed the evaluation with a combination of usage statistics, survey data, gradebook information, and student and faculty interviews. The results presented here are a subset of the broader evaluation data, more of which is included in Orange et al. (2011). Because the HigherEd 2.0 paradigm rests upon such a

[4] It is worth noting that when we started developing the HigherEd 2.0 paradigm in 2006, we had to provide training to students on video production using tools like GarageBand. Now, in 2011, no such training is required, and students often simply use their mobile phone cameras to capture video solutions written on paper or a white board.

strong pedagogical foundation (Section 3), for the rest of this section we focus on high-level conclusions about student participation, satisfaction with the learning environment, and overall rates of adoption of the technologies for learning.

6.1.1 Usage data

Student usage of the course blog and multimedia learning materials has remained consistently high throughout implementation of the HigherEd 2.0 program. Student usage of the blog (Figure 2) is typically cyclic but strong, averaging about 5-8 visits per week per student for the entire semester; students are clearly avid blog users. While students routinely view the blog, their comment rate appears to be quite sensitive to the local student environment and the set of incentives in place to promote active participation. The *student environment* concerning collaboration is important; in settings with a very small student population, it is not uncommon for students to collaborate almost exclusively face-to-face. However, with a larger student population, asynchronous collaboration via blogging, text messaging, etc. is much more common.

Perhaps more importantly, *incentives* provide an important impetus for students to actively use certain technologies, and our experience with blogging clearly shows the impact of incentives. For both Purdue courses and the Spring 2011 UVa course in Table 3, a small portion of the final course grade (3%) was tied to blog participation and asynchronous collaboration via commenting in threaded discussions on the course blog. The Spring 2009 UVa course used no incentives for blog participation. We discuss the role of incentives more in Section 6.2.2, but both our usage data, as well as student interview data detailed in Section 6.1.3, suggest that a course-grade-related incentive is an important motivator of early and active blog participation by students. When students are sufficiently motivated, fruitful discussions take place on the blog (Figure 1).

Site/Semester	*#comments*	*#comments/student*
UVa, Spring 2011	1012	9.45
Purdue, Spring 2011	2904	9.50
UVa, Spring 2009	26	0.40
Purdue, Spring 2009	1764	7.41

Table 3. Comparison of blog comments and per capita comment rate over two sites and two semesters.

6.1.2 Survey data

Survey data captures student attitudes about the HigherEd 2.0 paradigm and its perceived usefulness in helping them achieve course learning outcomes. Here we present a *very high-level summary* of the trends we have observed in our survey data, which has been collected over at least 6 semesters of HigherEd 2.0 courses at multiple institutions. Students across all semesters perceive the *lecture videos* to be of low-to-medium value, and this is largely because the lecture videos capture conceptual information and derivations. Students perceive this information to be less germane to their problem solving efforts in homework and exams, and therefore typically only consult lecture videos when they miss class due to illness or travel. Students report that they generally appreciate the *animations, simulations, and case studies* as

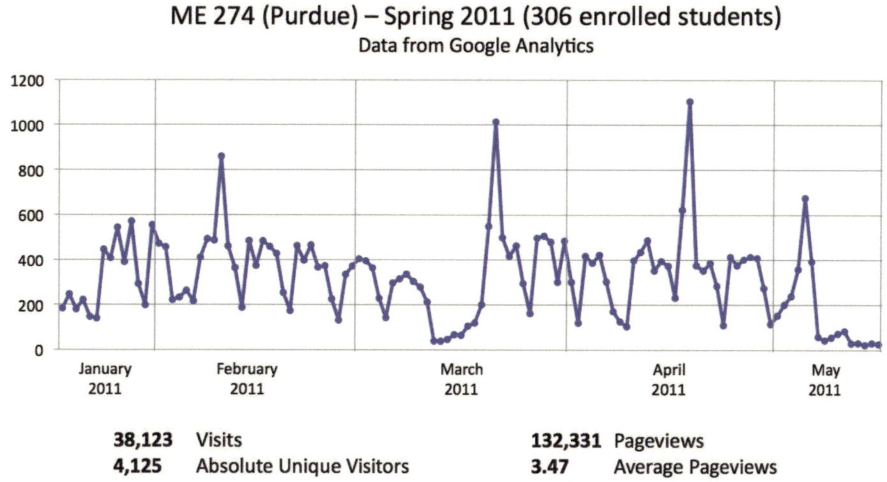

(a) Spring 2011 blog usage for Purdue (8.3 visits per week per student).

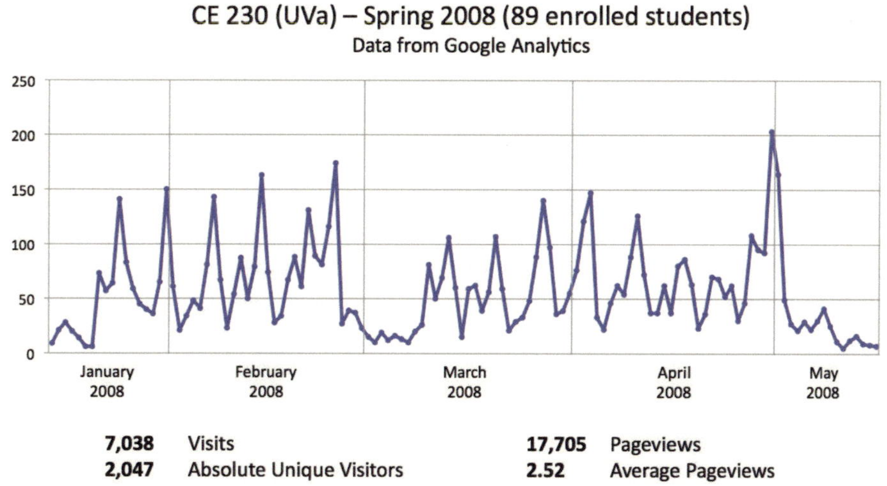

(b) Spring 2008 blog usage for UVa (5.3 visits per week per student).

Fig. 2. Blog usage during two semesters at two different sites.

valuable tools for a better conceptual understanding of the material. However, they also report that these components should be more closely integrated into course assignments in order for the learning impact to be maximized.

On the other hand, both the *course blog* and the *video solutions* are perceived to be of high value to students. Student report strong usage of the blog and typically find the anytime, anywhere collaboration through threaded discussions on the blog to be useful. Moreover, they report strong satisfaction with the learning environment shaped by the course blog. Students indicate that they appreciate the easy navigation, excellent organization, and convenient access. Video solutions are viewed similarly, with students generally appreciating their ease of use, expert perspective, and constant availability. Students report that the value of the video solutions increases as the course material become more conceptually complex (Orange et al., 2011) and the germane cognitive load therefore becomes higher.

6.1.3 Interview data

Student interview data reveals that the course blog and video solutions are considered extremely valuable by the majority of students. Purdue students offered comments like this about the course blog: "The discussions on the blog were very beneficial to view...I was promptly helped by both Prof. Krousgrill and other students." The virtues of video solutions were also recognized: "Helpful, good explanations, [I] would not get grade I am going to have without [the] videos", or "Very useful, well put together, easy to follow", or "They're super effective". On balance, student qualitative data is overwhelmingly positive about these and other features of the HigherEd 2.0 program. Nonetheless, students also recognize that social tools (such as the course blog) require a critical mass of users in order to deliver maximum value: "It's [the blog] only helpful if everyone uses it." Comments like these have stimulated our use of incentives to promote participation, yielding comments like this one from a Purdue student: "Assigning a portion of the course grade to blog posting made me look at the blog. Once I was there I wanted to post on the blog."

Students also describe their experience with technology adoption, specifically their gradual adaptation to using the technology for learning. A UVa student: "I was really resistant to it [using the technology] last semester, but I now see the value and efficiency of it. There's definitely an adjustment period to get comfortable though." Another UVa student: "I didn't have Dr. Berger for Statics last semester, so the blog and related tools forced me to change the way I use technology in support of learning. There was a slight learning curve/adjustment period at the beginning, but now I'm a pretty big fan of the blog...". The data from the Spring 2009 UVa course in Table 3, from a semester when no blog participation incentives were in place, bear out this general feeling from students. Incentives certainly promote technology adoption, and they therefore help to create the user base necessary for social tools like the blog to be truly beneficial to students as a collaboration tool.

6.2 A conceptual framework for technology adoption

The diffusion of innovation framework provides a useful lens through which to view the HigherEd 2.0 program and our evaluation data. Rogers' theory states (Rogers, 2003) that diffusion is "the process by which an innovation is communicated through certain channels over time among members of a social system" (p.5). Rogers further explains the five key characteristics of innovations, and managing these characteristics has a profound effect on the rate of diffusion: (i) *relative advantage* (RA) is the value of an innovation compared to available alternatives; (ii) *compatibility* (Cp) captures the consistency of an innovation with the prevailing values of the user community; (iii) *complexity* (Cx) represents the perceived difficulty in using an innovation; (iv) *trialability* (T) refers to an innovation's ability to be used experimentally by the user base; and (v) *observability* (O) denotes the visibility of the innovation's impact on the community. The goal for any innovation is obviously to present high RA, Cp, T, and O, while introducing low Cx.

These characteristics, the goal of any innovation seeking widespread adoption, and the ways the HigherEd 2.0 paradigm expresses them, are shown in Table 4 and discussed in more depth in Sections 6.2.1 and 6.2.2.

HigherEd 2.0 feature	*RA*	*Cp*	*Cx*	*T*	*O*
goal of innovation	↑	↑	↓	↑	↑
blogging					
-communication	↑	↑	↓	↑	↑
-collaboration	–	–	↓	↑	↑
lecture videos	–	–	↓	↑	↑
video solutions	↑	↑	↓	↑	↑
student-generated content	–	–	–	↑	↑

Table 4. Summary of HigherEd 2.0 approaches within the diffusion of innovation "5 characteristics" framework (Rogers, 2003). [↑=high value, ↓=low value, – = neutral]

6.2.1 Complexity, trialability and observability

The shared, collaborative nature of HigherEd 2.0 strategies and resources essentially guarantee that the *trialability* and *observability* goals are met. Students perceive the course materials to be available for usage and experimentation anytime, anywhere, and (because of the public nature of the course blog) the impacts of this educational approach have high visibility among the student population. As described in the Introduction, the *complexity* associated with web 2.0 tools is generally low, but students do initially reserve some skepticism for the SGC components of their work. Because creating multimedia content for their peers typically presents a new approach to learning, students are not immediately confident that they will be able to successfully navigate the technology and produce a quality product. They quickly–and with little training–overcome this perception, but it nonetheless requires careful and frequent encouragement from the instructor to ensure that students understand and exploit the simplicity of current authoring tools.

6.2.2 Relative advantage and compatibility

In two technology areas (communication via blogging and video solutions), both the *relative advantage* and *compatibility* of the technology are essentially self-evident to students. Video solutions allow students to access expertise in problem solving when they need it, providing both a relative advantage and compatibility. The video solutions are a favorable alternative to time-constrained office hours, offer expertise that a student's peers might not possess, and fit smoothly into both the workflow and digital lifestyle of today's students. Students can simply download the videos to their portable device and use them anytime, anywhere. The course blog, with its RSS technology, platform-independence and robust navigation features, fits easily within students' daily workflow, and these features typically provide a performance advantage over a traditional course management system (CMS). However, for collaboration, students do not always perceive a relative advantage to the threaded discussions on the blog, nor does it always fit with their conception of what collaboration in course work looks like. Our experience has shown that students sometimes prefer synchronous, in-person collaborations with their peers on problem sets and exam preparation. Here, we have found that *incentives* are usually needed to jump-start student excitement about asynchronous collaboration via the course blog. A small amount of course credit can be awarded to promote participation in blog discussions. Remember also that although students frequently use social technologies, their attitudes about such technology for purely social purposes versus academic purposes can be quite different (Cole, 2009).

The lecture videos, according to student perceptions, possess little relative advantage compared to attending class meetings in person. Moreover, the length of the lecture videos (up to about 40 minutes) is somewhat incompatible with students desires; students would rather navigate directly to the section of the video with which they need help, instead of watching the entire video. While the lecture videos serve students well in specific circumstances (e.g., when they miss class due to illness), they generally are not compatible with student needs and therefore do not enjoy significant usage.

Student-generated content presents perhaps the most challenges to widespread adoption, and the mechanisms are largely about context. Students taking a HigherEd 2.0 course are likely also enrolled in non-HigherEd 2.0 courses as well. The dearth of usage of active learning techniques in higher education is well documented (DeAngelo et al., 2009), so it should be no surprise that the general learning environment often does not challenge students to create and share educational materials for their peers. In addition to students' perceptions about the complexity of producing multimedia materials, they are typically unconvinced of its relative advantage versus other approaches to learning, and often find it incompatible with the prevailing educational environment of which they are a part. Our work has shown that instructors can convince students of the benefits of SGC by explaining SGC pedagogy, modeling clear examples of good multimedia materials (such as video solutions), and providing user-friendly authoring options.

7. Summary and conclusion

The HigherEd 2.0 program has been deployed since 2006 in engineering education classrooms with strong success. The course blog provides the critical course backbone, from which instructors can serve multimedia content, and on which students can have productive asynchronous discussions. The HigherEd 2.0 paradigm is built upon the scholarship in engineering education, educational psychology, and cognitive science. In particular, it represents a real-world deployment of such powerful learning approaches as the worked-example effect. When placed in a cognitive load theory framework, the HigherEd 2.0 program clearly seeks to optimize cognitive load on the learner by adhering to best practices in multimedia production (Table 1) and blog usage (Table 2), both of which are built upon our extensive experience and evaluation data as well as the scholarship of multimedia pedagogy. When viewed through a diffusion of innovations framework, the HigherEd 2.0 program largely follows Rogers' "5 characteristics" framework (Table 4), with incentives and consistent coaching/reinforcement from the instructor motivating students to begin active use of the technology resources.

As new tools and technologies become available, their use in higher education will continue to evolve. The prevailing trend of increased "socialization" of technology, as well as its commoditization, will make the HigherEd 2.0 paradigm even more relevant in the future. The coming ubiquity of mobile tablet devices presents an essential opportunity for educators to transform the way they teach, engage students, share information, and collaborate. We suggest further, detailed evaluation of our strategies with diverse student populations, in multiple settings, and a variety of subject areas. Careful studies in real higher education environments, such as semester-long courses, will inform the on-going conversations about thoughtful technology deployment, and will surely suggest lively areas for future research.

8. Index of embedded hyperlinks

- ❶ sample lecture video: `http://people.virginia.edu/~ejb9z/Media/Sample_media/lecture_video_example.mov`
- ❷ sample video solution: `http://people.virginia.edu/~ejb9z/Media/Sample_media/vibrations_homework`
- ❸ sample learning module: `http://people.virginia.edu/~ejb9z/Media/Sample_media/impact_problems`
- ❹ sample case study: `http://people.virginia.edu/~ejb9z/Media/Sample_media/merry_go_round`
- ❺ sample use of color in video: `http://people.virginia.edu/~ejb9z/Media/Sample_media/p5_23_snippet.mov`
- ❻ video description of HigherEd 2.0 course blog: `http://people.virginia.edu/~ejb9z/Media/Sample_media/blog_description.mov`
- ❼ sample student-generated content: `http://people.virginia.edu/~ejb9z/Media/DynProb16_134.mov`

9. Acknowledgment

We gratefully acknowledge the financial support of the National Science Foundation under grant DUE-0717820. Any opinions, findings, and conclusions or recommendations expressed in this material are those of the authors and do not necessarily reflect the views of the National Science Foundation. We also reserve our greatest thanks for our students, who have engaged deeply in the HigherEd 2.0 program, provided essential feedback, and demonstrated that the web 2.0 era empowers everyone to author great content.

10. References

Annis, L. F. (1983). The processes and effects of peer tutoring, *Human Learning: Journal of Practical Research & Applications* 2(1): 39–47.

Benware, C. A. & Deci, E. L. (1984). Quality of learning with an active versus passive motivational set, *American Educational Research Journal* 21(4): 755–765.

Berger, E. J. (2007). Podcasting in engineering education: A preliminary study of content, student attitudes, and impact, *Innovate–the Journal of Online Education* 4(1).

Berger, E. J. (2009). Highered 2.0: Enhanced and video podcasts in engineering mechanics, *Academic Intersections* 1(3).

Cole, M. (2009). Using wiki technology to support student engagement: lessons from the trenches, *Computers & Education* 52: 141–146.

DeAngelo, L., Hurtado, S., Pryor, J. H., Kelly, K. R. & Santos, J. L. (2009). *The American college teacher: national norms for the 2007-2008 HERI faculty survey*, Higher Education Research Institute, UCLA, Los Angeles.

Garrison, D. R. & Aykol, Z. (2009). Role of instructional technology in the transformation of higher education, *Journal of Computing in Higher Education* 21: 19–30.
URL: *doi 10.1007/s12528-009-9014-7*

Gregory, A., Walker, I., McLaughlin, K. & Peets, A. D. (2011). Both preparing to teach and teaching positively impact learning outcomes for peer teachers, *Medical Teacher* 33: e417–e422.
URL: *DOI: 10.3109/0142159X.2011.586747*

Grossman, L. (2006). You–yes, you–are time's person of the year, *Time* .
URL: *http://www.time.com/time/magazine/article/0,9171,1570810,00.html*

Halic, O., Lee, D., Paulus, T. & Spence, M. (2010). To blog or not to blog: student perceptions of blog effectiveness for learning in a college-level course, *Internet and Higher Education* 13: 206–213.

Hamuy, E. & Galaz, M. (2009). Information versus communication in course management system participation, *Computers & Education* 54(1): 169–177.
URL: *http://dx.doi.org/10.1016/j.compedu.2009.08.001*

Hernández-Serrano, M. J. (2011). Chapter 17: Progressing the social dimension toward the collaborative construction of knowledge in 2.0 learning environments: a pedagogical approach, *in* B. W. et al. (ed.), *Social media tools and platforms in learning environments*, Spring-Verlag, Berlin Heidelberg, pp. 289–310.

Holmes, B., Tangney, B., FitzGibbon, A., Savage, T. & Mehan, S. (2001). Communal constructivism: students constructing learning for as well as with others, *Proceedings of the 12th International Conference of the Society for Information Technology & Teacher Education (SITE 2001)*, SITE, Charlottesville, VA.

Hsiao, Y. P., Brouns, F. & Sloep, P. (2010). Effect of using peer tutoring to support knowledge sharing in learning networks: A cognitive load perspective., *ICO-Toogdag* .
URL: *http://hdl.handle.net/1820/2932*

Huang, T.-C., Huang, Y.-M. & Yu, F.-Y. (2011). Cooperative weblog learning in higher education: Its facilitating effects on social interaction, time lag, and cognitive load, *Educational Technology and Society* 14(1): 95–106.

Huang, Y.-M., Huang, Y.-M., Liu, C.-H. & Tsai, C.-C. (2011). Applying social tagging to manage cognitive load in a web 2.0 self-learning environment, *Interactive Learning Environments* pp. 1–17.
URL: *http://www.tandfonline.com/doi/abs/10.1080/10494820.2011.555839*

Kalyuga, S., Chandler, P., Tuovinen, J. & Sweller, J. (2001). When problem solving is superior to studying worked examples, *Journal of Educational Psychology* 93(3): 579–588.

Kerawalla, L., Minocha, S., Kirkup, G. & Conole, G. (2008). Characterising the different blogging behaviours of students on an online distance learning course, *Learning, Media and Technology* 33(1): 21–33.
URL: *http://dx.doi.org/10.1080/17439880701868838*

Kerawalla, L., Minocha, S., Kirkup, G. & Conole, G. (2009). An empirically grounded framework to guide blogging in higher education, *Journal of Computer Assisted Learning* 25: 31–42.
URL: *doi: 10.1111/j.1365-2729.2008.00286.x*

Kim, H. N. (2008). The phenomenon of blogs and theoretical model of blog use in educational contexts, *Computers & Education* 51: 1342–1352.

Krathwohl, D. R. (2002). A revision of bloom's taxonomy: an overview, *Theory into Practice* 41(4): 212–218.
URL: *http://www.jstor.org/stable/1477405*

Lambert, J., Kalyuga, S. & Capan, L. (2009). Student perceptions and cognitive load: what can they tell us about e-learning using web 2.0 course design?, *e-Learning* 6(2): 150–163.
URL: *http://dx.doi.org/10.2304/elea.2009.6.2.150*

Mayer, R. E. (2009). *Multimedia Learning (2e)*, Cambridge University Press, New York.

Mayer, R. E. & Moreno, R. (2003). Nine ways to reduce cognitive load in multimedia learning, *Educational Psychologist* 38(1): 43–52.

McLoughlin, C. & Lee, M. J. W. (2008). Mapping the digital terrain: new media and social software as catalysts for pedagogical change, *Hello! Where are you in the landscape of educational technology? Proceedings ascilite Melbourne 2008*, Melbourne, Australia.
URL: *http://www.ascilite.org.au/conferences/melbourne08/procs/mcloughlin.html*

Moreno, R. (2006). When worked examples don't work: Is cognitive load theory at an impasse?, *Learning and Instruction* 16: 170–181.
URL: *doi:10.1016/j.learninstruc.2006.02.006*

Moreno, R., Reisslein, M. & Delgoda, G. M. (2006). Toward a fundamental understanding of worked example instruction: impact of means-ends practice, backward/forward fading, and adaptivity, *Proceedings of the 36th ASEE/IEEE Frontiers of Education Conference*, IEEE, San Diego, CA.

Multon, K. D., Brown, S. D. & Lent, R. W. (1991). Relation of self-efficacy beliefs to academic outcomes: a meta-analytic investigation, *Journal of Counseling Psychology* 38: 30–38.

Nielsen, J. (2005). Talking-head video is boring online, *Alertbox* .
URL: *http://www.useit.com/alertbox/video.html*

Orange, A., Heinecke, W., Berger, E., Krousgrill, C., Mikic, B. & Quinn, D. (2011). An evaluation of highered 2.0 technologies in undergraduate mechanical engineering courses, *Advances in Engineering Education* in press.

Renkl, A. & Atkinson, R. K. (2003). Structuring the transition from example study to problem solving in cognitive skills acquisition: a cognitive load perspective, *Educational Psychologist* 38: 15–22.

Rogers, E. M. (2003). *Diffusion of Innovations (5e)*, Free Press, New York.

Roscoe, R. & Chi, M. (2007). Understanding tutor learning: knowledge-building and knowledge-telling in peer tutors' explanation and questions, *Review of Educational Research* 77(4): 534–574.
URL: *doi: 10.3102/0034654307309920*

Schnotz, W. (2005). Chapter 4: An integrated model of text and picture comprehension, *in* R. E. Mayer (ed.), *Cambridge Handbook of Multimedia Learning*, Cambridge, New York, pp. 289–310.

Sim, J. W. S. & Hew, K. F. (2010). The use of weblogs in higher education settings: a review of empirical research, *Educational Research Review* 5: 151–163.

Sorden, S. (2005). A cognitive approach to instructional design for multimedia learning, *Informing Science Journal* 8: 263–279.

Sweller, J. (2006). The worked example effect and human cognition, *Learning and Instruction* 16(2): 165–169.
URL: *http://linkinghub.elsevier.com/retrieve/pii/S0959475206000193*

Sweller, J. (2010). Element interactivity and intrinsic, extraneous, and germane cognitive load, *Educational Psychology Review* 22: 123–138.
URL: *DOI 10.1007/s10648-010-9128-5*

Sweller, J., Ayres, P. & Kalyuga, S. (2011). *Cognitive Load Theory*, Springer, New York.

Sweller, R. (1988). Cognitive load during problem solving: Effects on learning, *Cognitive Science* 12(2): 257–285.

Vygotsky, L. S. (1978). *Mind in Society: The Development of Higher Psychological Processes*, Harvard University Press, Cambridge.

Wagner, M. & Gansemer-Topf, A. (2005). Learning by teaching others: a qualitative study exploring the benefits of peer teaching, *Landscape Journal* 24(2): 198–208.

Wheeler, S., Yeomans, P. & Wheeler, D. (2008). The good, the bad, and the wiki: evaluating student-generated content for collaborative learning, *British Journal of Educational Technology* 39(6): 987–995.

Yale, M. S., Bennett, D., Brown, C., Zhu, G. & Lu, Y.-H. (2009). Hybrid content delivery and learning styles in a computer programming course, *Proceedings of the 39th IEEE International Conference on Frontiers in Education*, IEEE Press, Piscataway, NJ.

6

Multimedia Approach in Teaching Mathematics – Examples of Interactive Lessons from Mathematical Analysis and Geometry

Marina Milovanović[1], Đurđica Takači[2] and Aleksandar Milajić[3]
[1]*Faculty of Real Estate Management, Union University, Belgrade,*
[2]*Faculty of Natural Sciences, University of Novi Sad, Novi Sad,*
[3]*Faculty of Management in Civil Engeneering, Union University,*
Serbia

1. Introduction

Research on multimedia approach efficiency was carried out using lessons about the definite integral and isometric transformations (line and point reflection, translation and rotation), since these areas are among the basic ones in the fields of mathematical analysis and geometry. These topics are also important because of their presence in the mathematics programmes in the great majority of high schools and faculties, both directly and through their multipurpose character. Consequently, proper approach in presenting these topics is one of the most important segments of teaching mathematics on all educational levels.

In teaching mathematics, it is remarkably important to avoid so-called 'knowledge/ information adoption' as the only way of work. Students often solve problems mechanically, by following the algorithm steps without real awareness of their actual meaning. For example, in case of the definite integral, one of the common problems is that students calculate its value by following steps of the algorithm, without real understanding of its definition, the meaning of upper and lower limit or relation between the definite integral and the size of an area or a volume etc. In case of isometric transformations, it was noticed that students learned what are line and point reflection, translation and rotation, but the problem appeared when they have been faced to the realistic task, where they were supposed to use the adopted knowledge. One of the most important aims of the modern approach in teaching mathematics is to combine information adoption with so-called 'knowledge transfer', i.e. learning through defining the facts and explaining their interrelations.

Mathematics teachers show great interest in visualisation of the mathematical terms and emphasize that visualised lectures are of the great help in abstract thinking in mathematics (Bishop, 1989; Tall, 1986) believes that it is of the major importance to connect the existing pictures that students have on certain terms in order to develop them further and to enable students to accept the further knowledge. Therefore, in teaching mathematics it is necessary to combine the picture method and the definition method in order to improve the existing knowledge and to enlarge it with the new facts, which is one of the points of the cognitive theory of multimedia learning (Mayer, 2001, 2005).

Nowadays, use of different kinds of multimedia is largely included in the education because it allows the wider spectrum of possibilities in teaching and learning. Visualisation is very useful in the process of explaining mathematical ideas, abstract terms, theorems, problems etc.

Experience in work with students showed that they are highly interested in modern methods in learning which include all kinds of multimedia, such as educational software, internet, etc.

Modern methods in multimedia approach to learning include the whole range of different possibilities applicable in mathematics lectures for different levels of education and with different levels of interactivity (Deliyiannis et al. 2008a, 2008b; D. Đ. Herceg, 2009; Milovanovic, 2005, 2009; Milovanovic et al., 2011; Takači, et al., 2003, 2004, 2006, 2008). The authors usually work on suggestions on using different kinds of software in education, especially in the field of mathematics: geometry, algebra, numerical analyses etc. (Deliyiannis et al., 2008a, 2008b; D. Đ. Herceg, 2009; Milovanovic, 2005, 2009; Milovanovic et al., 2011), as well as the definite integrals and isometric transformations.

All the above-mentioned resulted in an idea of making applicative software which would be helpful in modern and more interesting approach to the field of teaching mathematics and rising the students' knowledge from the scope of definite integrals and isometric transformation to a higher level. The aim of our research was to recognize the importance of multimedia in the teaching process as well as to examine the students' reaction to this way of learning and teaching. Therefore, we have developed experimental software with multimedia lessons about the definite integral and isometric transformations and tested them in class in order to see how they would affect teaching process and results.

2. Multimedia presentation of given problems from the fields of integrals and isometric transformations

We would like to emphasize the importance of using computers, i.e. multimedia software in teaching and learning in the both areas, because visual presentation offers much more possibilities. Beside that, using multimedia lessons on isometric transformations enables students to actually see not only the final solution, but also the „movements" that have led to it.

2.1 Multimedia presentation of the area calculation

The problem of area calculation in the filed of integration calculations lead us directly to the definition of the definite integral. The basis for the defining and calculation of the definite integrals was made by Archimedes[1] and his quadrature of the parabola. Because of that, we decided to use modern, multimedia approach in explaining Archimedes' quadrature of the parabola to the students. In order to use PC as a teaching aid, we were led by suggestions of Tall (Tall, 1991), who emphasized the importance of PC in the teaching because of its great possibilities in the scope of visual presentations.

[1] Archimedes of Syracuse (Greek: Ἀρχιμήδης; c. 287 BC – c. 212 BC) was a Greek mathematician, physicist, engineer, inventor, and astronomer.

The quadrature of the parabola problem is formulated as follows: *For any given parabola $y = x^2$ and rectangle with nodes $A(0,0)$, $B(a, 0)$, $C(a, a^2)$ and $D(0, a^2)$, $(a > 0$)the parabola divides the rectangle in two zones of which the area of one is twice bigger than the area of the other one.*

Given problem is show on Figure 1[2]. The area of the rectangle is:

$$P = a \cdot a^2 = a^3 \tag{1}$$

If we mark the zone under the parabola - limited by sides AB and BC of the rectangle and the arc AC - with S, and the other one with P, our next task is to prove the following equation:

$$S:(P-S)=1:2\text{, i.e. } S=\frac{1}{3}P=\frac{1}{3}a^3 \tag{2}$$

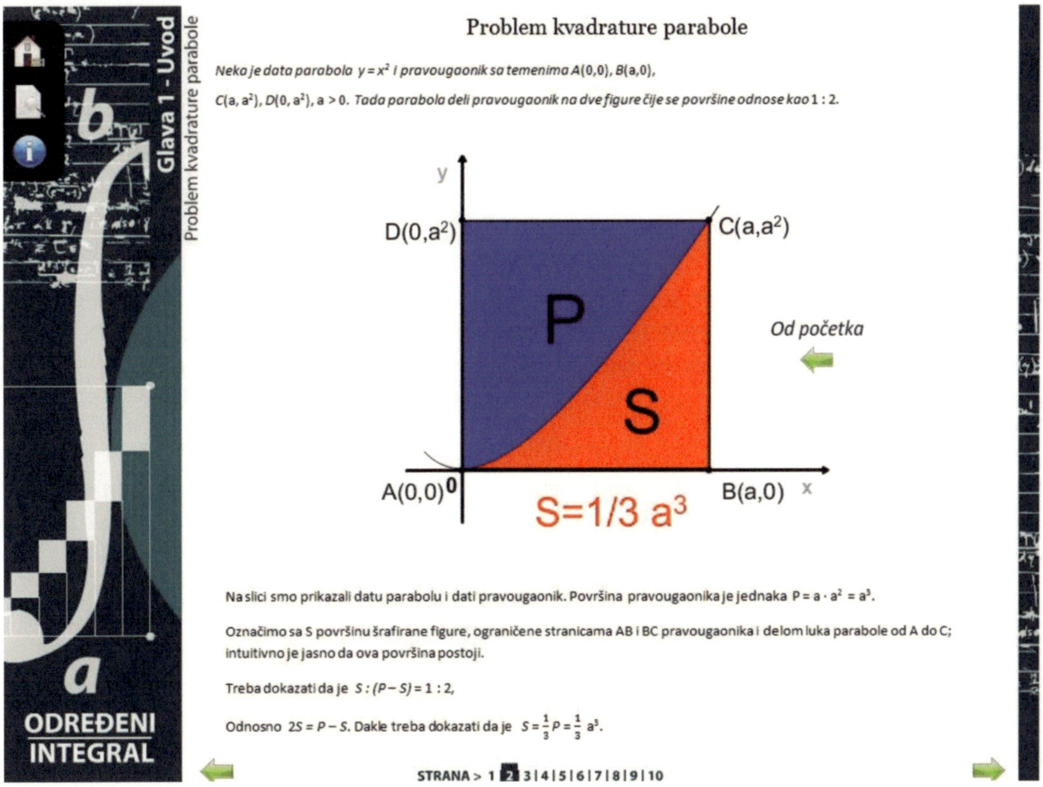

Fig. 1. Illustration of given problem taken from the multimedia lesson about the definite integrals

The next step is to divide the interval [0, a] of the *Ox* axis in *n* equal parts of length *a/n*, where *n* is a natural number, which should be shown to the students by animation (step-by-step), as shown in Figure 2a. Within each of these intervals, we construct two rectangles:

[2] Figure 1 is taken from the multimedia lesson about the definite integrals.

'circumscribed' one, with upper right vertex on the parabola (the animation of this step is shown on Figure 2b), and 'inscribed' one, with upper left vertex on the parabola (shown on Figure 2d). It is obvious that the first part have no inscribed rectangle. The heights of these rectangles are shown on Figure 2b, and their areas are as follows:

$$\frac{a}{n}\cdot\left(\frac{a}{n}\right)^2, \frac{a}{n}\cdot\left(2\frac{a}{n}\right)^2, \ldots, \frac{a}{n}\cdot\left((n-1)\frac{a}{n}\right)^2, \frac{a}{n}\cdot\left(n\frac{a}{n}\right)^2.$$

(Part of this animation is shown on Figure 2c.). Area of each inscribed rectangle is difference between the area of adjoining circumscribed rectangle and the area of 'added' rectangle (part of this animation is shown on Figures 2d and 2e).

It is obvious that:

$$P_U < S < P_O \tag{3}$$

Therefore: $\frac{a^3}{3}-\frac{a^3}{2n}+\frac{a^3}{6n^2} < S < \frac{a^3}{3}+\frac{a^3}{2n}+\frac{a^3}{6n^2}$, that is: $-\frac{a^3}{2n}+\frac{a^3}{6n^2} < S-\frac{a^3}{3} < \frac{a^3}{2n}+\frac{a^3}{6n^2}$.
These inequalities are correct for any given natural number n.

Since $\lim_{n\to\infty}\left(-\frac{a^3}{2n}+\frac{a^3}{6n^2}\right)=\lim_{n\to\infty}\left(\frac{a^3}{2n}+\frac{a^3}{6n^2}\right)=0$, we can conclude that:

$$S=\frac{1}{3}P=\frac{1}{3}a^3 \tag{4}$$

This was the solution of the given problem via numerical method, but we can offer much more by using the multimedia lessons. In animation shown on Figure 3, students can clearly see that with increasing of n, i.e. the number of circumscribed and inscribed rectangles, these areas will get closer and closer, until they, according to our intuition and visual perception, both become equal to the area S.

Led by the similar idea as in previous example, we will try to calculate the area of the curvilinear trapezium (students will see it in animation, as shown in Figure 4a and b, etc.) formed by the graph of the function $y=f(x), x\in[a,b]$, the abscissa's segment $[a,b]$ and the two segments of the lines $x = a$ and $x = b$ making the figure closed (Figure 4a).

If the values $x_0, x_1, \ldots, x_{n-1}, x_n$ define points on x axis as follows:

$$a = x_0 < x_1 < \ldots < x_{n-1} < x_n = b$$

these points divide interval $[a, b]$ into n sub-intervals:

$$[x_0, x_1], [x_1, x_2], \ldots, [x_{n-1}, x_n].$$

Therefore, we can name the $(n+1)$-plet $(x_0, x_1, \ldots, x_{n-1}, x_n)$ as *division of interval* $[a,b]$. For simplification, we will mark it as $\Pi = (x_0, x_1, \ldots, x_{n-1}, x_n)$.

If we choose any of these sub-intervals (Figure 4b), for example (x_{i-1}, x_i), and if ξ_i is arbitrary value within that sub-interval, the area of the rectangle whose basis is sub-interval $[x_{i-1}, x_i]$ and height is $f(\xi_i)$. can be calculated as:

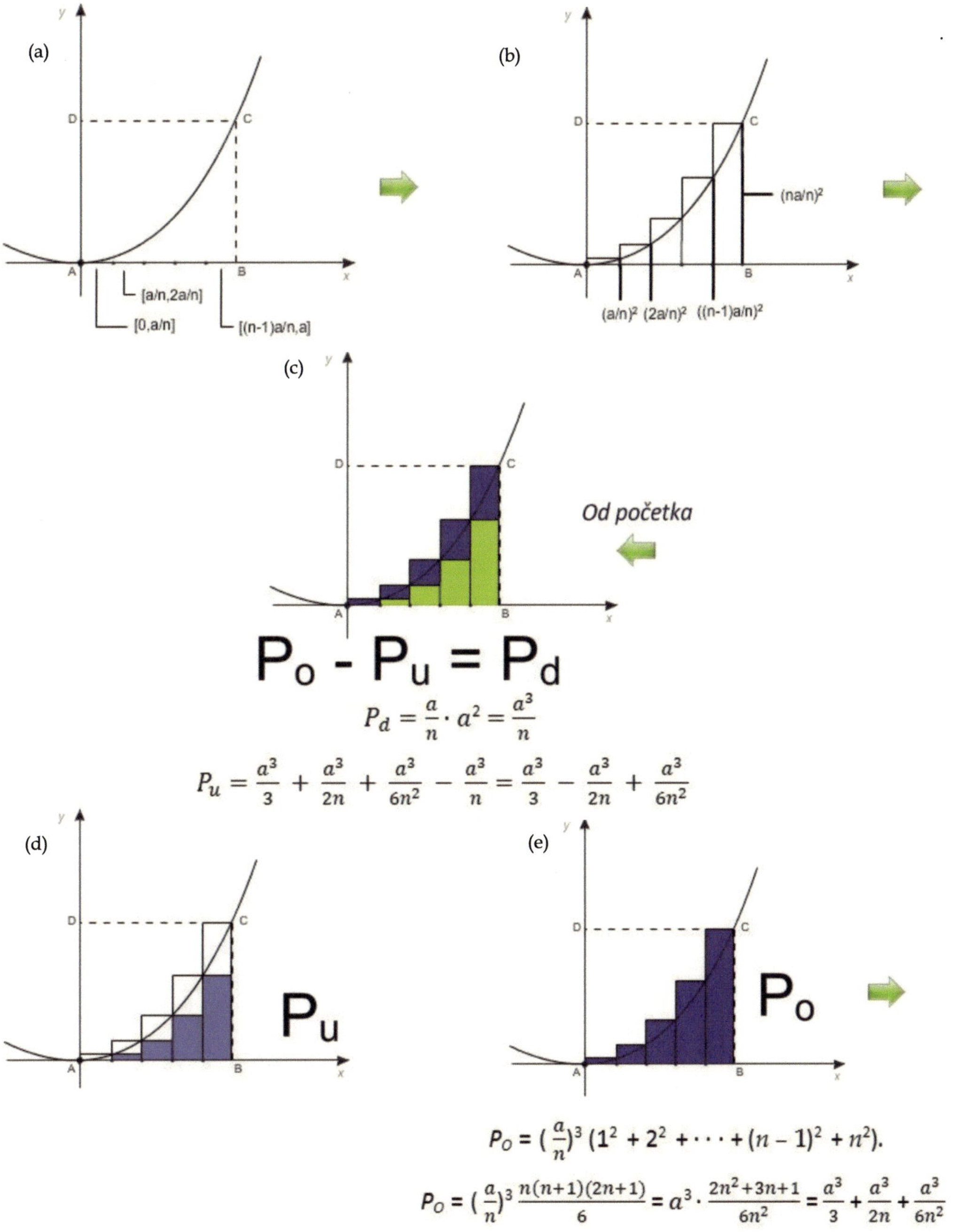

Fig. 2. Illustrations of the quadrature of the parabola problem taken from the multimedia lesson about the definite integrals

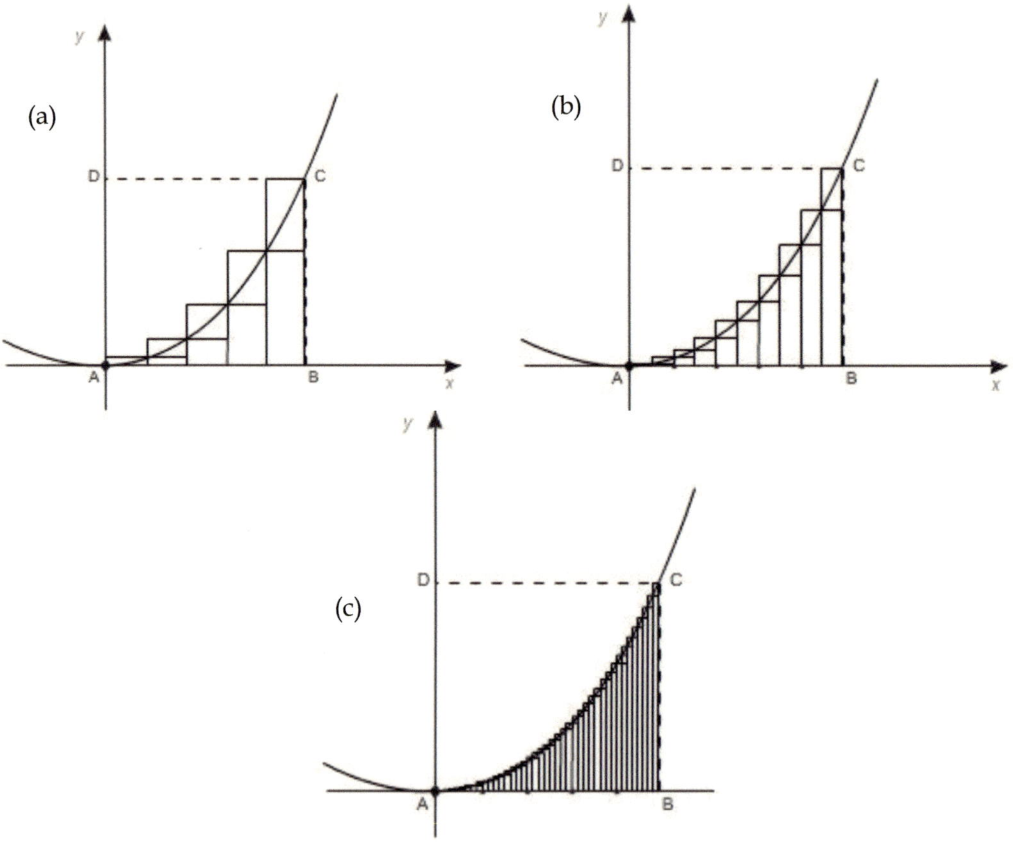

Fig. 3. Illustration of the quadrature of the parabola problem taken from the multimedia lesson (step-by-step)

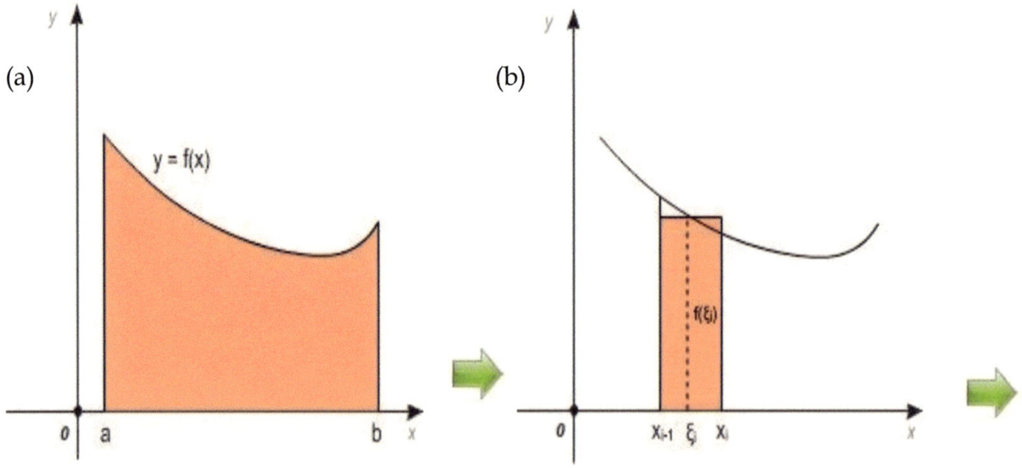

Fig. 4. The first part of solution of the quadrature of the parabola problem taken from the multimedia lesson (step-by-step)

$$P_i = f(\xi_i)(x_i - x_{i-1}) \tag{5}$$

If we do the same with every sub-interval $[x_{i-1}, x_i]$, $i = 1,2,...,n$, we will get the series of rectangles - figure S - with total area:

$$P(S) = \sum_{i=1}^{n} P_i = f(\xi_i)(x_i - x_{i-1}) \tag{6}$$

For a given curvilinear trapezium - i.e. for given interval $[a,b]$ and given function $f(x)$ - the shape of figure S depends on division Π = $(x_0, x_1, ..., x_{n-1}, x_n)$ and on choice of values $\xi_i \in [x_{i-1}, x_i]$, $i = 1,2,...,n$. Let us mark this n-plet of choices as $\xi = (\xi_1, \xi_2 ..., \xi_n)$. If all the sub-intervals $[x_{i-1}, x_i]$, $i = 1,2,...,n$, are 'small', shape of figure *S* will be 'very' similar to the curvilinear trapezium *F* (which are shown on Figures 5 and 6a).

If we mark value of $\Delta x_i = x_i - x_{i-1}, i - 1,2,...n$, than set $\{\Delta x_1, \Delta x_2, ..., \Delta x_n\}$ is finite set of positive numbers, and consequently has the largest element, which we will mark as *d*:

$$d = d(\Pi) = \max\{\Delta x_1, \Delta x_2, ..., \Delta x_n\}$$

If the value of *d* is small enough natural number, it means that sub-intervals are smaller and the division Π is 'fine'. If we introduce new breaking points, *d* gets smaller and smaller so the division gets finer. Consequently - and according to our intuition and multimedia presentation - figure *S* will get more and more similar to the curvilinear trapezium, so we can conclude that following definition of the area of the curvilinear trapezium *F* is valid:

Definition 1: Real number S is the area of the curvilinear trapezium F if for every $\varepsilon > 0$, there exists $\delta > 0$, such that for every division Π for which $d(\Pi) < \delta$ and for any chosen set of values $\xi = (\xi_1, \xi_2 ..., \xi_n)$ in correspondent sub-intervals:

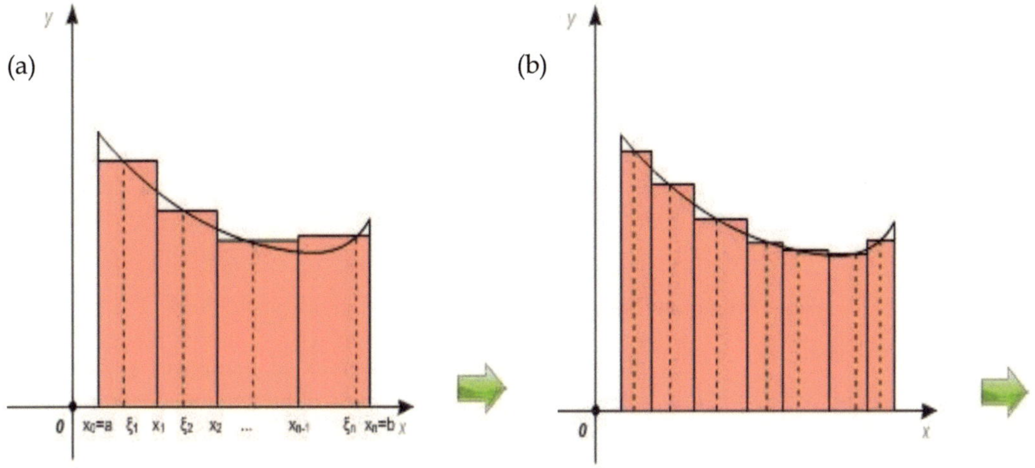

Fig. 5. The second part of solution of the quadrature of the parabola problem taken from the multimedia lesson (step-by-step)

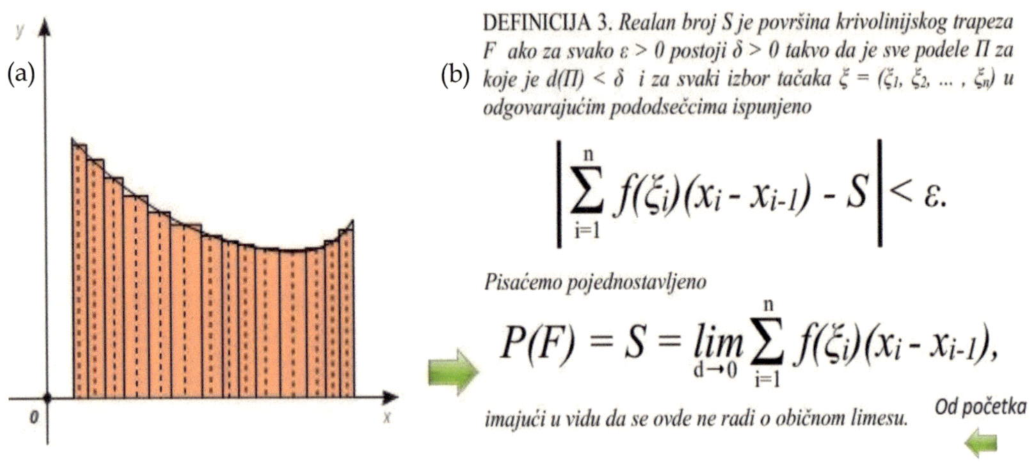

Fig. 6. *Definition* 1: Area of the curvilinear trapezium F – visualization method

$$\left|\sum_{i=1}^{n} f(\xi_i)(x_i - x_{i-1}) - S\right| < \varepsilon \tag{7}$$

Or it is simplified as:

$$P(F) = S = \lim_{d\to 0}\sum_{i=1}^{n} f(\xi_i)(x_i - x_{i-1}), \text{ i.e.} \tag{8}$$

Definition 2: Let the real-valued function *f* be defined on interval $[a,b]$. The real number *I* is definite integral of the function *f* on the interval $[a,b]$ if for every $\varepsilon > 0$, there exists $\delta > 0$, such that for every division $\Pi = (x_0, x_1, ..., x_{n-1}, x_n)$, $a = x_0 < x_1 < ... < x_{n-1} < x_n = b$ for which $d = d(\Pi) = \max\{\Delta x_1, \Delta x_2, ..., \Delta x_n\} < \delta$ and for any chosen set of values $\xi = (\xi_1, \xi_2 ..., \xi_n)$, $\xi_i \in [x_{i-1}, x_i]$, $i = 1, 2, ..., n$ (animation, Figure 7 shows further development step-by-step).

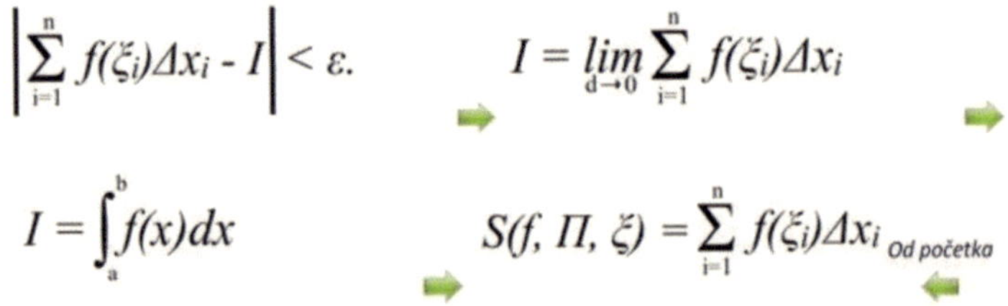

Fig. 7. *Definition 2:* Area of the curvilinear trapezium F – visualization method

With numerous visual presentations, animations, illustrations and examples we can also introduce and explain *integrability, integral sum, integrand, limits of integration, Newton-Leibniz formula, applications of integrals,* etc.

Example: Determining the area of plane figure.
Task: Determine the area of the figure in the *xOy* plane bounded by the curves $x - y = 0$ and $x - y^3 = 0$.

Solution: Animation shows the graphs of given curves (Figure 8a) and their intersection points *A(1, 1)*, *O(0, 0)* and *B(-1, 1)* (with numerical and graphic presentation). We can see that given figure consists of two identical parts. The next step in the animation is solving the given problem step-by-step. The final result is illustrated on Figure 8b.

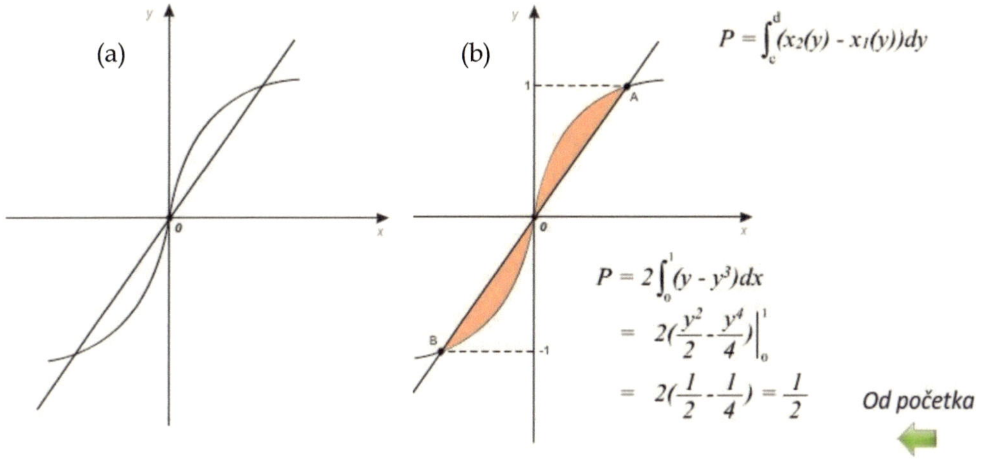

Fig. 8. Animation parts which represents the graphs of the given task and solution in determining the area of a plane figure

In a similar way as shown for determining the area of a given figure, we used multimedia animations to explain application of the determined integrals for calculus of volumes of solids, as well as volumes of solids of revolution obtained by revolving a plane figure around *Ox* or *Oy* axis.

Example: Determining the volume of body by revolving.
Task: Determine the volume of a right circular cone with altitude *h* and base radius *r*.
Solution: The cone is generated by revolving the right-angled triangle *OAB* around the *Ox*-axis (Figure 9a), which can be clearly shown by using animation (Figures 9b, and 9c). Animation parts which represents the given task and the triangle revolution.

Numerical solution of given problem is also shown step-by-step, by using animation.

Slant height of the cone is defined as line:

$$y = x \cdot tg\alpha = \frac{r}{h} \cdot x$$

Therefore, according to the formula for calculus of volume:

$$V = \pi \int_0^h (\frac{r}{h} \cdot x)^2 dx = \frac{\pi \cdot r^2}{h^2} \cdot \frac{x^3}{3}\Big|_0^h = \frac{\pi \cdot h \cdot r^2}{3}.$$

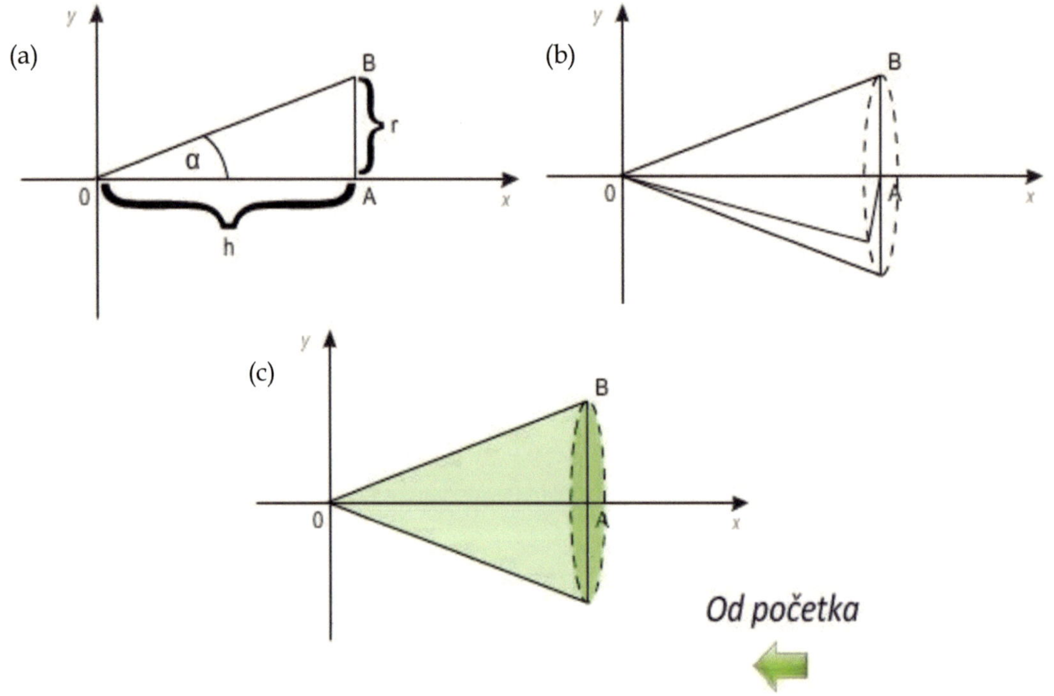

Fig. 9. Animation parts which represents the graphs of the given task and solution in determine the volume of a right circular cone with altitude h and base radius r

2.2 Assorted examples and problems from multimedia lectures on isometric transformations

Our lectures on isometric transformations (homepage shown on Figure 10), consist of four units: line and point reflection, translation and rotation. Every transformation is presented by the following chapters:

1. Basics
2. Examples
3. Some characteristics
4. Exercises
5. Problems
6. Examples from everyday life

Since the field of isometric transformations is very broad, we have conducted the research in only one area - line reflection. Multimedia lessons in line reflection are presented here by characteristic examples which have enabled us to use different, multimedia approach than in classical lectures.

Great advantage of multimedia lessons is particularly evident in chapter *Basics*, because the definitions of line reflection, axis of symmetry etc. are not only 'given' (written and drawn), but also illustrated by numerous animations which show 'movements', i.e. isometric transformation. We have also paid special attention to enabling students to find out the solutions by themselves.

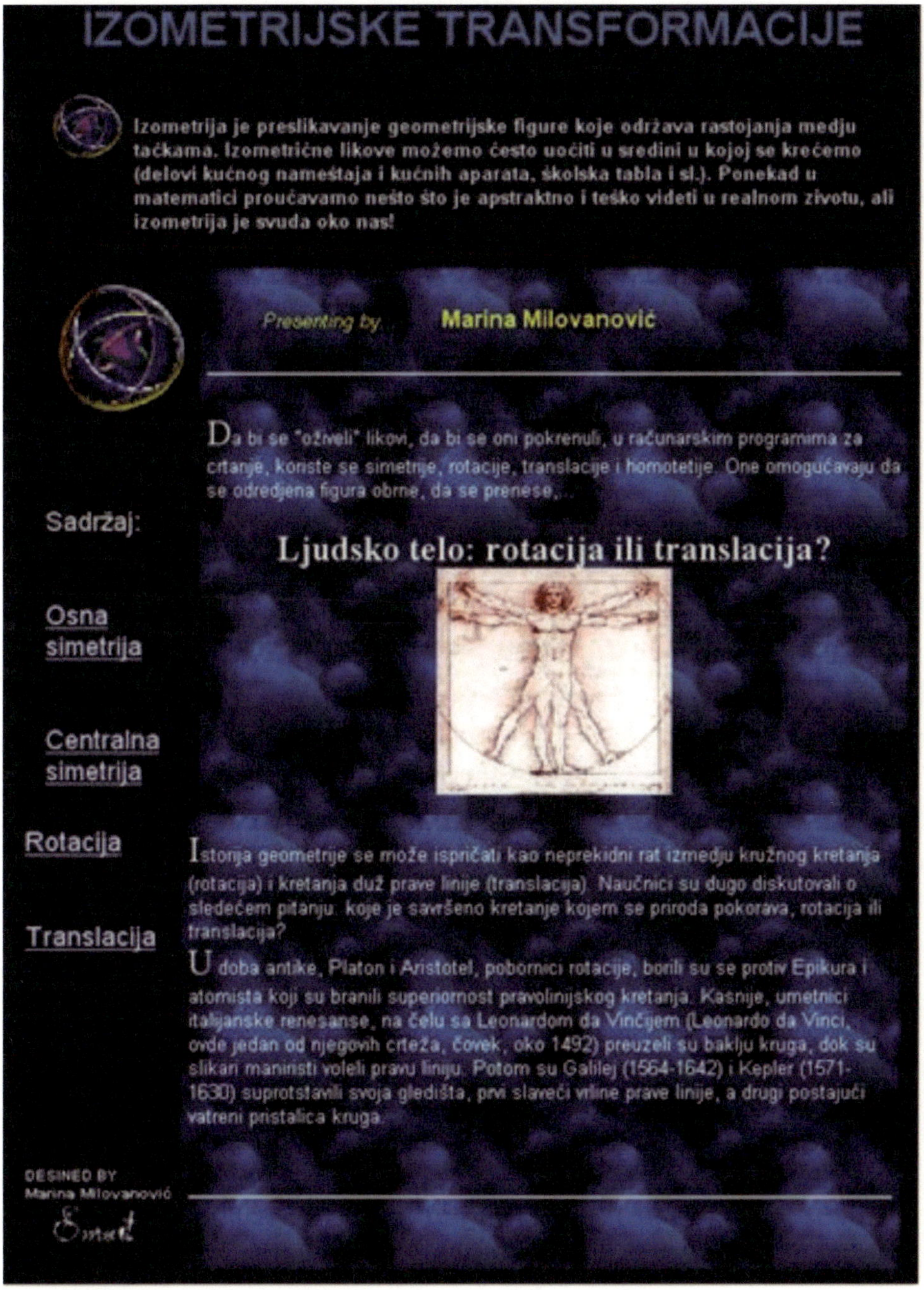

Fig. 10. Homepage of animation about isometric transformations

Example: Basic idea of this example is to help students to see, comprehend and implement the line reflection in different cases before giving them the exact definition. In the first task (Figure 11a), students were asked to recognize the common characteristic of given figures and to find which two of them do not belong in the group. After that, the solution was offered (for all the figures except the third and the last one) in which it was shown that there is at least one line along which we can fold the paper and every point from one side would fall on corresponding point on the other side (Figure 11b).

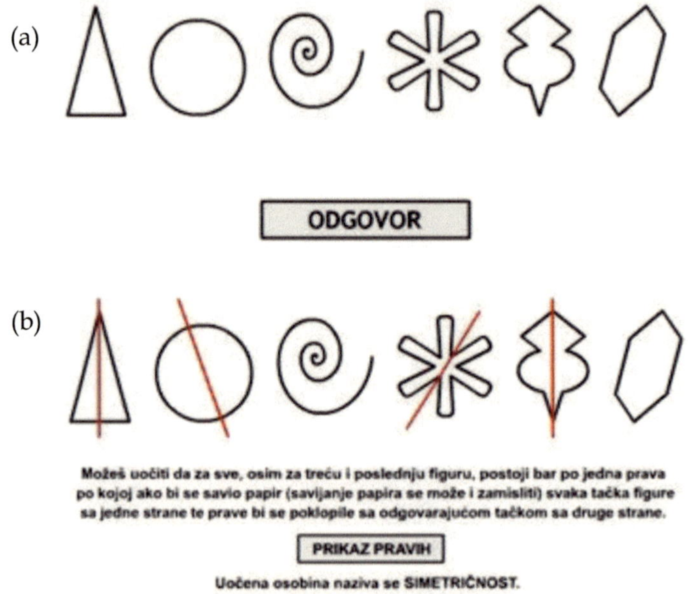

Fig. 11.

In next step, students were asked to look at the figures shown on Figure 12a and to find out if there is an axis of symmetry for any given pair of figures. Afther that, multimedia animation led them to the correct answer (Figure 12b)

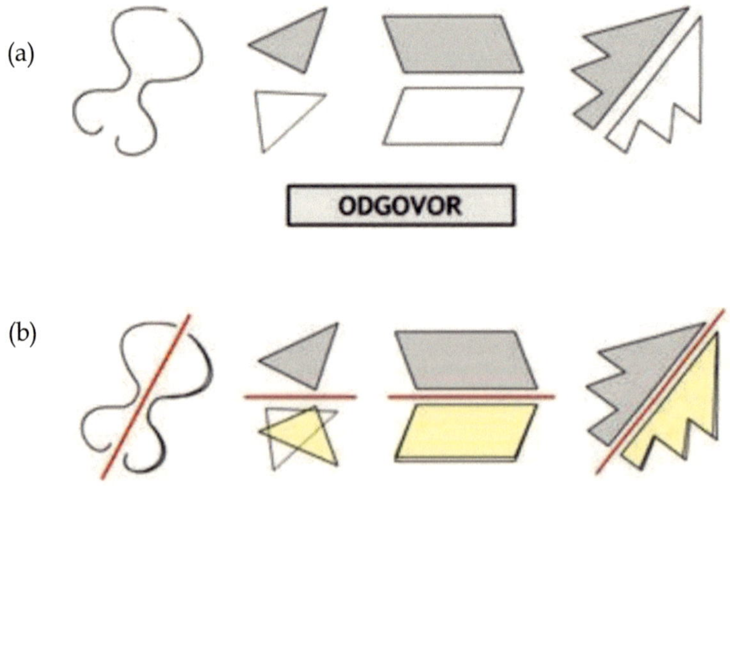

Fig. 12.

In chapter 'Examples', we have used series of animations to ask different questions, such as which of the given figures are symmetrical, how many axis of symmetry they have etc. All the answers were illustrated by complete multimedia presentations of isometric transformations. (Figure 13)

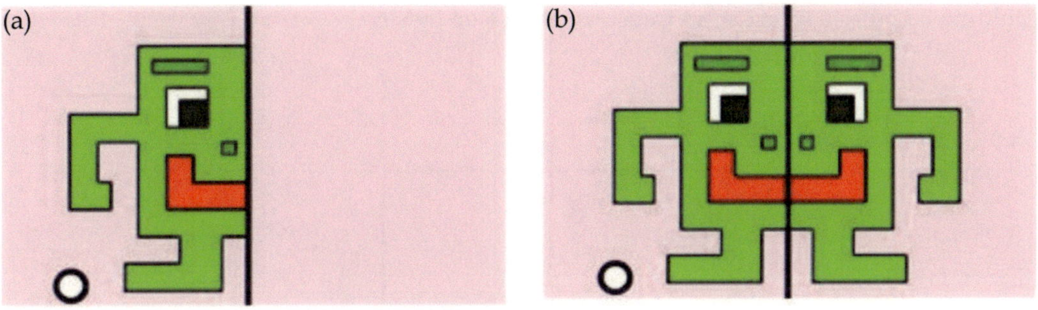

Fig. 13. Example of symmetrical figure (b), which is obtained by animated isometric transformation of picture (a), point by point, by pressing the button (left)

Chapter 'Exercises' offers variety of multimedia Q/A, quizzes and tests with purpose of resuming and exercising adopted knowledge.

One of the examples is presented in Figure 14. Its purpose was to use an interesting example from the everyday life in order to enable students to resume their knowledge.

Fig. 14. Task: How many axes of symmetry have these flags?

Chapter 'Problems' include variety of different interesting tasks, ranged from easier to more complex ones. All tasks are solved, majority with complete solutions and some with instruction how to solve them. The main idea was to enable student to get to the right solution individually, before he or she see it on the screen. Animations do not offer complete solution instantly, but gradually, step-by-step. Some of tasks are typical ones, as in traditional classes, but there are also non-standard tasks taken from the mathematics competitions.

Example: Two billiard balls, A and B, are on the rectangular table, as shown on figure. How should we hit the ball A if we want it to strike all four rails before hitting the ball B?

Let us mark the rectangle (billiard table) as XYUV, and $A'=I_{XV}(A)$, $A''=I_{XY}(A')$, $B'=I_{UV}(B)$, $B''=I_{UY}(B')$.
(Multimedia presentation shows transformation step by step.)

(a)

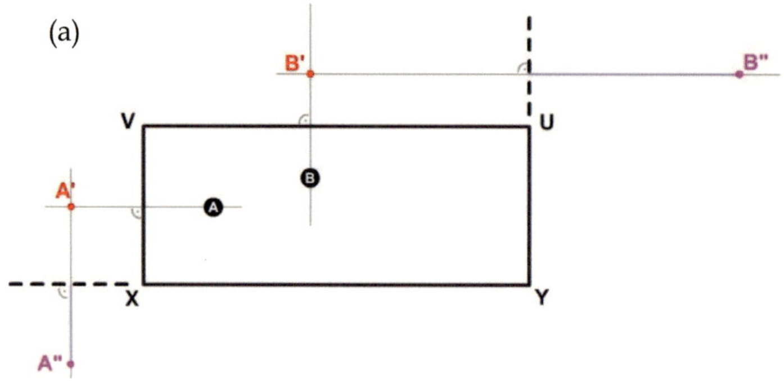

If we mark the intersection of lines A''B'' and XY as M, the intersection of lines A''B'' and UY as N, the intersection of lines A'M and XV as P, and the intersection of lines B'N and UV as Q, it can be noticed that the following angles are equal: APV=A'PV=XPM, PMX=XMA''=NMY, MNY=B''NU=UNQ, and NQU=B'QV=VQB.

(Multimedia presentation shows drawing of every line and their intersections, i.e. above mentioned points)

(b)

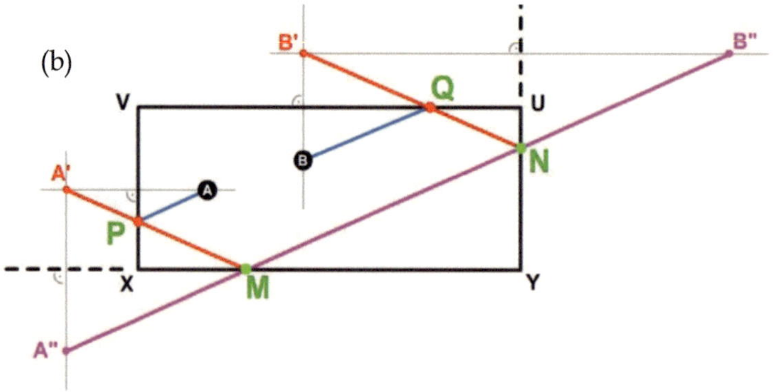

Therefore, ball in point A should be hit in such a way that would send it through points P, M, N and Q, and it will finally hit the ball in point B.

(c)

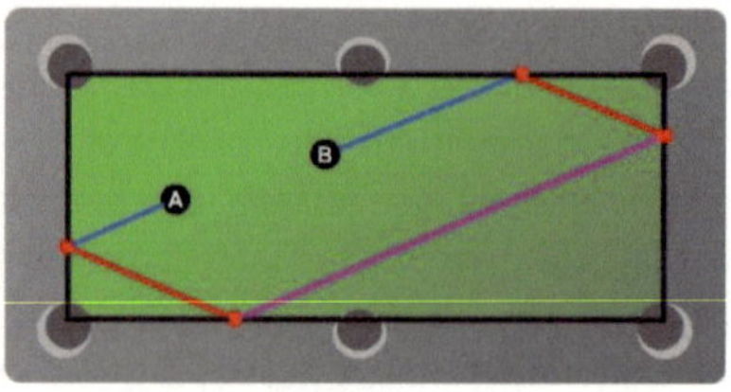

Fig. 15. Solution of a given task given by the multimedia animation

In teaching mathematics, we are sometimes supposed to explain abstract terms that rarely or hardly can be seen in reality, but students often ask for proof that theory can be seen and implemented in everyday life. With help of multimedia aids, we can show numerous examples of symmetry in architecture, art, nature, psychology, religion, etc.

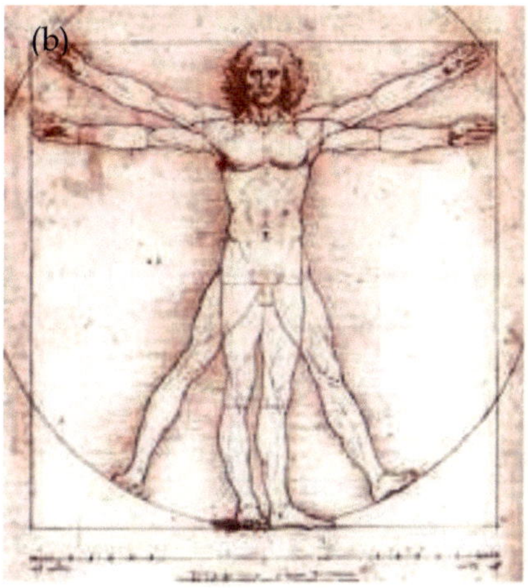

Fig. 16. Examples of symmetry in everyday life: (a) This photograph of the Taj Mahal has two axes of symmetry; Beside the vertical one, there is also a horizontal one, along the water line; (b) Famous Leonardo da Vinci's drawing The Vitruvian Man is also called Canon of Proportions or Proportions of Man. It shows the symmetry of the human body

3. Research methodology

3.1 Aim and questions of the research

Thanks to the experiences of some previous researches and results, some of the questions during this research were as follows:

1. Are there any differences between results of the first group of students, who had traditional lectures (control group - *traditional group*) and the second group, who had multimedia lectures (experimental group - *multimedia group*)? Where were these differences the most obvious?
2. What do students from the experimental group think about multimedia lectures? Do they prefer this or traditional way and why?
3. In students' opinion, where did multimedia learning help them more, in geometry or analysis (based on lessons on the definite integrals and the isometric transformations)?
4. Do students think it is easier to understand and learn the matter individually and during the classes by multimedia lectures?

3.2 Participants of the research

The research was conducted on two groups of 50 students, divided on subgroups of 25, at two faculties: the Faculty of Architecture and the Faculty of Civil Construction Management of the UNION University, Belgrade, Serbia. In both cases, one subgroup, consisting of 25 students, had traditional lectures while the other one had multimedia lectures. Groups were formed randomly, so the previous knowledge needed for the lectures about limited integrals and isometric was practically the same, which was confirmed by pre-test. The pre-test included tasks from the area of the continuous functions (analysis and graph-drawing), as well as the tasks about the basic figures in analytic geometry (circle, ellipse, parabola etc.). Average score of this pre-test was practically equal in these groups (I: 72.35, II: 71.25 out of 100).

3.3 Methods, techniques and apparatus

Lectures in both groups included exactly the same information on given topics, i.e. axioms, theorems, examples and tasks. It is important to emphasize that the lecturer and the number of classes were the same, too. The main information source for the multimedia group was software created in Macromedia Flash 10.0, which is proven to be very successful and illustrative for creating multimedia applications in mathematics lectures (Bakhoum, 2008). Our multimedia lecturing material was created in accordance with methodical approach, i.e. cognitive theory of multimedia learning (Mayer, 2001, 2005), as well as with principles of multimedia teaching and design based on researches in the field of teaching mathematics (Atkinson, 2005). This material includes a large number of dynamic and graphic presentations of definitions, theorems, characteristics, examples and tests from the area of the definite integrals based on step-by-step method with accent on visualisation. An important quality of making one's own multimedia lectures is the possibility of creating combination of traditional lecture and multimedia support in those areas we have mentioned as the 'weak links' (definite integral definition, area, volume, etc.)

After the lectures were finished, all students had the same tests consisting of tasks on definite integrals and isometric transformations. Besides that, students were interviewed after the classes and transcripts of the most characteristic opinions are also included here. In order to get as objective results as possible, participation in the interviews was voluntary and anonymous, and the interviewer was not a member of the teaching staff at any of the faculties.

Test 1 – Definite integral:

1. Use Archimedes' method to determine the area of plane figure bounded by the Ox-axis, line $x = a$, and part of the curve $y = x^3$ for $0 \le x \le a$.
2. Write the definite integral definition.
3. Determine the definite integral $\int_0^{\pi/4} \sin x \cdot \cos^2 x dx$.
4. Determine the area of the plane figure F bounded by Oy axis, graph of the function $y = x^2$ and the tangent on this graph in point (1, 1).
5. Determine the volume of the body of revolution obtained by rotating figure F bounded by parabolas $y^2 = 8x$ and $x^2 = y$ in the xOy plane around the Oy axis.

Test 2 – Isometric transformations:

1. Which of the following figures are symmetrical:
   - Ray

- Circle
- Line
- Parallelogram
- Isosceles triangle
- Isosceles trapezium
- Kite

2. Line reflection:
   a. is a plane isometry
   b. is not a plane isometry

   How many axes of symmetry are there in the circle?
   a. 2
   b. 4
   c. Infinite number

   Immovable lines in the line reflection are:
   a. parallel with axis
   b. intersect axis
   c. rectangular with axis
3. How many axes of symmetry are there in the following alphabet letters?

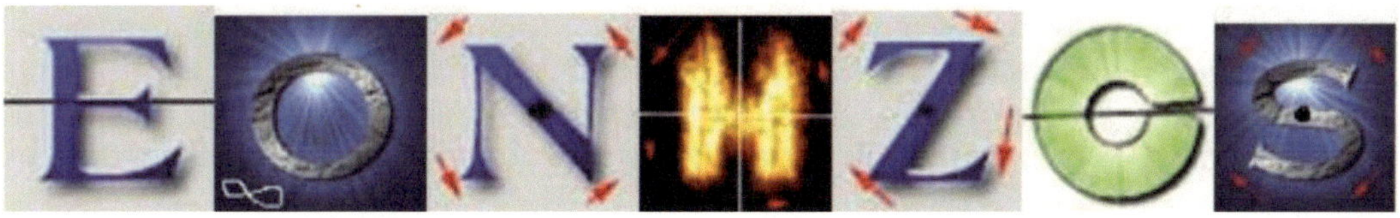

Fig. 17.

4. For given sharp angle *aOb* and point *C*, find the points *A* and *B*, such that *A* belongs to *Oa*, *B* belongs to *Ob*, and the triangle *ABC* has the minimal possible circumference.

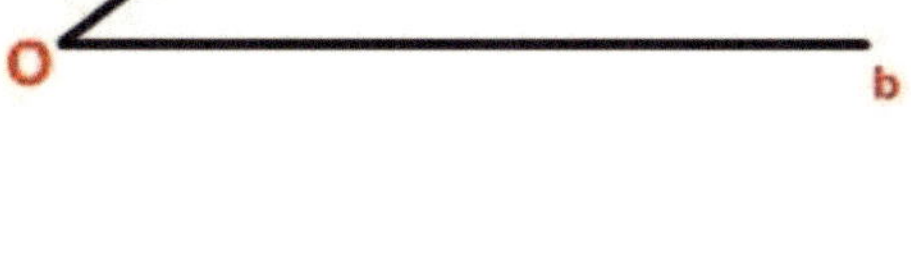

Fig. 18.

5. For given line *p* and points *A* and *B* on the same side of *p*, find the point *P* on the line *p*, so the ray of light which starts in point *A* hits the point *P* and passes through the point *B*. (Use the fact that entering ray is symmetrical with reflected ray.)

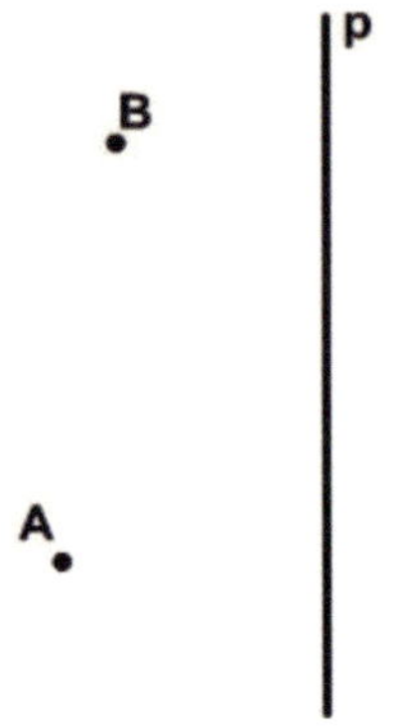

Fig. 19.

Both tests were scored within the interval from 0 to 100 (20 points per task) and the average scores in both tests separately were calculated for the traditional and the multimedia group.

Results were analysed with *Student's t-test for independent samples* using SPSS (version 10.0) software. The result was considered significant if the probability *p* was less than 0.05.

3.4 Results

At the Faculty of Architecture, average score on Test 1 (definite integrals) in the traditional group was 67.75 with standard deviation 14.51, and in the multimedia group, average score was 83.21 with standard deviation 15.01. Average score on Test 2 (line reflection) in the traditional group was 76.04 with standard deviation 15.25, and in the multimedia group, average score was 87.92 with standard deviation 12.5. (Figure 20)

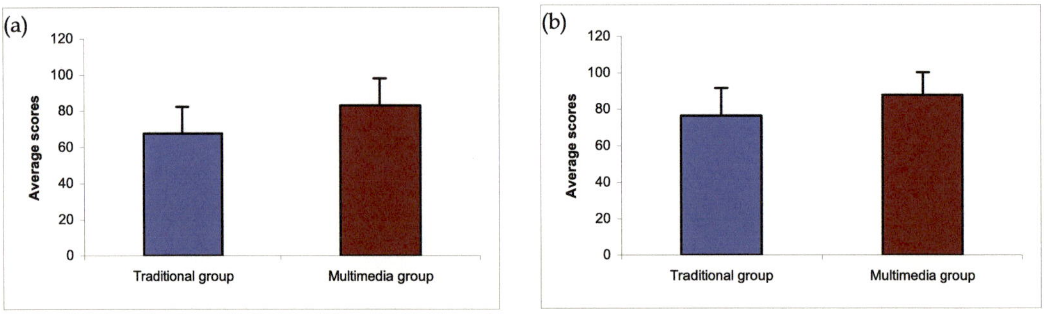

Fig. 20. Total average test scores for (a) Test 1 (definite integral) and (b) Test 2 (line reflection) for traditional and multimedia groups at the faculty of Architecture

At the Faculty of Civil Construction Management, average score on Test 1 (definite integrals) in the traditional group was 60.04 with standard deviation 16.2, and in the multimedia group, average score was 76.37 with standard deviation 19.13. Average score on Test 2 (line reflection) in the traditional group was 72.21 with standard deviation 17.32, and in the multimedia group, average score was 84.37 with standard deviation 15.27. (Figure 21)

In all groups, statistical comparison with t-test for two independent samples showed that multimedia groups had remarkably higher score in comparison with the traditional groups, with statistical significance $p < 0.05$.

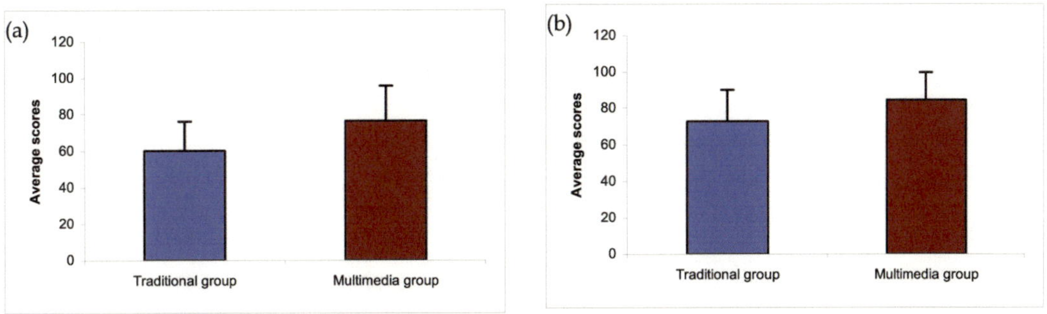

Fig. 21. Total average test scores for (a) Test 1 (definite integral) and (b) Test 2 (line reflection) for traditional and multimedia groups at the Faculty of Civil Construction Management

Test scores by tasks for all groups are given in Figures 22 and 23.

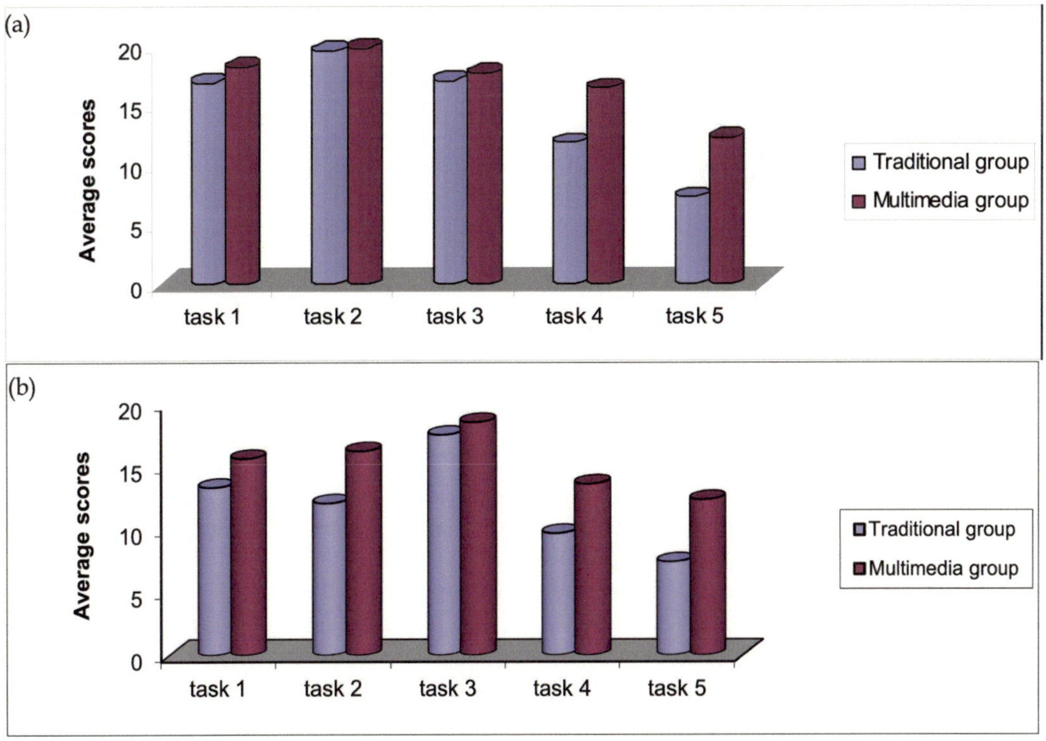

Fig. 22. Average test scores by single tasks for (a) Test 1 (definite integral) and (b) Test 2 (line reflection) for traditional and multimedia groups at the faculty of Architecture

When asked whether they prefer classical or multimedia way of learning, 12% (3 students) answered classical and 82% (22 students) answered multimedia at the Faculty of Architecture, while at the Faculty of Civil Construction Management 20% (5 students) answered classical and 80% (20 students) answered multimedia, explaining it with the following reasons:

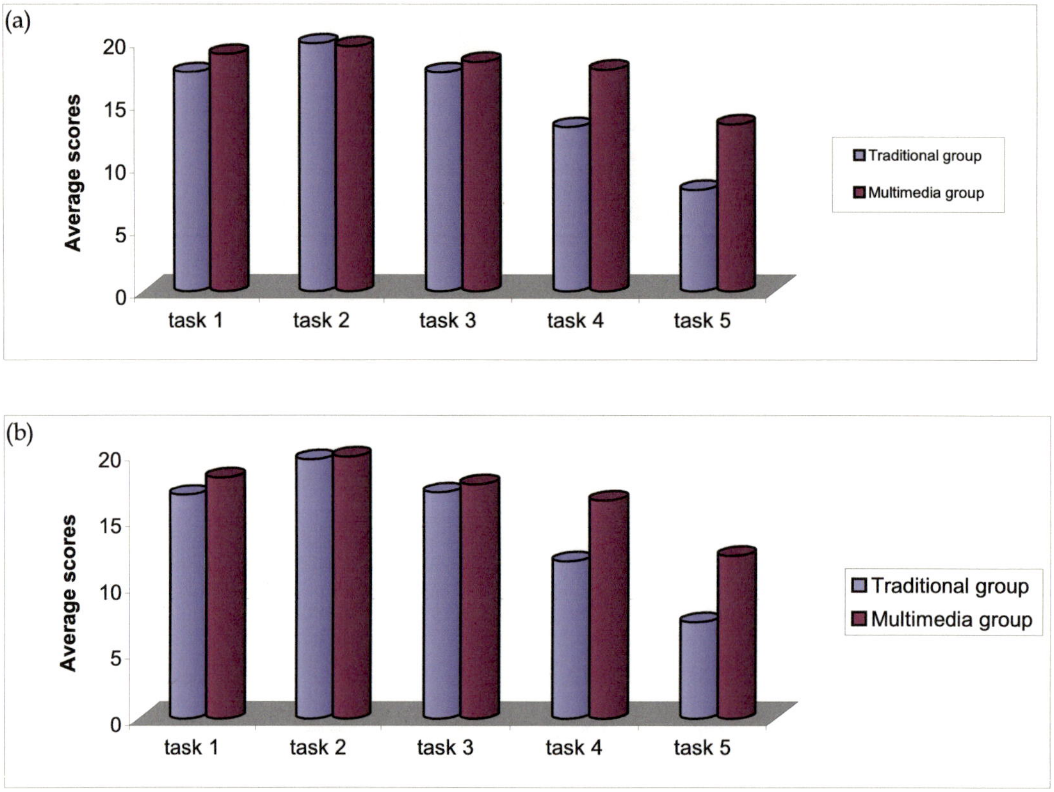

Fig. 23. Average test scores by single tasks for (a) Test 1 (definite integral) and (b) Test 2 (line reflection) for traditional and multimedia groups at the Faculty of Civil Construction Management

- 'It is much easier to see and understand some things, and much easier to comprehend with the help of step-by-step animation.'
- 'Much more interesting and easier to follow, in opposite to traditional monotonous lectures with formulas and static graphs.'
- 'More interesting and easier to see, understand and remember.'
- 'I understand it much better this way and I would like to have similar lectures in other subjects, too.'
- 'This enables me to learn faster and easier and to understand mathematical problems which demand visualisation.'
- 'Quite interesting, although classical lectures can be interesting - depending on teacher.'

Students have also commented in which area (analyses or geometry) multimedia lessons were more helpful:

- 'Multimedia lessons certainly make learning easier, especially in the fields which are more abstract and which are better understood with help of pictures and animations, such was the one about the integrals.'

- 'I have comprehended the integrals much better now than in the high school, while in case of symmetry it was much easier to understand and solve more difficult problems with help of multimedia.'
- 'Line reflection is not very difficult to understand and learn, but it was much easier and even funny through the multimedia lessons. I have always thought that integrals are horrible, but now I understand them and know how to calculate area or volume by drawing a figure.'

When asked whether it was easier for them to learn, understand and solve problems after having lectures and individual work with multimedia approach, students answered the question as shown in Figure 24:

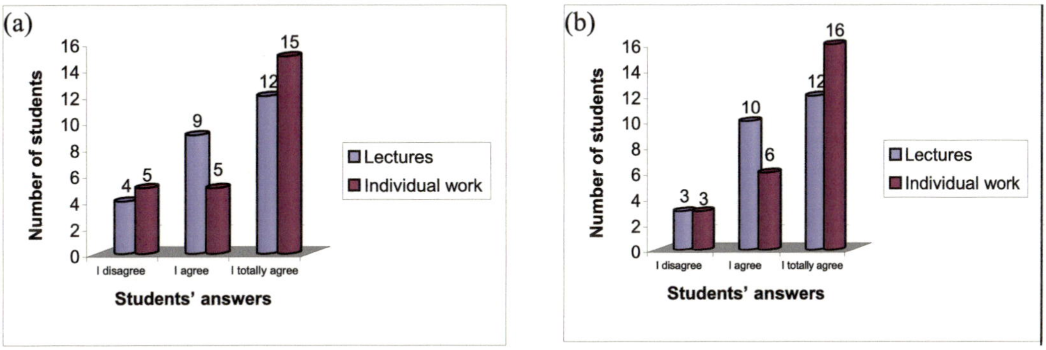

Fig. 24. Students' answers to the question: Should PC be used in lecturing and learning mathematics? (a) Architecture; (b) Civil Construction Management

4. Discussion and conclusions

During past few years, multimedia learning has become very important and interesting topic in the field of teaching methodology. Researches conducted by Mayer (Mayer, 2001, 2005) and Atkinson (Atkinson, 2005) resulted in establishing the basic principles of multimedia learning and design, which were confirmed in our research, too. Multimedia lessons about the definite integrals and the isometric transformations, created in accordance with these principles, proved to be successful. According to the students' reactions, highly understandable animations from multimedia lessons are the best proof that a picture is worth a thousand words. Their remark, and consequently one of this research's conclusions, was that there should be much more of this kind of lessons in education, made - of course - in accordance with certain rules and created in the right way. Many research works in different scientific fields, including mathematics, have proven that multimedia makes learning process much easier.

The tests of adopted knowledge conducted during this research showed that students from multimedia group had much higher average scores in comparison with students from traditional group, which also correspondents with results of some other authors (D. Đ. Herceg, 2009; Wishart, 2000). At the Faculty of Architecture, average score on Test 1 (definite integrals) was 15.49 points greater in multimedia group than in traditional group, while the average score on Test 2 (line reflection) was 11.52 points greater in multimedia group. At the Faculty of Civil Construction Management, average score was 15.97 points greater on Test 1 and 12.6 points greater in multimedia group.

Research on learning the definite integrals with software packages Mathematica and GeoGebra (D. Đ. Herceg, 2009) has shown that students who had used PC in learning process had higher scores on tests. Although this research was conducted with different multimedia teaching tools for the same subject - the definite integral as one of the most important areas in mathematical analyses - our results only proved the universality of multimedia in the process of teaching mathematics.

According to Figures 22a and 23a, which show average scores in single tasks from the field of definite integral, we can conclude that students from multimedia group were remarkably more successful in problems which demand visual comprehension (tasks 1, 2, 4 and 5), while the average score in the third task was practically the same on the both groups. Additionally, according to Figures 22b and 23b, which show average scores in single tasks from the line reflection, it can be seen that the students from multimedia groups at both faculties were remarkably more successful in solving the tasks that demanded visual comprehension, as well as in using the adopted knowledge for more complicated problems (tasks 4 and 5), while the average scores for other tasks were not significantly different.

Wishart's (Wishart, 2000) research included analyses of comments on how much multimedia approach affects teaching and learning processes. Teachers emphasized that multimedia lectures have made their work easier and have proved to be motivating for students, while students said that multimedia lessons, in comparison with traditional methods, have offered better visual idea about the topic. As shown in Figure 24, a great number of them insisted that multimedia tools enabled easier understanding, learning and implementation of knowledge. Students' remark, and consequently one of this research's conclusions, was that there should be more multimedia lessons, i.e. that multimedia is an important aspect of teaching and learning process.

One of this research's conclusions can be put in the way one student did it during the survey (by answering the question: What is multimedia learning): 'Multimedia learning is use of multimedia as an addition to the traditional way of learning. Multimedia enables us to have better understanding of many mathematical problems and to experiment with them.'

Since the experimental lessons on definite integral and isometric transformations have proven to be very successful, we have decided to continue our work and to develop similar multimedia lessons for other areas of mathematics (where applicable) and to make them available for other researchers and teachers when the whole package is ready for publishing.

5. Guidelines for further researches

During our research, several new questions appeared that should be solved in the future: (a) In which scientific fields does the multimedia approach give the best results? (b) How much success of the multimedia approach depends on an individual student's ability and how much on a teacher's skills? (c) How can we improve the understanding of lectures by using the multimedia approach, because our aim is learning and understanding, not the multimedia *per se*.

6. References

Atkinson, R. (2005.). Multimedia Learning of Mathematics in *The Cambridge handbook of Multimedia Learning,* Mayer, R. pp. 393-408., Cambridge University Press, ISBN 0-521-54751-2, United States of America

Bishop, (1989.). Review of research on visualization in mathematics education, *Focus on Learning Problems in Mathematics,* 11 (1), pp. 7-16. ISSN 0272-8893

Damjanović, B. (2005). *Matematička analiza,* GND Produkt, ISBN 86-904989-1-5, Belgrade, Serbia.

Deliyannis, I., Vlamos, P., Floros, A. & Simpsiri, C. (2008). Teaching Basic Number Theory to Students with Speech and Communication Disabilities using Multimedia, *International Conference on Information Communication Technologies in Education* (ICICTE 2008), 10-12 July, Corfu, Greece. ACON-05 I.

Deliyiannis, I., Floros, A., Vlamos, P., Arvanitis, M. & Tania, T. (2008). Bringing Digital Multimedia in Mathematics Education, *The 7th European Conference on e-Learning,* Agia Napa, Cyprus, on 6-7 November 2008

Herceg, D. & Herceg, Đ. (2009.). The definite integral and computer, *The teaching of mathematics,* Vol. 12, No.1, pp. .33-44. ISSN 0351-4463

Mayer, R. (2005.). *The Cambridge handbook of Multimedia Learning,* Cambridge University Press, ISBN 0-521-54751-2, , New York, United States of America

Mayer, R. (2001.). *Multimedia Learning,* Cambridge University Press, ISBN 0-52178-749-1, New York, United States of America

Miličić P.M. & Ušćumlić, M.P. (2005.). *Zbirka zadataka iz više matematike I,* GK, ISBN 86-395-0450-4, Belgrade, Serbia

Milovanovic, M. (2005.). *Коришћење мултимедија за учење изиметријских трансформација,* Математички факултет Универзитета у Београду, master thesis

Milovanovic, M. (2009.). Multimedijalni pristup nastavi matematike na primeru lekcije o osnoj simetriji, *Inovacije u osnovnoškolskom obrazovanju-vrednovanje,* pp. 580-588, ISBN 978-86-7849-136-8, Belgrade, Serbia, october, 2009.

Milovanović, M., Takaci, Đ. & Milajic, A. (2011.). Multimedia Approach in Teaching Mathemathics - Example of Lesson about the Definite Integral Application for Determining an Area, *International Journal of Mathematical Education in Science and Technology,* Vol. 42, No. 2, pp. 175-187, ISSN 0020-739X

Takači, Dj. & Pešić, D. (2004.). The Continuity of Functions in Mathematical Education-Visualization method, *The Teaching of Mathematics,* Belgrade, Vol. 49, No.3-4, pp. 31-42, ISSN 0351-4463

Takači, Dj. , Pešić, D. & Tatar, J. (2006.). On the continuity of functions, *International Journal of Mathematical Education in Science & Technology*, Vol. 37, No.7, pp. 783-791, ISSN 0020-739X

Takači, Dj., Pešić, D. & Tatar, J. (2003.) An introduction to the Continuity of functions using Scientific Workplace, *The Teaching of Mathematics,* Belgrade, Vol. 6, No.2, pp. 105-112. ISSN 0351-4463

Takači, Dj.. Stojković R. & Radovanovic, J. (2008.). The influence of computer on examining trigonometric functions, *Teaching Mathematics and Computer Science,* Debrecen, Hungary, Vol. 6, No.1, pp. 111-123. ISSN 1589-7389

Takači., Dj., Herceg D. & Stojković, R. (2006.). Possibilities and limitati-ons of ScientificWorkplace in studying trigonometric functions, *The Teaching of Mathematics*, Belgrade, Vol. 8, No.2, pp. 61-72. ISSN 0351-4463

Tall, D. (1991.). *Advanced mathematical thinking*, Springer, ISBN 978-0-7923-2812-4, New York, United States of America

Tall, D. (1986.). *A* graphical to integration and fundamental theorem, *Mathematics teaching*, 113, pp. 48-51, ISSN 0025-5785

Wishart, J. (2000.). *Students' and Teachers' Perceptions of Motivation and Learning Through the Use in Schools of Multimedia Encyclopaedias on CD-ROM*, Journal of Educational Multimedia and Hypermedia Vol. 9, No.4, pp. 331-345, ISSN 1055-8896

E. Bakhoum, (2008.). Animating an equation: a guide to using FLASH in mathematics education, *International Journal of Mathematical Education in Science and Technology*, Taylor & Francis, Vol. 39, No.5, pp. 637–655. ISSN 0020-739X

7

Multimedia Teaching Contents: Creating and Integrating Activities in New Learning Environments

Manuela Damiana Guedes and Pedro Almeida
University of Aveiro, Portugal

1. Introduction

New technologies in addition to being one of the pillars of information and knowledge society are also an important factor of change in a cultural and social way and they are present in all stages of social life, businesses, public services, cultural activities and inevitably in Education and in the School. The changes that higher education has gone through, in particular and more recently with the Bologna process, are having consequences in the teaching/learning (T&L) process with particular focus on the contents and the way they relate to teachers and students.

The contribution of new technologies in this process of change at school, as well as its role in society, will be essential.

"Higher education is in the midst of transformative (but exciting) change. Over the next decade, the practices of teaching and learning will undergo fundamental change as universities and colleges respond to global, social, political, technological, and learning research trends. A duality of change – conceptual and technological – faces higher education".

(Siemens, G., 2009)

Teachers have one more challenge in hands: seek to encourage more students to a new learning environment characterized by a breakdown of the increasing expectations of students compared to traditional practices of teaching and learning. We consider that the teacher by integrating new technologies in the T&L process will meet the conditions to improve the relationship with their students, engaging deeper in their learning. In this scenario, there is the need to adjust and adapt the format of learning content as well as the channel through which it is distributed, the proposed activities and assessment methodologies.

We face a new group of students, with a digital literacy which, sometimes, is higher than of their teachers.

"New technologies will not be tools to help the teacher but rather elements that need to be present during the daily school activities to, together with teachers, introduce new factors, creativity add-ons, in this new way of producing knowledge, teaching and learning".

(Pretto, N., 2001)

Casting technologies consist of publishing audio content, video and picture on the Internet. This resource has been highlighted for its potential to generate richer learning scenarios, in distance learning or face to face modalities. This led us to carry this research and reflect on its potential exploitation in the context of T&L. These tools and technologies provide many possibilities for use/application in education, including the ability to have access to class contents anywhere and anytime and, in some cases, in open formats, and to enable the improvement and development of individual skills.

"Faced with a rapid development of knowledge is important that primary education by the acquisition of intellectual capacity needed to learn to learn throughout life, gathering information digitally stored, recombining it and using it to produce knowledge for the desired objective in every moment."

(Castells, M., 2004)

This integration of technology leads teachers to assume new roles and tasks at a professional level. Therefore, the teacher ceases to be just the one who teaches, but the one who co (learns) and drives the learning process.

"Teachers know that their work is changing, as well as the context in which they do it (...) The world rules are changing. It's time for the rules of teaching and work to change ".

(Hargreaves, A., 1998)

Zhao (2007) stresses that the key factors leading to successful learning with technology are related with the knowledge that the teacher has of technology and its experience in using it.

This study is being conducted from a perspective of technology and services/tools in order to assess the educational impact of the use of emerging casting technologies is in the context of T&L in higher education, focusing on the students and teachers capabilities, practices and expectations.

The various possibilities that lie ahead for emerging casting technologies in the classroom together with the lack of research studies that address this problematic, led us to carry out this study.

2. Aims and goals

This study tries to promote the use and integration of emerging casting technologies in the classroom and outside it, as tools to support the construction of educational content and as tools for building collective knowledge.

We also want to evaluate its integration not only as a support to classes but as a strategic option of the T&L process which may contribute, promote, encourage and motivate students to learn and improve their skills. We believe that the development of this study may promote the use of these technologies by teachers in the classroom but also in other places and contexts by students to carry out, as an example, broadcasting of events and/or the creation of an online TV channel for the school.

Therefore, the mail goal of this study is:

To identify opportunities and practices for the teaching/learning process in higher education as a result of the integration of Podcasts, Vodcasts, and Screencasts and other emerging casting technologies.

It is intended to develop and achieve the following specific goals:

1. To access the expectations and beliefs teachers have about integrating casting technologies in the T&L process;
2. To test technology integration strategies and evaluate the practices that are generated by it;
3. To assess how the practices of using casting technologies are recognized/valued by teachers and students and to identify the improvements in the T&L process.

2.1 Characterization and use of casting technologies

Students and teachers roles in the school, namely in the classroom, are well established, traditionally it is expected that the teacher teaches and that the student learns. But the new approaches to T&L demand from students an active role in building their own learning which can be supported by the use of technologies. This challenges students, teachers and also the school to adopt new roles in a more student centred learning.

Among the technologies that can contribute to this change, casting technologies may act as means for the creation of new learning scenarios or as means to improve existing scenarios for more efficient T&L practices. This gains more importance when distance or blended-learning scenarios are at stake as (casting) content has the ability to contribute for the referred creation of new learning scenarios, adding time and place flexibility and contributing for collaborative learning practices.

We believe that the integration and use of casting technologies in schools may act as as positive ingredient for T&L and that the sucess of its aplication depends on the involvement of all actors. The goal *"to test technology integration strategies and evaluate the practices that are generated by it"* is strictly related with our choices about the technologies and tools to use in the current research, as we target to try different technological and pedagogical strategies and evaluate their impact in the T&L process.

The ease with which one can publish and edit podcasts or vodcasts has proven to be an important factor for the increasing integration in higher education contexts (Chan, A., & Lee, MJ, 2005; Boulos, M., et al, 2006; Chan, A., et al. 2006; Frydenberg, M., 2006). Several research projects have tried to understand this growth and the implications for T&L process (Edirisingha, P., et al, 2007; Guertin, L.A., et al, 2007; Lee, M.J. & Chan, A., 2007; Nathan, P., & Chan, A., 2007; Salmon, G., et al, 2007).

"Educators have also taken an interest in podcasting. Some have started broadcasting, such as at McMaster, where engineering professors now host an online show."

"This approach to learning means that learning content is created and distributed in a very different manner. Rather than being composed, organized and packaged, e-learning content is syndicated, much like a blog post or podcast. It is aggregated by students, using their own personal RSS reader or some similar application. From there, it is remixed and repurposed with the student's own individual application in mind, the finished product being fed forward to become fodder for some other student's reading and use."

(Downes, S. 2011)

The students' needs motivated by the technological changes along with the will of teachers to create alternative strategies in the context of their practice, has led more and more teachers to integrate them as a support tool in their classrooms.

"Rooted in emerging technologies which are often transparent to their users, podcasting in an academic setting has become an accepted one-way channel of communication between teacher and students, as faculty have seen the potential impact of creating podcasts of lectures and other course materials".

(Frydenberg, M., 2006)

Emerging casting technologies may turn out to be excellent teaching resources in different areas both at distance and local learning scenarios:

"Academics from many areas of education are showing interest in podcasting for education and the first results of research in this field point towards the benefits to learners".

(Edirisingha, P., et al, 2007)

"Each of the educator and learner tasks can be augmented through use of different technologies. For example, educators can provide a short lecture via a podcast, learners can respond to course materials through a blog post or through a short recording in a tool like Jing."

(Siemens, G., 2009)

For Siemens, podcasts can be used for teaching and learning to:

"Record lectures, include external presenters, evaluation and feedback, learner created reflections and interviews, interviews with notable contributors to a particular field, news or course-related updates and to short introductions to new subject areas".

(Siemens, G., 2009)

2.1.1 Podcast: Definition and concept

The term podcast is the result of the addition of the word iPod and broadcasting and its creation dates back to 2004 when its creator, DJ Adam Curry and Dave Winer decided to publish in the Internet their radio show. Although sometimes there is an indiscriminate use of terms, it is important to clear that the term podcasting refers to the act of publishing in the Internet while the term podcast refers to the content itself.

Concerning the format of the Podcast it can be audio, video or a combination of images and voice, which Edirisingha & Salmon (2008) refer to as "enhanced podcast". If the podcast includes video then is called vodcast or vidcast (Salmon, G., & Edirisingha, P., 2008). When the video content refers to screen captures along with vocal descriptions it is called screencast. This type of casting is particularly relevant for demonstrations on how to use software. Once produced, the podcast can be reused in different contexts and for different audiences. From the perspective of the student, podcasts can be heard or seen, "when and where you want "(Carvalho, A.A., 2008).

Kaplan-Leiserson (2005) also states that some students prefer to listen instead of reading. To Steizinger (2006) podcasts may help in creating a social presence and according to

Salmon et al (2007) it may help teachers and students to reinforce ties and improve their relations.

3. Podcasts and vodcasts in higher education in Portugal and the world: Local input and experiences

There are already several universities that recognize the potential of podcasts and have integrated them mainly because they consider that the fact that the students listen to their MP3 players is an asset.

Thus, some universities even provide their freshmen iPods (Kaplan-Leiserson, E., 2005) in order to benefit from the fact that some teachers record their classes to subsequently make it available online (Frydenberg, R.N, 2006; Guertin , L.A. et al, 2007).

In the next section we present a review of some key studies on the use and integration of podcasts and other forms of casting. These studies are organized accordingly to subject areas, uses or levels of education.

Studies about content production by academics:

- Kingston University (United Kingdom)

In the Kingston University podcasts were used in two courses: English Language and Communication and Earth Sciences and Geography. In the first case the podcasts were intended to support students in the tasks of creating portfolios and presentations and had a non-binding character. In the class of Earth Sciences and Geography the podcasts were used to address key dataterms during class and to make an introduction to the next lesson with the teacher recording the classes so the students can review them (Edirisingha, P., C. Rizzi, & L. Rothwell, 2007).

- University of Leicester (United Kingdom)

The university did a study of the podcasts in two classes: fiber optics communication systems and genetics. In the first course podcasts served to guide students in the activities held during the week (Edirisingha et al, 2007) and in genetics the students created podcasts related to ethical issues in genetics.

- University of Nottingham (United Kingdom)

They conducted a study that integrated ten case studies in five universities (Salmon et al, 2007). The authors concluded that students have difficulty using their MP3 players and heard podcasts and saw or heard vodcasts mainly if they were required in the course.

- University of Leicester (United Kingdom)

The study presents and describes 12 experiments performed using podcasting in higher education (Edirisingha, P. & Nie, M. 2008).

- Carrick Institute for Learning and Teaching in Higher Education (Australia)

"Questioning the net generation: a collaborative project in Australian higher education", describes a project that sought to identify how the tools supported by technologies of a new generation can be used successfully in higher education (Kennedy, G., Krause, K.-L., Gray, K., Judd, T., Bennett, S., Maton, K., Dalgarno, & B. Bishop, A., 2006).

Studies about content production in secondary levels:

- University of Minho (Portugal)

The project "Correspondance Scolaire" took place in 2005-2006 involving the teaching of French and the eTwinning project. It carried several activities involving Portuguese and Belgian students in an online space using a forum, blog, wiki, chat and podcasts (Moura & Carvalho, 2006a).

- University of Minho (Portugal)

The study, "The Use of Podcasts in Education and Learning Sciences: a study with students from 9th grade on topics of the Human Body/Health," focused on the use of podcasts in the natural sciences. The students used nine podcasts about contraceptive methods and two related to the theme of the cardiovascular system (Carvalho, J. 2009).

- University of Minho (Portugal)

In the study presented by Moura & Carvalho (2006b), students had access to class related recordings in Podomatic and could hear them whenever they wanted, according to their pace and learning needs. Working students, with difficulties in attending all classes, saw a chance in podcasts to hear the contents given in their absence.

- University of Minho (Portugal)

In the project "Podcast: A Powerful web tool for learning history" students listened to an activity proposed by the teacher to undertake the course of history and, subsequently, they were asked to produce their podcasts, in pairs, on the curricula they were studding (Cruz, S. & Carvalho, A.A., 2007).

- Duquesne University (USA) and Allegheny Singer Research Institute - Center for Genomic Studies (USA)

This US project aimed specifically to understand the use and development of podcasts by students and its impacts on learning in a science class (Piecka, D., Studnicki, & Zuckerman-Parker, M. 2008).

- University of Gloucestershire (UK)

In the study carried out in this University podcasts had duration of 10 minutes and were aimed at making a first approach regarding the environment and sustainability as well as help students improve their study skills.

Final notes:

The most widely used type of podcasting in higher education, as Evans reports (2007) has been recorded lectures. MIT, Stanford and other universities have regular practices of making available their lectures. In b-learning and e-learning scenarios podcasts can provide several advantages and be an asset in the T&L process. Some universities use podcasts in these flexible learning scenarios like: Charles Sturt University - Australia (Chan, A., & Lee,

M., 2005; Chan, A. et al, 2006; Lee, M., & Chang, A., 2007; Nathan P . & Chan, A., 2007 or University of Minho (Carvalho, A.A., 2008).

4. Research methodology

As previously referred, this study tries to promote the use and integration of emerging casting technologies. It is being carried at the School of Technology and Management of Lamego - Polytechnic Institute of Viseu - Portugal. The study is structured accordingly to an action research methodology.

In the current study students have been gradually exposed to various types of content according to its technical complexity and novelty and in the following order: 1º: audio podcasts, 2º: vodcasts and screencasts and in a future research cycle, yet to be carried, broadcasting (live TV).

In addition to this gradual introduction of different type of multimedia content, it is our purpose, in the next research cycle, to adopt strategies for the use of casting tools outside the T&L context, including its application in the support of some institutional services.

The action research methodology, adopted in this study, is characterized for its spiral approach, always focusing on a problem and interactively alternating between action and critical reflection.

Dick, B. (1999) argues: "The methods, data and interpretation are refined in later cycles, continuously based on experience and knowledge achieved in the previous cycle". Several authors consider Kurt Lewin, a social psychologist and educator who developed his work in action research in the United States of America in the 40s, the pioneer in this methodology.

Fig. 1. Action-Research according to Kurt Lewin (*adaptation*).

One of these authors, Esteves (1986), classifies action-research as a "realistic action always followed by a self-critical reflection, and an evaluation of the gathered results sustained in a triangle action research and learning".

For data collection and analysis, this study adopted questionnaires, interviews with users and teachers, gathered statistics (from the supporting web sites) and will perform qualitative evaluation of the content that is produced.

4.1 Target audience and phases of the study

This research, applied in the undergraduate School of Technology and Management of Lamego, involves the researcher as coordinator of the multimedia division, teachers and students from the same institution.

The study is structured in different stages as follows:

Step 1: The first step was focused in the literature review on the area.
Step 2: The second stage was focused in the analysis and evaluation of the most adequate technologies to be adopted in the study. For this purpose a benchmarking grid was created and used.
The selected tools were then tested before the following stage of development.
Step 3: The stage were the strategy and planning for the integration of the tools was defined.
Step 4: This stage is focused in the production of the multimedia content.
The content is being produced in a first step by the researcher and it is focused on the use/explanation of the various technologies involved. The goal is that students and teachers gradually learn how to create their own podcasts and learn it through the use of podcasts and vodcasts.For the publication of these casting content, a on-lineplatform was created, supported by Grouply, at: http://estgl-criar-aprender-partilhar.grouply.com/

Fig. 2. Main Page of Community:" estgl_criar_aprender e partilhar"

Step 5: This phase consists of the field work, namely providing the casting content in a gradual way, along with the evaluation in each sub-step.
Step 6: This phase will be targeted at processing and analysing the collected data.
Step 7: Finally, the study results will be inferred.

5. About the different tools and technologies being adopted

The study aims to promote the use of emerging casting technologies as enablers for the production of educational content and collective knowledge, not only in the context of the classroom by the teacher but also in other initiatives carried by the students. One of the aims of the study is that students and teachers create their own multimedia content, so we had to take into consideration when choosing the tools to use that most of them do not have high computer literacy. For choosing the tools to be used in the study we defined the following characteristics as demanding:

- Open source: free to use based on open technologies;
- Intuitive, practical and functional;
- Easy to setup.

In the next section we will present the tools selected.

5.1 Choosing the tools to produce podcasts (audio)

For the production of audio castings (podcasts) the following tools were analysed and compared: Audacity, Sony Sound Forge and Adobe Audition. The decision went to Audacity.

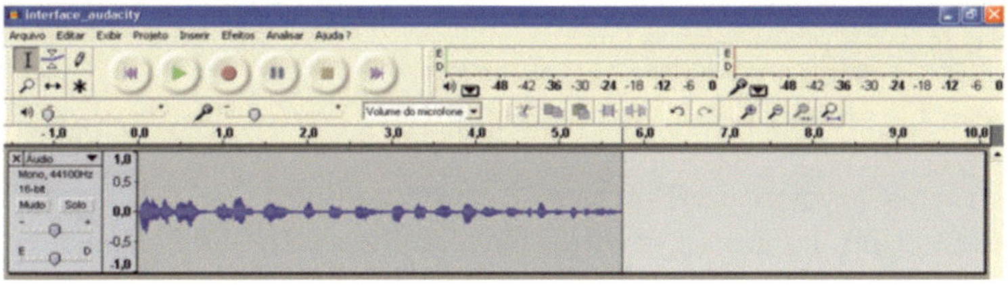

Fig. 3. The Audacity Interface

Choosing Audacity was based on its features and advantages over the others, namely: the fact that it is open source, free to use, easy to configure along with the integration of the usual tools of professional software.

5.2 Choosing the tools to produce vodcasts and screencasts

For the creation of screencasts and vodcasts the analysis was made on three tools: Jing, Camtasia Studio 6.0.3 and Screentoaster. After analysing the characteristics and capabilities of each of the tools Jing was the chosen one for being open source, easy to use, with the ability to capture, edit and share the content.

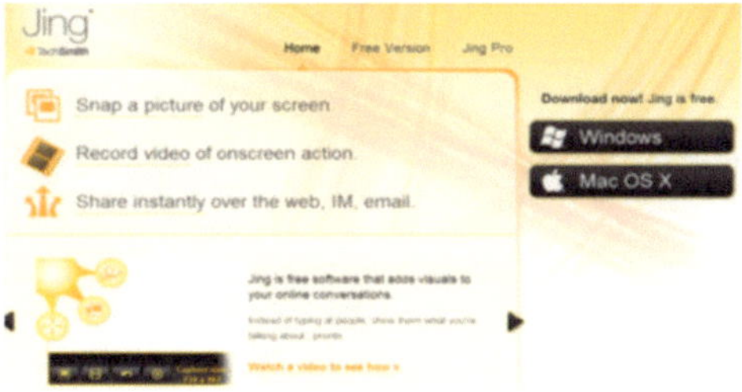

Fig. 4. Homepage of Jing

5.3 Choosing the tools for broadcasting

Regarding the tools for Broadcasting we chose to analyse and compare three: Livestream +Procaster, Stickam and Ustream.tv. This choice took also into account the popularity of the tool, an indicator that minimizes the risk of discontinuation of the service.

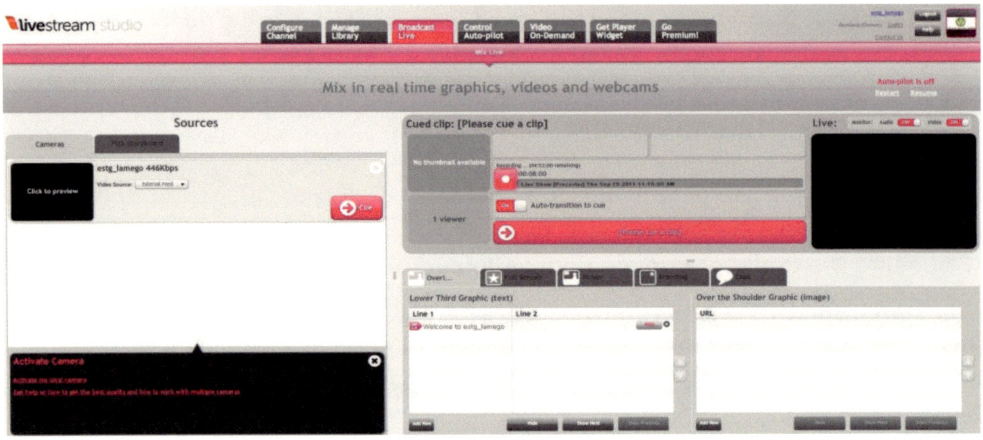

Fig. 5. Interface of Livestream/Procaster - Studio

The chosen one was Livestream+Procaster a more complete solution when compared to Ustream.tv and Stickam, including features such as the availability of an interactive on-line studio and the flexibility of the broadcasting tools that allows to adapt to different needs like classes, conferences or workshops.

5.4 Choosing the tools for content aggregation

All tools are relevant, with advantages and disadvantages as well as distinct features that correspond to different situations. The importance they have depends on the use and context the user wants to do with them.

To select a platform for aggregating multimedia content we also produced a table for a comparative analysis which included: Ning, Elgg, Moodle, Facebook and Grouply. The choice was toward the last one: Grouply.

Fig. 6. One of the Groups created on "estgl_criar_aprender e partilhar": Upload multimedia content

The Grouply platform has advantages such as the fact that it is intuitive to use, very functional and allows to set different graphic templates. On the other hand, Ning platform is not free and Moodle is difficult to configure, and has limited support for Web 2.0 features.

6. Preliminary results

As preliminary results we can point out the curiosity and motivation, either from teachers or students to produce and integrate various types of multimedia content in their courses.

The study involved, so far, and during the school year of 2010-2011,the participation of a majority of the undergraduate courses available at the school, namely: Tourism Information (1st, 2nd and 3rd years), Tourism, Cultural and Heritage Management (1st and 2nd years), Accounting and Auditing (2nd year), Accounting and Auditing - evening course (1st year), Administration Secretariat - evening course (2nd year), Management and Computer Sciences (1st and 2nd years) and a group of Erasmus students. It involved also several teachers who gave their contribution. It is also expected that during the current school year 2011-2012 an increase in the participation and collaboration of teachers.

To evaluate the opinions of teachers and students about their use of casting technologies, a questionnaire was released on-line (in Google Docs). The process of data collection is still taking place during the preparation of the chapter, but we can indicate some preliminary data on the basis of one hundred percent of teachers who responded and in the universe of two hundred seventy-six students responded one hundred seventy-for.

6.1 The students' opinion

About the development of skills in multimedia content creation and present/future use:

Students considered having an increase in their skills to produce digital resources (e.g. documents, presentations, audio podcasts, video podcasts, screencasts, vodcasts, etc.) as shown in graphic 1.

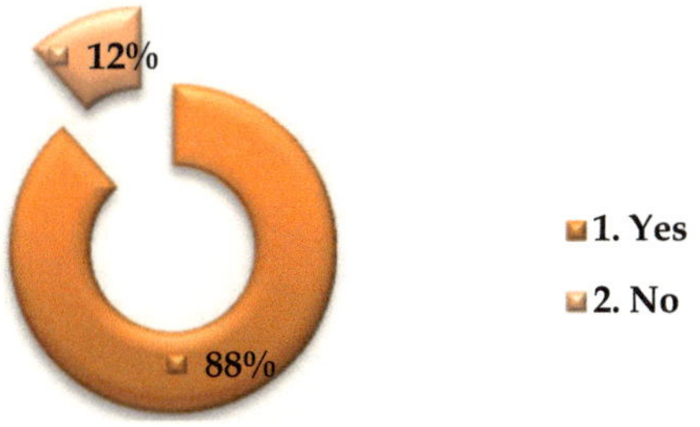

Graph. 1. Part II - Question E: Using the casting technologies improved my ICT?

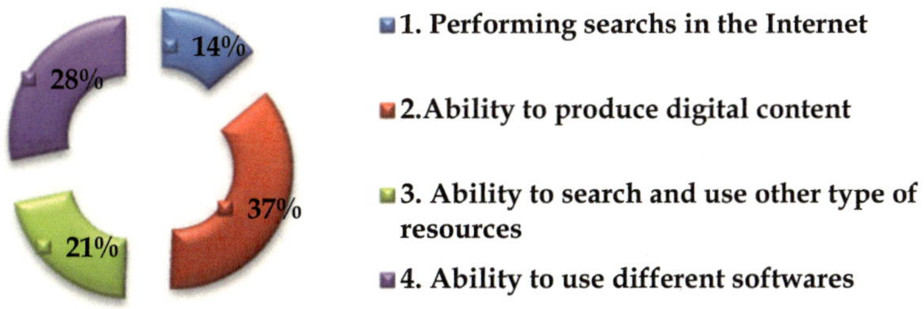

Graph. 2. Part II - Question F: *If so, in what area(s)?*

- Ability to use different types of software with varied functions (Audacity, Jing, YouTube, AuthorStream, Prezi, etc.):

When asked if the casting technologies and content could be an improvement to the classes 98% referred yes. As referred an on-line community portal was built to support the dissemination of the produced content. Considering its uses, the students were asked if they preferred that the portal acted more as a deposit of information or as a space for sharing experiences and discussions on the use of casting content. Graphic 3 shows that the majority preferred the discussion and interactive format.

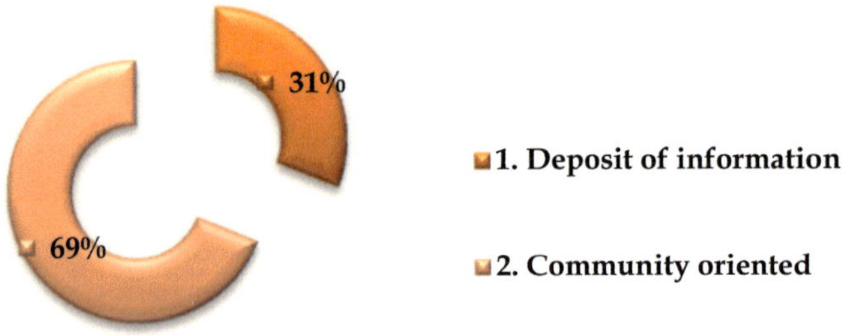

Graph. 3. Part III – Question E: What is the preferred role for the portal "estgl_criar_aprender e partilhar": a) deposit of information; b) community oriented.

Considering the willingness to publish content in the portal, 84% referred that they will do it in the future and 95% referred the expectation to get more content from this community.

6.2 The teachers' opinion

Skills development of multimedia content creation and present/future use:

- Increased production skills of digital resources (eg. documents, presentations, audio podcasts, video podcasts, screencasts, vodcasts, etc.):

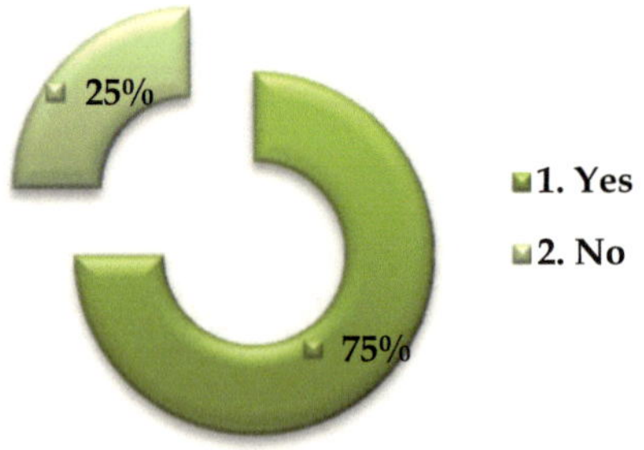

Graph. 4. Part II – Question E: Using casting technologies the ICT competences get better?

- Ability to use different types of software with varied functions (Audacity, Jing, YouTube, AuthorStream, Prezi, etc.):

Considering the willingness to use, create and publish content in the portal, 100% responded yes.

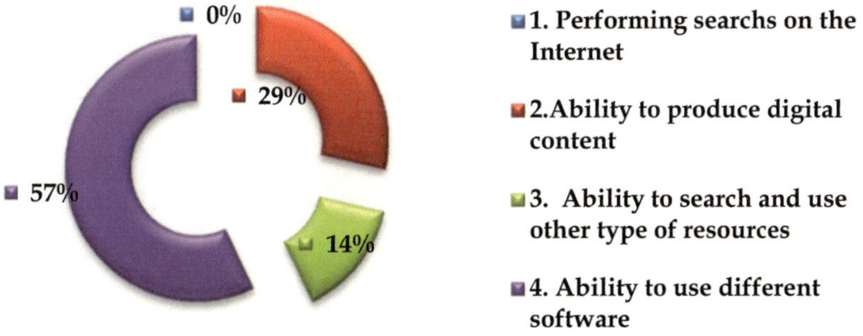

Graph. 5. Part II – Question F: *If so, in what area(s)?*

- Preference in the Community "estgl_criar_aprender and share" to have more support for discussions/interactions of the class that are taken in the context of classroom or other platforms such as Moodle over an optical function more content repository:

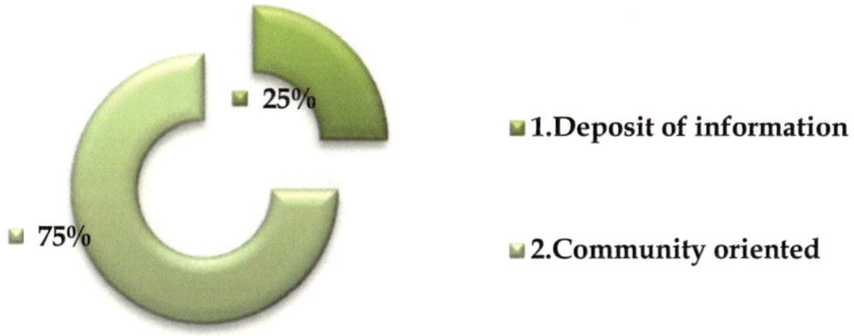

Graph. 6. Part III – Question E: What is the preferred role for the portal "estgl_criar_aprender e partilhar": a) deposit of information; b) community oriented.

About the ability for the teachers to get multimedia content and casting supporting software for their classes in the portal, all referred the support for this initiative.

Finally considering the perceived impact of using multimedia/casting technologies in the classed all teachers referred that it had a positive effect on student´s motivation in the classes (Graphic 7).

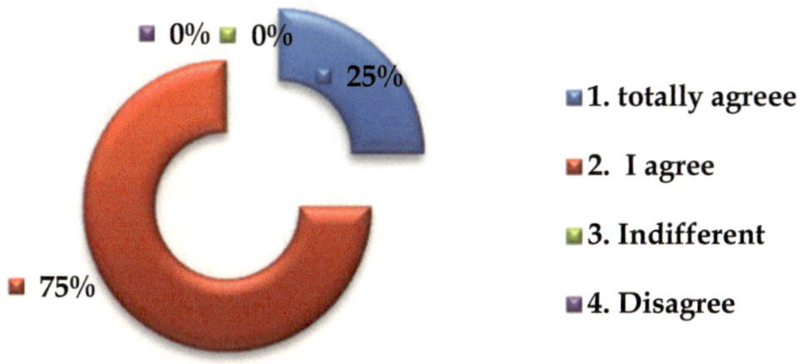

Graph. 7. Part IV – Question M: Using technologies in my class got an extra motivation for the students?

They all agreed that the *"estgl_criar_aprender e partilhar"* community played an important role of the positive feedback of students:

7. Conclusions

The development of this project includes several stages and a constant adaptation according with the gathered and perceived results. Some important stages are already concluded but others remain active, like the field work. Nevertheless, we were able to gather some results that indicate positive feedback from teachers and students.

All they perceive the relevance for classes of introducing casting content and technologies. These preliminary results obtained allow us to face the next steps of the study with optimism.

8. Future work

Some of the work is still to be carried, namely the full evaluation of students and teachers practices and opinions concerning the use of casting technologies. This will provide us with a better understanding of the impact of these tools in the T&L process.

As future work for this project, in order to increase its positive impact, we aim to increase the number of members of the community involved - teachers and students - by providing increasing the awareness towards the project along with better technical and human support that may allow more activities for the creation, development and sharing of multimedia content in their classes, ultimately targeted at providing a better T&L process.

All the activities being carried are aimed to promote the use of these technologies not only in the classes but also in other extra-curricular activities. We aim to provide conditions to the creation and development of an on-line TV channel for the institution that will allow the dissemination of the activities and events carried in the institution.

9. References

Boulos, M., Maramba, I. & Wheeler, S. (2006). Wikis, blogs and podcasts: a new generation of Web-based tools for virtual collaborative clinical practice and education. *BMC – Medical Education*, 6 (41), pp. 1-8. Available from: <http://www.biomedcentral.com/content/pdf/1472-6920-6-41.pdf>

Carvalho, A. A. (2009). Grelha para classificar Podcasts. Available from: < http://www.iep.uminho.pt/podcast/grelha_podcasts.docx>

Carvalho, A.A (2008). Os Podcasts no Ensino Universitário: Implicações dos Tipos e da Duração na Aceitação dos Alunos. *In* A. A. Carvalho (org), *Actas do Encontro sobre Web 2.0*. Braga: CIEd, Universidade do Minho, 179-190. Available from: <http://hdl.handle.net/1822/8558>

Carvalho, A. A.; Aguiar, C.; Carvalho, C. J.; Oliveira, L. R.; Cabecinhas, R.; Marques, A.; Santos, H. & Maciel, R. (2008). *Taxonomia de Podcasts*. Available from: <http://sisifo.fpce.ul.pt>

Carvalho, J. (2009). O Uso de Podcasts no Ensino e na Aprendizagem das Ciências Naturais: um estudo com alunos de 9º ano sobre temas do Corpo Humano/Saúde

Ozarfaxinars: e-revista do CFAE_Matosinhos. e-revista ISSN 1645-9180, nº8. Available from: <http://www.cfaematosinhos.eu/O%20Uso%20de%20Podcasts%20no%20Ensino%20e%20na%20Aprendizagem_08.pdf>

Castells, M. (2004). *A Galáxia Internet.* Lisboa: Fundação Calouste Gulbenkian.

Chan, A.,Lee, M. J. W. & McLoughlin, C. (2006). Everyone's learning with podcasting: A Charles Sturt University experience. *Proceedings of the 23rd annual conference: Who's learning? Whose technology?. ASCILITE 2006.* The University of Sydney. pp. 111-120.

Chan, A. & Lee, M. J. W. (2005). An MP3 a Day Keeps the Worries Away: Exploring the use of podcasting to address preconceptions and alleviate pre-class anxiety amongst undergraduate information technology students. *Student Experience Conference 2005 - Good Practice in Practice.* Charles Sturt University, pp. 59-71.

Cruz, S. & Carvalho, A. A. (2007). Podcast: a powerful web tool for learning history. In M. Nunes & M. McPherson (eds). *IADIS International Conference, e-Learning 2007-Proceedings.* Lisboa: IADIS, 313-318.

Dick, B. (1999). *What is action research?* Available from: <http://www.scu.edu.au/schools/gcm/ar/whatisar.html>

Downes, S. (2011). *Acess: Future- Practical Advice on How to Learn and What to Learn.* Canada: National Research Council of Canada. Available from: < http://www.downes.ca/files/AccessFuture.pdf >

Edirisingha, P. & Nie, M. (2008). *Podcasting in Higher Education - 12 approaches.* UK: University of Leicester. Available from: <http://www2.le.ac.uk/projects/impala/presentations/mlearn-2008-impala-workshop/materials/03.1%20Podcasting%20approaches_06Oct2008.pdf>

Edirisingha, P., Rizzi, C., & Rothwell, L. (2007). Podcasting to provide teaching and learning support for an undergraduate module on English language and communication. *Turkish Online Journal of Distance Education,* 8 (3), 87-107. Available from: <http://www.eric.ed.gov/ERICWebPortal/custom/portlets/recordDetails/detailmini.jsp?_nfpb=true&_&ERICExtSearch_SearchValue_0=ED498818&ERICExtSearch_SearchType_0=no&accno=ED498818>

Evans, C. (2007). The effectiveness of m-learning in the form of podcast revision lectures in higher education. *Computers & Education,* 1-8. Available from: <http://uwpodcast.pbworks.com/f/Podcast_Effectiveness.pdf>

Esteves, A., J. (1986). *A investigação-acção.* Em A. Santos Silva e J. Madureira Pinto. *Metodologia das Ciências Sociais.* Porto: Afrontamento.

Frydenberg, M. 2006. Principles and pedagogy: The two P's of podcasting in the information technology classroom. In *Proceedings of ISECON 2006,* ed. D. Colton et al. §3354. Chicago: AITP. Available from: <http://www.webcitation.org/5YEq6awtl>.

Guertin, L. A., Bodek, M. J., & Zappe, S. E. & Kim, H. (2007). Questioning the Student Use of and Desire for Lecture Podcasts. *MERLOT – Journal of Online Learning and Teaching,* 3(2), pp.1-9. Available from: <http://jolt.merlot.org/vol3no2/guertin.htm>

Hargreaves, a. (1998). *Os Professores em Tempos de Mudança: o Trabalho e a Cultura dos Professores na Idade Pós-Moderna.* Lisboa: McGraw-Hill.

Kaplan-Leiserson, E. (2005). Trend: Podcasting in Academic and Corporate Learning. *Learning Circuits.* Available from: <http://www.astd.org/LC/2005/0605_kaplan.htm>

Kennedy, G., Krause, K.-L., Gray, K., Judd, T., Bennett, S., Maton, K., Dalgarno, B. & Bishop, A. (2006). Questioning the Net Generation: A collaborative project in Australian higher education. In L. Markauskaite, P. Goodyear & P. Reimann (Eds.), *Who's learning? Whose technology? Proceedings of the 23rd Annual Conference of the Australiasian Society for Computers in Learning in Tertiary Education* (pp. 413-417). Sydney: Sydney University Press.

Lee, M. J., & Chan, A. (2007). Reducing the Effects of Isolation and Promoting Inclusivity for Distance learners Through Podcasting. *The Turkish Online Journal of Distance Education*. 8 (1), 85-104. Available from: <http://www.eric.ed.gov/ERICWebPortal/custom/portlets/recordDetails/detailmini.jsp?_nfpb=true&_&ERICExtSearch_SearchValue_0=ED494811&ERICExtSearch_SearchType_0=no&accno=ED494811>

Moura, A.,& Carvalho, A.A. (2006a). Podcast: Potencialidades na Educação. *Revista Prisma.com*, nº3, 88-110.

Moura, A.,& Carvalho, A. A. (2006b). Podcast: para uma Aprendizagem Ubíqua no Ensino Secundário. *In* Alonso, L. P. *et al.* (eds), *8th International Symposium on Computer in Education*. León: Universidad de León. (Vol. 2, pp.379-386).

Nathan, P. & Chan, A. (2007). Engaging undergraduates with podcasting in a business subject. *Proceedings ASCILITE*. Singapore, pp. 747-751.

Piecka, D., Studnicki, E. & Zuckerman-Parker, M. (2008). A proposal for ozone science podcasting in a middle science classroom. *AACE Journal, 16*(2), 203-233.

Pretto, N.; Serpa, L.F. (2001). A Educação e a Sociedade de Informação. In Dias, P; Freitas, C.V. (Org.) *Actas da II conferência internacional de tecnologias de informação e comunicação na educação, Challenges 2001*. Braga: Universidade do Minho: 21- 41.

Salmon, G. & Edirisingha, P. (2008). *Podcasting for Learning in Universities*. Berkshire: McGraw-Hill.

Salmon, G., Nie, M., & Edirisingha, P. (2007). *Informal Mobile Podcasting And Learning Adaptation (IMPALA)*. e-Learning research Project Report 06/07. Beyond Distance Research Alliance. University of Leicester. Available from: <http://www2.le.ac.uk/projects/impala>

Siemens, G. & Tittenberger, P. (2009). *Handbook of emerging technologies for learning*. Available from: <http://www.elearnspace.org/blog/2009/03/11/handbook-of-emerging-technologies-for-learning/>

Y. Zhao. (2007, março, 15). Social Studies Teachers' Perspectives of Technology Integration. *Journal of Technology and Teacher Education*, pp. 311-333.

Part 3

Interfaces and Interaction

8

Developing Attention-Aware and Context-Aware User Interfaces on Handheld Devices

Massimo Ancona[1], Betty Bronzini[1], Davide Conte[2] and Gianluca Quercini[3]

[1]*University of Genoa, Department of Computer Science, Genoa*
[2]*Eurocontrol SpA, Genoa*
[3]*University of Maryland, Institute for Advanced Computer Studies, College Park, MD*
[1,2]*Italy*
[3]*USA*

1. Introduction

I do not fear computers. I fear lack of them. - Isaac Asimov

In today's modern societies the lack of computers feared by Asimov is not an imminent danger thanks to the advance of mobile technology in the last two decades. According to several market surveys, sales of handheld devices, especially smartphones, are growing at an incredibly fast rate and are expected to exceed those of any other electronic device by the end of 2011 [1]. This success is far from surprising, as today's handheld devices feature high computational power and provide a wide range of applications that go beyond the traditional use of a phone. Examples are *mHealth*, a term coined by Istepanian et al. (2005) that refers to the use of mobile applications in healthcare, and *augmented reality*, defined by Azuma (1997) as a variation of *virtual reality* that "allows the user to see the real world, with virtual objects superimposed upon or composited with the real world". Essentially, handheld devices fit in a pocket and provide most of the functionalities of a bulky computer. Their small size, however, is a mixed blessing, as it imposes serious limitations on usability, which is the focus of this chapter. In particular, we discuss two important aspects of the interaction with handheld devices, namely *context-awareness* and *text entry*.

Context-aware computing, introduced by Schilit et al. (1994), is a major achievement in mobile computing. In fact, unlike desktop computers, handheld devices work in dynamic environments, where user's context and/or location is likely to rapidly change. Based on the information derived from the context, applications can automatically change their interface or behaviour accordingly. For instance, the context-aware application described by Ancona et al. (2006) senses that a certain area of an archaeological site is crowded at a certain time of the day and suggests the visitor to modify his/her visit path. Similarly, the location-aware application presented by Ancona et al. (2003; 2001) understands which ward a doctor is walking in and proposes an appropriate list of drugs that can be rapidly selected to fill in a prescription. Essentially, context-aware applications minimize or remove, if at all possible, the need to interact with the device, by automatically updating its interface and behaviour.

[1] `http://www.gartner.com/it/page.jsp?id=1550814`

Context-awareness can also help to ease tasks that demand a continuous attention of the users, such as *text entry*. Since most handheld devices do not have a hardware keyboard, which would limit their portability, text entry is usually performed by using either a virtual keyboard or a handwriting recognition system. However, neither the former nor the latter stands out in the same way as the *Qwerty* keyboard does for desktop computers.

The remainder of the chapter is organized as follows. In Section 2 we describe the main features of today's smartphones, which are the most popular handheld devices on the market. In Section 3 we discuss issues related to the design of context aware applications, along with examples drawn from our own past research projects *Agamemnon*, *Past* and *WardInHand*. We note that when we worked on those projects, smartphones were not equipped with the sophisticated sensors they feature today. Consequently, the development of context-aware applications was much more challenging than today, as we detail in Section 4. In Section 5 we analyse the problem of text entry and describe a context-aware text entry tool named *WtX* that we developed few years ago. Finally, Section 6 concludes the presentation.

2. Smartphones: an overview

A *smartphone* is a cellular phone integrating standard mobile phone capabilities with the advanced computing ability and peripherals of a personal digital assistant (PDA), like a camera, an advanced (touch)screen, a (virtual) keyboard and a compass. Users can interact with the touchscreen either through their fingers or a tiny pen, generally referred to as a *stylus*; the use of a smartphone with a stylus is generally referred to as *pen computing*. Like PDAs, smartphones offer a full featured operating system and an advanced platform for application development.

Although the term *smartphone* was used for the first time in 1997, when Ericsson launched the concept phone GS88, it came into use later in early 2000. Since their early commercial introduction (end 90s-early 2000), smartphones have evolved at an incredible fast pace. In the design phase of our project *Agamemnon*, started on January 2004, we envisioned to use the *Nokia 6600* and we finally resorted to its successor, the *Nokia 6630*, for the implementation phase. After only 7 years, both devices are obsolete and appear like archaeological finds compared to the *Apple iPhone 4*, the *Samsung Galaxy S2 Smartphone* and the *Nokia 3720 Classic*, which are the best selling smarphones on the market at the time we are writing. IMS research states that up to 420 million smartphones (28% of the mobile phone market) will be sold by the end of 2011 and predicts that annual sales will surpass one billion devices (50% of the mobile phone market) by the end of 2016 [2]. According to Gartner, in the first quarter of 2011 *Nokia* is still the worldwide leader of the smartphone market, although its market share considerably declined in favour to *Samsung* [3]. Although *Apple* market share is only 3.9%, it doubled the sales of *iPhones* since 2010. Still referring to the first quarter of 2011, *Android* and *Symbian* dominate the operating system market, but *Apple iOS* is keeping the pace.

A particularly popular smartphone is the *camera phone*, which can be defined as a smartphone with limited capabilities featuring a medium/high resolution camera. According to the latest

[2] http://imsresearch.com/press-release/Global_Smartphones_Sales_Will_Top_420_Million_Devices_in_2011_Taking_28_Percent_of_all_Handsets_According_to_IMS_Research

[3] http://www.gartner.com/it/page.jsp?id=1689814

report by *Strategy Analytics* [4], worldwide camera phone sales will exceed 1 billion units in 2011. The fastest growing segment will be the high-tier camera phone market with sensors of eight megapixels and above.

Clearly, the evolution of smartphones is primarily due to electronic miniaturization that allows powerful processors in small devices. The computing power of smartphones is almost comparable to that of computers that were sold few years ago, which paves the way to applications that were virtually unthinkable before. Consequently, smartphones and PDAs are not only passive devices waiting for any input to perform an action, but they actively support users in such activities as visiting a city or monitoring their health.

2.1 Sensors

Sensors can be either *mobile,* if they are installed on mobile devices, or *fixed,* if they are stationary; mobile devices can typically access fixed sensors via a communication network such as *UMTS, GPRS, WiFi* or *Bluetooth.* Today's smartphones feature a number of different sensors, including GPS receivers, accelerometers, gyroscopes, digital compasses, proximity and ambient light sensors. The *iPhone* features a relatively new sensor, named *Asahi Kasei's azimuth magnetometer,* which determines the orientation of the phone.

The role of sensors is crucial in mobile computing, because, unlike desktop computers, handheld devices are meant to support users in their interaction with the external environment besides the "virtual world" trapped inside the machine. Not surprisingly, sensors greatly simplify the design of context and location aware applications. For instance, by combining information from a GPS receiver and a magnetometer, an application can easily determine not only the position of the user, but also what s/he is currently looking at.

Interestingly, most of the peripherals of handheld devices, such as a camera, are meant to point to the real world, as opposed to peripherals of desktop computers, such as a mouse. For example, *TinyMotion,* described by Wang et al. (2006), is a software that detects in real time a person's hands movements by using the camera of a mobile phone. Similarly, Ancona et al. (2007) described a system, of which an overview is presented in Section 4, that uses the camera of a smartphone and image recognition techniques to determine the position and the orientation of a person. In the first case, the camera is used as an accelerometer, while in the second as a GPS receiver and a magnetometer. We note that it is not appropriate at all to define the camera as a sensor, but many applications use it as such, although from the users' perspective it is merely a tool to take photos.

The camera is not the only example of a device that can be used as a sensor even if it is not its primary purpose. In a cellular network the position of a mobile phone can be estimated based on the knowledge of the *base station* to which the phone is connected. In a sense, the *base station* is used as a location sensor. The location accuracy is about 1km (0.6 mi) in cellular networks based on *microcells,* such as *GPRS,* and only 100m (328 feet) in networks based on *picocells,* such as *UMTS.* These location methods cannot achieve the accuracy of GPS and are typically used when a device does not have a GPS receiver, which was the case of most smartphones and PDAs few years ago, or GPS is not available.

A complete discussion about the role of sensors is outside the scope of this presentation. For further details, we refer the interested reader to the paper written by Lane et al. (2010).

[4] http://www.strategyanalytics.com/default.aspx?mod=reportabstractviewer&a0=6216

3. Context aware applications

As already noted by Turk & Robertson (2000), human-computer interaction is still dominated by the "typing, pointing and clicking" paradigm, which works well with desktop or laptop computers, but reveals all its limitations with handheld devices, due to their limited size.

One way to ease the interaction with a handheld device is to design *context-aware applications*, which "adapt according to the location of use, the collection of nearby people, hosts and accessible devices as well as to changes to such things over time", as defined by Schilit et al. (1994). Context-awareness proved to be particularly effective in healthcare, as witnessed by the wealth of projects and applications that have been proposed in the last decade, of which a good review has been written by Bricon-Soufand & Newman (2007). The ability of an application to automatically change its behaviour based on the context is particularly helpful in handheld devices, as they reduce the number of interactions with the device. To this extent, several models of user interfaces have been introduced, in particular:

- **Perceptual interfaces**, described by Turk & Robertson (2000) as being able to add human-like perceptual capabilities to an application. For instance, an application may be aware of what the user is saying or what the user's face, body, and hands are doing.
- **Computer vision-based interfaces**, presented by Turk (2004) as those that "look at people" and aim at determining the user's focus of attention based on visual clues.
- **Attentive interfaces**, that, as pointed out by Vertegaal (2003), aim at understanding what the user might be interested in at a given time and context and generate relevant information accordingly.
- **Multimodal interfaces**, that integrate, in an homogeneous way, different human communication mechanisms like speech, gestures and eyes and body movements. An overview is presented by Oviatt & Cohen (2000).

Most of the applications we developed are based on attentive interfaces. For instance, our text entry tool *WtX* (Section 5.4) only suggests words that are appropriate to the user's context; the *Agamemnon* system (Section 3.3) guides tourists through an archaeological site by showing on the screen of their smartphones only the information relevant to the monuments which they are currently looking at.

3.1 Design principles of a context aware HCI

The design of mobile applications is significantly different from that of desktop applications, which can rely on powerful devices connected to a power outlet and equipped with keyboard, mouse, plenty of storage space and a wide screen to visualize as much information as needed. As opposed to that, handheld devices have a limited autonomy, they lack effective text entry tools and their screen size is typically very small, which poses serious challenges to applications; the *iPhone* 4 screen, for example, is only 3.5 inches. As a result, applications need to visualize as little information as possible in order to avoid visual clutter. On the one hand, providing all information in just one page is not an option, as users would be forced to use such graphical widgets as scrollbars, which are very difficult to handle in small devices. On the other hand, partitioning the information into many pages could make the navigation hard and force users to continuously switch pages. A feasible solution consists of a compromise between the two approaches: grouping only the most significant data in a page while showing the rest only upon users' request.

Here context and location awareness can contribute to simplify the HCI of mobile applications. Consider, for example, the case of an application on a PDA that supports doctors and nurses while filling in prescriptions for their patients in a hospital. In order to optimize the space on the screen, the application only visualizes information about patients in the ward in which the doctor or the nurse is, while other data, if needed, can be visualized through a limited number of taps. Or, the application may be smart enough to understand which ward the doctor is in and automatically update the information on the screen without the explicit request of the doctor.

In this section we show how context and location awareness can be integrated in the design of the HCI. We say that a component of the interface is *horizontal* if it provides utilities that are likely to be shared by several applications. Examples of horizontal components are virtual keyboards, Web browsers, word processors and editors. Similarly, a *vertical* component is one that is linked to a specific application. Here we give to the HCI a very wide meaning by including in it any tool supporting data I/O between a user and a software application or component. This distinction is useful for designing a Service Oriented Architecture (SOA) where the horizontal components identify services i.e. units of computer work, while vertical components identify modules or objects inside a single service.

Today, in the development of the HCI for a wide range of applications, including industrial control systems, power system automation and telemedicine, there is the tendency to shift from ad-hoc solutions to Web services. This is motivated by the wide portability of web browsers that offer almost the same interface on every system - from powerful servers to small handheld devices. Major advantages of web browsers are:

- *No cost*, due to the availability of free software available on all platforms;
- *Intuitiveness*, as web browsers are well-known by any computer user and thus can be considered as a universal interface;
- *Scalability and portability*, as browsers are available for every architecture, from supercomputers to desktop PCs and handheld devices.
- *Open architecture*, as several open and standard systems are available (e.g., Javascript, Java, HTML, XML etc.);
- *Reusability*, as browsers reduce the risks of obsolescence.

An example of Web-based application is *WardInHand*, described in greater details in Section 3.2, that runs under *Windows* and *Linux* and on several devices, from palmtops (small laptops), to full featured notebooks. We successfully experimented it on a *iPAQ* running *Familiar Linux* with the *Konqueror* Web browser. By enhancing the use of horizontal interfaces like web browsers, supported by open software architectures, and by extending the capabilities of existing ones (see *WtX* described later), the application presents an easy-to-learn standard interface with almost the same look-and-feel on every kind of available device. As a result, the software is scalable and reusable and its implementation is exposed to a limited risk of obsolescence, as most of its (horizontal) components are regularly updated.

3.2 *WardInHand*

WardInHand (abbreviated as WIH) was a three-year EU co-funded IST project (IST 10479, 2000-2002), whose objective was to support the daily activities of doctors and nurses in a hospital. WIH provides a tool for workgroup collaboration and ubiquitous access to the patient's clinical records at every point-of-care through the use of HP iPAQ pocket PCs.

The project has been completed at the end of March 2002 with the release of a system prototype improved with all suggestions and feedbacks collected during the testing phase and evaluation activities extensively performed by the three end users.

WIH belongs to a relatively new class of "everyday and everywhere" applications. In 1999-2000, wireless networks and handheld devices were a completely new technology, making data ubiquity in hospitals a reality, which saves doctors' time and makes handheld devices part of the usual doctors' equipment. On the downside, handheld devices have limited autonomy, especially when they use intensively a wireless network to send and receive data, they provide a small screen real estate and, as already explained, they are hard to interact with. In general, we noticed that the short battery life did not pose any serious problem, mostly because the personnel of the hospital needs WIH only for short time intervals, namely when visiting patients and prescribing treatments.

In order to improve the interaction with the system in uncomfortable situations, we tested some natural interfaces, which, as explained by Abowd & Mynatt (2000), "facilitate a richer variety of communications capabilities between humans and computation". For example, we tested speech recognition technologies as well as handwriting recognition systems, which require less attention from the user than a virtual keyboard to enter a text. We based our HCI on Web technologies integrated with two small components dedicated respectively to textual data input and speech recognition.

The WIH system is composed of a server that hosts a *MySQL* database storing all patients' records and a *Patient Record Manager* (PRM), a Java servlet application managing the clinical data. The PRM interface supports three pen-based mechanisms for data input: icon clicking, selection of items in (pop-up) menus or lists and alphanumeric data input in forms, by using either a virtual keyboard or a handwriting recognition system or *WtX* (Section 5.4). The patient record is composed of six sections, personal info, physiological signs, treatments, tests, annotations and historical info; each is represented as an icon in the application. The interface of PRM visualizes a weekly summary of each physiological sign and treatment, that gives a comprehensive overview of the patient's current health status. A daily overview is also provided, detailing all physiological signs occurred in the last 24 hours. Finally, an interface is provided to update the patient's record with new information, such as new physiological signs and/or prescriptions. We note that the interface of the PRM makes an heavy use of menus and lists, which reduces the need of typing long words.

Further details about WIH are provided by Ancona, Dodero, Minuto, Guida & Gianuzzi (2000).

3.3 *Agamemnon* and *Past*

Agamemnon (IST-508013) [5], described in details by Ancona et al. (2006), was a research project co-funded under the 6th Framework Program of the European Commission (January 2004 - June 2006), aiming at the development of a dynamic electronic tourist guide to support visits to archaeological sites. It has been successfully tested in two of the most important archaeological sites in the Mediterranean area, namely Paestum (Italy) and Mycenae (Greece). *Agamemnon* is a software system based on a *client-server* architecture. The client is a a *Java* application, running on smartphones with *Symbian* OS 6, that drives the user through the site by displaying information about the monuments being visited; the server is a set of

[5] `http://services.txt.it/agamemnon/`

applications running on workstations, that manage all the cultural data about the site and the requests from the clients. Clients communicate with the server applications via the UMTS network. Before the visit, the user needs to install the application on her phone and fill in a form to let the system know some personal data and preferences, such as her age, cultural background, cultural preferences and available data. Based on the user profile, the *Visitor Profiler*, a software module of the server, creates a personalized path through the site; if the user changes her path, the system modifies the initial path accordingly, adapting it to the user's current choices. The initial path may also be changed autonomously by the system to delay the visit to certain monuments if they are too crowded at a given time.

One of the most interesting and novel aspects of *Agamemnon* is the possibility for the user to take a photo at a monument with the camera integrated in the smartphone and have the system recognize the monument to get additional information about it. The *Agamemnon* image recognition system, described in greater details by Pittore et al. (2005), is based on statistical pattern recognition and realized by using multi-class *support vector machines*. The system is able to recognize not only a monument, but also a detail of it, such as a column, which is useful when the user is not only interested in a generic description of the monument, but wants also to know details about its architecture.

We note that *Agamemnon* represents an evolution over a traditional audioguide that is often rented to visitors in museums and archaeological sites. First of all, an audioguide does not suggest any personalized path through the site, as *Agamemnon* does. Moreover, audioguides are expensive for both the site and the visitors, who usually need to pay an extra cost to rent it; as opposed to that, the *Agamemnon* client application can be freely downloaded from the Internet and installed on the phone of the visitor. The only cost comes from the use of the UMTS network. At the time we developed *Agamemnon* the use of wireless networks was not so widespread as today, especially in the countries where we tested the application, which explains why we resorted to the UMTS network. However, today it is not unrealistic to assume that an archaeological site has a wireless network that visitors can use with little or no cost at all.

Agamemnon is the natural evolution of a previous project named *Past* (IST-1999-20805) [6] that aimed at supporting context and location aware visits to archaeological sites. Similarly to *Agamemnon*, the *PAST* consortium included three archaeological sites, namely *Bibracte* (France), *Toumba* (Greece) and *Passo di Corvo* (Italy). Visitors are given a PDA, which in our case was an *HP iPAQ*, with an application that guides them through the site. The application communicates via a wireless *IEEE 802.11b* network with a server application that tracks the position of the visitors at any time to display content relevant to what they are currently seeing. As in *Agamemnon*, the application suggests a visit path based on personal preferences. We explored different technologies to determine the location of a visitor, namely GPS, triangulation of the distances between the visitor and multiple WiFi access points and comparison between images taken by the PDA's webcam and known profiles. One negative aspect of *PAST* is the use of ad-hoc devices, such as PDAs, owned by the archaeological site, not by visitors, as in the case of *Agamemnon*. As a result, the archaeological site must bear the cost of renting devices. Further details on *Past* are provided by Ancona, Dodero, Gianuzzi, Bocchini, Vezzoso, Traverso & Antonacci (2000).

[6] `http://www.beta80.it/past/index.htm`

4. *Agamemnon in City*: Context-awareness without sensors

One of the weak points of *Agamemnon* is the need of installing a full application on the visitor's mobile phone, with all that implies in terms of compatibility, software maintenance and user assistance. For this reason, we implemented and successfully tested an extension to *Agamemnon* that only requires a MMS enabled camera phone to support users in their visit to a city. More specifically, the user can take a photo at a monument and submit it via a MMS message to a predefined server application, which recognizes the monument and sends back some information about it, as shown in Figure 1. In some sense, the camera is used as a

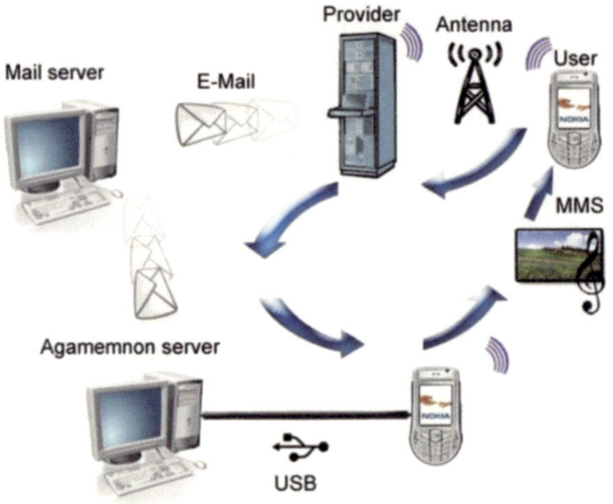

Fig. 1. Architecture of *Agamemnon in City*.

"virtual eye" of the system that tracks what the user is interested in or, in other words, his/her *focus of attention*. We note that we developed this prototype in 2007, when smartphones were not equipped with any sophisticated sensor. In our prototype, the camera itself is used as a sensor to understand both the exact location and the orientation of the user at the same time; in other words, the camera is used as a GPS receiver and a magnetometer, which was the main novel aspect of our prototype. During a cultural visit to a city people are constantly on the move, going in and out of buildings and stopping to admire the main landmarks. While moving people may see something that captures their attention and want to know immediately what it is. Our prototype *Agamemnon in City* aims at satisfying this need and in a sense it can be considered as the natural evolution of a traditional audioguide.

The *Agamemnon in City* prototype is based on the *Agamemnon* image recognition system, which proved to be effective in recognizing monuments of two archaeological sites, namely Paestum and Mycenae. Understanding the user focus of attention from a photo is an intriguing goal with a lot of issues that need to be taken care of. Recognizing objects in a photo is a hard problem for which no system is known to achieve a 100% accuracy. Recognizing monuments is even more challenging, due to the visual similarities shared by landmarks of the same type, such as statues. As a result, the system may not be able to send any information in response to a MMS, which is likely to irritate the sender. Our prototype uses techniques, explained in Section 4.2, to understand the approximate location of the user so as to send, in case a photo cannot be recognized, a list of monuments that are nearby.

4.1 Heavy-client *Vs.* light-client

Agamemnon is a *heavy-client* system, in which the client application provides a rich interface and advanced features. In our view, the need of installing an application on the visitor's phone is the inherent weakness of the *heavy-client* approach, as the application may not be compatible with all phones and multiple versions need to be developed to run on different platforms and operating systems. In other words, the application implies a cost, which depends on its complexity. In the specific case of *Agamemnon*, we also found some problems due to the choice of *Java* as the main programming language used to develop the client application. *Java*, in fact, imposes some limits on handling high-resolution images, which was a serious problem for the *Agamemnon* image recognition system. Finally, we found that the client application in *Agamemnon* was too demanding in terms of the interaction requested to the user. Therefore, users would spend more time looking at the phone screen than enjoying their visit. In other words, *Agamemnon* does not provide a "eyes-free user interface", in the sense explained by Raman & Chen (2008). These considerations are the rationale for our choice of developing *Agamemnon in City* as a *thin-client system*, where most of the computation is demanded to the server application. In *Agamemnon in City* the phone only needs to be equipped with a camera and to be able to send MMS messages, two requirements that are met by virtually all mobile phones on the market today.

4.2 Geolocation

At the time we developed *Agamemnon in City*, it was quite clear that soon most of the smartphones would feature at least a GPS receiver, although the first release of the *iPhone*, dating back to January 2007, did not include one. Therefore, we were interested to see how the knowledge of the user location improves the recognition of the monuments in the photos. To this extent, we modified the prototype to allow users to specify their coordinates while sending a photo to the server application. The server application uses the geographic coordinates to help the image recognition system to correctly interpret the monument in the photo. For example, if the system selects two different monuments as possible interpretations, the one that is far from the user's position is discarded.

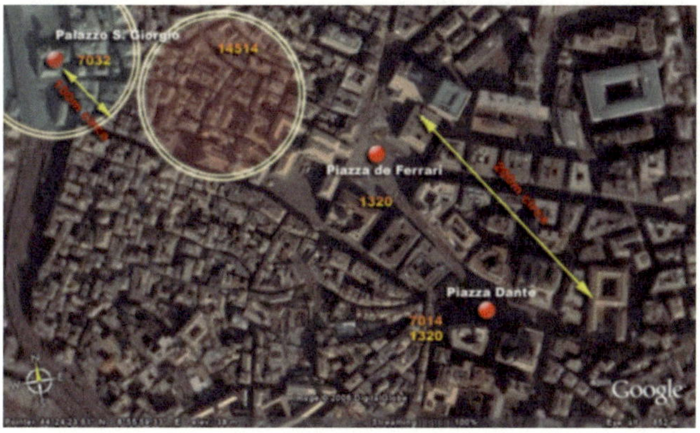

Fig. 2. Mapping UMTS cells to landmarks in Genoa, Italy.

Since the mobile phones used for *Agamemnon in City* had no GPS receiver, we used en external one that we interfaced with the phone via *Bluetooth.* The GPS coordinates could be read on the screen of the phone, so that the user could include them manually in the MMS. We note that with today's smartphones, the geographic coordinates would be automatically integrated in the photo, so there would be no need to specify them manually. One of the problem of the GPS receiver we used is that it did not receive properly the signal from the satellites in the narrow streets of the old town of Genoa (Italy), the city where we tested the prototype.

For this reason, we also used another geolocation technique termed *Cell-ID*, of which an interesting discussion is provided by Warrior et al. (2003). Basically, *Cell-ID* consists in locating a phone based on the cell to which the phone is connected. The location accuracy is acceptably good, as the radius of the area covered by a UMTS cell is approximately 100 meters. By using a free software, we mapped the main landmarks of Genoa to the identifier of the UMTS cells covering the area where they are, as shown in Figure 2. We note that by using *Cell-ID* we do not need any additional hardware, but we need a simple software that shows on screen the identifier of the cell to which the phone is connected. Obviously, *Cell-ID* is suitable in cities, where landmarks are usually spatially dispersed, but is useless in the archaeological sites such as the ones in Paestum and Mycenae, because there may be more than one monument within 100m.

There are several other geolocation methods, of which an overview is presented in Table 1. *GPS*, *Cell-ID* as well as *DGPS* and *WAAS*, which are enhancements of *GPS*, are *global*

Technology	Accuracy (m)	Cost	Coverage	Pros	Cons
GPS	10	High *	Unlimited	Accurate	Costly *
Cell-ID	100	None	Unlimited	No hardware	Unaccurate
DGPS	0.1	High	Unlimited	Very accurate	Costly
WAAS	2	Very high	Unlimited	Accurate	Costly
Bluetooth	20	Low	Indoors	Popular	Limited range
WiFi	20	High	Indoors	Fast	Complex
RFID	0.01	Low	Indoors	Precise	Limited range

* Referred to when we developed the prototype

Table 1. Comparison of geolocation methods.

positioning systems, as they provide a global coverage and they are indeed used to track devices outdoors. In particular, *DGPS* and *WAAS* are very accurate but their cost prevents their use in applications such as our prototype *Agamemnon in City*. On the other hand, *Bluetooth*, *WiFi* and *RFID* are *local positioning systems* that use a set of beacons that only detect devices that are nearby. Since *Bluetooth* is provided in the vast majority of mobile devices, including the old ones, it is more cost-effective than both *WiFi* and *RFID*.

As a side project of *Agamemnon in City*, we experimented a local positioning system based on *Bluetooth* in the *Galata Museum of the Sea* in Genoa, with the aim of supporting the visit of tourists. The system is composed of a set of *Bluetooth*-enabled devices, which we term *base stations* for convenience, scattered around the museum, that constantly listen for new incoming devices. Each base station knows its own position and that of the nearby base stations; a *Bluetooth* device communicates its position to another by using the *Bluetooth Local Positioning Profile*, a protocol that specifies standard data formats and interchange methods for local positioning information. In order to determine the position of a device, we resort to the *triangulation* technique via *lateration*, which uses multiple distance measurements between the

Landmark	No geolocation	With geolocation
Basilica S.S. Annunziata	82.3	88.2
Porta dei Vacca	0	93.8
Genoa University Admin.	50	50
Genoa University Art Dept.	85.7	85.7
Palazzo Balbi	75	75
University Library	50	88.9
St. George Palace	75	100
Genoa Cathedral	80	100
Doge's Palace	100	100
Porta Soprana	100	100
Piazza de Ferrari fountain	100	100
Carlo Felice theater	100	100
San Matteo Church	100	100
Accuracy	65.6	83.2

Table 2. Accuracy of *Agamemnon in City* with and without geolocation.

device and the base stations. The distance between a device and a base station is measured with a technique similar to that described by Feldmann et al. (2003).

4.3 Experiments

We tested *Agamemnon in City*, with and without geolocation, in Genoa by simulating a typical visit of a tourist, wandering around the streets of the city and taking photos at 13 selected landmarks to have them recognized by the system. For each landmark we took 100 photos and measured the *success rate* as the number of photos in which the landmark was correctly recognized; the *accuracy* of the system is the *average success rate* over all landmarks. The results, shown in Table 2, where the accuracy is reported in the last row, show that geolocation considerably improves the accuracy of the system, as expected. However, we point out the the poor accuracy of the system without geolocation is due to few monuments, such as "Porta dei Vacca" and "University Library", which seems to suggest that we failed to train the image recognition in a proper way. Moreover, the image recognition of *Agamemnon in City* is the same as the one developed for *Agamemnon*, which was specifically tailored for recognizing monuments in archaeological sites. Finally, while *Agamemnon* has been always tested in ideal conditions, with monuments being clear of obstacles such as crowds, *Agamemnon in City* has been used in a urban environment, where often cars got in the way between the camera and the monument.

5. Text entry in handheld devices

I was afraid of the internet... because I couldn't type - Jack Welch

While we can still rely on keyboard and mouse to interact with a desktop PC or a laptop, there is a urgent need to find valid text entry tools for handheld devices. Small hardware or software keyboards are only good to write short texts; handwriting recognition systems do not always interpret correctly users' input and generally limit users' writing speed much more than keyboards do, as pointed out by Zhai & Kristensson (2003); speech recognition systems are far from being accurate as well. We note that most today's smartphones are likely to be used to write long texts, such as emails, text documents and spreadsheets, while early mobile phones were just meant for phone calls and short text messages, for which a small keyboard coupled with *T9* was more than enough.

We now survey some of the text entry tools that have been proposed in recent years, focusing our attention on keyboards and handwriting recognition systems and leaving aside other technologies, such as eye-tracking and speech recognition, that are considerably less popular. At the time we are writing, *Apple* announced the release of the *iPhone 4S*, which features a promising speech recognition system called *Siri*. However, no matter how good a speech recognition system will be, it will never replace a keyboard or a handwriting recognition system, as there are situations where users do not want to annoy people nearby with their voices or let them know their personal matters.

5.1 Hardware keyboards

Until recent years mobile phones were almost all equipped with a keypad with 12 keys, each associated to more than one character. Since each key is ambiguous, one needs to tap on a key multiple times to insert a single character, which MacKenzie & Tanaka-Ishii (2007) refer to as the *multitap* method. As a result, the typing speed is very limited, which makes the keypad suitable only to write short messages or notes.

Despite the introduction of *T9* and other text prediction techniques, such as *LetterWise*, presented by MacKenzie et al. (2001), the keypad does not suit the needs of today's handheld devices users. Smartphones such as the *Blackberry* feature a small-size *Qwerty* keyboard, where keys are generally small, which poses serious challenges to people with thick fingers. Some vendors propose portable keyboards whose size is acceptably large, as they are independent of the device, and can be either plugged to the device or connected to it via *Bluetooth*. While portability may not be an issue, as some of them are even foldable, these keyboards can only be used at a desk or in situations where users can comfortably sit. Same considerations apply to infrared laser keyboards.

5.2 Virtual keyboards

Virtual or software keyboards are conceived to ensure the portability of handheld devices, while providing a familiar and easy-to use interface. Basically, a *virtual keyboard* is a software that displays the image of a keyboard on the screen which is interacted with by using either a finger or a tiny stylus. The action of pressing a key on a virtual keyboard is usually referred to as a *tap*. Virtual keyboards have the following advantages over their hardware counterparts:

- They do not increase the size of the device.
- Two or more virtual keyboards can be installed in the same device and chosen from by users.
- They can be interacted with by using a stylus, which is independent of the size of users' fingers.

On the downside, virtual keyboards need space on the screen, which is usually already pretty limited, and may not be clearly visible under adverse light conditions. Moreover, hardware keyboards give an immediate tactile feedback to users, which cannot be mimicked in virtual keyboards. Despite this, virtual keyboards are quite popular among handheld devices users. Here we survey some of the most known virtual keyboards that have been proposed over the years. Due to space constraints, the survey is not meant to be exhaustive; for further details we refer the interested reader to Zhai & Kristensson (2003). Without lack of generality, we assume that the domain of characters is limited to the 26 letters of the English alphabet and the space character, which is the usual approach. Indeed special characters and punctuation marks, except the most used ones such as comma, period, colon and semi-colon, are rarely displayed in a virtual keyboard and a key is usually provided to visualize them upon user's request.

5.2.1 Qwerty

Commercial handheld devices provide a *Qwerty* virtual keyboard, as users are usually acquainted with it (Figure 3). However, *Qwerty* is meant to be used with two hands rather than a stylus. Since one needs to move the stylus over the keyboard in order to select characters,

Fig. 3. The *Qwerty* keyboard.

the distance between keys is a critical issue in a virtual keyboard. We remark that *Qwerty* has a landscape orientation, which means that the distance between two keys is typically large. Moreover, letters that form frequent digraphs (i.e. pairs of letters) in English, such as "at" and "in" are distant, which intuitively results in a slower typing speed. Although Baber (1996) claims that the *Qwerty* layout is the result of a random choice, it is common belief that the letters forming frequent digraphs in English have been placed on purpose far from each other to prevent jams in old typewriters, caused by back to back pressures of two close keys. However it is, *Qwerty* was devised well before the advent of handheld devices, thus it is not optimized at all for a pen-based interaction.

5.2.2 Fitaly

Fitaly (Figure 4) is a virtual keyboard specifically optimized for pen-based text entry [7]. It has been designed by Jean Ichbiah, better known as the inventor of Ada, and today is commercialized by *Textware*, a company founded by Ichbiah himself.

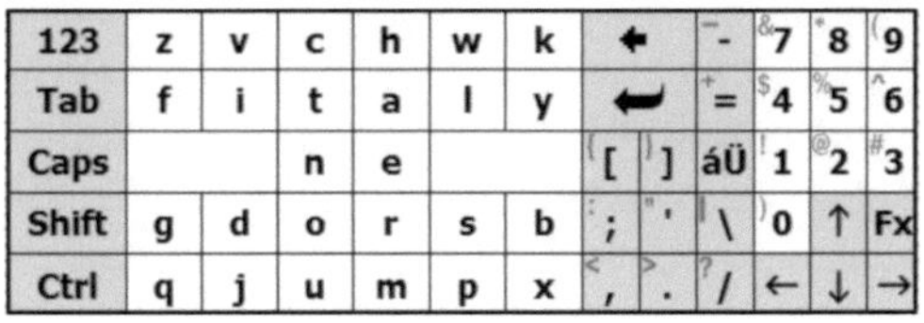

Fig. 4. The *Fitaly* keyboard.

Similarly to *Qwerty*, *Fitaly* owes its name to the concatenation of six adjacent letters in the second row of the keyboard. Unlike *Qwerty*, *Fitaly* has a portrait orientation, which results in a more compact layout. Thus the average distance between two keys is considerably smaller than in *Qwerty*, which results in a minimization of the movement of the hand to jump from

[7] `http://www.fitaly.com`

one letter to another. Moreover, frequent letters, such as *t*, *a*, *n*, *e*, *o*, *r*, which have a cumulative frequency of 40% according to the tables of Mayzner & Tresselt (1965), are arranged in the middle of the keyboard, while less frequent letters, such as *z* and *x* appear at the edges. As a result, the movements of the stylus are limited in a small area around the centre of the keyboard, and only rarely need to expand to the edges. Finally, two large keys (the ones with no label) are dedicated to the space character; this choice is based on the observation that the space character is much more frequent than any other; in fact, according to the tables of Mayzner & Tresselt (1965), the space has a frequency of 18%, while "e", the second most frequent character, has "only" a frequency of 10%. As of today, *Fitaly* features also a technology known as *Instant Text*, that allow the use of abbreviations to insert words, which further decreases the writing speed.

<table>
<tr><td>q</td><td>f</td><td>u</td><td>m</td><td>c</td><td>k</td><td>z</td></tr>
<tr><td colspan="2">space</td><td>o</td><td>t</td><td>h</td><td colspan="2">space</td></tr>
<tr><td>b</td><td>s</td><td>r</td><td>e</td><td>a</td><td>w</td><td>x</td></tr>
<tr><td colspan="2">space</td><td>i</td><td>n</td><td>d</td><td colspan="2">space</td></tr>
<tr><td>j</td><td>p</td><td>v</td><td>g</td><td>l</td><td>y</td><td></td></tr>
</table>

Fig. 5. The *Opti* keyboard.

5.2.3 *Opti*

The layout of *Opti*, visualized in Figure 5, is based on the same considerations as *Fitaly*'s, with the difference that *Opti* also accounts for the frequency of English digraphs, as explained by MacKenzie & Zhang (1999). *Opti* has been obtained by first placing the ten most frequent letters in the middle of the keyboard and arranging the other letters based on the most frequent English digraphs. Up to four keys are dedicated to the space character. It is immediate to see that letters forming frequent digraphs such as *th*, *in* and *of* are spatially proximate in the keyboard.

5.2.4 Automatic generation of virtual keyboards

The three keyboards described above have been designed by trial-and-error, which means that different key arrangements have been tried before obtaining a satisfactory one. The optimality of the final layout is only based on the designer judgment. Ideally, one would need to try all possible layouts to pick the best one. However, there are potentially infinite ways of arranging keys in a keyboard, and the keyboard itself may come in shapes other than a rectangle. Obviously, we cannot expect that an algorithm is able to generate all possible layouts of a keyboard; nonetheless, it can try many more than a human in much less time. The generation of a keyboard layout can be modelled as an optimization problem, where typically the values of some parameters can be manually tuned to obtain a layout that meets some predefined constraints.

To the best of our knowledge, the first algorithm that generates a virtual keyboard is described by Getschow et al. (1986). The algorithm sorts the list of the letters of the English alphabet (including the space character) by decreasing frequency and creates three partitions of equal size, the first containing the top-9 letters and the others containing the remaining. For each partition independently the algorithm tries all possible arrangements of 9 letters in a 3x3 grid and keeps the best. The best layouts of each partition are combined together to form the final keyboard.

The keyboard described by Lewis et al. (1999) is obtained from the analysis of the frequency of the English digraphs. First, a matrix is created containing the relative frequency of unordered English digraphs; the matrix is then used to generate a minimally connected network, with a node for each letter and an edge only between nodes representing letters of digraphs having a frequency above a certain threshold. Each edge of the network has also a weight, representing the strength of the link between two nodes/letters. Finally, a keyboard is created where the distance between two letters connected by an edge with strong weight is minimized.

An original and elegant way to create an optimized virtual keyboard is to resort to physics inspired techniques. The *Hooke* keyboard, proposed by Zhai et al. (2000), is obtained from a mechanical simulation of a mesh of springs, each connecting two characters and tensioned proportionally to the frequency of the digraph formed by the endpoints. The rationale of the approach is that strings connecting two characters that form a frequent digraph need to be pulled together with greater force than two characters in a digraph that rarely occurs. The springs are stretched and then released to obtain the final layout. The layout of *Metropolis* is based on the *Metropolis* algorithm, which is normally used to search for the minimum energy state in a physical system, as described by Binder & Heermann (1988). Since a keyboard must support fast typing, the keys need to be arranged so as to minimize the average time needed to type a word. Suppose that a keyboard is a molecule, the keys are its atoms and the energy of the molecule is the average time to type a word; searching for an optimal layout of the keyboard is tantamount to searching for the arrangements of the atoms that minimize the overall energy of the molecule, which is exactly what the *Metropolis* algorithm is intended for. The average time to type a word can be estimated by using the Fitts (1954) law, as pointed out by Soukoreff & MacKenzie (1995). Fitt's law states that the time required to move from a source to a target area is proportional to the distance between the two areas and inversely proportional to the size of the target area (the smaller is the target area, the more difficult is to hit it). In a virtual keyboard, the time to move the stylus from key i to key j is given by:

$$MT = a + b\log_2\left(\frac{D_{ij}}{W_j + 1}\right) \tag{1}$$

where D_{ij} is the distance between i and j on the keyboard, W_j is the width of j and a, b are two constants whose value is empirically determined, as discussed by Soukoreff & MacKenzie (1995). Usually, a is set to 0. If P_{ij} denotes the frequency of the digraph composed of key i and j, the average time in seconds for typing a character in a keyboard is:

$$t = \sum_{i=1}^{27}\sum_{j=1}^{27} b \cdot P_{ij}\left[\log_2\left(\frac{D_{ij}}{W_i} + 1\right)\right] \tag{2}$$

If we assume that English words on average have 5 characters (including space), the number of words that can be written in a minute is $60/5t$.

Finally, we note that recently a 16-year-old high school student, Natalie Nash, created an optimized keyboard layout for people with disabilities by using the simulated annealing algorithm. This story is covered by Krakovsky (2011).

5.3 Handwriting recognition systems

Hardware and virtual keyboards are generally considered the fastest way to input text over any other tool, probably due to the fact that people are usually acquainted with them. Ideally, however, it would be nice to input text in a device in the same way as we write on a paper. This explains the flurry of research in handwriting recognition, which is brilliantly surveyed by Plamondon & Srihari (2000) and Tappert & Cha (2007). A handwriting recognition system aims at converting an handwritten text to a digital form, which is a very difficult problem given that humans themselves sometimes cannot interpret the handwriting of somebody else. There are two main research areas: *offline* and *online* recognition. The former refers to the conversion of an handwritten document after the writing is completed, and has numerous applications, such as, but not limited to, reading postal addresses, forms and signatures. The latter refers to the recognition of characters while they are written and is applied in recognition softwares for handheld devices, as users generally prefer to have an immediate feedback of what they write. We here give some details on online recognition and shortly describe softwares that are today used in handheld devices.

5.3.1 How online recognition works

An important concept in online recognition is that of a *stroke*, which refers to any mark made with the pen without lifting it. Information such as the speed of the pen within each stroke, the number of strokes as well as the order and direction of each one are used to considerably improve the accuracy over offline recognition. Online recognition works through three main steps: preprocessing, segmentation and recognition.

The *preprocessing* deals with noise removal, normalization and smoothing. Noise may be due to several reasons, including inaccuracies of the digitization process as well as irregular hand movements; the normalization corrects any irregular slant of the strokes, due to the different handwriting styles of people; finally, smoothing eliminates any blob in the contours of the marks.

Segmentation is by far the most challenging problem in handwriting recognition. Usually, a person writes multiple characters without lifting the pen, therefore the recognition must understand which character or group of characters are associated to each stroke. Numerous techniques have been proposed, which we omit here due to space constraints and we refer the interested reader to Liu et al. (2003); Plamondon & Srihari (2000); Tappert & Cha (2007).

Finally, the *recognition* step assigns the segmented marks to characters and/or words. Early recognition systems were based on simple rules, which described the shape of characters based on their geometric features. For instance, a rule that describes the character x may be: "x is two lines that mutually cross and have an inclination of 45 and 135 degree respectively". Such rules are not quite effective to capture the complexity of handwriting and are not used in any commercial products we are aware of. Statistical methods are more efficient, even though they are computationally more expensive and need a lot of training data. Popular techniques are based on artificial neural networks, time-delay neural networks and hidden Markov models. Again, further details can be found in Plamondon & Srihari (2000).

5.3.2 Shorthand writing

Two major obstacles to the development of an ideal handwriting recognition system are the variability in handwriting and segmentation. One way to overcome both is to ask users to collaborate and adapt their handwriting in order to make the recognition task easier. This is the rationale of *shorthand writing*, pioneered in the pen computing domain by Goldberg & Richardson (1993), who proposed *Unistroke* (Figure 6). *Unistroke* defines a set of symbols, each associated to a character of the alphabet, which are easy to be recognized. To avoid the problem of segmentation, the user is asked to insert each symbol with just one stroke, hence the name *Unistroke*. Compared to a handwriting recognition system using the regular English alphabet, *Unistroke* proved to be twice as faster, as pointed out by Goldberg & Richardson (1993) themselves. However, besides the fact that people may not like the idea of lifting the

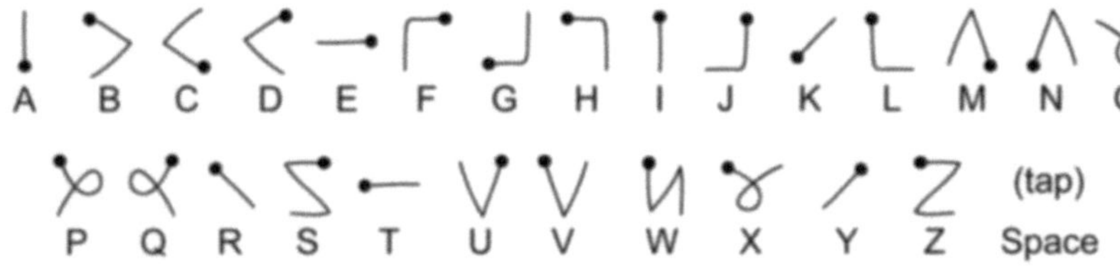

Fig. 6. The *Unistroke* alphabet.

stylus after writing each character, the symbols associated to the alphabet letters need to be learned, which is not always obvious, as most of them do not look like the corresponding character at all. *Unistroke* symbols, indeed, have been devised to be easy to recognize by an algorithm and, more importantly, to be written with just one stroke, rather than to be easy to learn.

Graffiti, developed at *Palm Inc.* to run on PDAs based on *Palm OS*, was a major improvement over *Unistroke*, because the symbols have a good visual similarity with the associated characters and consequently can be memorized more easily. However, Fleetwood et al. (2002) found out that *Qwerty* is more efficient than *Graffiti*. First, expert users can write only slightly faster with *Graffiti* than with *Qwerty*, while novice users are considerably slower with *Graffiti*; second, the learning curve is slow, because users take three to six months before writing with *Graffiti* at a speed comparable to that with *Qwerty*; finally, even expert users commit considerably more errors with *Graffiti* than with *Qwerty*.

Other shorthand recognition systems include *Cirrin*, proposed by Mankoff & Abowd (1998), and *Shark*, discussed by Zhai & Kristensson (2003), which associate predetermined gestures to whole words, *Quickwriting*, due to Perlin (1998), which associates strokes to single characters and *Dasher*, described by Ward et al. (2000), which allows writing word with continuous gestures, without lifting the pen at each character or word.

5.4 The *WtX* system

WtX is a context aware text entry tool for PDAs that we initially developed to support archaeologists taking notes at the excavations, in the context of a project called *RAMSES*, discussed in details by Ancona et al. (1999). The current version runs only on PDAs with the *Windows Mobile* operating system, but we are working on an implementation for both *iPhone* and *iPad*. *WtX* is designed to be a *comfortable*, *easy-to-use* and *flexible* text entry tool, that meets the needs of as many users as possible. *WtX* uses predictive text techniques to enter most of the words by specifying only few letters, hence the comfort; it has a simple interface, that can be used with little or no training at all, hence the ease-of-use; finally, it provides either a virtual keyboard or a handwriting recognition system, based on users' preferences, hence

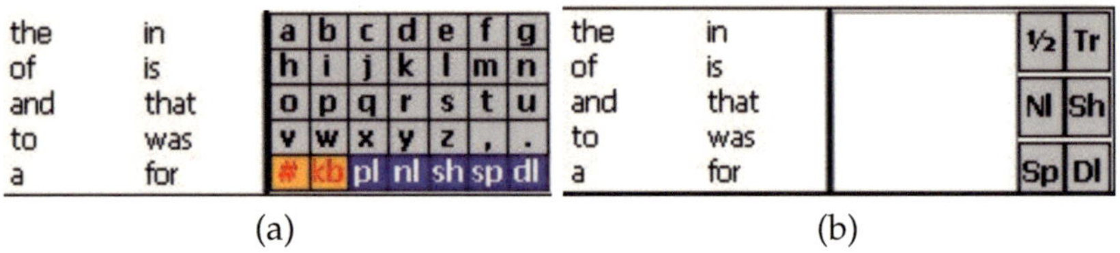

Fig. 7. WtX interface with a virtual keyboard (a) and with HRS (b).

the flexibility. Figure 7 shows the interface of *WtX* with a virtual keyboard (a) and with a handwriting recognition system (b).

Basically, *WtX* is composed of two side-by-side areas of equal size; the one on the left side is called *selection area*, and contains up to 10 words loaded from a dictionary, while the one on the right side is called *composition area* and displays either a virtual keyboard or a handwriting recognition system. When a sequence of characters is inserted by using either tool of the composition area, the selection area shows the most frequent words having the sequence as a prefix. Therefore, a word can be inserted by either tapping on each character, if the word is not in the dictionary, or by selecting it when it shows up in the selection area, in which case a space character is automatically appended. We note that at the startup the selection area displays the ten most frequent words in English, that can therefore be selected with just one tap.

Finally, the selection area and the composition area can be swapped upon users' request, so that the former appears on the right side and the latter on the left side of the screen. This option is based on the observation that if the selection area is on the left side left-handed people cover it with their hand, which makes hard to check whether the word being typed shows up. We now describe in greater details some important aspects of *WtX*.

5.4.1 The keyboard

The width of the composition area of *WtX* is only half of that normally dedicated to a virtual keyboard, because of the presence of the selection area. Consequently, *Qwerty* is not a good choice for *WtX*, due to its landscape orientation. Initially, we devised a partial keyboard similar to *DotNote* [8], displaying only the most frequent characters in English and one shift key to visualize the others upon request. However, preliminary experiments showed that such a keyboard results in frequent shifts between the two layouts, which considerably decreases the writing speed. Instead, we opted for an alphabetic keyboard, displaying all letters, the space character (the key labelled *sp*) and the two most used punctuation marks (period and comma), as shown in Figure 7 (a).

Although an alphabetic keyboard is not optimized for pen-based entry in the same way as *Opti* or *Fitaly* are, it is still better than *Qwerty*, as discussed by Mackenzie & Soukoreff (2002), and it is easy to learn, as keys are arranged in an intuitive way. The keys in the last row are assigned to special functions. From left to right, the *hash* and *kb* keys are respectively used to display a keypad with numbers and one with special symbols; the *pl* key triggers a function that changes the last inserted word to its plural form; the *nl* key inserts a new line character; the *sh* key activates/deactivates the *FTL* rule, which will be discussed in Section 5.4.4; finally,

[8] *DotNote* is produced by Utilware (`http://www.utilware.com`), a description can be found in Mackenzie & Soukoreff (2002).

the *sp* and *dl* keys are used to insert a space character or delete the last inserted character respectively.

5.4.2 The handwriting recognition system

The small size of the composition area severely limits the size of the keyboard, which is likely to make text entry tedious and slow. For this reason we included in *WtX* a handwriting recognition system, based on *Graffiti*, whose interface consists of just one blank box, where users write the characters, and few special keys, as shown in Figure 7 (b). As a result, the composition area does not look as cluttered as with a virtual keyboard. Moreover, an handwriting recognition system, as opposed to a virtual keyboard, is a "heads-up text entry tool", as pointed out by Goldberg & Richardson (1993), meaning that users can write without even looking at the device. Consequently, users' attention must only focus on the selection area. On the downside, *Graffiti* has a low accuracy and frequently misinterprets the characters written by the user.

5.4.3 The dictionary

In the current version the *WtX* dictionary includes about 14.000 words, each associated with their frequency of use, based on the *British National Corpus*, discussed by Leech et al. (2001). The small size of the dictionary is due to the memory limitations of the devices for which *WtX* was developed. However, in the new releases, notably for *iPhone* and *iPad*, the dictionary will include more words. In main memory the dictionary is represented as a *trie*, which is an ordered rooted tree, where edges are labelled with one letter and each node represents a string, given by the concatenation of the letters on the path from the root to the node. The leaves of the trie represent the words of the dictionary.

5.4.4 The *FTL* rule

The goal of text prediction is the minimization of the number of taps or strokes needed to insert a word. In the *WtX* dictionary the average word length, weighted by word frequency, is 4.4 characters; words show up in the selection area after an average of 2.43 taps or strokes. In order to further decrease the average number of taps/strokes, we propose what we term the *First-Third-Last* (*FTL*) rule, which asks users to write a word by specifying its first, third and last character before specifying the others, starting from the second one, in the order in which they appear. *FTL* is based on the observation that any three-letter sequence is likely to match a considerably higher number of words of the dictionary if the characters of the sequence are interpreted as their prefix than if they are interpreted as their first, third and last ones. This fact is illustrated in Figure 8(a), which plots every possible three-letter sequence against the number of words of the dictionary matched by the sequence with (blue line) and without (transparent red line) the *FTL* rule.

In other words, the *FTL* rule acts as a powerful filter on the dictionary, by selecting, for any given three-letter sequence, a small number of words, thus improving the likelihood that a word shows up in the selection area after only three taps, no matter how long the word is. As shown in Figure 8(b), up to 87.50% of the words of the dictionary show up in the selection area after only three taps if the *FTL* rule is used; this number drops to 64.50% if the *FTL* rule is not used.

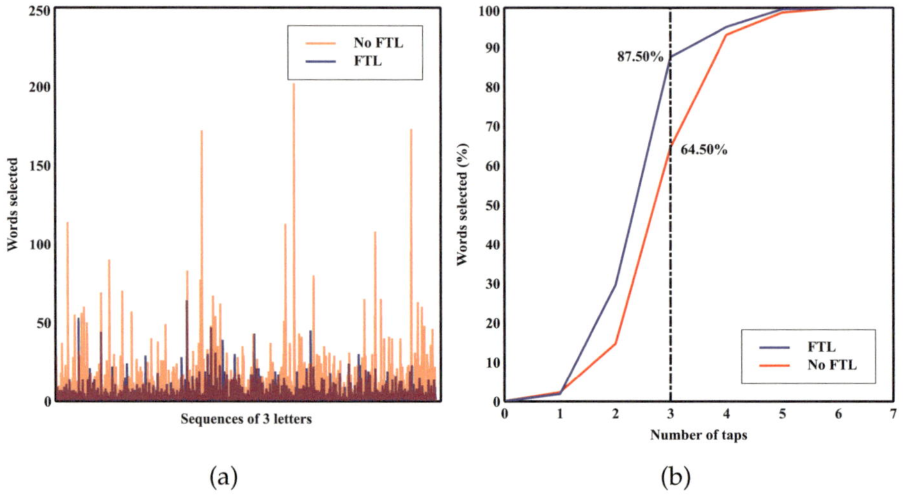

Fig. 8. The effect of using the FTL rule.

We note that we need on average 2.32 taps/strokes to insert a word of the dictionary with the *FTL* rule, which is only slightly better than the 2.43 taps/strokes needed without it. This is certainly due to the fact that the average number of taps/strokes is weighted by the frequency of the words and the *FTL* rule is not effective on frequent words, because they are usually very short. Indeed, the average length of the 100 most used English words, which have a 50% cumulative frequency, is 3.35 characters, which is considerably less than the non-weighted average of all English words (5 characters).

FTL is similar in spirit to abbreviation systems such as *InstantText* of Fitaly, where a word is inserted by specifying its first letter and one or more non necessarily consecutive letters in the order in which they appear. For instance, the word "dichlorodifluoromethane" can be inserted as "didime", "dcfm", or "doooh". However, once a character is inserted, the system has no clue to know its position within the word, which is likely to make the selection of the words from the dictionary more ambiguous than with *FTL*. We may also argue that from a user standpoint it might be easier to know that there is only one way to write a word, as in the case of *FTL*, instead of countless abbreviations, as in *InstantText*. However, we cannot draw any conclusion at this point, as we have not compared yet *FTL* against *InstantText*, although it is part of our future work.

5.4.5 Context-awareness

One important aspect of *WtX* is that we designed it to be context aware, which, to the best of our knowledge, is a novelty for a text entry tool. More specifically, *WtX* can handle multiple dictionaries and select the words from the one that is more appropriate to the current user's context. Consider the example of a doctor who uses *WtX* to either send emails to his friends or fill in the medical record of one of her patients. While in the first case a general English dictionary suits perfectly her needs, in the second case a dictionary of medical terms is much more appropriate, because it contains words that may not be found in a general purpose dictionary and it does not contains words that are unlikely to be used in a medical record. The second aspect is particularly important, as ideally the selection area of *WtX* should suggest only words that are appropriate to a given context. Context awareness in

Session	Speed	Accuracy	Comfort
Qwerty	**13.33**	0.43	0.02
WtX + Keyboard	**9.64**	4.55	**0.03**
WtX + *FTL* + *Graffiti*	6.43	3.57	**0.03**

Table 3. *WtX* experiment results.

WtX is realized through an Application Programming Interface (API) that allows third-party applications to communicate to *WtX* any change of the context and how the dictionary should change accordingly. We experimented the *WtX* context-awareness in *WardInHand*, where the dictionary automatically changes according to the position of the doctor within an hospital; this provides the doctor with a dictionary of terms appropriate to a specific ward, without the need of manually selecting it.

5.4.6 Experiments

A text entry tool is typically evaluated by asking a group of people to type a sample text and measuring two parameters, namely *speed* and *accuracy*. The first is usually measured as number of words per minute averaged on all users, while the second as the inverse of the number of misspelled words. We introduce *comfort* as a third parameter, which we define as the tiredness perceived by the user while writing a long text.

The measurement of *comfort* is complicated, because, as opposed to speed and accuracy, it is a subjective parameter. Speed alone can not be a reliable measure of comfort. Indeed, the average speed of a user may be high because s/he inserts quickly the very first sentences of the sample text and slows down on the subsequent sentences because of tiredness. The experiments described by Ancona & Quercini (2009) showed indeed that there is a correlation between speed variation over time and comfort; the higher the variation, the lower the comfort. Therefore, we measure comfort as the inverse of the average speed variation over the time taken to write the sample text.

In our experiments we selected 10 participants and we asked them to write a sample text with 454 words by using, in the order, *Qwerty*, *WtX* with the virtual keyboard and *WtX* with *Graffiti* and *FTL*. More details on the settings of the experiments can be found in Ancona & Quercini (2009). The results are shown in Table 3. As expected, participants wrote more quickly when using *Qwerty*, as they were familiar with it. However, accuracy is low and speed variation is high, which means a low level of comfort. With *WtX*, accuracy remarkably improves, as most of the words are directly selected from the dictionary, and comfort benefits from it. Despite the high number of misspelled words due to *Graffiti*, users reported to feel less tired when using *WtX* with *FTL* and *Graffiti*. Although we are planning to further investigate this point in the future, we are convinced that the *FTL* rule plays an important role in improving comfort, due to the minimization of the average number of taps needed to insert words.

6. Concluding remarks

In this chapter we covered two important aspects of the interaction with handheld devices, namely *context-awareness* and *text entry*. We analysed the key challenges in the design and implementation of context-aware applications, with a particular focus on our past research projects, namely *WardInHand*, *Agamemnon* and *Past*. We surveyed the most popular text entry tools, especially virtual keyboards and handwriting recognition systems, and described *WtX*, a context-aware text entry tool for PDAs that we developed few years ago.

The recent advent and success of sophisticated and economic smartphones, such as the *iPhone*, calls for a revitalization of our past research projects, that have been developed when the technology was not mature enough to fully support all their innovative ideas. Sensors, for instance, extremely simplify the implementation of context-aware applications, as we illustrated in several examples throughout this chapter. Moreover, natural user interfaces, such as speech recognition softwares, have been improved a lot in the last decade and start to appear in commercial products, such as the *iPhone 4S*, released in October 2011. Finally, smartphones' computational power has been increasing at a high pace, which paves the way to applications that were virtually impossible only a decade ago.

7. References

Abowd, G. D. & Mynatt, E. D. (2000). Charting Past, Present, and Future Research in Ubiquitous Computing, *ACM Trans. Comput.-Hum. Interact.* 7: 29–58.

Ancona, M., Cappello, M., Casamassima, M., Cazzola, W., Conte, D., Pittore, M., Quercini, G., Scagliola, N. & Villa, M. (2006). Mobile Vision and Cultural Heritage: the AGAMEMNON Project, *in* B. Schiele, L. Paletta & L. V. Gool (eds), *First International Workshop on Mobile Vision*, pp. 3–17.

Ancona, M., Conte, D., Quercini, G. & Casamassima, M. (2007). Attention-Aware Cultural Heritage Applications on Mobile Phones, *IEEE International Symposium on a World of Wireless, Mobile and Multimedia Networks*, IEEE, pp. 1–8.

Ancona, M., Coscia, E., Rubattino, C. & Megliola, M. (2003). Horizontal Versus Vertical Development of the HCI in the Ward-in-Hand Project, *4th International IEEE EMBS Special Topic Conference on Information Technology Applications in Biomedicine*, IEEE, pp. 27–30.

Ancona, M., Dodero, G. & Gianuzzi, V. (1999). RAMSES: a Mobile Computing System for Field Archaeology, *in* Hans-W.Gellersen (ed.), *Handheld and Ubiquitous Computing*, Vol. 1707 of *Lecture Notes in Computer Science*, Springer Verlag, Heidelberg, pp. 222–233.

Ancona, M., Dodero, G., Gianuzzi, V., Bocchini, O., Vezzoso, A., Traverso, A. & Antonacci, E. (2000). Exploiting Wireless Networks for Virtual Archaeology: the PAST Project, *VAST: International Symposium on Virtual Reality, Archaeology and Intelligent Cultural Heritage*.

Ancona, M., Dodero, G., Minuto, F., Guida, M. & Gianuzzi, V. (2000). Mobile Computing in a Hospital: the WARD-IN-HAND Project, *Proceedings of the 2000 ACM Symposium on Applied Computing - Volume 2*, SAC '00, ACM, New York, NY, USA, pp. 554–556.

Ancona, M., Locati, S. & Romagnoli, A. (2001). Context and Location Aware Textual Data Input, *Proceedings of the 2001 ACM Symposium on Applied Computing*, SAC '01, ACM, New York, NY, USA, pp. 425–428.

Ancona, M. & Quercini, G. (2009). Text Entry in PDAs with WtX, *The Ergonomics Open Journal* 2: 185–195.

Azuma, R. T. (1997). A Survey of Augmented Reality, *Presence* 6: 355–385.

Baber, C. (1996). *Beyond the Desktop: Designing and Using Interaction Devices*, Academic Press.

Binder, K. & Heermann, D. (1988). *Monte Carlo Simulation in Statistical Physics*, SpringerVerlag.

Bricon-Soufand, N. & Newman, C. R. (2007). Context Awareness in Health Care: a Review, *International Journal of Medical Informatics* 76: 2 – 12.

Feldmann, S., Kyamakya, K., Zapater, A. & Lue, Z. (2003). An Indoor Bluetooth-Based Positioning System: Concept, Implementation and Experimental Evaluation, *International Conference on Wireless Networks*, ICWN '03, CSREA Press, pp. 109–113.

Fitts, P. M. (1954). The Information Capacity of the Human Motor System in Controlling the Amplitude of Movement, *Journal of Experimental Psychology* pp. 381 – 391.

Fleetwood, M., Byrne, M., Centgraf, P., Dudziak, K., Lin, B. & Mogilev, D. (2002). An Analysis of Text-Entry in Palm OS: Graffiti and the Virtual Keyboard, *Proc. of the 46th Human Factors and Ergonomics Society Annual Meeting*, pp. 617–621.

Getschow, C. O., Rosen, M. J. & Goodenough-Trepagnier (1986). A systematic Approach to Design a Minimum Distance Alphabetical Keyboard, *Proceedings of RESNA (Rehabilitation Engineering Society of North America) 9th Annual Conference*, pp. 396–398.

Goldberg, D. & Richardson, C. (1993). Touch-typing with a Stylus, *Proceedings of the INTERCHI '93 conference on Human factors in computing systems*, INTERCHI '93, IOS Press, Amsterdam, The Netherlands, pp. 80–87.

Istepanian, R., Laxminarayan, S. & Pattichis, C. S. (eds) (2005). *M-Health: Emerging Mobile Health Systems*, Springer.

Krakovsky, M. (2011). Success at 16, *Commun. ACM* 54: 20–20.

Lane, N. D., Miluzzo, E., Lu, H., Peebles, D., Choudhury, T. & Campbell, A. T. (2010). A Survey of Mobile Phone Sensing, *Comm. Mag.* 48: 140–150.

Leech, G., Rayson, P. & Wilson, A. (2001). *Word Frequencies in Written and Spoken English: Based on the British National Corpus*, Longman, London.

Lewis, J. R., Kennedy, P. J. & LaLomia, M. J. (1999). Development of a Digram-based Typing Key Layout for Single-Finger/Stylus Input, *Human Factors and Ergonomics Society 43rd Annual Meeting*.

Liu, Z.-Q., Cai, J. & Buse, R. (2003). *Handwriting Recognition: Soft Computing and Probabilistic Approaches*, Springer.

MacKenzie, I. S., Kober, H., Smith, D., Jones, T. & Skepner, E. (2001). LetterWise: Prefix-Based Disambiguation for Mobile Text Input, *Proceedings of the 14th Annual ACM Symposium on User Interface Software and Technology*, UIST '01, ACM, New York, NY, USA, pp. 111–120.

MacKenzie, I. S. & Zhang, S. X. (1999). The Design and Evaluation of a High-Performance Soft Keyboard, *Proceedings of the SIGCHI Conference on Human Factors in Computing Systems: the CHI is the Limit*, CHI '99, ACM, New York, NY, USA, pp. 25–31.

MacKenzie, I. & Tanaka-Ishii, K. (2007). *Text Entry Systems*, Morgan Kaufmann.

Mackenzie, S. I. & Soukoreff, W. R. (2002). Text Entry for Mobile Computing: Models and Methods,Theory and Practice, *Human-Computer Interaction* 17(2 & 3): 147–198.

Mankoff, J. & Abowd, G. D. (1998). Cirrin: a Word-level Unistroke Keyboard for Pen Input, *Proceedings of the 11th Annual ACM Symposium on User Interface Software and Technology*, UIST '98, ACM, New York, NY, USA, pp. 213–214.

Mayzner, M. S. & Tresselt, M. E. (1965). Tables of Single-Letter and Digram Frequency Counts for Various Word-Length and Letter-Position Combinations, *Psychonomic Monograph Supplements* 1(2): 12 – 32.

Oviatt, S. & Cohen, P. (2000). Perceptual User Interfaces: Multimodal Interfaces that Process What Comes Naturally, *Commun. ACM* 43: 45–53.

Perlin, K. (1998). Quikwriting: Continuous Stylus-Based Text Entry, *Proceedings of the 11th Annual ACM Symposium on User Interface Software and Technology*, UIST '98, ACM, New York, NY, USA, pp. 215–216.

Pittore, M., Cappello, M., Ancona, M. & Scagliola, N. (2005). Role of Image Recognition in Defining the User's in 3G Phone Applications: the AGAMEMNON Experience, *IEEE International Conference on Image Processing*, ICIP 2005, pp. 1012 – 1015.

Plamondon, R. & Srihari, S. N. (2000). On-Line and Off-Line Handwriting Recognition: A Comprehensive Survey, *IEEE Trans. Pattern Anal. Mach. Intell.* 22: 63–84.

Raman, T. & Chen, C. (2008). Eyes-Free User Interfaces, *Computer* 41(10): 100 –101.

Schilit, B. N., Adams, N. & Want, R. (1994). Context-Aware Computing Applications, *Workshop on Mobile Computing Systems and Applications*, WMCSA '94, IEEE, pp. 89–101.

Soukoreff, R. W. & MacKenzie, I. S. (1995). Theoretical Upper and Lower Bounds on Typing Speed Using a Stylus and Soft Keyboard, *Behaviour & Information Technology* 14: 370–379.

Tappert, C. C. & Cha, S.-H. (2007). English Language Handwriting Recognition Interfaces, *in* I. S. MacKenzie & K. Tanaka-Ishii (eds), *Text Entry Systems: Mobility, Accessibility, Universality*, Morgan Kaufmann, chapter 6, pp. 123–137.

Turk, M. (2004). Computer Vision in the Interface, *Commun. ACM* 47: 60–67.

Turk, M. & Robertson, G. (2000). Perceptual User Interfaces (Introduction), *Commun. ACM* 43: 32–34.

Vertegaal, R. (2003). Attentive User Interfaces, *Commun. ACM* 46: 31–33.

Wang, J., Zhai, S. & Canny, J. (2006). Camera Phone Based Motion Sensing: Interaction Techniques, Applications and Performance Study, *Proceedings of the 19th Annual ACM Symposium on User Interface Software and Technology*, UIST '06, ACM, New York, NY, USA, pp. 101–110.

Ward, D. J., Blackwell, A. F. & MacKay, D. J. C. (2000). Dasher - A Data Entry Interface Using Continuous Gestures and Language Models, *Proceedings of the 13th Annual ACM Symposium on User Interface Software and Technology*, UIST '00, ACM, New York, NY, USA, pp. 129–137.

Warrior, J., McHenry, E. & McGee, K. (2003). They Know Where You Are, *IEEE Spectrum* 40: 20–25.

Zhai, S., Hunter, M. & Smith, B. A. (2000). The Metropolis Keyboard - An Exploration of Quantitative Techniques for Virtual Keyboard Design, *Proceedings of the 13th Annual ACM Symposium on User Interface Software and Technology*, ACM, New York, NY, USA, pp. 119–128.

Zhai, S. & Kristensson, P.-O. (2003). Shorthand Writing on Stylus Keyboard, *Proceedings of the SIGCHI Conference on Human Factors in Computing Systems*, CHI '03, ACM, New York, NY, USA, pp. 97–104.

9

Multimedia Design Decisions, Visualisations and the User's Experience

Sue Fenley
University of Oxford
United Kingdom

1. Introduction

This chapter analyses of the types of design decisions that have been made in interactive multimedia and large Internet resources, and how these designs affect both how users navigate through the package, and the information they obtain from using the resource. The chapter starts with an introduction of its scope and content and its relationship to the rest of the book. The literature on multimedia design and use are then reviewed, concentrating on navigation tools, design elements and human computer interaction. The chapter will then look at design decisions and how these affect users, before outlining good quality and more problematic design decisions. Visualisations of how users have used the software and the navigational tools used will follow, before recommendations for design and user assistance and finally a way forward for designers is proposed.

The chapter contains screen views of parts of multimedia packages and an assessment of what elements of the design have been successful. It will also investigate designs where the user has misinterpreted what the designer portrayed and how that has led to a misuse of the full potential of the package. The research in the chapter reflects back on doctoral work of the researcher which involved assessing over 100 multimedia products to ascertain which navigational methods the packages allow, how the users employ these, and how they should have been designed to make full use of all the features and the full resource.

Several of the examples are from the Open University and the BBC which were both used in the research. The Open University produces large quantities of excellent educational material and the design decisions process there could be used to assist other designers. Commercial software producers have also been included as some of the popular commercial packages would have benefited from more careful design decisions.

The chapter will review the literature on multimedia and Internet resource design, investigate how design decisions affect how the resource is used, give examples of good and poor quality design and give recommendations for future design decisions. An aspect of the research in this area that will be covered is the use of visualisations in how people approach the software, and this is augmented with both comments and information on the navigation methods and tools used. The chapter will give detailed information on specific packages and how designs have encouraged or prevented the development of good techniques in their usage. Examples of the type of package used will include: Medieval Realms, Carbon Cycle, Homer, Encarta, and Eyewitness History among others.

2. Aim of the chapter

The aim of the chapter is to investigate navigational patterns employed by users while exploring multimedia and Internet resources. The objectives of the chapter are:

- To investigate which navigational patterns are used and the best methods of utilising the resource,
- To encourage the use of newer or more efficient methods of navigating and visualising resources,
- To promote a toolkit of specified navigational tools as a transferable toolkit or palette for users,
- To demonstrate how visualisation techniques can inform users, tutors and software designers of the methods used to interrogate resources.

3. Scope and content of the chapter

The scope and content of the chapter is aimed at students using educational resources and designers of software, who can objectively look at the research that has been done and begin to apply it to their own design work. Designing multimedia and resource packages for different groups of people involves many different processes. However the key process is to test it with groups of users of similar age and ability to those that are expected to use the resource, and to keep doing this. Educators also need to be made aware of some of these issues, so that the resource is used to its most effective presentation, that the students or adults are given sufficient introduction in its usage but also to allow for some self discovery and personal opinions. Interestingly trying out novice users on a new resource, most people would investigate it initially to see if it contained something they knew a lot about. This seemed to ground them in their opinion of the package, so first impressions were important, and successful initial searches usually meant a greater involvement with, and use of, the package. This chapter is a practical review of the work on the designing of multimedia and of design decisions that were made for specific projects. Analysing these decisions and seeing the reaction of students when using them, have given greater insights into multimedia and large internet resources in terms of their structure, navigation methods, use of the material and areas of little use. This sort of analysis should enable designers to create better, user friendly and informative resources and give educators additional knowledge in how using the resource affects the amount of information searched for and found, the receptiveness of the user and it's learning potential.

4. Background to the research

It is important to first ground this in the research literature. Researchers such as O'Malley (2002) have stated that the designs need to be transparent. This means that the tools needed to use the software and the way users navigate within the package should be naturalistic and intuitive, i.e. they should not find the controls or navigation methods intrusive and they should be easy to use and learn. One solution to this problem is to develop a generic tool kit that could be used for a number of different multimedia resources. This means the user would not have to re-learn how to use specific tools - such as how to navigate within the package, how to follow specific routes, how to return to previous searches, the quickest way to specific information, the structure of the package and so on.

Another area that needs more design work is computer games software. Much of the software has been developed to provide high quality graphic images and relatively little design time has been spent on exactly how they will be used. Many games designers do not actively test the product with users within the targeted age group and a more sensitive design brief would overcome many of the initial problems in using the package. What should be straightforward design decisions, if wrongly interpreted, can adversely affect the take-up of commercial software and there is a real need to fully developed the testing, redesign and audit trail procedures for this type of product. Giving designers an insight into how packages are used in educational settings, the skills required to use them and the learning processes used may make the designers more aware of the design constraints and the real need to fully test the resource with users.

5. Literature review of the area

A review follows of the available literature on multimedia design and use, in thematic areas such as navigation tools, design elements, and human computer interaction.

5.1 Digital natives

The research on Digital natives (user who have grown up using digital materials), was started by Prensky in 2001 when he stated that the Digital Natives had "spent their entire lives surrounded by and using computers, videogames, digital music players, video cams, cell phones, and all the other toys and tools of the digital age" (Prensky, 2001, p.1). Prensky proposed that the Natives exposure to digital culture and environment had changed the way they think: "It is now clear that as a result of this ubiquitous environment and the sheer volume of their interaction with it, today's students think and process information fundamentally differently from their predecessors." (p.1). Prensky's digital natives are meant to: prefer receiving information quickly; be adept at processing information rapidly; prefer multi-tasking and non-linear access to information; have a low tolerance for lectures; prefer active rather than passive learning, and rely heavily on communications technologies to access information and to carry out social and professional interactions. Prensky had a view on these student's educators, called Digital Immigrants - foreigners in the land of the Net Generation. Prensky's view, supported by other researchers such as Oblinger (2003) and work by Frand (2000) along the same lines was, that educators need to adjust their pedagogical models to suit these new kinds of learners. Students according to Prensky are already "adopting new systems for communicating (instant messaging), sharing (blogs), buying and selling (eBay), exchanging (peer-to-peer technology), creating (Flash), meeting (3D worlds), collecting (downloads), coordinating (wikis), evaluating (reputation systems), searching (Google), analysing (SETI), reporting (camera phones), programming (modding), socializing (chat rooms), and even learning (Web surfing)" (p8).

Many researchers are now harnessing the technologies that students are finding more comfortable. These include the expected mobile technologies, social networking software such as Facebook and MySpace, sharing digital files and web usage. However, the information on producing (rather than reading) blogs, RSS feeds usage, and conferencing is more variable and may have different skill levels. It is arguable that students have better skills at the social software and less developed skills with the more work/education oriented systems such as virtual learning environments, immersive environments, virtual reality, role play, strategy games (such as economic modellers), interviewing skills and intelligent tutors. If Prensky is to be followed completely we as educators may overestimate the abilities and skills of the Digital Natives and their skill at accessing and manipulating software which may camouflage their reduced ability to understand and be creative within a totally new environment. Having the prior knowledge of a range of software may though lessen the learning curve and enable rapid uptake of any new technology, and students may not necessarily judge which technology is best for a specific purpose or to be able to assess how useful a new technology is for a specific educational activity.

5.2 Design decisions

The design decisions that will be reviewed in this chapter concern the choices that designers of multimedia and large resources have to make. There are generally in terms of the restrictions they place on movement, the structure of the package and what the user is allowed to do within the package. There is a great deal of work in the human computer interaction field that investigates and researches on these areas. Examples of good current thinking in this area are Shneiderman, the textbook by Dix, Finlay, Abowd and Beale, and that of Benyon, Turner and Turner. These core works move on from the earlier work of gurus such as Norman and Jacob Nielsen who were the original proponents of the need to organise the resource properly. Neilsen thought that all designs need to be tested - early and often, rather than the industry norm of testing once the design is complete.

Donald Norman's work involves the advocacy of user-centered design. His books all have the underlying purpose of furthering the field of design, from doors to computers. Norman has recently been controversial in saying that the design research community has had little impact in the innovation of products, and that whereas academics can help in refining existing products, it is technologists that accomplish the breakthroughs.

An example of Neilsen's work in this area is the 'Test your design' paper where he takes a basic web site and works with the designers to improve it. The changes he makes are usually quite simple, for instance, the overall impression is less cluttered, especially with text. Nielsen is adamant with clients that they need to rethink their approach to textual communication on Web sites and emphasize powerful headlines, summaries, and bullet points, not long blocks of text that annoy and put off readers. Gouma's notes: "On the original version, you'll note that there are hundreds more words. There's a quarter of the words and number of ideas on the newer site. That was definitely based on feedback." There were a series of other changes:

- The colour of the navigation bar and words on it shifted to a more readable blue, and the language was changed to become clearer.
- More effort was made to distinguish in different places between registration, which is aimed at first-time visitors, and log-in, which is for returning visitors.
- The testimonial photograph was made smaller and dropped on the page, and the eyes are averted to keep from trapping users' eyes.
- It's clear from the headline and the treatment of the top left-hand box that that's where one "starts" on this page.
- Finally, one change (not apparent here) went to the heart of the process by which users were guided through the site. Originally, Ideas.com featured "wizards" that used

shortcuts based on user responses to various questions. However, the wizards did not test well. "We learned they actually made it too simple," says Goumas. "Users wanted more hand-holding and walking-through the process."

Work by Shneiderman has further revolutionized specific areas in particular that of health and health records. Since 1991 his major focus has been information visualisation, beginning with his dynamic queries and starfield display research that led to the development of Spotfire. Shneiderman developed the treemap concept which inspired his research and commercial implementations. The University of Maryland's Treemap 4.0, developed in cooperation with Catherine Plaisant, remains available for educational and research purposes. Shneiderman advised Smartmoney which implemented the widely used MarketMap for stock market analyses. Later information visualisation work includes the LifeLines project for exploring a patient history, and its successor project, PatternFinder, which enables searches across electronic medical records. Searching for patterns in numerical time series data was enabled by three versions of TimeSearcher, which was applied for stock market, auction, genomic, weather, and other data.

The Hierarchical Clustering Explorer supports the discovery of features in multi-dimensional data, especially for gene expression data, using the powerful rank-by-feature framework. Three current projects focus on network visualisation: Network Visualisation by Semantic Substrates, SocialAction, and NodeXL. These tools are being applied for citation analysis and social network analysis, especially for the iOpener project, STICK (Science Technology Innovation Concept Knowledge-base), and ManyNets (explores & visualises many networks at once) projects. A new direction is based on applying social media to national priorities such as the 911.gov article in Science, which led to work on emergency and disaster response: Community Response Grids. Raising awareness of the need for expanded research was accomplished by the iParticipate report.

5.3 Navigational patterns research

Research on navigational patterns investigated patterns that other researchers had recognized with users in multimedia, hypertext and Internet resources. Research undertaken by Horney (1993), and Canter, River and Storrs (1985), both recorded and discussed the navigational paths of individual users. Research by Simpson and McKnight (1990) on how users preferred to navigate looked at different structures within a hypertext system. They varied the structures and cues for the subjects from alphabetical indexing to hierarchical structuring, using typographical cues and giving provision for position indicators. Their results showed users had preferences for hierarchies. When researching different navigation methods, Henderson (1993) commented that the prevalent characteristic of the modern worldview was the dependence on the conceptual view of information as being hierarchical, and that this conflicted with an alternative conceptual view, that of time, which produced a linear and sequential pattern. It was this dichotomy that Henderson considered made the investigation of multimedia packages more difficult, as users wanted to use the resource hierarchically, but moved through it sequentially. The user's perspective and gradual acquisition of navigational skills and awareness were emphasised by McKnight, Dillon and Richardson (1990): "Acquisition of navigational knowledge proceeds through several development phases from the initial identification of landmarks in the environment to a fully formed mental map" (p.69).

This area brings in another area of my research that of using landmarks within multimedia and Internet research, so that users can navigate within the resource and be aware of their physical place within this resource. This is in much the same way as a games user can fix their position in a game either by geographical landmarks or by placing themselves within a maze or 3D map. The concept of a mental map related to navigation patterns to the mental processes involved in working through software, and with physical awareness of where the user was in the package. Shum (1990), discussing navigating in multimedia and the user's acquisition of spatial knowledge as a two-step process, produced similar results to Simpson and McKnight (1990). Shum explained the first step as the acquisition of route knowledge, where the information was context dependent, and the second step as the acquisition of map knowledge, in which the individual understood the global spatial relationships, navigation was then world centred.

Using audit trails or server log files it is possible to back up this more esoteric research with objective behavioural data however, the data files are not easy to capture, analyse and interpret. The greatest problem to these scanned and audio files though is the time that it takes to analyse these sufficiently in order that robust statements can be made backed by actual data. This problem has been recognized by other researchers (c.f. Spiliopoulou, et al. 1999) who developed methodological procedures for visualizing and analysing log file data for data mining purposes. However, there are a few methods that have been developed which would enable the navigational behaviour of individuals to be analysed using the methods of the psychological researcher, such as using a range of different task demands and conditions (Unz & Hesse, 1999).

6. Investigating navigational patterns

Research was conducted into the methods users employ in navigating through multimedia and internet resources. The three elements of the research into these patterns consisted of:

A taxonomy of multimedia packages - concentrating on the navigation paths and available tools

A First Study - of school pupils using multimedia packages (2-3 packages for each pair - 23 pairs)

A Second Study - of adults using a specific encyclopaedic multimedia resource - 20 individuals.

The taxonomy was useful as it revealed how the design of a range of multimedia packages affected how these resources could be used. The second study on schoolchildren fits in well with the scope of this chapter as the children could be termed digital natives but as they were young, they had not experienced the full effect of the digital revolution, in terms of access to and use of computers, mobile devices and the Internet. The third study looked at adults and although they ranged from novice to expert, they ranged from being digital natives to the digital immigrant range of Prensky's work (2001). An interesting point here is that novices were able to benefit from the more experienced experts and it is possible that digital immigrants could learn usage and navigation techniques from digital immigrants in the same way. The other key aspect of this research is the nature and amount of learning that took place and how the navigation patterns used affected what information was retrieved and the sections that were used within the resources. The most important of these three areas of study for this chapter is the last of these. In this research, each user was given three tasks within the same extensive encyclopaedic package. For each of these tasks a 2D chart was produced. From these navigation charts (60 in all) each users navigation patterns and preferences were assessed.

These charts also enabled comparison of different users across each task. Using the scanned records of each user's progression through the software and these navigation charts, it was possible to create a range of the different types of navigation pattern found. The list of navigation types was then compared to the other patterns, which are shown in the list below. From these scanned records or audit trails of each user and the subsequent charts it was possible to build taxonomy of navigation patterns. These included nine main types (with several sub types).

7. Recognising navigational patterns

The following navigation patterns were recognised from the initial empirical work and these were then further tested in the second study. These navigational patterns were put into a definitive list and a graphical version of the patterns was prepared.

1. Linear - path on one level, using tools e.g. index, time line, or word search, one direction
2. Linear extra - paths lead away from basic linear pattern, returning to the linear path, usually at the same place or the next node to their original leaving point.
3. Circular - initially recognised as linear, but circular if completed, one/two-way dependent on software design, may be represented by an ellipse/multifaceted shape e.g. an octagon.
4. Star - movement initially linear but implies a change in level, going into second level areas from the first level and returning, one way or two way.
5. Star extra - a development or extension of the star pattern, movement into the second or third level of the package, i.e. into an additional level, beyond the usual star pattern, one or two way, and the extra depth may only be used for part of the route.
6. Hierarchical - movement down the hierarchy, with a possible return along the same path, to go down one or more branches of a tree structure. Progressing one way down the structure and across to the next branch of the tree, can be two-way, can return to the original starting point, retracing path.
7. Hierarchical - extra - movement along multiple hierarchies usually with different subject/themes, usually in the same way, returning to the same tree or continuing onto a linked or associated tree.
8. Complex - Chaotic - movement follows a series of different paths, usually in rapid succession, random and erratic navigation, frequent changes of route and searching method, may be a mixture of the above types.
9. Complex - Planned - sequence of moves following established path, sometimes including definite patterns, using a mixture of different types, but following an ordered route.

The list of navigational patterns above shows all the subdivisions of each pattern type, these should mean that the navigational patterns are clear and that the classification can be used with many different types of digital resources. This is especially useful for educational resources when the user may not be aware of how the package/ resource are structured or how to find the information required.

8. Recognising design decisions and the effect of these on how users use the software – Good design practice and problem designs

8.1 British Library Medieval Realms

The excellent British Library's package has been developed over a long period to include: historical information, real documents, music, arts and poetry but had a complex interface. Aimed at school pupils, the package assumed knowledge in many of these specific fields in order to be able to select information. During testing of the package with the planned age group this knowledge was not apparent and they spent a lot of time trying to work out how to find the material. Giving the developers an idea of how complex they found the package, and the types of searches or information the users needed, allowed a total redesign of the interface. Keeping the high quality underlying information base meant that the redesign was specifically targeted at the interface. The redesign made the resource easier to use and with far greater hit rates for the relevant searches.

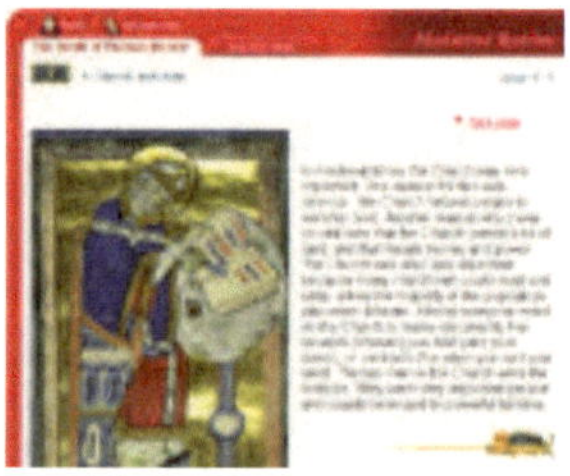

Fig. 1. Screen shot from Medieval Realms, British Library

Perseus is an interactive guide to Classical Greece which includes various items such as maps, photographs of sites, datasets of coins and sculpture, as well as texts in Ancient Greek and translations. This has been designed for university students, but again the sources are very text based. The resource has now been developed into a website, called the Perseus Digital Library.

Perhaps one of the problems of moving from a library or text resource is how to make the resource more interesting and the methods of linking different types of media to make a full multimedia product.

There are many other multimedia packages with a historical or archaeological theme. One of these is Viking World produced by the York Jorvik Centre as a commercial venture. This uses a large image database but presently has little information on each of the artefacts. Other products from the British Library include Inventors and Inventions, The Patent Express Jukebox and the Electronic Beowulf. The latter of which has received critical acclaim.

8.2 The Open University Carbon Cycle

The Carbon Cycle software was part of a larger Science introductory course from the OU comprising over 100 CD's. The carbon cycle was receiving mixed responses as users had spent a long time exploring all the options before eventually going through the one correct route to achieve the required completion of the task. Redesigning the interface meant that the majority of students followed the most suitable route and much less time was taken to complete the section of the work.

The chapter includes the detail of both the initial design and of how the improvements affected the usage, together with tips for future design decisions. It is intended that some visualisations of how users have navigated through specific packages will be included, as well as visual images of different methods of designing the package to allow easier navigation and use.

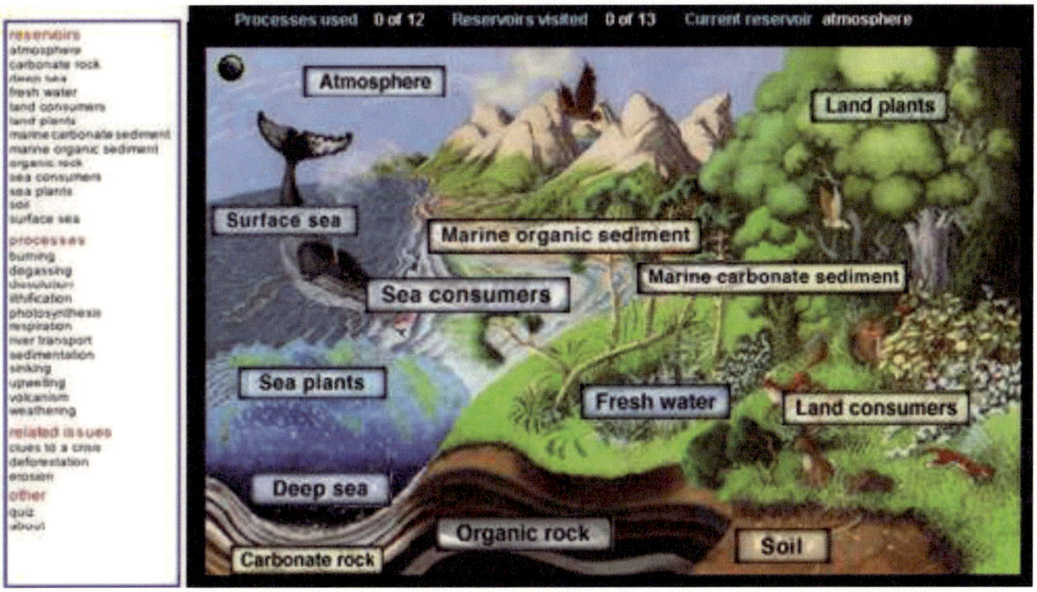

Fig. 2. Screen shot from the Open University Carbon Cycle

8.3 The Homer package

The Open University have developed a multimedia package for the course 'Homer: Poetry and Society', which looks at the nature of the relationship between the Homeric poems and the archaeological data on Ancient Greece.

The course is taught currently through print (poems, commentaries, essays, study guide), video (of archaeological sites, site plans, excavations, material objects) and audio (readings of poetry, expert discussions). In the format of these narrative media, a section of the teaching will have quite a complex structure, with different media (printed study guide, video of archaeological site, students' notes, published text) carrying different parts of the storyline. An example of this would be, for example:

1. Hypothetical question – in the Guide
2. Critique of assumption – in the Guide
3. Presentation of evidence - view the Video
4. Elicited student's response – put into the Notes
5. Interpretation of evidence – checking in the Guide
6. Contradictory evidence – reading about other evidence - Text
7. Interpretation of evidence – reviewing interpretation - Guide
8. Synthesis at higher level – being able to synthesise the information - Guide

Fig. 3. Screen shot from A295 Homer: Poetry and Society

From the illustration of the Homer multimedia package it can be seen that the structure of the work packages relates to each week of the course and these have been organized as an introduction and then six weekly sessions.

The icons under the Trojan horse image are links into other areas of the package. These include detailed archaeological tools, showing the user how these are employed and the methods used with them, maps and bird's eye views of the sites, notes and historical information as well as all the poems and associated works. This resource is an amazing, complex resource for Homer. However the way it has been designed with a controlling tutorial workload restricts the use the student can make of it. For instance only the tools which are needed for each week are introduced and certain areas are restricted until the course has arrived at this stage. This limits the amount of serendipity for the student and puts all the resources in the hands of the programme director. This also effectively blocks re-use as it would be necessary to go through the course again. This would have been better designed with the information resource available and the course as a prescribed route for first time users. I would suspect that the majority of the users would do this the first time but not be prepared to go through this again, hence limiting the use and usability of the package. The amount of work which has gone into developing it is therefore wasted and should have been allowed to augment and support the learning rather than control it.

8.4 The Sonoran Desert

The Sonoran desert multimedia package has been produced by the BBC and is advertised as being able to 'Explore one of the world's most fascinating deserts, accompanied by an experienced desert guide'. The Desert multimedia has been arranged as if the user was going on a multimedia field trip to the Cactus Desert of Arizona, south western United

States (2010). The software consists of over 400 desert scenes, with narrated information, images, sound clips and video. The Gila field centre allows the user to discover more about the desert including ecology, climate and geography. The user can learn what you should take with you on a field trip, conduct experiments, look up information and run their own slide show. The CD also features 100 video sequences from the BBC Natural History Unit, 800 sound clips and narrated tours, 1,300 photographs and illustrations and allows both a scrapbook and print option as well 'satellite links' to other deserts and laboratory experiments

This package was designed with a strong route defined basis. The routes were selected from a compass point system. The user could choose to start off North, South, West or East. However as most users are very organised into a top to bottom and left to right orientation in terms of movement through material, the most popular initial route was North. Giving people a choice without being aware of their natural preferences is not helpful, as in this instance introductory information was given for each of the routes. If everyone using the package is going to select a first route, i.e. North then this route and this route only, could have the introductory information. Giving multiple repetitions of the basic information (or even of similar interfaces) is likely to either annoy the user or to totally put them off using the package further.

Fig. 4. Screen shot from the Sonoran Desert

An alternative design would be for the introductory section to appear which ever route is chosen first, but not repeated in subsequent route choices. This though would involve getting the student/user to register with the package before using it. Most of the people using educational packages would be doing this as part of their courses this might not be an issue, but for courses where a high throughput is needed this might create a time delay. This sort of decision is particularly important for software designed for younger children, who might spend some valuable time filling out a form and have less time in the interactive package. In primary schools where pupils need to share limited resources this could be difficult balance to resolve. Obviously if the package performs some sort of testing or assessment then the registering of the user is important, or in some cases essential, as with online or lifelong learning courses where progress is measured electronically. However in these cases it should be possible to keep the registration required to a minimum.

9. Problems with design decisions

This section deals with examples of software where the design of the package has caused problems or significantly affected how the resource is used.

Investigating large resources has highlighted a series of problems that are common with both multimedia and large resources generally. Both of these resources need to be fully indexed and it is necessary to be able to search for and find, specific items reasonably accurately and quickly. Many of the problems of using the resources are based in the slow speed of searching and the poor quality of the results obtained. Much of this is due to the key wording and other selection techniques, but some is due to poor structural design of the package. In examples such as the British Library Medieval Realms, the initial package was very difficult to navigate and the detail involved did not match the age range of the material it was targeted at. Hence areas within the resource such as the Black Death which were taught to second and third year secondary students required a real knowledge of the period and the events and people in order to access the information. Giving feedback to the British Library meant that they went through a period of testing and then of redesigning the original interface to make it more comprehensible to the pupils it was meant to help.

The other main issue of any large and rich resource is that of serendipity. Rather than going to a specific area of the resource it is helpful for beginners to obtain an idea of the wealth and depth of the resource. Allowing students to browse or offering a quick tour, or better still a random review of the material may allow them to view or be interested in something they might not otherwise have discovered. One of the issues with using specific software in a school context is both the limited number of computers with the software - which restricts the amount of time they can spend on it, but also the time constraints of having to find the right material to answer the questions as quickly as possible. The result of this is that each student's experience of using the resource is likely to be similar, hurried and very rapid with no browsing or discovery time.

10. Visualisation

Another area of interest in this research is visualisations of how the users have approached the software, comments on these and developing tools for visualisation.

In the main research work each of the pairs and the individuals were mapped using the software. This was done by recording a scanned progress of the user through the software so that each step they took and the time taken on each screen was recorded. Additionally interviews were held with the users to determine why they decided to follow a specific route and to ask questions such as had they found what they were looking for, was there sufficient depth and if they were aware of specific types of routes they were using. One interesting outcome of this was that the younger children thought they had investigated a large proportion of each of the resources they had used, whereas in fact they had been through relatively small amounts of the whole resource.

In some resources a key issue was whether or not the resource was at the right level or had sufficient content to both interest them and hold their attention. In some packages notably the Eyewitness series the information stopped at the point where they were becoming most interested - so it was rather too shallow. If this is likely to be the case then linking the resource to more detailed web pages or sites may be an answer, allowing the keen student to develop their knowledge further. In some cases the front end (the interface) was too simplistic - such as the Peanuts cartoon interface on a math resource. Younger students liked the cartoon interface, but found the math underneath too difficult, and getting the answers wrong repeatedly meant they rapidly dropped out of the package. In the opposite way - a too simple front end with complex information underneath - the resource The Way Things Work, again had a cartoon front end and simple cartoon like diagrams of how they worked, but the physics described was of a much higher standard. This package also had a workshop front end which made a series of noises - very upsetting to students trying to work nearby and causing laughter and playful behaviour from its devotees! Again testing this in a school environment would have immediately shown up these problems - even the children were aware of them and stated that it was interesting but noisy.

11. Navigational tools – Investigating navigation tools

Further development of the navigation tools would necessitate knowing information on each node and where the information is found within the resource. This information proved difficult to find for commercial resources and so a new resource would need to be developed around this basis. Research by McGuffin and Schraefel (2003) called Hyperstructures has involved representing information on the web. Hyperstructures which include component models such as Zzstructures and mSpaces are described using graph theory. These structures use hypertext structures like the web and hypertext links to show links between pages but also the multiple relationships between information within the pages. The INTENTS project from the University of Dublin (2007) involves the design of a series of intelligent knowledge based tools to assist in the construction, navigation and management of hypertext documents. Examples of these tools are 1) Creation of a framework which gives conceptual structure to a document corpus which can then be interrogated by an intelligent hypertext browser or 2) A knowledge based browser, using metadata from other tools in the series, as well as document management and authoring tools, and user behaviour tools. Developments of this nature would allow further exploration of individual's preferences and behaviour when using navigation tools.

The next part of the research was to develop a list of the most essential navigational tools to be used by designers in the construction of multimedia/Internet resources. This list gives an overview of the necessary component parts of good quality interactive multimedia. These resources are a good example of how digital natives could be used to determine the nature and extent of what they would prefer to have in their own toolkit.

1. Navigational tool Diagrams or Map
2. Known material
3. History
4. Audit Trails - navigational paths
5. Time line
6. Activities - Worksheet/ Task
7. User Levels
8. Individual student records/histories
9. Customobility issues
11. Curriculum research
12. Off-line facilities
13. Internet links
14. Expert guide, tour, induction/ tutorial
15. Intelligent Tutor

This list can be used by designers as a check to ensure that as many of these as feasible are built into the new software package. Some of these are reasonably straightforward but other items such as the intelligent tutor involve more detailed construction and facilities and substantial input from the tutor(s) to make this effective. If the navigation tools are produced as a series of device independent software tools then these could be added onto each resource and the user allowed to select from the available palette.

12. Navigational tools – and how these relate to the resources used – Producing new navigation tools

The newer navigational tools consist of the following: beacons, landmarks, breadcrumb trails, searchlights, intelligent agents, 2D and 3D maps and interactive guides. Beacons allow significant items or areas to be highlighted or lit up for particular students, or for whole classes or for specific search areas. Landmarks relate to the resource in the same way as physical resources, by providing points at which users can recognise that they have been there or they have gone past this point. These can be colour markers or set up as points within the resources so that users can find them again easily. A simple map could involve reproducing a schematic image of these and putting these landmarks on to a virtual map of the entire resource. Searchlights can be used with or without a search engine and can highlight just the relevant section or be used within areas where specific references are made to the search term. Breadcrumb trails enable a series of markers (with the breadcrumbs left at strategic points, i.e. whenever a user flags this area or screen, or would want to return to it. These trails could be set up either with different markers/ objects or colours or for specific trails. For instance, while searching for a particular set of images the user may find several that are useful for another project and they could then use several different breadcrumb trails while researching in the same resource. The example used is of a geographical resource with breadcrumb tails in different colours. It should be possible to create a similar navigation tool within a multimedia or internet based resource so that individual routes through the resource are detailed as a distinct route and can then be viewed on an overview map. New technologies such as geo-location, the facilities of smart phones and usage knowledge by digital natives could all be used to make learning more interesting, relevant and available ubiquitously and whenever needed.

13. Recommendations – General

New research using this information on preferred navigation and tools usage, together with the visualisation of the routes has been applied to new resources. The large catalogue of Arts and Humanities material created by the Intute project based at Oxford has created a large body of Internet accessible web sites with information on their quality and content and their applicability to UK HE courses. This resource is now being made available to a community for further enhancement and expansion. This community is based on lecturers and researchers in the arts and humanities area. The Arch project is now developing this resource further, to include both an interface for the community to add and develop content, but also a series of demonstrators to show what is possible when using large resources. The project also brings together research on tools and suitable software packages.

The demonstrators for this project, include an outline of the tools presented, but also an interactive reconstruction of a house/museum format to store the exhibits. Previous work on the use of metaphors in multimedia has shown that although there are problems in using familiar structures such as a house that some users fail to realise that each room has a different function. The aim of this project is to help with the navigation and visualisation of the information resource but to make this discovery process interactive. The research will include both diagrams and images of these navigational routes, but also how these tools can be used and the type of structure for the resources that would aid discovery and usage in education.

Analysing multimedia and Internet resources has highlighted several problems, which were common across many resources. These include: insufficient or inadequate capabilities for navigation, the lack of awareness of where the user is in the package, and misconceptions of the amount of the resource they had investigated. Many of these problems could be resolved with better interfaces and more adequate testing; however allowing the users to develop navigational skills and providing them with a toolkit to do this may have longer term and more developmental benefits. These navigation tools are also meant to give an ability to the user to navigate on a physical level, and to do physical actions such as they might do in exploring a physical resource. Common actions in this environment would be walk, look around, zoom, pan, orbit, examine (as well as pick up/ inspect) fly - or bird's eye view, and turntable. Using this type of physical approach may lessen the need for specific navigational tools but support a toolbox or palette of navigational tools approach and the time investment needed is reduced if these tools are re-usable over a wide array of resources.

The standard types of navigational tool hence include indexes, search engines, maps, plans, timelines, histories and directional devices. There is however, a whole range of more innovative tools that could be developed for multimedia and Internet resources. The development of Open Source software has meant that it would be possible to develop a set of tools, which conform to XML or Java formats. This would mean that these tools could be freely available and added in with the minimum of effort. The newer tools include breadcrumbs, searchlights, beacons, landmarks, 3-D mapping, trackers, location finders, compasses, and route maps. Breadcrumbs are paths selected by the user of the key screens they have visited and can be set up to record different aspects of the search or information retrieval, Searchlights and beacons allow selected searches to be highlighted. There are ranges of direction/ map finders from games software where compass type location finders, and 2-D plans of the whole resource, help locate the user and allow them to find specific areas of the resource.

14. Recommendations for design and user assistance

The previous sections detailed current research on navigation patterns, new navigation tools and an outline of possible directions in visualizing these with some visualisation examples across a range of disciplines.

These new areas of research in visualisation which would have significant impact when applied to multimedia and internet resources and these techniques would allow an expansion of the possible views or investigations possible within interactive media resources. Much of this work is being done in the field of social networking. In this research the connections that people make over work or research is mapped and different methods of visualising these as maps, charts, patterns etc. give a different perspective on potential analysis methods. The key point of the chapter is the need to assess navigation abilities of students, even of digital natives, to develop their skills and abilities in this area and to give them a set of device independent navigation tools that they can use in many different resources.

The benefits of the visualisations are that these are easy to understand and to remember and a graphical image is easier to retain in the memory. Allowing students to link work areas together and to see the benefit of the work they have done is very important. The Internet will remain a source of information resources and users need to be fully equipped to use these and to make the best use of limited time. Allowing them the facility to re-use information and skills is equally essential and developing an appropriate set of tools into a tool bag or palette would be a useful skill set to take with them into employment or further study.

15. Conclusions and a way forward for designers

The conclusions from the research described in this chapter cover several areas, such as user preferences, potential navigation routes, testing designs and providing both flexibility and generic tools to assist the user.

Firstly, in the user preference areas, the research has shown that each individual user has very distinct preferences in how they navigate. Most users would perform some sort of linear route and most would do some hierarchical searching. Some users wanted to complete every section, or to cover all the screens in a particular sector, however the expert users were usually less systematic and would search for exactly what they wanted. It is therefore important to design different routes and paths through the resource.

Secondly the potential navigation routes in some multimedia and Internet resources were very restricted often with only one main route, forcing users to go through the resource in a specific way. This may be acceptable for introductory sessions but becomes very limiting in terms of exploring or self discovery modes. Ideally several different ways of navigating should be built in to the resource, with at least linear and hierachical routes being available.

Thirdly echoing Neilsen's work it is essential that developers test the design and the resource at every stage of its development, with the same age and experience for the target audience.

Finally producing a palette or toolkit of suitable navigation and visualisation tools that could be generic would be very useful for most users. Using the same tools over a series of resources would be less time consuming and far more productive, as users would not have to relearn another method of navigating. Ideally these tools should be created to work with a whole range of different software packages.

Following these recommendations would mean that better, more user oriented software would be produced that was easy and intuitive to use and allowed rapid and successful searches in the minimum of time.

16. Acknowledgments

The doctoral research quoted in this chapter was completed with a scholarship from the Engineering and Physical Science Research Council (EPSRC). My supervisors for the doctorate were Professor Josie Taylor, Dr Ann Jones and Professor John Richardson from the Open University.

17. References

Benyon, D Turner, P and Turner, S (2005) Designing Interactive Systems: People, Activities, Contexts, Technologies Addison Wesley, London

Canter, D., Rivers, R., & Storrs, G. (1985) Characterising user navigation through complex data structures. *Behaviour and Information Technology*, 4 (2), 93-102

Chambers, E. & Rae, J. (1999) Evaluation of the Homer CD-ROM: Final Report. Milton Keynes: Open University. http://kn.open.ac.uk/public/getfile.cfm?documentfileid=111

Dix, A, Finlay, J Abowd, G and Beale, R (2003) Human-Computer Interaction, Prentice Hall, London

Fenley, S (2004) Metaphors in interactive multimedia. Workshop paper for Human Computer Interaction Conference (HCI2003), University of Bath. Internet publication Spring 2004.

Fenley, S. (2006) *Navigational patterns in interactive multimedia.* PhD thesis, Open University

Frand, J. L. (2000) The information-age mindset. Changes in students and implications for higher education. *EDUCAUSE Review*, 35(5), 15-24. ERM0051.pdf a/a

Horney, M.A. (1993) Case Studies of Navigational Patterns in Constructive Hypertext. *Computers & Education* 20 (3), 257-270

Henderson, L. (1993) Interactive multimedia computer courseware and culturally appropriate ways of learning. In C. Latchem, J. Williamson, & L. Henderson-Lancett (Eds.), *Interactive multimedia: Practice and promise,* 189-203 London: Kogan Page

Jacob Nielsen web site http://www.useit.com/

Laurillard, D (1998) Multimedia and the learner's experience of narrative. Computers & Education, 31, (2), 229-242

Laurillard, D, ( ) Multimedia and the learner's experience of narrative

McGuffin, M. J. & Schraefel, M.C. (2004) A Comparison of Hyperstructures: Zzstructures, mSpaces, and Polyarchies. In: ACM Conference on Hypertext and Hypermedia, 2004, Santa Cruz, California, USA, 153-162

McKnight, C., Dillon, A.P. & Richardson, J.H., Eds. (1993) *Hypertext: A Psychological Perspective*, Ellis Horwood, Chichester, England

Nielsen, J (2002) Building Web Sites With Depth (Web Techniques, Feb 2001)By Dr. Dobb's Journal

Nielsen, J (1995) Navigating Large Information Spaces In *Multimedia and Hypermedia.* San Diego, CA: Academic Press

Nielsen, J (1999) Designing Web Usability: The Practice of Simplicity, by New Riders Publishing, Indianapolis

Norman, D (1988) The Design of everyday things Newprint 2002

Oblinger, D. (2003) Boomers, Gen-Xers & Millennials.Understanding the new students. *EDUCAUSE Review,* 38(4), 37-47. www.educause.edu/ir/library/pdf

Prensky, M. (2003) Digital game-based learning Computers in Entertainment (CIE), 2003 - portal.acm.org

Prensky, M. (2005) *Listen to the natives Educational Leadership*, 2005 - centre4.core-ed.net

Shneiderman, B Plaisant, C Cohen, M Jacobs, S (2010) Designing the User Interface: Strategies for Effective Human-Computer Interaction, Pearson, London

Shum, S. (1990) *Real and Virtual Spaces: Mapping from Spatial Cognition to Hypertext.* Hypermedia, 2 (2), 133-58

Simpson, A., & McKnight, C. (1990) Navigation in hypertext: structural cues and mental maps. In R. McAleese and C. Green (eds.) *Hypertext: State of the Art.* Oxford: Intellect, 73-83

Spiliopoulou, M., Faulstich, L. C., and Winkler, K. (1999) A Data Miner analysing the Navigational Behaviour of Web Users. In *Proc. of the Workshop on Machine Learning in User Modelling of the ACAI'99* Int. Conf., Greece.

Unz, D., & Hesse, F. (1999) The use of hypertext for learning, *J. of Educational Computing Research*, 20(3) 279-295

10

Digital Scope on 2D Communication Sheet for Location-Specific Multimedia Service

Bing Zhang[1], Youiti Kado[1], Kiyohiko Hattori[2] and Jiang Yu Zheng[3]
[1]*National Institute of Information and Communication Technologies*
[2]*University of Electro-Communications*
[3]*Indiana University Purdue University Indianapolis,*
[1,2]*Japan*
[3]*USA*

1. Introduction

In recent years, multimedia data have explosively increased in the web environment for education, investigation and exploration. At the same time, augment reality research has paid a great attention to providing views and contents in a real setting to enhance the perception of environments and spaces. A basic function — position aware display is demanded in such systems for many applications. Examples include finding location-specific data in a map [1-5], exploring media related to an object [6-7], viewing process at a spot, watching structure and diagnosing a part of human body, simulating various effects in a designed space, etc.

Position indexing has been realized on normal computer screen by reading various input devices. However, such systems are not sufficient for indexing details from a large map or hierarchical maps. The windows showing different media such as a map and a street view are usually displayed separately and it requires some effort to correspond the location between two windows [2]. This design has been generalized to many machine interfaces with large scale where the hand movement is tracked by cameras and the detected position drives scenes on another separate screen. In the tabletop projections, two views with different resolutions and media are combined [8-10] with a projector and sensor systems. In this chapter, we construct a platform on which users can watch details just as a magnificent by touching a special sheet.

To develop a new communication technology that complements wired and wireless communications, a special physical medium has been developed to perform both data and power transmission inside a 2D sheet [11]-[13]. Through a connector put on the top of sheet, an electromagnetic (EM) proximity connection is obtained to receive and send the electromagnetic signals, while moving the connector mounted device away from the sheet disconnects the transmission [14]. The size of a sheet can be as wide as several meters and is inexpensive in production. The signal transmission is different from the wireless communication that overwhelms the entire 3D space; it covers a wide surface or on partitioned surfaces to facilitate information transmission and visualization. The sheets can be laid on a table, wall, and floor in living and working spaces. By putting a display device onto the sheet, we can look into the information at that position by receiving the signal from a computer transmitted via the sheet.

We design and build a system that can enlarge details at a location or show related media data without directing viewer's focus to separated screens or windows. The system has a function of magnifier or scope to pin-point locations with a small display on a surface. Moreover, because there has no successful example of curved screens that can fit on a curved body for clicking and display, we can then wrap a surface with this two dimensional sheet for signal transmission. By placing a small high-resolution LCD on the sheet, we will be able to see position specific information and media detailed in resolution in contrast to a global map laid on the surface. In this chapter, we introduce the design and implementation of a platform that can look into a 2D or even 3D space by touching the surface sheet with a small display. Several tasks will also be examined to evaluate the performance of the platform. Figure 1 shows such an idea to magnify details at designated locations of an atlas.

Fig. 1. Digital scope on a communication sheet to view media contents at indicated locations in an atlas.

2. The sheet as communication medium

A 2D communication system (2DCS) consists of two components: a sheet and a connector. Figure 2 illustrates the basic structure of the 2D sheet, which contains three layers in order: conductive layer, dielectric layer and mesh conductive layer from the bottom. The conductive fabric is usually copper or aluminum, whereas the dielectric material is polystyrene. With this layered composition, an electromagnetic wave can be confined within the 2D sheet depending on the relatively permittivity of dielectric layer and mesh size of conductive layer. The interval and width of mesh structure are determined from the wave length of the electromagnetic wave. In the case of 2.4GHz microwave, the interval and width of the stripes in mesh structure are designed to be 7mm and 1mm respectively, as shown in Fig.2 (Top). The electromagnetic field seeped out from the sheet is called as "evanescent wave" as shown as Fig.2 (Bottom), which spreads only to the vicinity of the sheet. When the connector is brought close to the sheet, the energy is transmitted to the connector through the evanescent wave.

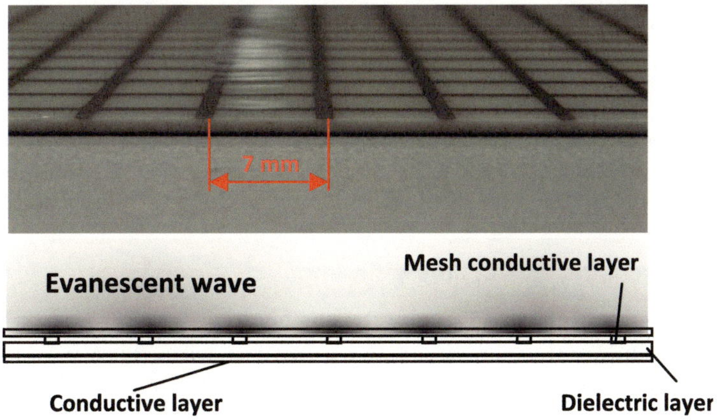

Fig. 2. Two dimensional communication sheet. (Top) 2D sheet construction; (Bottom) The electromagnetic wave seeping out from the 2D sheet.

Meanwhile, the connector is an antenna by which an electromagnetic wave is extracted from or inserted into the 2D sheet. An example of the connector was designed and proposed by Yamahira et al. [14]. The proposed connector consists of metal, dielectric material with the relative permittivity of 10.5, and a subminiature type-A (SMA) connector. The radius of the connector was also determined so that the reflection of the electromagnetic wave from the connector to a cable is minimized at the frequency of 2.4 GHz.

Besides the communication, the power can also be supplied through the 2D communication sheet. A device such as PDA can be put anywhere on the sheet to work without extra wires and batteries, which forms a very flexible system of distributed displays. The sheet can be manufactured in a very low cost affordable to be put on table top, walls, and poster boards. The connector is an antenna by which an electromagnetic wave is extracted from or inserted into the 2D sheet. The connector is manufactured in a small piece to contact the sheet for receiving and passing signals. Figure 3 shows a set of connector (each piece is 25x70x3mm and weights 2g) and a small display (LCD of 800x480 pixels) that can be put on any position of the communication sheet to receive data and power signals.

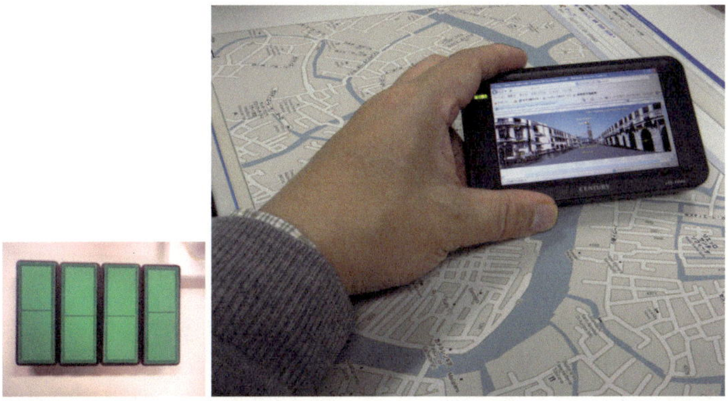

Fig. 3. Digital scope by a lightweight high-resolution display receiving data signal through the 2D sheet. The connector for the display contacts the sheet to receive the power signal.

3. Position detection on communication sheet

To develop the location-specific multimedia applications for 2D communication system, it is highly important to accurately estimate the position where the display is placed over the sheet. Here, two position identification approaches are examined in our platform: (a) position sensing the arrival time difference between the infrared and ultrasound waves, and (b) position sensing the arrival phase difference between the multiple radio inputs.

3.1 Positioning by sensing arrival time difference

The first approach uses infrared and ultrasound technologies. Two kinds of transmitters are adopted to send the infrared and ultrasonic waves, which are mounted on the display. A sensor bar including two kinds of receivers sensing the infrared and ultrasonic waves is set up on one side of the 2D communication sheet. Upon receiving the infrared and ultrasonic signals from transmitters, the distance between display and sensor bar is acquired from the arrival time difference of two waves. Figure 4 shows the mechanism that the relative position of transmitter is calculated from S_0, S_1, and W, which are the distances between the transmitter and ultrasonic receiver, transmitter and another ultrasonic receiver, and two ultrasonic receivers, respectively, as follows

$$y = \frac{s_0^2 - s_1^2 + W^2}{2*W} \tag{1}$$

$$x = \sqrt{s_0^2 - y^2} \tag{2}$$

Through the above Trilateration, the location of the transmitter can be determined.

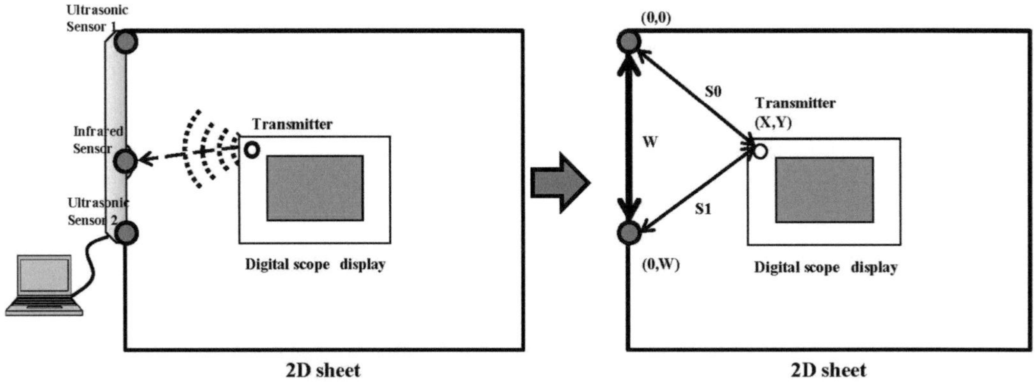

Fig. 4. Acquiring the relative position by the arrival time difference between the infrared and ultrasound waves.

To obtain the orientation of the display in addition to the position, two positioning sets are mounted on two corners of the display. Since the sensor bar cannot simultaneously receive the location information from two positioning sets, a relay switch is built into the display side, as shown in Fig. 5. The relay switch on the display receives the ZigBee signal from the computer via the communication sheet and then controls the turn of the transmitters in sending pulses. The positions of transmitters are linked as a vector that defines the

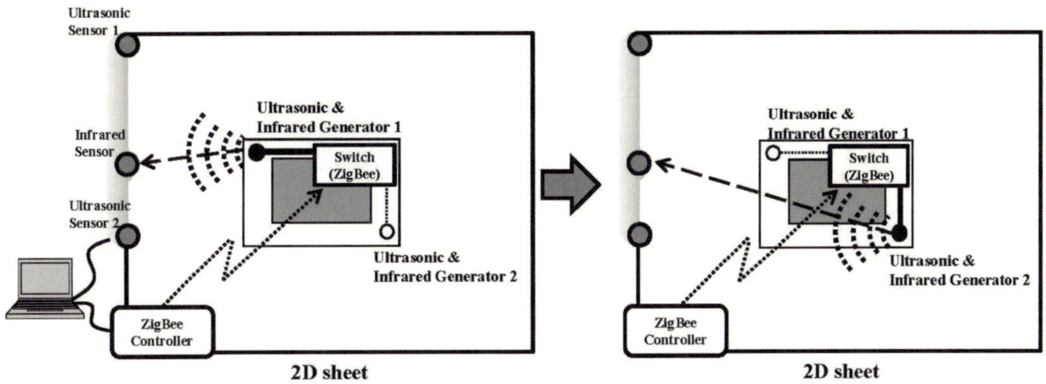

Fig. 5. The signals from two positioning sets are alternatively sent to the receivers by using the wireless Zigbee switch controller. (a) The positioning set 1 is turned on switched by Zigbee controller, (b) The positioning set 2 is turned on.

orientation of the display. The temporal output of the vector provides a trace of orientation moving on top of the communication sheet as depicted in Fig. 6. The drawbacks of this approach are the necessity of the additional sensor devices to generate and sense the infrared and ultrasound waves, as well as the influence from surrounding objects and human bodies, because the reflection of beams from other objects makes the signal noisy when reaching the receivers.

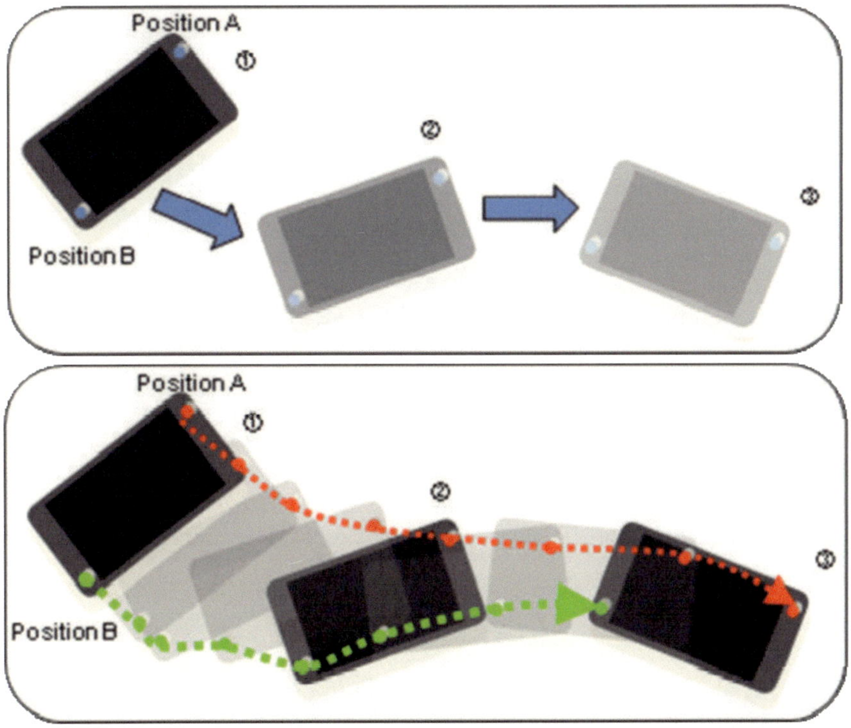

Fig. 6. Obtaining location and orientation of a display device on the 2D sheet.

3.2 Positioning by sensing arrival phase difference

To avoid the interference to the other radio communications performed outside of the sheet, the second approach sends signal within the communication sheet. To aim at a simple system, instead of the utilization of the extra infrared and ultrasound waves mentioned in subsection 3.1, we directly employ the microwaves applied in the 2D communication system for position estimation. We employ a small signal emitter mounted on the scope device that is called target device, and attach the multiple microwave receiving electrodes on the sides of the communication sheet, as shown in Fig. 7. As the microwave runs much faster than the ultrasonic wave, even when the time clock is 3.4GHz achieved by the chip-scale atomic clock in one of DARPA projects in 2007 [15], the precision of the measured distance computed by the arrival time of radio beacon is about 10 cm. Instead of directly measuring the arrival time of microwave, we here examine another approach in which we measure the phase difference arriving at the different abovementioned electrodes, by transmitting the pilot signal from the target device.

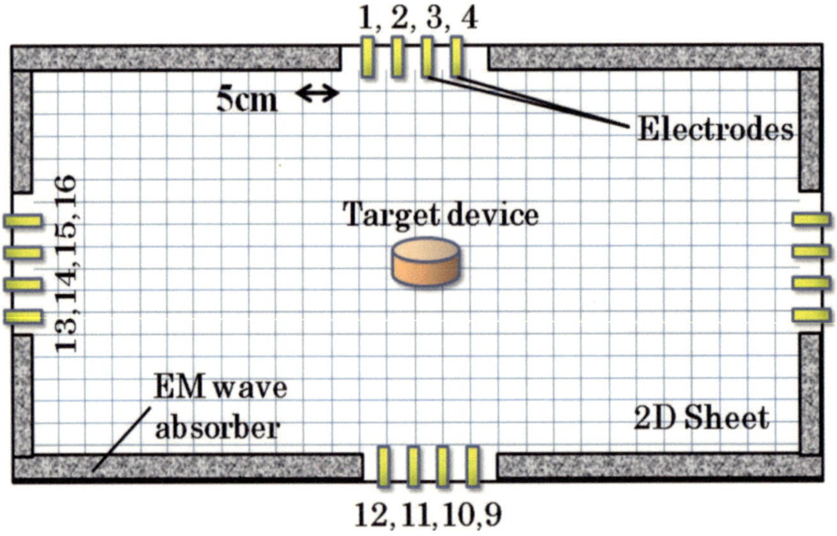

Fig. 7. Positioning of target device using phase difference of electrode array on 2D Communication sheet.

When a sinusoidal wave at radio frequency is transmitted from a targeted device via a coupler on the 2D sheet, it is propagated through the 2D sheet as a cylindrical wave. Figure 8 schematically shows how the phase shift and difference of received signal strengths (RSS) occur between two electrodes at different distance d_1 and d_2 from the target device on a 2D sheet under the ideal condition. The waveform in the 2D sheet can be approximated by the following equation.

$$f = A(d)e^{i(kd-\omega t+\varnothing)} \tag{3}$$

Where d is the distance from the target, $A(d)$ is amplitude corresponding to the distance, k is wave number associated with the wavelength, ω is the angular frequency of the waveform, t is the time and ϕ is the initial phase. The phase difference between the electrodes does not change with time, which changes in the range from 0 to 360 angular degrees. From a practical point of view, however, since there exist reflected waves from the edges of the 2D sheet, the EM absorber is attached to the sides of 2D sheet to mitigate the deviation of the RSS at electrodes.

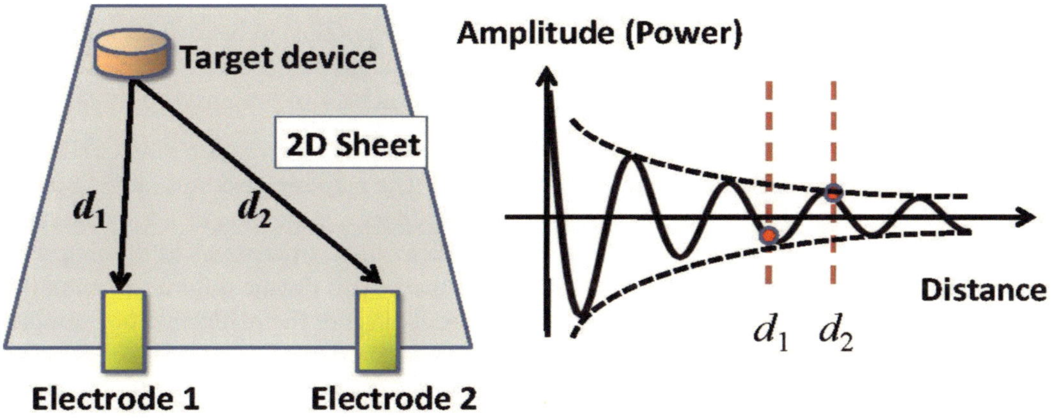

Fig. 8. Difference of received phase and signal strength in the 2D sheet.

Our proposed position identifying method works in two stage processes: the first stage is the database creation stage by preliminary experiment measurement, and the second stage is the position determination stage by comparing the online data with the database of phase difference at each electrode. In the database creation stage, the pilot signal is sent from reference points on the 2D sheet to obtain the mapping database of RSS and phase difference. After constructing the mapping database, the maximum likelihood is utilized to locate device at the online position determination stage.

Because the radio signal in the 2D communication sheet is less influenced by the outside noises, the RSS captured by the electrode shows a stable distribution with respect to the position of target device. Thus, a likelihood method can be employed to estimate the corresponding positions of target device. However, the inner factors such as reflections at the sides of the sheet or shadows caused by the connectors of the target device influence the propagation of the EM wave to some extent. To confirm such influence level, we have conducted some simulations concerning radio propagation in the 2D communication sheet where reflections and shadowing effects are taken into account [16]. The results show that the positioning method using the arrival phase difference provide the adequate estimation of location, and the less the reflection coefficient, the better the accuracy. We also evaluate our proposed method by performing actual position measurement on a 30 cm x 30 cm area, where the phase differences are measured by eight array electrodes corresponding to 2.44GHz pilot signal. In order to identify the position by sensing the arrival phase difference between any neighboring two electrodes, we first calibrate the phase patterns at all possible positions of target device placed on the top of communication sheet. At each position p, we record an array of multi-receiver output, and memorize them as database. The measuring process is done by a motor driven X-Y translator moving to every position on the sheet. The experiment results reveal that our method can detect position at resolution of 2.5 cm square grid perfectly.

4. Digital scope system on the sheet

4.1 Scope display for visualizing location-specific contents

A large and coarse level map is overlaid on the communication sheet or is projected onto it, and the small display device is placed on the sheet. The printed map has no influence on the electromagnetic wave. Because the communication sheet is possible to be made transparent, the coarse map can also be projected from back of the sheet. Hence, the sheet can be attached on screen or table glass as well with the map projected from back or bottom respectively.

The map overlaid on the sheet can be an atlas of world, city, convention site, exhibition room, designed interior space, human body, etc [3]-[5]. The map can also be a table of items as a brief index of categories. Such a map or table can cover a large area or a big collection that a normal PC screen has insufficient resolution to include. In contrast to the map, the underlying media data to display can be selected as those with drastic differences from the map in resolution or type in order to achieve the special effect of the platform. For example, a street view can be displayed according to the position and orientation of the scope display on a road map. Moving the scope display along a street in the map will update the street view in it. This setting can benefit virtual navigation in a large city, which is not flexible on a normal PC window that displays only a limited part of map and the corresponding street view side-by-side. Because the small display of the scope shows details without changing the large map, the user has a good understanding on his/her global location during the exploration of in-depth data.

Another advantage of the scope display is the possibility for visualizing subjects in different modes or media. Figure 9 shows a table for a children's museum on what it becomes when the egg hatched, and how the living species grow up with the scope displays. The map can also be zoomed in on the display and eventually cross different media to visualize a spot, as displayed in Fig. 10. This type of system best fits into a quiz-and-answer diagram and arouses people's curiosity in exploring topics of interest. User can glance over a large category in exposition and then dig into details by placing the display at an interesting spot.

Fig. 9. Scoping details from a category using the communication sheet.

Fig. 10. Zooming in a map across media for location-specific information visualization. (left) from map to scene, (right) how a bird grows up.

4.2 Data transmission to multi-users

The system is designed for multi-users, i.e., multiple persons can look at different information at separated locations in the map, which cannot be achieved by a flat screen or touch panel. To meet this goal, multiple media streams have to be sent to the corresponding multiple displays. The design of the platform is depicted in Fig. 11. Here we can employ different channels to send signals to individual displays.

Two approaches are examined here. The first one uses location-free-servers which receive analogue signals from PC output, and convert them to digital signal in IEEE 802.11A (5.2GHz). In such a framework, the same number of location-free servers as the number of users is needed to send multi-channel signals. Heavy graphics or video contents may even need multiple PCs to render scenes on separated displays. We feed the signals into the sheet through the clip connectors (antenna), and the signals reach everywhere in the sheet for displays to pick up.

The second approach is to use Windows sub-monitors to distribute different contents to displays. Multiple USB LAN output are fed into the sheet by clip connectors and sent to individual displays. The displays that have USB as their input are connected to antenna and is required to register their IDs on the PC first via the communication sheet. This approach requests less resource but can only be used for a few users because of the limitation in the rendering power of a single PC.

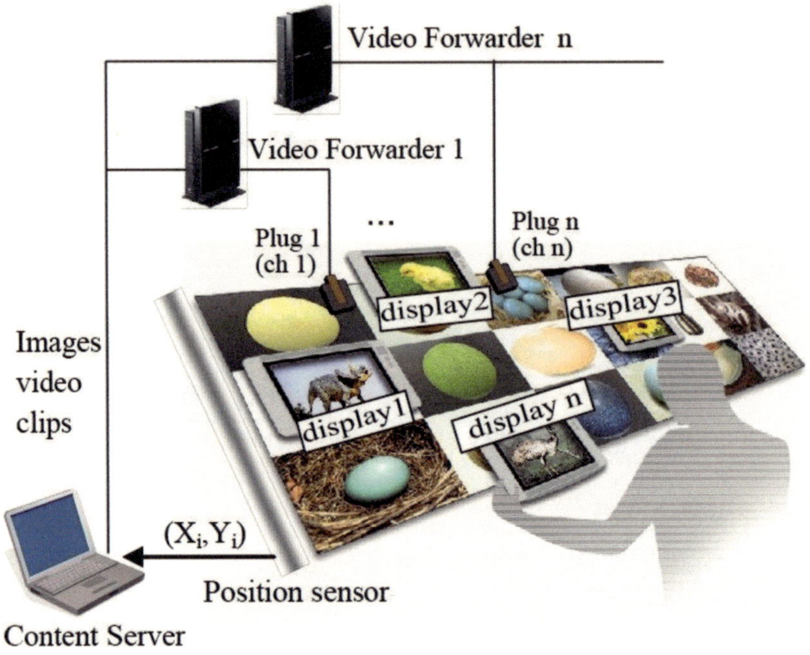

Fig. 11. The system design in which the multimedia signals are sent to individual displays for detailed content visualization according to the positions of displays on the communication sheet.

5. System construction for education and exposition

The system platform uses a communication sheet originally developed for communication and power supply, which has 2mm thickness and a mesh interval of 7mm. Figure 12 shows power supply via the communication sheet to small devices including speakers, LED lights, monitors, etc. Currently, the communication sheet can be printed at a width of 1m and a length of 2m for experiments. The cost of such a sheet is low and will be dropped further in mass production for home and office use.

The digital scope display is a Century 4.3 inch screen driven by USB input and the resolution is 800*480 pixels. The connector developed is attached to the display from back and it contacts the sheet to pick up signals via the communication sheet. We use a position sensing device reconstructed from MIMIO [17], which has the granularity of 100dpi. A circuit is designed to switch between multiple infrared-ultrasound generators to send out pulses alternatively. The signal reaching the receivers is then sent to computer via USB connection. The position estimation on the computer is programmed with MIMIO SDK. The frequency to compute the position of one generator is 87Hz, and the Zigbee switching between two positioning sets is 10Hz.

We have experimented on several types of media contents and demonstrated the functioning system. The contents include a world map with 42 topics in famous sightseeing cities and spots, six categories of living species (41 species ranging from animals to plants) and their growing process exhibited in museum. The system is a new type of interface for users to move on a large map space and peek in detailed information at different locations.

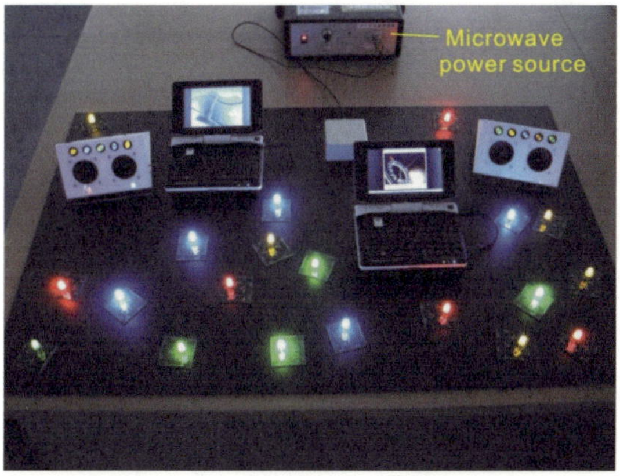

Fig. 12. Power supply via the communication sheet to small devices including speakers, LED lights, monitors, etc.

The large map underlying the small display solves the problem of location/orientation perception in multiwindow system on PCs. For multi-user on the same sheet, we prepare multiple displays connected to a PC for media presentation. The current response time for video clip, however, is a bottleneck that affects the usability of the system. A high performance PC and customized software will be developed to solve this problem.

Based on the estimated positioning data of the display with the reconstructed MIMIO system, the location-specific media details can be magnified and displayed as a digital scope to learning materials, catalogs, tourists guide, X-ray image of building, and various other purposes. For example, as shown in Fig.13, we have developed a digital scope system called

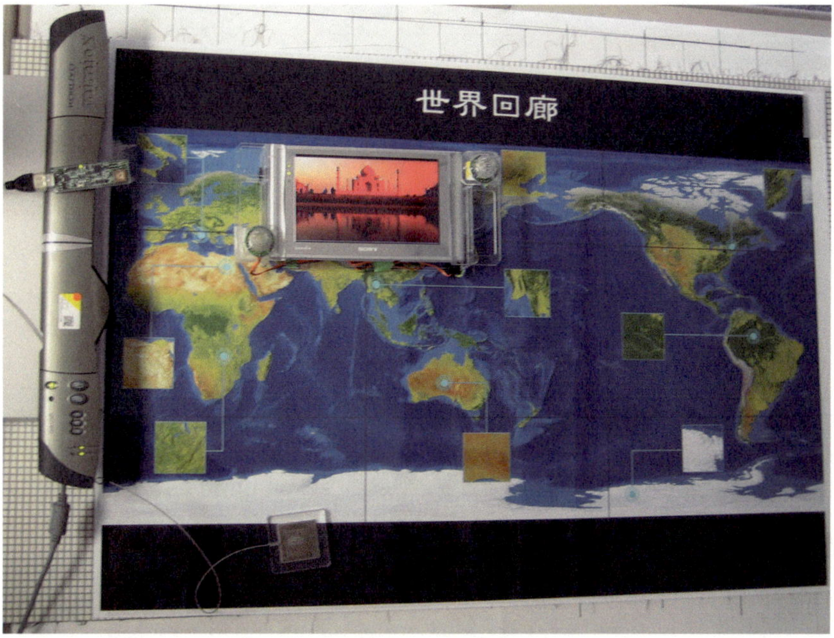

Fig. 13. Digital scope system called "World Corridor".

"World Corridor." Along the "World Corridor," we can enjoy an around-the-world trip with family and friends while staying at home. Depending on the position where the display is placed, the scenery image of the place on the map can be gradually magnified by zooming in; details of living creatures in the sightseeing spots can also be visualized. We have also developed another digital scope system for children's education materials. Figure 14 shows a picture book of various eggs and species on what it will become when it grows up. For example, as shown in Fig. 14 , when the display is placed in the middle of 2D sheet, the motion pictures are displayed on how the baby chicken were hatched from eggs, grow up and finally develop to adult chicken.

Fig. 14. Digital scope system for children's education materials on what it will become when it grows up.

6. Discussion and future work

The proposed digital scope platform is an interface composed of a physical medium and multiple displays to reveal details behind a global map or a general category. It separates the presentation of a map and in-depth data to different media, one on printed paper and others on small screens. This reduces the burden in using a large display or projector in presenting both large map and multiple scope views. A few servers can handle multi-user tasks, which is more flexible than employing a wall of monitors or an array of projectors in conventional setting. It is also energy saving because the signal spread within the communication sheet has less loss than in the air, and in our case only low power signal is sent for communication. The entire system is also convenient to be set anywhere on flat surfaces.

The scope displays are not wired to ensure their free movement on the 2D surface. On the other hand, this platform can send multi-channel signals in the closed sheet by utilizing wider bandwidth than wireless. Multi-channel video can be distributed to different displays simultaneously. Moreover, the communication sheet has the location dependent property as compared to wireless in the air; a display placed over different sheets can receive different signals. By partitioning a large space into sheet patches that correspond to regions of interest, a display can receive region-specific data on the patches and will show nothing if it is away from the sheet. This also improves the security in the information access in a large space. The future works include the accuracy improvement of the position sensing on the sheet, which will increase the granularity of the map for dense location information retrieval; lightweight display design for mobility on the sheet; building stereo display with a lenticular sheet for visualizing 3D urban scenes on the map; and adding touching panel on the display to allow viewing different media. We will further consider extending the map to curved surfaces on human body or various objects. For example, partitioned sheets can be wrapped on each part of a manikin or on surfaces of a car to form 3D surface maps. By contacting displays onto surfaces, people will be able to see internal structures, which will help education in engineering and medical areas.

7. Conclusion

This chapter describes a multimedia interface platform on the communication sheet named digital scope for visualizing location-specific information. The platform contains small high-resolution displays, a large communication sheet, and location sensors. The sensed position of each display is sent to the server and the related media data are transmitted to the display via the communication sheet. Functioning as a scope, users can move the small displays over a large map and look into details at different locations. The multi-channel media data are distributed to facilitate multi-user's interaction. Because of the large map, the location-related data are more perceivable in a global layout than in a single screen as current PC that has to present different media at a location side-by-side. The platform is also power efficient than a wall of monitors in achieving the same goal. It will enhance many applications in education and exposition.

8. References

[1] J. Y. Zheng, X. Wang, " Pervasive Views: Area exploration and guidance using extended image media ", ACM Multimedia 05, 986-995, 2005.
Google Map: http://maps.google.com.
[2] J. Y. Zheng, B. Zhang, H. Cai," Pervasive scene map on wireless devices for city navigation ", NBiS 2009, 75-82.
[3] H. Cai, J. Y. Zheng," Key views for visualizing large spaces ". Journal of Visual Communication and Image Representation 20(6): 420-427 (2009).
[4] J. Y. Zheng, M. Shi, Mapping cityscapes into cyberspace for visualization, J. of Visualization & Computer Animation, 16(2), 97-107, 2005.
[5] C. Pinhanez, M. Podlaseck, R. Kjeldsen, A. Levas, G. Pingali, N. Sukaviriya, "Ubiquitous interactive displays in a retail environment", SIGGRAPH'03 Sketches. San Diego, California.
[6] M. Podlaseck, C. Pinhanez, N. Alvarado, M. Chan, E. Dejesus, "On interfaces projected onto real-world objects", CHI'03. Florida, 2003

[7] C. H. Hsiao, L. W. Chan, T. T. Hu, M. C. Chen, J. Hsu, Y. P. Huang, "To move or not to move: a comparison between steerable versus fixed focus region paradigms in multi-resolution tabletop display systems", 153-161, CHI09.

[8] S. Izadi, S. Hodges, S. Taylor, D. Rosenfeld, N. Villar, A. Butler, J. Westhues, "Going beyond the display: a surface technology with an electronically switchable diffuser" UIST 2008: 269-278.

[9] P. Steurer et al., "System design of smart table", IEEE Int. Conf. on Pervasive Computing and Commun. (PerCom), March 2003.

[10] H. Shinoda, "Sensor networking based on two-dimensional signal transmission technology", SICE-ICASE Int. Joint Conf. 2006.

[11] H. Shinoda et al., "Surface sensor network using inductive signal transmission layer," Conf. INSS, pp.201–206, 2007.

[12] Bing Zhang, Azman Osman Lim, Youiti Kado, Hiroto Itai, Hiroyuki Shinoda, "An efficient power supply system using phase control in 2D communication", INSS2009 (Sixth International Conference on Networked Sensing Systems, Pittsburgh, USA), 2009-06.

[13] N. Yamahira, Y. Makino, H. Itai and H. Shinoda," Proximity connection in two dimensional signal transmission", SICE-ICASE Int. Joint Conf., pp.2735-2740, Korea, 2006.

[14] S. Knappe, V. Shah, V. Gerginov, A. Brannon, L. Hollberg, and J. Kitching, "Long-term stability of NIST chip-scale atomic clock physics packages",PTTI2006(38th Annual Precise Time and Time Interval Meeting), 2006-12.

[15] Youiti Kado, Toshifumi Oota, Azman Osman Lim, Bing Zhang, "A simulation study for position estimation of multiple devices in 2D communication system,"in Proc. of the International Symposium on Antennas and Propagation (ISAP), pp.1095-1098, Bangkok, Thailand, 20-23 Oct. 2009.

[16] MIMIO: http://www.mimio.com

11

Building Adaptive Rich Interfaces for Interactive Ubiquitous Applications

Carlos Eduardo Cirilo, Antonio Francisco do Prado,
Wanderley Lopes de Souza and Luciana Aparecida Martinez Zaina
*Federal University of São Carlos (UFSCar),
Brazil*

1. Introduction

The emerging of the Web 2.0 (O'Reilly, 2005) has allowed users more interactivity with Web applications. Among the striking features of Web 2.0 applications, the use of rich interfaces that afford users a more meaningful experience with these applications stands out. In this context, the so-called Rich Internet Applications (RIAs) have transposed the boundaries of simple interfaces built only in HyperText Markup Language (HTML). Through the adoption of technologies that enable creating more advanced interfaces with interactive resources, such as asynchronous communication, drag-and-drop components, audio and video players, among others, RIAs resemble the appearance, behavior and usability of desktop applications (Deitel & Deitel, 2008).

The miniaturization of computational devices for personal use along with recent advances in wireless communication technologies and the maturing of Ubiquitous Computing (Weiser, 1991) have significantly expanded the access possibilities to a wide range of applications in several fields (Forte et al., 2008; Souza et al., 2011). Until recently, there were few ways to access online content, among which the main one was through personal computers. However, this situation has changed quickly. Nowadays, for instance, it is possible to read e-mails, make financial transactions, share resources (hardware, software and data), access multimedia content, and enjoy a variety of other applications through a small cell phone or a sophisticated smartphone, either the user is stationary or moving, whether at home, on the street or at work. In this scenario the vision of Ubiquitous Computing, introduced by Mark Weiser about two decades ago, has been driven by new technological achievements that enable easy access to information anywhere, anytime and through any device at user's disposal (Araújo, 2003; Hansmann et al., 2003).

Nevertheless, the dynamic nature of Ubiquitous Computing environments imposes a series of challenges and additional requirements to software development (Garlan & Schmerl, 2001; Spínola et al., 2007). One of the critical aspects in developing applications for operating in ubiquitous environments is the premise that they should be able to run and to adapt themselves to the diversity of users' computational devices as well as to the environment in which they are immersed (Gajos & Weld, 2004). Given the diversity of devices, access networks, environments and contexts, providing applications that meet the peculiarities of each access device, while one maintains a consistent appearance and coherent behavior in view of changes occurring in the surrounding environment, has become a difficult task for software engineers (Eisenstein et al., 2000; Paternò et al., 2008; Singh, 2004). In the case of interactive Web 2.0 applications, this task becomes even more complex due to the need of preserving interaction aspects that afford users a richer experience.

In this universe, building and maintaining specific application versions to meet the particularities of each interaction context have become a challenge to be overcome. Among other problems, this cross-context design requires high investments, demands large development efforts, and still can result in inconsistent application versions. Furthermore, the existence of multiple application versions hinders the maintenance, since modifications and changes will have to be managed separately (Eisenstein et al., 2000; Singh, 2004). In this sense, it is important to provide developers with an appropriate software process which can guide them through the establishment of activities and artifacts that give support in meeting the adaptation requirements demanded by a ubiquitous environment, considering the different contexts involved in the application execution (Serral et al., 2010).

Faced with these challenges, a software process named Model Driven RichUbi (Model Driven Process to Construct Rich Interfaces for Context-Sensitive Ubiquitous Applications) was proposed (Cirilo et al., 2010a). The process aims at supporting the development of rich interfaces for interactive ubiquitous applications that adapt themselves when viewed on different types of devices. Based on the conceptions of Model Driven Development (MDD) (France & Rumpe, 2007) and Domain-Specific Modeling (DSM) (Kelly & Tolvanen, 2008), the process defines activities and artifacts that aid the modeling and the partial code generation of rich interfaces for different platforms. These artifacts include a Rich Interfaces Domain metamodel which expresses the abstract syntax of a Domain-Specific Language (DSL) (Sadilek, 2008) to support the rich interfaces modeling, and Model-to-Code transformations for code generation. Besides, dynamic content adapters that refine the produced interface versions are also employed in the process, so that the developed interfaces can adapt to the peculiarities of the access device identified from the interaction context at runtime. The process' computational support focused on the Rich Interfaces Domain - a cross-cut domain to the application domains - enables its reuse on the development of adaptive rich interfaces for interactive ubiquitous applications of several fields, which contributes to effort reduction and productivity increasing.

The approach employed in the Model Driven RichUbi to adapt the content of the developed rich interfaces leaps out. Aiming to overcome the individual shortcomings of the purely static adaptation strategy (construction of several interface versions at development time) and the purely dynamic one (adaptation of the whole code at execution time) (Viana & Andrade, 2008), and to reduce the number of versions to be developed, the process employs a hybrid adaptation approach (Cirilo et al., 2010b). This approach combines code generation from modeling at development time (facilitated by the metamodel and transformations reuse) with code generation at runtime (facilitated by the content adapters reuse). This way, just a few generic interface versions are built, each one appropriated to a particular group of devices, instead of a specific device (static adaptation). The dynamic content adapters supplement the adaptation during the application execution, by repurposing the interface's contents - when necessary - according to the peculiarities of the current access device (dynamic adaptation). Thus, the development becomes simplified, since a smaller number of versions can be designed and developed.

Therefore, the purpose of this chapter is to present the Model Driven RichUbi process, detailing its activities and support mechanisms that simplify the development of adaptive rich interfaces for interactive ubiquitous applications. Moreover, in order to evaluate the feasibility of the process, an experimental study, following the experimental methodology proposed by Wohlin et al. (2000), is also presented. In this study the impact of the Model Driven RichUbi on the efficiency of teams developing adaptive rich interfaces was evaluated. The study's results, even in a university context, highlight the potential of the process to collaborate for increasing the teams' efficiency in building adaptive rich interfaces for interactive ubiquitous applications in terms of spent time and productivity.

The sequence of this chapter is organized as follows: Section 2 provides a theoretical background on the issues which this work deals with; Section 3 presents the Model Driven RichUbi process and the mechanisms developed to support it; Section 4 addresses the process' evaluation; Section 5 discusses some related work; and Section 6 presents concluding remarks and further work.

2. Theoretical background

This section introduces the main concepts in which the developed work is based on. Whereas the proposed process aims at supporting the development of adaptive rich interfaces for interactive applications, Section 2.1 briefly presents the concepts related to Web 2.0 and Rich Interfaces. Section 2.2 deals with concepts associated with Model-Based User Interface Development, employed in the static content adaptation part of the hybrid adaptation approach applied in the process. Since the dynamic interface adaptation part relies on contextual information obtained at runtime, Section 2.3 broaches the conceptions regarding Context-Sensitive Applications.

2.1 Web 2.0 and rich interfaces

The term Web 2.0 has been created to refer to a new generation of Web applications mainly characterized by providing support for collaboration and sharing of user-generated content (Norrie, 2008). Usually, companies developing applications for Web 2.0 use the Web as a platform to create collaborative and community-based websites, such as social networks, blogs, wikis, and others. The idea is to make the online environment more dynamic, where users can play a more active role and work together for producing and organizing the content, unlike the traditional Web (Web 1.0) where users are mostly readers of information.

Besides harnessing collective intelligence, the Web 2.0 encompasses a number of other principles (O'Reilly, 2005), among which the use of rich interfaces in applications for allowing a more meaningful user experience stands out. The so-called Rich Internet Applications (RIAs) have adopted technologies that enable the creation of more attractive user interfaces, providing the sensitivity, features and functionalities that resemble desktop applications. Features like asynchronous communication with Asynchronous JavaScript and XML (AJAX) (Zakas et al., 2007), drag-and-drop components, sliding panels, components to capture and display videos, maps, online spreadsheets and text editors, are examples of rich interface components which enable greater interactivity and improve the overall users' experience (Gaspar et al., 2009).

Another important Web 2.0 principle refers to the multi-device-oriented development (O'Reilly, 2005). The Web 2.0 is no longer limited to the PC platform, which means these applications are able to run on different types of device and over any operating system. In fact, any Web application already meets this requirement, once it just requires one computer hosting a server and a client equipped with a Web browser regardless the underlying platform. However, in the context of Web 2.0 this concept goes a step beyond, in the extent that Web 2.0 applications are not restricted just to the conventional client-server architecture, but are also capable to run in several other architectures, such as Peer-to-Peer (P2P), or even on a myriad of distinct hardware platforms, like mobile devices (Gaspar et al., 2009).

2.2 Model-based user interface development

The Model-Based User Interface Development (MB-UID) (Viana & Andrade, 2008) explores the idea of using declarative interface models, which allows the definition of the different aspects of a user interface in an abstract way, regardless the implementation platform. This strategy facilitates the transformation of the abstract interaction components represented in the models into concrete components of the target-platforms (Vellis, 2009). Thus, developers can focus on the conceptual definition of interfaces rather than on technical details of implementation (Bittar et al., 2009).

The approach employed by the MB-UID is known as Model-Driven Development (MDD) (France & Rumpe, 2007), in which software engineers do not need to interact manually with the entire application's source code, but they can concentrate on models of higher abstraction level. Transformation mechanisms (code generators) are used to generate code from models. In this scenario, the models not only guide the development and maintenance tasks, but are also part of the software being developed just as the source code, since they are used as input by code generation tools to distil part of the application's code; it, in fact, contributes to reduce developer's efforts (Bittar et al., 2009).

In the MB-UID the user interface modeling involves the creation of knowledge bases expressed in a hierarchy of models that describe the various aspects of the interface, such as presentation, dialog and user tasks structure (Paternò et al., 2008). The models provide an infrastructure for building methods and tools for automatic generation of the interface's final presentation (Viana & Andrade, 2008). This way, by applying the appropriate Model-to-Code (M2C) transformations, it is possible to generate the entire or most of the code for different platforms and implementation technologies in order to obtain the executable interface with little or no manual change (Cicchetti et al., 2007).

2.2.1 Domain-specific modeling

Following the same direction of MDD and addressing specific problem domains, there is the Domain-Specific Modeling (DSM) (Kelly & Tolvanen, 2008). In DSM the application's models are built by using Domain Specific Languages (DSLs) (Sadilek, 2008), which can be defined through metamodels that represent the knowledge of a particular domain. The use of DSLs for modeling, rather than general purpose languages like the Unified Modeling Language (UML), allows the expression of solutions in the language and abstraction level of the problem domain. This reduces efforts in translating the concepts of that domain into concepts of the computational solution (Chavarriaga & Macías, 2009). Thus, in DSM the models become more specific and complete, and resources such as frameworks, design patterns and components are included in the modeling in order to generate more code with better quality.

The use of specific models of the Rich Interface Domain can raise the abstraction level during application design so that users and developers can clearly see how the application's requirements are mapped into interfaces. The interface models are created in a more intuitive way and are less associated with technical implementation details. This way, developers can focus on high-level conceptual aspects of the interaction. Moreover, since the models are not related to a specific platform, it is also possible to reuse the interface's specifications in different projects (Bittar et al., 2009).

2.3 Context-sensitive applications

Context sensitivity (or context awareness) is related to the adaptation of an application according to its location of use, the nearby people or objects, as well as the changes occurring in the surrounding environment over time (Baldauf et al., 2007). A Context-Sensitive Application (CSA) is able to adapt its operations without explicit user intervention, providing information and services that are relevant for users to perform their tasks using information taken out of the interaction context (Dey, 2001; Serral et al., 2010).

In this sense, context plays a key role to enable applications to refine available information into relevant one, to choose appropriate actions from a list of possibilities, or to determine the optimal method of information delivery. Accordingly, context guides the variations in application's behavior, enriching the user interaction either by influencing recommendations or by enabling adaptations of any kind (Vieira et al., 2011).

2.3.1 Computational context

Many definitions for context have been proposed to make it an operational concept (Bazire & Brézillon, 2005). A widely referenced one states that context is any information that can be used to characterize the situation of an entity. This entity may be a person, place or an object that is considered relevant to the interaction between a user and an application, including themselves (Dey, 2001).

Similarly, Brézillon (1999) considers context as a set of relevant conditions and influences that make possible the understanding of a situation, where such conditions and influences act directly on entities of the considered domain. In addition, Brézillon & Pomerol (1999, as cited in Vieira et al., 2011) introduced the notion of focus, which determines what should be considered as relevant in a given context. According to this definition, the focus, for instance, can be a task to be performed, or a step in a problem solving or in a decision making process.

A more recent definition, derived from the previous ones, suggests the explicit distinction between context - a dynamic concept - and contextual element (CE) - a static concept - in order to improve developers' understanding about context and to facilitate its usage in applications (Vieira et al., 2011). In such definition, a CE is considered as any piece of information which characterizes an entity in a domain (e.g. device's screen resolution width, user's location). On the other hand, the context of an interaction between an agent (human or software) and an application, with focus on a task, is stated as the set of instantiated CEs that are necessary to support the task to be performed (e.g. "300 pixels", "São Carlos - Brazil"). This definition makes it easier for a developer to enumerate the context of a certain application scenario at development time. In this sense, if a given piece of information characterizing an entity in an interaction is useful to support the task at hand (e.g. content adaptation), then this information makes up the context of that particular interaction.

3. Model Driven RichUbi process

The Model Driven RichUbi (Cirilo et al., 2010a) is a software process conceived specifically to support the development of adaptive rich interfaces for ubiquitous applications in the field of Web 2.0. Considering the ideas from MB-UID and DSM, in the Model Driven RichUbi the interface modeling is performed from a Rich Interfaces Domain metamodel. This facilitates the translation of application requirements into interface models, and also enables code generation for several implementation technologies. Besides, part of interface adaptation is dynamically performed through the usage of content adapters. In this sense, the process employs a hybrid adaptation strategy by joining static with dynamic adaptation: during the development, the application's requirements are mapped into a few generic interface versions, each one appropriated for a particular group of devices (static adaptation); at runtime, the content adapters select the version which best fits the device profile recovered from context, and adapt the code snippets that need to be refined so as to meet the access device's characteristics (dynamic adaptation).

As shown in the Structured Analysis and Design Technique (SADT) diagram (Ross, 1977) in Figure 1, the process is performed in two main steps: Domain Engineering (DE) and Application Engineering (AE). The process begins in the DE, where the metamodel to support the modeling of the applications' interfaces is built from the requirements of the Rich Interfaces Domain. The metamodel is built in such a way to allow the reuse of the Rich Interface Domain knowledge on application projects of several areas, and to provide a useful infrastructure to automate most of interfaces' code generation. Also in the DE, based on the rich interface components represented in the developed metamodel, the M2C transformations and the dynamic content adapters are built to act as support mechanisms in the development of rich interfaces in the AE step.

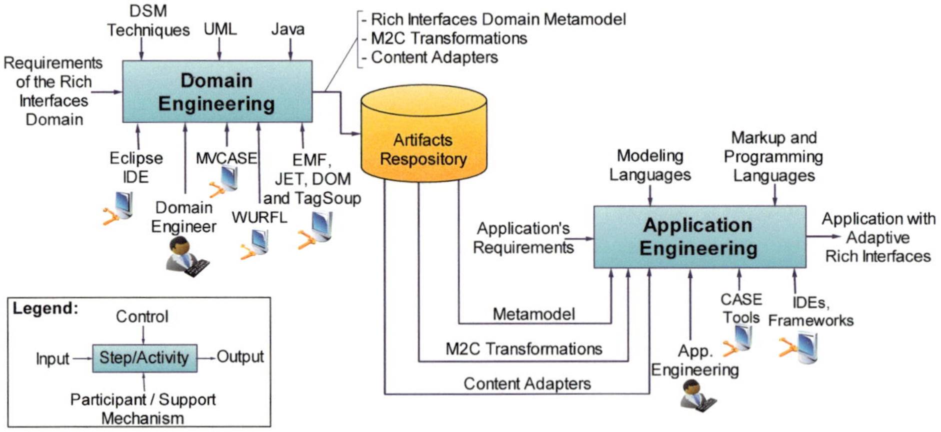

Fig. 1. High-level overview of the Model Driven RichUbi process

The AE, in turn, includes activities for developing applications with reuse of the artifacts produced in the DE. In such step, the Rich Interfaces Domain metamodel is used to instantiate the applications' interface models to simplify the mapping of requirements into interface components that fulfill them. Once the models are not associated with a specific implementation platform, one can generate code for different technologies by applying the M2C transformations, which reduces efforts in the development of the interface versions for different groups of devices. The content adapters are used to further refine the interfaces at runtime according to specific characteristics of the access device dynamically identified. The activities of the DE and AE are detailed in the following subsections.

3.1 Domain Engineering (DE)

The DE focuses on the development of software artifacts for posterior intensive reuse. Overall, the DE is a process for identifying and organizing the knowledge about a class of problems - the problem domain – in order to support its description and solution. The DE's goal is to systematize the creation of domain models, architectures and sets of software artifacts to aid building applications in a particular problem domain (Blois et al., 2005).

Figure 2 shows the SADT diagram detailing the activities defined for the DE in the Model Driven RichUbi. The activities on the left-hand side correspond to the construction of the metamodel to support rich interfaces modeling. The activities on the right-hand side refer to the construction of the M2C transformations for partial generation code (upper activity) and the content adapters for dynamic adaptation of the developed interfaces (bottom activity). Since these latter depend on the metamodel's implementation as input artifact, the activities for constructing the metamodel must precede all other activities of the Domain Engineering.

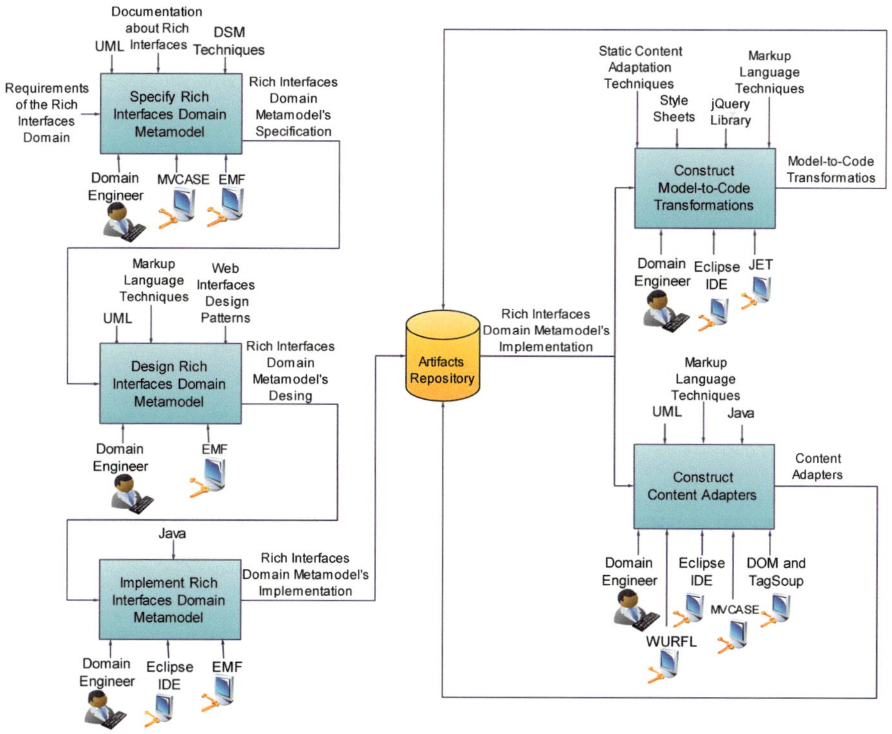

Fig. 2. Domain Engineering step

3.1.1 Specify rich interfaces domain metamodel

The goal of this activity is to identify, from the requirements of the Rich Interfaces Domain, the interface components that are useful for the construction of Web 2.0 ubiquitous applications. These components are elicited, specified, analyzed and translated into meta-constructs in a Rich Interfaces Domain metamodel. One means to accomplish such identification is to study the interface components available on several Web development environments, like the Adobe Dreamweaver[1] and the MS Visual Studio[2], along with other documentation about rich interfaces[3, 4, 5]. Through these studies, the Domain Engineer can identify the components commonly used in building rich interfaces and model their structural and behavioral similarities. The UML is used to support the modeling and specification of the components.

Figure 3 shows, for example, an excerpt of a class diagram that specifies some interface components identified from this activity, which range from ordinary form controls (`Button`, `TextField`, and `Select`) to advanced rich interfaces widgets (`TabbedPanel`, `AccordionPanel`, `MessageDialog` and `DatePicker`). During this modeling task, the Domain Engineer is assisted by the Mutiple-View CASE (MVCASE) (Lucrédio et al., 2003), a Computer-Aided Software Engineering (CASE) tool currently available as an Eclipse workbench[6] plug-in to support UML modeling.

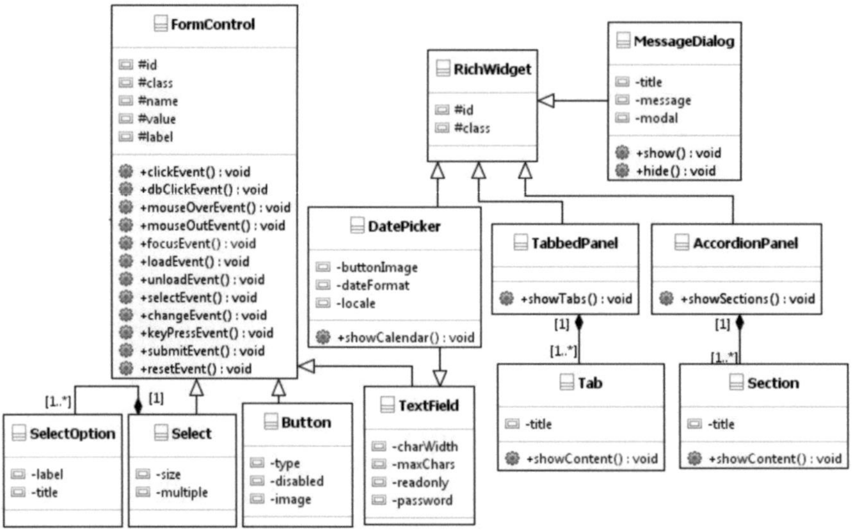

Fig. 3. Interface components' specification

The Domain Engineer then specifies the Rich Interfaces Domain metamodel by defining its metaclasses, meta-attributes and meta-relationships based on the interface components' specification. In the Model Driven RichUbi, the metamodel is built through the Ecore's

1 http://www.adobe.com/products/dreamweaver/.
2 http://www.microsoft.com/visualstudio/en-us/.
3 http://www.jboss.org/richfaces/docs.html.
4 http://jqueryui.com/demos/.
5 http://www.asp.net/ajax/AjaxControlToolkit/Samples/.
6 http://www.eclipse.org/.

metamodeling constructs from the Eclipse Modeling Framework (EMF)[7]. As illustrated in the excerpt of the metamodel's specification in Figure 4, the interface components specified in the class diagram of Figure 3 were mapped into homonymous metaclasses. The `id`, `class` and `label` attributes from the `FormControl` class have been factored, respectively, into the `IdentifiableComponent`, `ClassifiableComponent` and `Label` metaclasses. In addition, the `FormControl` class' event-handling methods formed the `EventType` meta-enumeration and the `Event`, `EventComponent` and `Script` metaclasses. Metaclasses to address the interface's data input constraints were also included in the metamodel, such as the `ValueConstraint`, `NumberValueConstraint`, `RequiredFieldConstraint` and `ValidDateConstraint` ones.

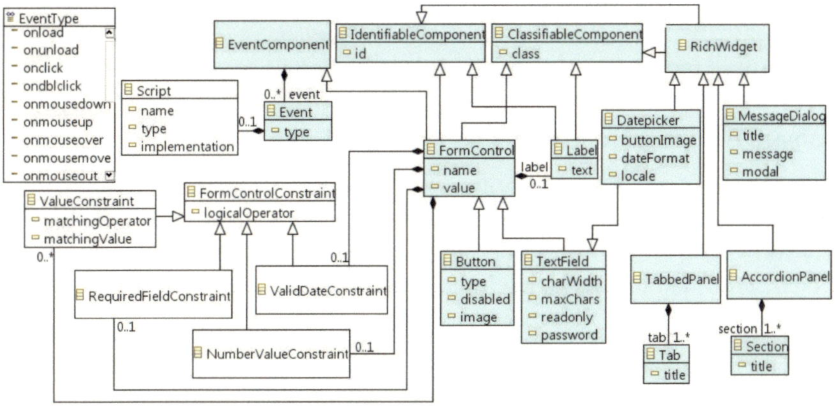

Fig. 4. Rich Interfaces Domain metamodel's specification

3.1.2 Design rich interfaces domain metamodel

The goal of this activity is to define standards, technologies, as well as hardware and software platforms that enable the construction of the metamodel. Through these design decisions the Domain Engineer refines the Rich Interfaces Domain metamodel's specification produced in previous activity.

For example, Figure 5 shows part of the metamodel refined with the employment of the Web interfaces design pattern called *Portal Site*[8]. This pattern, represented on the right-hand side of Figure 5, defines the header, navigation, content, search and footer regions of a Web portal. On the left-hand side, the refined metamodel is shown with the inclusion of new metaclasses (shaded), whose stereotypes indicate their association with the Web portal's regions.

Moreover, metaclasses for suiting the metamodel to the XHTML documents' structure were included in the metamodel during the refinements (e.g. `Document`, `Form`, and `Fieldset`). The definition of compounding relationships between these metaclasses has also been performed in accordance with the XHTML specification. These refinements allowed structuring the way in which the rich interface components are arranged and organized in the interface models which will be instantiated from the metamodel.

---

[7] www.eclipse.org/emf/.

[8] http://www.welie.com/patterns/showPattern.php?patternID=portals.

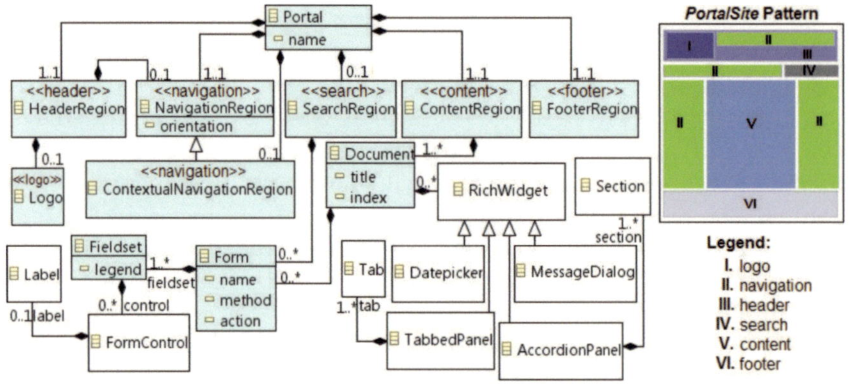

Fig. 5. Refinement of the metamodel by applying the *PortalSite* pattern

3.1.3 Implement rich interfaces domain metamodel

In this activity the metamodel is implemented from the metamodel's design resulting from previous activity. The metamodel's implementation aims at obtaining software components which fairly reflect the entities and relationships represented in the metamodel's design so that it can be instantiated to create rich interfaces models in the AE step.

In the process, the EMF framework is also employed for implementing the metamodel. It allows automatically generating the Java code of both the metamodel and an associated model editor that will assist in the instantiation of the metamodel to create the rich interfaces models. In the generated editor the instantiated models are persisted in XML Metadata Interchange (XMI)[9] format, which is a standard from Object Management Group (OMG) used to represent models through eXtensible Markup Language (XML). This format defines an XML document structure that considers the relationship between the model's data and their corresponding metadata, which facilitates mapping models into code for the definition of M2C transformations.

In this work, the metamodel's implementation along with the model editor were deployed as Eclipse plug-ins and integrated into the MVCASE tool in order to support the rich interfaces modeling in the process' AE step.

3.1.4 Construct model-to-code transformations

The goal of this activity is to build the transformations to be applied on the interface models for automated code generation in the Application Engineering's implementation activity.

Among the techniques for constructing transformations, the use of templates stands out (Lucrédio, 2009). A template is a text file instrumented with constructs for selecting and expanding code. These constructs perform queries on a given input (e.g. a XMI file representing a model) and use the outcome as parameter to produce custom code in any textual language (Czarnecki & Eisenecker, 2000, as cited in Lucrédio, 2009). So, a template is usually composed of fixed parts, which always are included in the output code, and variable parts, which depend on the information contained in the input model to be generated.

[9] http://www.omg.org/spec/XMI/2.1.1/

The proper implementation of transformations relies on the knowledge of the language's syntax in which the input models are created, i.e., the metamodel. Hence, the metamodel's implementation is used as input in this activity so that the transformations are built in a compatible way with the developed Rich Interfaces Domain metamodel. In the process, the transformations are implemented as templates by using the Java Emitter Templates (JET) framework[10], which provides a library of metaprogramming markups that implement conditional, looping and formatting statements, as well as other useful functions to query the input rich interfaces models and generating code.

In this work, two types of transformations were built: one that generates XHTML code for desktops; and another one that generates XHTML code for smartphones by applying static content adaptation techniques for mobile devices, such as single-column content presentation and splitting of large forms (Paternò et al., 2008; Viana & Andrade, 2008). In order to give an initial layout formatting to the generated interfaces, references to prefabricated style sheets were incorporated into the transformations' output code. In addition, aiming at creating advanced rich interface components, the jQuery[11] JavaScript library, which provides reusable functions for rendering such components, has also been integrated into the output code.

Figure 6 shows a fragment of the JET template which generates the XHTML code of the tabbed panel component for desktops. This figure also illustrates the template's execution process, in which each template's part is interpreted in order to query the input model (in XMI format) and then producing its corresponding code. So, whenever the mechanism that executes transformations (or template processor) finds the node representing the tabbed panel component in the XMI input model, the template's execution starts. The template's lines 1-12 generate the JavaScript code which invokes the jQuery's function to render the tabbed panel on the user's Web browser. Line 14 produces a `<div>` markup that makes up the tabbed panel's structure. This markup references the style class named `demo`, which is defined in the prefabricated style sheet copied into the application's project during the template's execution. In lines 16-19 and 21-28 iterations are made on the panel's tabs defined in the model to generate their content in the output code.

To support code generation in the AE step, the developed transformations have also been deployed as Eclipse plug-ins and integrated into the MVCASE tool. Since the models instantiated from the metamodel are platform-independent, it is possible to create several types of transformations for automatically generating code to a plenty of implementation technologies, such as Wireless Markup Language (WML), Voice XML (VXML), Compact Hypertext Markup Language (CHTML), and so on. By using this technique, the repetitive tasks associated with the coding of interfaces for different devices in Ubiquitous Computing are (semi)automated, which contributes to save development efforts. Therefore, the transformations along with the metamodel collaborate to simplify the static part of the interface adaptation in the hybrid approach employed in the process.

3.1.5 Construct content adapters

The goal of this activity is to build the content adapters which will perform the dynamic part of the interface adaptation considering the access device profile recovered from the

[10] http://www.eclipse.org/emft/projects/jet/.

[11] http://jqueryui.com/.

interaction context. This activity takes as input the Rich Interfaces Domain metamodel's implementation, which contains the definitions of all interface components to be adapted when rendered on devices with different characteristics.

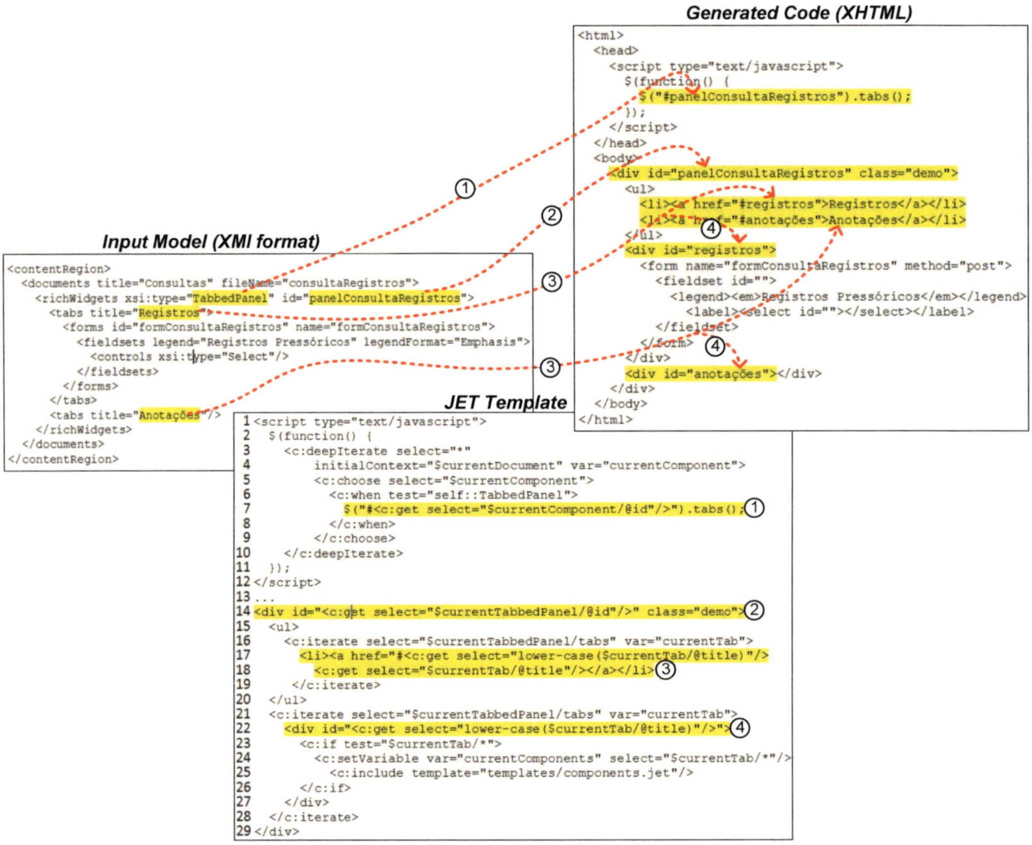

Fig. 6. Template-based code generation for the tabbed panel component

Before starting the content adapters' implementation, the Domain Engineer must specify, for each component represented in the metamodel, the adaptation requirements demanded when the interface is viewed on devices with distinct configurations. This specification is not a simple task and requires from the Domain Engineer a good technological vision about interfaces, devices available in the market and their capabilities that influence the adaptation. To support the Domain Engineer's work, the UML is used to specify and to design the interface adaptation. For example, Figure 7 shows one of the class diagrams for the content adapters' specification. Each method of the `ContentAdapter` class represents an adapter subroutine which performs the adaptation of a particular rich interface component represented in the metamodel. The `adapt` method performs the dynamic reading of the requested Web document and invokes the suitable `ContentAdapter`'s method to adapt its interface components. The Java API Document Object Model (DOM)[12] has been used to implement the dynamic adaptation. This API allows, at runtime,

[12] http://download.oracle.com/javase/7/docs/api/org/w3c/dom/package-summary.html.

manipulating XML documents that follow the World Wide Web Consortium (W3C)'s DOM recommendation, such as XHTML and HTML ones. It provides functionalities for reading and writing these documents in the Web server's memory by structuring them into a tree of DOM objects (e.g. `Node`, `Document`, `Element`). This capability makes possible to analyze and to modify dynamically the document's interfaces as necessary. In order to work properly the DOM API requires well-formed XML files as input. However, since many documents available on the Web do not satisfy this requirement, the TagSoup[13] parser was used to correct features like missing and mismatching tags in order to get the DOM tree of the corrected document before processing the dynamic interface adaptation.

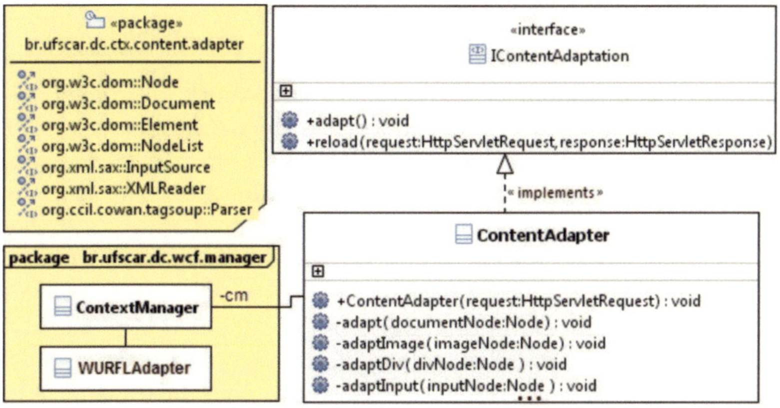

Fig. 7. Content adapters' specification

To guide the interface adaptation, the `ContentAdapter` class consumes contextual information on the current access device profile and adjusts the document's interface according to the device's peculiarities. As presented in the class diagram in Figure 7, this information is provided by the `ContextManager` class, which obtains the device profiles from the public XML database called Wireless Universal Resource File (WURFL)[14] using the services provided by the `WURFLAdapter` class. The WURFL stores the profiles of thousands[15] of devices from different brands and models and is used by software developers to guide the creation of appropriate solutions for specific devices. Because it is a public database, the WURFL receives updates on a daily basis by developers spread around the world interested in contributing to completeness and correctness of the information contained therein. As it receives continuous updates from the community development itself, the WURFL was adopted as the main context source from which the device profiles are acquired in this work.

Some of the content adaptation rules implemented in the content adapters are illustrated in Figure 8. For example, as in the first rule, the adaptation of the interface's input text fields (`inputNode`) will only occur if their length attribute (`size`) exceeds the number of visible columns on the current device's screen. The second rule states that any image in the interface (`imageNode`) should be adapted when its `width` and `height` properties exceed the screen resolution of the user's current device.

[13] http://home.ccil.org/~cowan/XML/tagsoup/.
[14] http://wurfl.sourceforge.net/.
[15] The last WURFL's update, available in August 29, 2011, contained about 15,093 device profiles.

```
Rule 1:
 Conditions
  inputNode.size > DEVICE_DISPLAY_COLUMNS_NUMBER
  AND (inputNode.type == "text" OR inputNode.type == "password")
 Actions
  adaptInput(inputNode)

Rule 2:
 Conditions
  imageNode.height > DEVICE_DISPLAY_RESOLUTION_HEIGHT
  OR imageNode.width > DEVICE_DISPLAY_RESOLUTION_WIDTH
 Actions
  adaptImage(imageNode)
```

Fig. 8. Content adaptation rules

Figure 9 illustrates the operation of the interface adaptation performed by the content adapters in a hybrid fashion. When a client accesses the application, the HTTP request is intercepted by an application *Servlet*[16] specifically designed to address the adaptations (①). The *Servlet* triggers the whole interface adaptation process by invoking the `ContentAdapter`'s `adapt` method (②). The `ContentAdapter` then asks the `ContextManager` the access device profile (③), which is retrieved from the WURFL database through the `WURFLAdapter` class (④). Next the static adaptation part is consummated with the selection and processing of the requested Web page from the most appropriate interface version, stored in the application's Web directory, according to the recovered device profile (⑤). Afterwards, in order to carry out the dynamic adaptation part, the `ContentAdapter` creates a DOM tree of the chosen page into the server's memory, corrects its ill-written excerpts, and identifies the interface snippets that need to be refined to meet the current device profile by applying the content adaptation rules implemented in the content adapters (⑥). The necessary adjustments are then applied, and the DOM tree of the adapted page is converted back into a Web page (⑦). Then, the page is written in the output stream of HTTP response by the `ContentAdapter` (⑧). Finally, the control flow is returned to the application *Servlet* (⑨) and the adapted page is sent to the user's device (⑩).

After performing the DE step's activities, there will be the artifacts that support the construction of adaptive rich interfaces for interactive ubiquitous applications of different application projects in the AE step. In the Model Driven RichUbi, the DE is performed whenever it is necessary to include new rich interface components in the metamodel (e.g. video display, drag-and-drop components), to build new M2C transformations (e.g. templates for generating WML code), and to implement new content adapters or to refine the existing ones.

3.2 Application Engineering (AE)

The main goal of the AE is to build applications of a certain problem domain focusing primarily on software reuse. In a general way, the AE is dedicated to the study of the best techniques, processes and methods for building applications based on the reuse of software artifacts. In this step, software components previously developed in the DE are reused for the development of applications in the focused problem domain (Griss et al., 1998).

---

[16] http://www.oracle.com/technetwork/java/overview-137084.html.

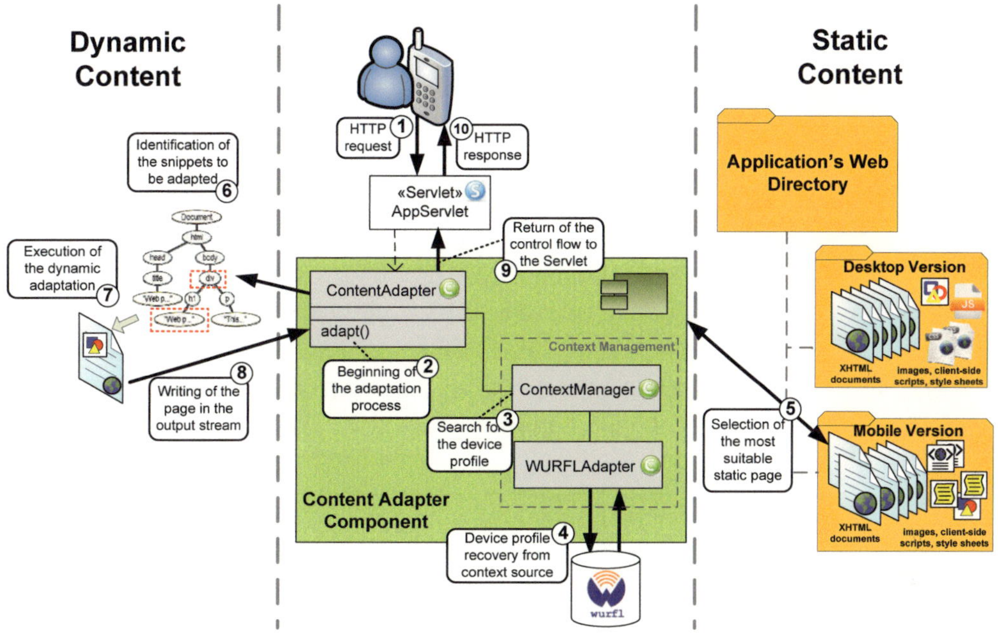

Fig. 9. Illustration of the hybrid adaptation operation

As shown in the SADT diagram in Figure 10, the activities defined for the AE step in the Model Driven RichUbi cover the Analysis, Design, Implementation and Testing disciplines from the software life-cycle. It extends the conventional software development processes by including the MDD and DSM conceptions, and it is focused on developing rich interfaces for interactive ubiquitous applications through the reuse of the artifacts produced in the process' DE step. The usage of the Rich Interfaces Domain metamodel in this step facilitates the application's interface modeling. Besides, the M2C transformations enable automating most of the interface's codification, which makes faster the Application Engineer's tasks. In addition, the content adapters provide decoupled functionalities for dynamic interface adaptation, allowing keeping focus on the development of features related to other application's functional and nonfunctional requirements.

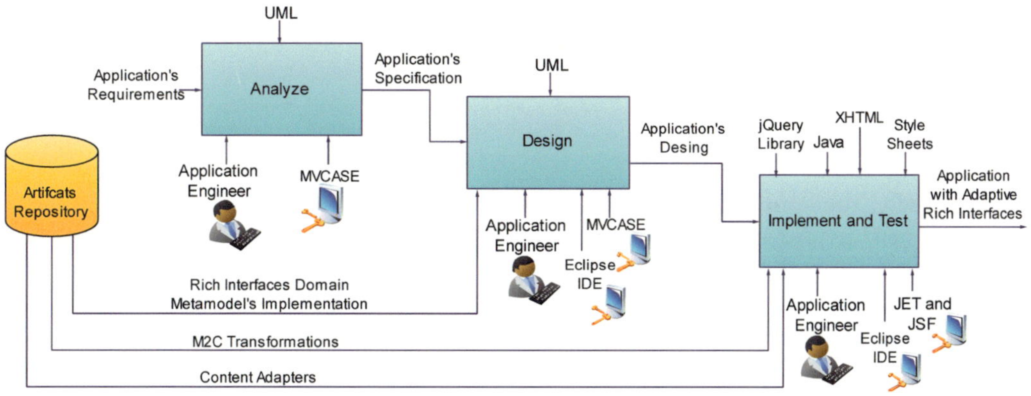

Fig. 10. Application Engineering step

In order to illustrate the description of each AE's activities, the Web module of a ubiquitous application from the Electronic Health Records (EHR) domain has been developed by reusing the metamodel, the M2C transformations and the content adapters. This application allows cardiologists and other healthcare professionals to monitor blood pressure data of their patients from anywhere through both desktops and smartphones (Menezes et al., 2011). Such an application consists of three distinct parts: the first one, which is installed on the patients' mobile devices, records the blood pressure data reported by the patients and transmits these data to a server; the second one, which runs on the server, handles the sent data and persists them in a database; and the third one, which also runs on the server, is the Web module, named WebRES, that provides an rich interface for allowing caregivers to remotely analyze the blood pressure status of their patients.

The SADT diagram in Figure 10 already reflects the AE step's instantiation with all technologies, controls and mechanisms necessary to build the WebRES.

3.2.1 Analyze

In this activity the application is specified according to its requirements. In the process, this specification can be accomplished by using UML techniques, such as class and use cases diagrams. For instance, Figure 11(a) shows a stretch of the use cases diagram developed by the Application Engineer through the MVCASE tool to specify the WebRES' requirements. These requirements include the nonfunctional ones, such as user authentication, and also the functional ones, like recovering the patients' blood pressure records. Figure 11(b) shows a class diagram that specifies some of the domain entities associated with the WebRES.

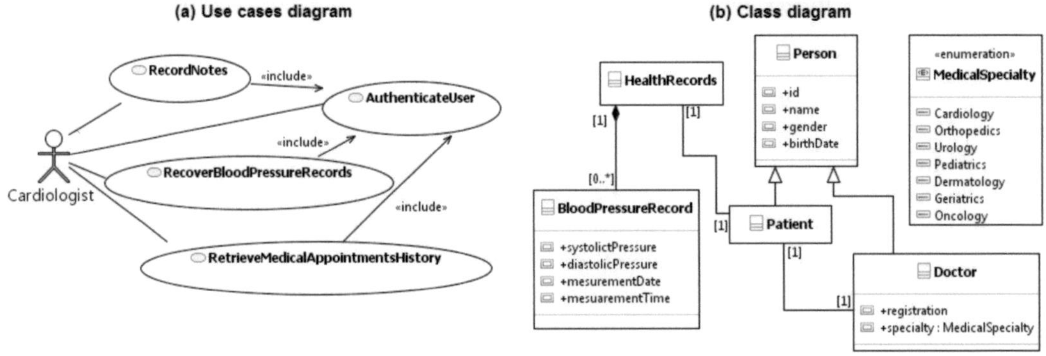

Fig. 11. WebRES' specification

3.2.2 Design

In this activity, the application's specification from previous activity is refined with design decisions, such as the inclusion of low-level details of technologies, and hardware and software platforms which enable implementing the application (e.g. Java EE[17] platform, JavaServer Faces[18] framework). Moreover, based on the specified use cases, the Application Engineer also performs the application's interface modeling by instantiating the Rich

[17] http://www.oracle.com/technetwork/java/javaee/index.html.
[18] http://www.oracle.com/technetwork/java/javaee/javaserverfaces-139869.html.

Interfaces Domain metamodel. In the models must be included appropriate rich interfaces components that meet, as much as possible, each of the specification's use cases.

For example, Figure 12 shows, on the left-hand side, the WebRES' interfaces model built through the model editor plug-in integrated into the MVCASE tool. On the right-hand side there is the components diagram illustrating the corresponding instantiation of the metamodel. In the editor the interface models are created in the Eclipse's default EMF tree view mode. The icons are shown in the model due to a light-weight mechanism for concrete syntax, which enabled associating one representative icon with each interface component defined in the underlying metamodel. As shown in the figure, the AuthenticateUser and `RecoverBloodPressureRecords` WebRES's use cases were mapped, respectively, into an authentication form inside a login page, and a search form inside a tabbed panel in a page designed for searching blood pressure records.

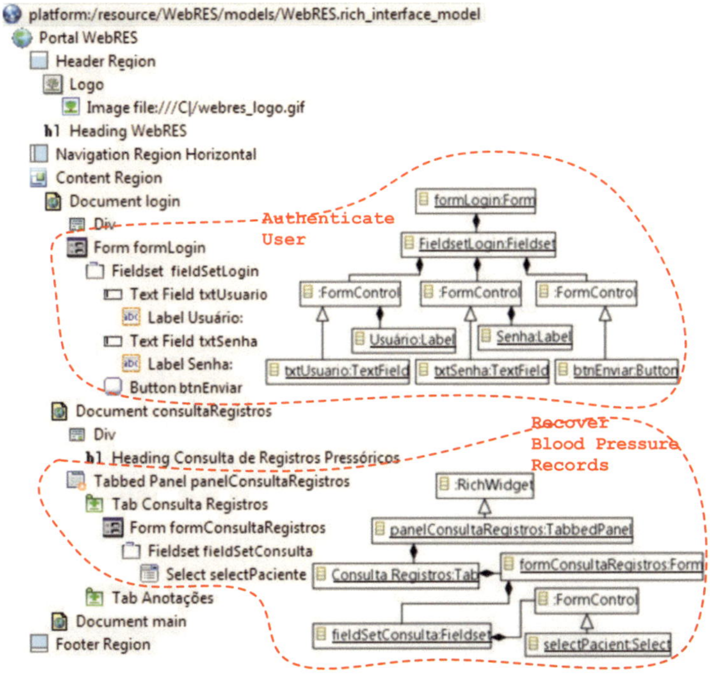

Fig. 12. WebRES' interfaces model instantiated from the Rich Interfaces Domain metamodel

3.2.3 Implement and test

In this activity the application's coding and testing are performed according to the application's design, focusing on the implementation of its adaptive rich interfaces.

By using the M2C transformations' plug-in in the MVCASE tool, the transformations are executed on the interface models in order to generate the partial code of the application's static interface versions. For example, for the WebRES the M2C transformations were used to partially produce its interfaces versions for desktop and smartphones. Afterwards, the output code must be manually complemented by the Application Engineer until finishing the application's interfaces. This task involves handwriting code of features not covered by the interface models, such as data retrieving from external sources, custom style sheets, JavaScript functions, business logic routines, navigability, and other necessary features.

Moreover, the dynamic content adapters are incorporated into the application in order to assign the adaptive behavior to its interfaces versions. Figure 13 shows, for instance, the code of the WebRES' *Servlet*, called `ContextServlet`, in which the reuse of the content adapters was accomplished in such application. The `doGet` method intercepts every HTTP requests and then invocates the `adapt` method from the `ContentAdapter` class in order to process the hybrid interface adaptation according to the current access device's capabilities.

```
package br.ufscar.dc.webres.servlets;
import br.ufscar.dc.ctx.content.adapter.ContentAdapter;
public class ContextServlet extends HttpServlet {
  private ContentAdapter ca;

  public ContextServlet() {
      super();
  }
  protected void doGet(HttpServletRequest request,
          HttpServletResponse response)
              throws ServletException, IOException {
      if (ca == null) {
          ca = new ContentAdapter(request, response);
      } else {
          ca.reload(request, response);
      }
      ca.adapt();
  }
}
```

Fig. 13. Content adapters reuse in the WebRES' *Servlet*

Finally, the tests of the interfaces provide feedback for the previous AE step's activities. Figure 14 shows the results of the tests with the WebRES' interfaces performed on an iPhone and a desktop. Figure 14(a) shows the execution of the page for searching blood pressure records on the iPhone emulator, to which the interface version for smartphones adapted in compliance to the iPhone's characteristics (e.g. screen width) was delivered. Figure 14(b) shows the same page viewed on a personal computer, to which the desktop version has been delivered.

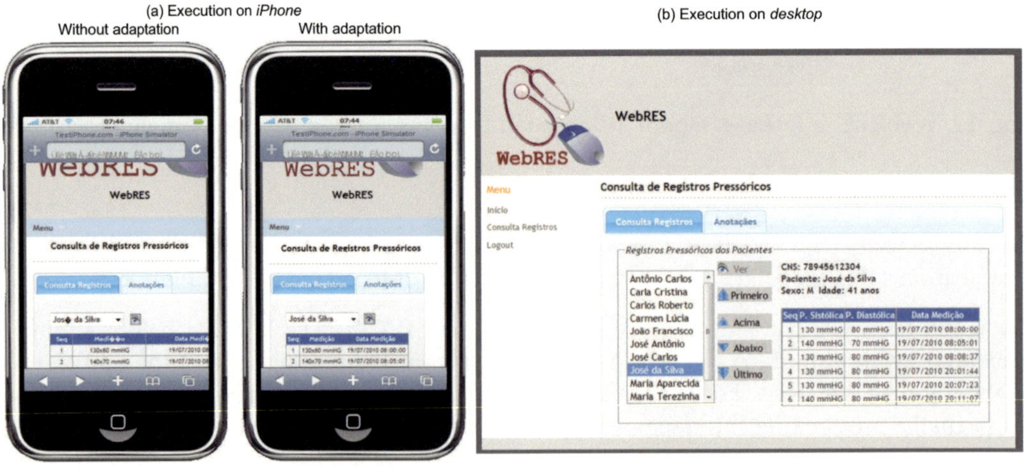

Fig. 14. Tests with the WebRES' interfaces performed on an iPhone and a desktop

4. Model Driven RichUbi evaluation

In order to assess the proposed process, an experiment was conducted following the Definition, Planning, Operation, and Analysis experimental phases, as defined in Wohlin et al. (2000). The experimentation was performed in the second semester of 2010 and consisted of a comparative study between the use of the Model Driven RichUbi for building adaptive rich interfaces and the non-use of a model driven process , based on the classic life cycle, for the same purpose.

To carry out the experiment, a ubiquitous application for tracking people, designed especially for the execution of the experiment, has been used. In such application, named TrackMe, the tracking is done based on the location of the Access Points (APs) in which users have connected recently. It consists of three distributed parts: the first one, running on the users' device, performs the users' registration in the nearest AP; the second one, which runs on a server, processes the users' records and stores them in a database; and the last one, also hosted on the server, is a Web module that provides a rich interface for visualizing the users' positions on the map of the locality in which the APs are distributed.

The experiment has been carried out in the Teaching Laboratory of the Computer Science Department at Federal University of São Carlos - UFSCar (Brazil). It was conducted with 31 volunteer students in 3rd and 4th years from Computer Science and Engineering undergraduate courses, enrolled in the Topics in Computer Science discipline. These students were split into 10 homogeneous groups according to their experience levels, so that each group had, as much as possible, similar experience level averages. The participants' experience was quantified by the participants' characterization form - document used to capture the participants' expertise with the subjects related to the study (e.g. MDD, Java, XHTML, CSS). The allocation of the participants in the groups was done in an unbalanced manner in order to reflect teams with varying numbers of members. The assignment of the groups to one of the process was accomplished in a completely random way so that the experiment's results were not biased.

The participants' task during the experiment operation was to develop part of the interface versions of the TrackMe's Web module, so that it could properly be viewed from both smartphones and desktops. These versions had been previously specified. This specification was delivered to the participants carry out the experiment. Moreover, since the focus of the study was on the application's presentation layer development, the aplication's features related to functional requirements had already been implemented. The groups then received the partially implemented application's project, which should be imported to their development environment for building the missing interfaces. Each group was provided with a support material with guidelines that aided them during the activities for building the interfaces.

The groups assigned to apply the Model Driven RichUbi followed the activities of the process' Application Engineering step for building the TrackMe's interfaces, starting from the Design activity. All the process' support mechanisms were provided to these groups, namely: the model editor and the M2C transformations Eclipse plug-ins integrated into the MVCASE tool, and the java archive of the content adapters for supporting the hybrid interfaces adaptation. On the other hand, the groups assigned to apply the classic life cycle performed the traditional Design, Implementation and Testing activities for developing the interfaces. In order to improve the comparison of the efficiency between the groups from both processes, the groups which followed the classic life cycle employed a purely static adaptation strategy to construct the interfaces. For simplicity, these groups should only develop two specialized interface versions: one for desktops and another one for iPhones.

During the experiment operation, all groups recorded in a form the start and finish times of each activity performed, and the number of lines of code (LOC) automatically and manually implemented. Only the code related to the rich interfaces has been considered during the LOC counting (e.g. XHTML code, JavaScript routines, custom style sheets). In the case of the groups assigned to the classic life cycle, which did not use transformations for code generation, it has been considered as automatically generated code the one created by the development environment itself, such as pre-fabricated Web page templates, standard style sheets, and others.

4.1 Experiment operation

The groups performed the experiment's trials as defined in the experimental plan. Table 1 presents the data collected by the groups in operating the experiment. The data are arranged in two blocks in the table: the upper part lists the data from the groups that have applied the Model Driven RichUbi process; and the bottom part shows the data from the groups which performed the classic life cycle. The table's columns labeled as "Total LOC", "Total Time (τ)" and "Productivity (þ)" represent, respectively, the total number of lines of code produced by the groups, the total time spent by them for constructing the interface versions, and the groups' productivity in terms of LOC produced per hour.

The groups were instructed to report technical problems faced during experiment operation. To this end, in the groups' data collection forms were placed appropriate fields in which the groups should fill out with the problems' description and their corresponding identification and resolution times. The total time spent by each group to solve problems is summarized in the "Problems" column in Table 1. This time was not deducted from the groups' overall time since technical problems may occur in any development process.

4.2 Results analysis and interpretation

From a preliminary analysis of the data presented in Table 1, some noticeable aspects could be remarked among the groups which applied both processes. The groups have spent similar times in designing and testing the developed interface versions. However, one can observe a significant effort reduction in the implementation for the groups that applied the Model Driven RichUbi in relation to the groups which followed the classic life cycle. While the latter spent, on average, 49 minutes for coding the interfaces, the former took, on average, only 18 minutes to complete that same task (63.3% reduction).

Even though having spent less time for implementing the interfaces, the groups of the Model Driven RichUbi were more productive (average of 301 LOC per hour) than the ones of the classic life cycle (average of 104 LOC per hour). The total LOC average of the groups which applied the Model Driven RichUbi was 277, while the other groups' was about 156. This inverse relationship between time spent and total LOC is due to the use of M2C transformations in the Model Driven RichUbi's implementation task. The data provide evidence that development efforts can be significantly reduced without adversely affecting

	Group	Design Start Time	Design Finish Time	Impl. Start Time	Impl. Finish Time	Test Start Time	Test Finish Time	Auto-matic LOC	Manual LOC	Total LOC	Prob-lems	Total Time (τ)	Produc-tivity (þ)
Model Driven Rich Ubi	G1	16:37	17:06	17:06	17:25	17:25	18:08	289	64	353	00:43	01:31	233
	G4	16:35	17:17	17:18	17:43	17:43	17:50	200	45	245	00:11	01:15	196
	G5	16:40	17:01	17:01	17:12	17:12	17:34	282	48	330	00:00	00:54	367
	G9	16:37	16:54	16:54	17:19	17:19	17:21	125	40	165	00:02	00:44	225
	G10	16:42	16:50	16:51	17:04	17:04	17:18	252	40	292	00:11	00:36	487
	Average	**00:23**		**00:18**		**00:17**		**230**	**47**	**277**	**00:13**	**01:00**	**301**
Classic Life Cycle	G2	16:30	17:15	17:15	18:00	18:00	18:15	0	232	232	00:35	01:45	133
	G3	16:37	16:52	16:52	18:03	18:03	18:11	12	75	87	00:34	01:34	56
	G6	16:40	16:41	16:41	17:40	17:40	18:10	24	149	173	00:30	01:30	115
	G7	16:40	17:33	17:33	18:00	17:53	18:04	26	94	120	00:38	01:24	86
	G8	---	---	16:42	17:27	17:28	18:00	36	132	168	00:32	01:18	129
	Average	**00:22**		**00:49**		**00:19**		**20**	**136**	**156**	**00:33**	**01:30**	**104**

Table 1. Experiment's data

the teams' productivity, since most of the coding tasks can be encapsulated in the transformations - which is usual in MDD-based processes. As shown in Table 1, on average, 83% of the code implemented by the groups of Model Driven RichUbi was automatically generated by the transformations (≈ 230 LOC). On the other hand, the groups of the classic life cycle, which did not use code generators, had, on average, only 13% of their code automatically generated by the development environment itself (≈ 20 LOC).

After these initial remarks, the step of obtaining the experimental findings from the research hypotheses was performed, as described in next subsection.

4.3 Research hypotheses testing

Three hypotheses regarding the effect of the development process on the experiment's results were prepared. To formulate these hypotheses, the following metrics were considered:

- τ - The total time spent by the team for building the adaptive rich interfaces versions;
- þ - The team's productivity in building the adaptive rich interfaces versions, in terms of produced LOC per time unit (þ = LOC/τ);
- μ_τ - The average time spent by the teams for building the adaptive rich interfaces versions; and
- $\mu_þ$ - The team's average productivity in building the adaptive rich interfaces versions.
  The null hypothesis (the hypothesis that one wants to reject) and its corresponding alternative ones (the hypotheses that one wants to check) are:
- Null Hypothesis (H_0): "In general, there is no difference between teams using the Model Driven RichUbi process and teams using the process based on the classic life cycle for building adaptive rich interfaces, with respect to the team's efficiency (Є)". H_0 can then be formalized as follows:
  H_0: $Є_{RichUbi} = Є_{Classic} \Rightarrow \mu_{\tau RichUbi} = \mu_{\tau Classic}$ e $\mu_{þRichUbi} = \mu_{þClassic}$
- First Alternative Hypothesis (H_1): "Teams using the Model Driven RichUbi process for building adaptive rich interfaces are, in general, more efficient than teams using the classic life cycle". It can be formally expressed in the following way:
  H_1: $Є_{RichUbi} > Є_{Classic} \Rightarrow \mu_{\tau RichUbi} < \mu_{\tau Classic}$ e $\mu_{þRichUbi} > \mu_{þClassic}$
- Second Alternative Hypothesis (H_2): "Teams using the classic life cycle for building adaptive rich interfaces are, in general, more efficient than teams using the Model Driven RichUbi process". It, in turn, can be formalized as follows:
  H_2: $Є_{RichUbi} < Є_{Classic} \Rightarrow \mu_{\tau RichUbi} > \mu_{\tau Classic}$ e $\mu_{þRichUbi} < \mu_{þClassic}$

In a preliminary analysis of the data collected in the experiment, one observes that the use of the Model Driven RichUbi process has apparently contributed for increasing the groups' efficiency. To demonstrate this effect in a statistical way, the *t-test* has been applied on the experiment's data. This parametric test is used to compare two independent samples by checking if their averages are statistically different at a given degree of significance. So, the test's goal is to verify whether the hypothetical effect can be demonstrated.

In the performed experiment, the samples were composed by the data concerning the groups' productivity (þ) as well as the total time (τ) spent by the groups to build the interface versions. Therefore, the *t-test* has been applied on samples' dataset in two separate steps. In the first one, the samples related to the groups' total times were compared. In the second one, the comparison was performed with the samples regarding the groups' productivity. The null hypothesis testing was based on the combination of the rejection criteria of the two test's steps. This way, H_0 would be rejected if, and only if, it could be rejected according to both total time and productivity criteria.

Test's 1st step: $H_{0\tau}$: $\mu_{\tau RichUbi} = \mu_{\tau Classic}$

By applying the *t-test* it has been possible to reject the null hypothesis that there is no difference between the groups' total times averages with $p < 0.05$ ($p = 0.03758509$).

Test's 2nd step: $H_{0þ}$: $\mu_{þRichUbi} = \mu_{þClassic}$

By applying the *t-test* it has been possible to reject the null hypothesis that there is no difference between the groups' productivity averages with $p < 0.05$ ($p = 0.02052551$).

Since the null hypothesis H_0 could be rejected at a lower degree of significance in the two test's step, it was possible to draw conclusions about the experiment's results. The test's results demonstrates that the alternative hypothesis H_1 can be validated rather the H_2, i.e., the data provide evidence which enable claiming that teams using the Model Driven RichUbi process for building adaptive rich interfaces are, in general, more effective than teams which use the classic life cycle one. This conclusion is in line with initial expectations about the experiment, although they have not been formally stated in the hypotheses. The expectations were that the reusable artifacts built in the Model Driven RichUbi's DE step (Rich Interfaces Domain metamodel, M2C transformations and content adapters) could make more agile the developers' tasks.

Finally, considering that the experiment was performed in-vitro under controlled conditions, it is important to notice the conclusions about the current results are limited to the scope of software developers in university environment in which this study was conducted. In order to expand the generalisability of the observed phenomenon, it is necessary new experiments to be conducted in other contexts for a more comprehensive validation of the research hypotheses.

5. Related work

Several works related to the development of adaptive interfaces and context-sensitive applications have been proposed by academic community, including processes (e.g. Vieira et al., 2011), tools (e.g. Viana & Andrade, 2008; Paternò et al., 2008; Gajos & Weld, 2004) and frameworks (e.g. Forte et al. 2008; Woensel et al., 2009).

Contextual Elements Modeling and Management through Incremental Knowledge Acquisition (CEManTIKA) (Vieira et al., 2011) is a generic approach proposed to support the design of context-sensitive applications in different domains. This approach has, among other components, a process that defines Software Engineering activities related to context specification and the design of context-sensitive applications.

XMobile (Viana & Andrade, 2008) is an environment for generating adaptive interfaces of form-based applications for mobile devices. It consists of a framework of abstract user interface components, which allows modeling the application interfaces, as well as a tool to support code generation at development time. Semantic Transformer (Paternò et al., 2008) is a tool used for automatic transformation of Web pages originally designed for desktop platform into Web pages suitable for mobile devices. This tool acts as a Proxy which detects HTTP requests originated from mobile devices and processes the requested Web page by placing it in an adequate format for viewing on mobile devices.

Extended Internet Content Adaptation Framework (EICAF) (Forte et al. 2008) is a framework for Web applications' content adaptation. EICAF applies ontologies for describing the profiles of devices, users and other relevant entities, and employs Web services for performing content adaptation by combining contextual information from the profiles.

Semantic Context-aware Ubiquitous Scout (SCOUT) (Woensel et al., 2009) is a framework for building context-sensitive applications for mobile devices. SCOUT allows mapping real world entities (e.g., people, places, objects) into virtual entities on the Web, so that the resources/services provided by these entities become location-specific and accessible when users are close to them.

The Model Driven RichUbi process presented in this chapter is based on several characteristics of the work described above. In addition, it has its own contributions through the evolution and adaptation of the related work's concepts. CEManTIKA, for instance, proposes a general-purpose approach, with recommendations for building context-sensitive applications for any domain. On the other hand, the Model Driven RichUbi focuses on the needs of a specific domain - the Rich Interfaces one -, providing suitable guidelines and artifacts closer to that domain's concepts in order to facilitate the development of adaptive rich interfaces. Regarding the XMobile and the Semantic Transformer tools, the proposed process is distinguished by combining the concepts of MB-UID, DSM and context sensitivity, furnishing support mechanisms that help automating most of the coding tasks for different technologies through the interfaces' modeling, and enable to adapt the interfaces' code in a hybrid manner. Both EICAF and SCOUT frameworks present contributions for software reuse in the context-sensitive ubiquitous applications development. The content adapters, which support the hybrid adaptation employed in the proposed process, extend these conceptions by adjusting them for the development of adaptive rich interfaces.

6. Conclusion

Ubiquitous Computing has imposed a series of additional requirements to software development. Among these requirements there is the need to adapt both application's content and behavior to the heterogeneity of users' computing devices and the environment in which they are immersed. In view of this, this work has proposed the Model Driven RichUbi process to address the rich interfaces adaptation issues for interactive ubiquitous applications. The process, which is based on the MDD and DSM conceptions, defines a domain metamodel that constitutes a DSL to support the application's rich interfaces modeling, and M2C transformations to semi-automate the interfaces' static coding for different devices. In addition, the Model Driven RichUbi also provides guidelines for building content adapters that will refine the developed interfaces at runtime according to the access device's capabilities dynamically retrieved from the interaction context. All of these artifacts, produced in the process' Domain Engineering step, can be reused by application engineers to simplify their development tasks.

Although the focus of this work has been held on the Rich Interfaces Domain, it was noticed the Model Driven RichUbi process can be generalized to serve other domains. Except for the Construct Content Adapters activity, the remaining activities of the DE step, if generalized, can address the development of DSLs and M2C transformations which can be applied to any application domain.

7. Acknowledgment

The authors are thankful for the scholarships provided by the Brazilian Coordination for the Improvement of Higher Level Personnel (CAPES) which supported this work. We are also grateful to the students from the 2010's class, enrolled in the Topics in Computer discipline at UFSCar, for participating in the experiment performed in this work. We specially thank to Mr. Waldomiro Barioni Júnior, statistical researcher at Embrapa - Cattle-Southeast[19], and to Dr. Cecilia Candolo, professor and researcher at the UFSCar's Statistics Department[20], for their kind support and valuable contributions in the experiment's data analysis.

8. References

Araújo, R. B. (2003). Ubiquitous Computing: principles, technologies and challenges (Computação Ubíqua: princípios, tecnologias e desafios), Proceedings of the 21st Brazilian Symposium on Computer Networks, short-term course: text book, pp. 1-71

Baldauf, M.; Dustdar, S. & Rosenberg, F. (2007). A survey on context-aware systems, Int. J. Ad Hoc Ubiquitous Comput., Vol. 2, No. 4, pp. 263-277

Bazire, M. & Brézillon, P. (2005). Understanding context before using it, Proceedingos of the 5th Int. and Interdisciplinary Conference on Modeling and Using Context, pp. 29-40

Bittar, T. J. ; Fortes, R. P. ; Lobato, L. L. & Watanabe, W. M. (2009). Web communication and interaction modeling using model-driven development, Proceedings of the 27th ACM international Conference on Design of Communication, pp. 193-198

Blois, A. P.; Werner, C. M. L. & Becker, K. (2005). Towards a components grouping technique within a Domain Engineering process, Proceedings of the 31st EUROMICRO Conference on Software Engineering and Advanced Applications, pp. 18-25.

Brézillon, P. (1999). Context in problem solving: a survey, Knowl. Eng. Rev., Vol. 14, No. 1, pp. 47-80

Chavarriaga, E. & Macías, J. A. (2009). A model-driven approach to building modern Semantic Web-Based User Interfaces, Adv. Eng. Softw, Vol. 40, No. 12, Dec. 2009, pp. 1329-1334

[19] http://www.cppse.embrapa.br/English.
[20] http://www.des.ufscar.br/.

Cicchetti, A. ; Di Ruscio, D. & Di Salle, A. (2007). Software customization in model driven development of web applications, Proceedings of the 2007 ACM Symposium on Applied Comput, pp. 1025-1030

Cirilo, C. E.; Prado, A. F.; Souza, W. L. & Zaina, L. A. M. (2010a). Model Driven RichUbi A Model Driven Process for Building Rich Interfaces of Context-Sensitive Ubiquitous Applications, Proceedings of the 28th ACM International Conference on Design of Communication, pp. 207-214

Cirilo, C. E.; Prado, A. F.; Souza, W. L. & Zaina, L. A. M. (2010b). A Hybrid Approach for Adapting Web Graphical User Interfaces to Multiple Devices using Information Retrieved from Context, Proceedings of the 16th International Conference on Distributed Multimedia Systems - Globalization and Personalization, pp. 168-173.

Deitel, P. J. & Deitel, H. M. (2008). AJAX, Rich Internet Applications, and Web Development for Programmers, Prentice Hall PTR

Dey, A. K. (2001). Understanding and using context, Personal Ubiquitous Comput, Vol. 5, No. 1, pp. 4-7

Eisenstein, J.; Vanderdonckt, J. & Puerta, A. (2000). Adapting to mobile contexts with user-interface modeling, Proceedings of the IEEE Workshop on Mobile Computing Systems and Applications, pp. 83-92

France, R. & Rumpe, B. (2007). Model-driven development of complex software: a research roadmap, Proceedings of the 29th International Conference on Software Engineering - Future of Software Engineering, pp. 37-54

Forte, M.; Souza, W. L. & Prado, A. F. (2008). Using ontologies and Web services for content adaptation in Ubiquitous Computing, Journal of Systems and Software, Vol. 81, No. 3, March 2008, pp. 368-381

Gajos, K. & Weld, D. S. (2004). SUPPLE: automatically generating user interfaces, Proceedings of the 9th International Conference on Intelligent User Interfaces, pp. 93-100

Garlan, D. & Schmerl, B. (2001). Component-based software engineering in pervasive computing environments, Proceedings of the ICSE Workshop on Component-Based Software Engineering, Comp. Certification and Syst. Prediction, pp. 1-4

Gaspar, T. C. ; Yaguinuma, C. A. & Prado, A. F. (2009). Development of synchronous collaborative applications in the Web 2.0 (Desenvolvimento de aplicações colaborativas síncronas na Web 2.0), Proceedingos of the 15th Brazilian Symposium on Multimedia Systems and Web, short-term course: text book, pp. 168-207

Griss, M. L.; Favaro, J. & Alessandro, M. d. (1998). Integrating feature modeling with the RSEB, Proceedings of the 5th international Conference on Software Reuse, pp. 76-85

Hansmann, U.; Merk, L.; Nicklous, M. S. & Stober, T. (2003). Pervasive Computing. Springer-Verlag, Germany

Kelly, S. & Tolvanen, J. (2008). Domain-Specific Modeling: Enabling Full Code Generation. Wiley-IEEE Computer Society Press

Lucrédio, D. ; Alvaro, A. ; Almeida, E. S. & Prado, A. F. (2003). MVCASE Tool - Working with Design Patterns, Proceedings of the 3rd Latin American Conference on Pattern Languages of Programming

Lucrédio, D. (2009). A model-based approache for software reuse (Uma abordagem orientada a modelos para reutilização de software), PhD Thesis, Universidade de São Paulo, Instituto de Ciências Matemáticas e de Computação, São Carlos, Brazil

Menezes, A. L. ; Cirilo, C. E. ; Moraes, J. L. C., Souza, W. L. & Prado, A. F. (2010). Using Archetypes and Domain Specific Languages on Development of Ubiquitous Applications to Pervasive Healthcare, Proceedings of the 23rd IEEE International Symposium on Computer-Based Medical Systems, pp. 395–400

Norrie, M. C. (2008). PIM Meets Web 2.0, Proceedings of the 27th International Conference on Conceptual Modeling, pp. 15-25

O'Reilly, T. (2005). What is Web 2.0: Design Patterns and Business Models for the Next Generation of Software, http://oreilly.com/web2/archive/what-is-web-20.html

Paternò, F.; Santoro, C. & Scorcia, A. (2008). Automatically adapting web sites for mobile access through logical descriptions and dynamic analysis of interaction resources, Proceedings of the Working Conference on Advanced Visual interfaces, pp. 260-267

Ross, D. T. (1977). Structured Analysis (SA): A Language for Communicating Ideas, IEEE Trans. Softw. Eng.. Vol. 3, No. 1, January 1977, pp. 16-34

Sadilek, D. A. (2008) Prototyping domain-specific language semantics, Proceedings of the 23rd Companion to the ACM SIGPLAN Conference on Object-Oriented Programming Systems Languages and Applications, pp. 895-896

Serral, E.; Valderas, P. & Pelechano, V. (2010). Towards the model driven development of context-aware pervasive systems, Pervasive Mobile Comp., Vol. 6, No. 2, pp. 254-280

Singh, G. (2004). Guest editor's introduction: content repurposing, IEEE Multimedia, Vol. 11, No. 1, pp. 20-21, January 2004

Souza, W. L.; Prado, A. F.; Forte, M. & Cirilo, C. E. (2011). Content Adaptation in Ubiquitous Computing, Ubiquitous Computing, Eduard Babkin (Ed.), ISBN: 978-953-307-409-2, InTech, http://www.intechopen.com/articles/show/title/content-adaptation-in-ubiquitous-computing

Spínola, R. O.; Silva, J. L. M. & Travassos, G. H. (2007). Checklist to characterize ubiquitous software projects, Proceedings of the 21st Brazilian Symposium on Software Engineering, pp. 39-55

Vellis, G. (2009). Model-based development of synchronous collaborative user interfaces, Proceedings of the 1st ACM SIGCHI Symposium on Engineering interactive Comput. Systems, pp. 309-312

Viana, W. & Andrade, R. M. C. (2008). XMobile: a MB-UID environment for semi-automatic generation of adaptive applications for mobile devices, Journal of Systems and Software, Vol. 81, No. 3, pp. 382-394, March 2008

Vieira, V. ; Tedesco, P. & Salgado, A. C. (2011). Designing context-sensitive systems: An integrated approach, Expert Syst. Appl., Vol. 38, No. 2, pp. 1119-1138

Weiser, M. (1991). The Computer for the 21st Century, Scientific American, Vol. 265, No. 3, September 1991, pp. 66-75

Woensel, W. ; Casteleyn, S. & Troyer, O. (2009). A Framework for Decentralized, Context-Aware Mobile Applications Using Semantic Web Technology, Proceedings of the Confederated int. Workshops and Posters on on the Move To Meaningful internet Systems, pp. 88-97.

Wohlin, C.; Runeson, P.; Höst, M.; Ohlsson, M.; Regnell, B. & Wesslén, A. (2000). Experimentation in Software Engineering: an introduction. Kluwer Academic Publishers, USA

Zakas, N. C.; McPeak, J. & Fawcett, J. (2007). Professional AJAX, Wrox

12

Using RFID/NFC and QR-Code in Mobile Phones to Link the Physical and the Digital World

Mabel Vazquez-Briseno, Francisco I. Hirata*,
Juan de Dios Sanchez-Lopez, Elitania Jimenez-Garcia,
Christian Navarro-Cota and Juan Ivan Nieto-Hipolito
*Autonomous University of Baja California,*CICESE,*
Mexico

1. Introduction

Today it is clear that the most widely used device in the world is the mobile phone. Phones are mostly voice-centric devices, but a wide range of mobile devices now exist on the market offering multiple services and functions. The term *smartphone* is now used to characterize a mobile phone with special computer-enabled features. Despite the mobile phone evolution, one of the main disadvantages of these devices is that they still have insufficient input capabilities, providing tiny keyboards to do manual entries. Fortunately most smartphones are now equipped with several sensors that can be used to enhance and create new users interfaces. This is the case for integrated cameras that can be used to read visual codes, like Quick Response (QR) Code as well as other sensing technologies such as Radio Frequency Identification (RFID) and the associated Near Field Communications (NFC). The use of these technologies does not only facilitate entering information, but it also allows using mobile phones for interactions with people, places and things, enhancing the usability and usefulness of these devices. The use of QR Codes and RFID tags has significantly evolve in the last decades, they were first used to track products in the industry, but now they have contributed to develop several new concepts that integrate the physical world with the virtual one.

In this chapter we describe RFID/NFC and QR-Code technologies. We present the methodologies and the software Application Program Interfaces (APIs) associated with these technologies for their use in mobile phones. QR-Code readers already available on mobile phones are also described and compared. In addition we present several mobile services and projects that base their functionality on the use of these technologies.

2. Identification, sensing and communication technologies

Automatic identification and data capture (AIDC) techniques provide fast, easy and accurate data collection methods. Once data is captured it can be stored or analyzed by a computer or another device. AIDC methods in general do not require human involvement

* Corresponding Author

in order to capture data, these methods include technologies like: barcodes, biometrics, RFID and others.

Today, AIDC techniques are mostly used on products for inventory control, quality control, and product life cycle management using devices specially designed for reading the corresponding tags including barcode scanners, magnetic stripe readers, among others. However, AIDC techniques can be used for many other applications not very well known. Recently the mobile industry is also considering the use of these methods, but some of them are not fully supported by all mobile phones. We consider that the most suitable AIDC methods for mobile phones are QR code and RFID/NFC. These technologies are described in the following sections.

2.1 Radio Frequency Identification (RFID) / Near Field Communication (NFC)

RFID is an AIDC method that uses radio waves to store and retrieve data from an identification chip. These chips are known as RFID tags. RFID is now widely used in the industry for several applications including security, access control, transportation and tracking of the supply chain. Usually an RFID system requires three main components: The reader/writer, RFID tag and application software for processing the information. The RFID reader comprises an antenna, a transceiver and decoder. The reader periodically transmits signals to search for tags in their vicinity. When it captures a signal from a tag, it extracts the information and passes the data to the processing subsystem. An RFID tag or transponder consists of an antenna, a radio transceiver and integrated circuit for storing and processing information. There are several types of tags. A tag contains writable memory where data is stored to be transfer later to RFID readers. The internal memory capacity of a tag depends on its model and varies from tens to thousands of bytes. RFID technology is classified into the short-range wireless communications, which are systems that cover distances of less than 100 meters. Others systems of this type are: Bluetooth, IrDA and Wi-Fi.

Near Field Communication (NFC) is also a short-range high frequency wireless communication technology which enables the exchange of data between devices at distances fewer than 10 cm. This technology is an upgrade to RFID technology; it was designed and marketed by the NFC Forum. Table 1 shows a comparison among different technologies of short-range communication. Bluetooth and IrDA are not compatible with NFC but they can be used in combination, for instance NFC can be used for pairing (authenticating) a Bluetooth session used for the transfer of data (Ortiz, 2008). On the other hand NFC is compatible with RFID and basically, both technologies use the same working standards. NFC can be seen as an evolution of RFID, both of them use radiofrequencies for communication; however RFID can operate in a long distance range, therefore it is not suitable for exchanging sensitive information since it can be vulnerable for various kinds of attacks. Contrary NFC has a very short transmission range, in this way NFC-based transactions are inherently secure.

The International Standard *Near Field Communication - Interface and Protocol, ISO/IEC 18092 (NFCIP-1)*, defines communication modes for NFC interface and protocol. According to this standard, NFC can operate in active or passive mode. In active mode, the devices generate their own electromagnetic field independently, while in passive mode only one of the devices is capable of generating an electromagnetic field and the other extracts energy from it to operate and transmit the required information. NFCIP-1 defines the following operating speeds: 106, 212, 424 and 848 Kb/s.

	NFC	RFID	IrDA	Bluetooth
Set-up time	<0.1 ms	<0.1 ms	~0.5 ms	6 s
Range	Up to 10 cm	Up to 3m	Up to 5m	Up to 30m
Usability	Human centric, Easy, intuitive, fast	Item centric, Easy	Data centric, Easy	Data centric, Medium
Selectivity	High, given, security	Partly given	Line of sight	non-selective
Uses cases	Pay, get Access, share, initiate service, easy set up	Item tracking	Control and exchange data	Network for data exchange headset
Consumer experience	Touch, simply connect	Get information	Easy	Configuration needed

Table 1. Comparing NFC to other close range communication technologies (Source: NFC Forum)

One of the key elements of NFC enabled devices is the ability to read different types of tags. This facility of NFC technology is a key enabler for many applications. NFC tags are passive devices with no power of their own. In order to read a tag the users almost touches it with an NFC-enabled device. A small amount of power is taken by the NFC tag from the reader/writer to power the tag electronics. The tag is then enabled to transfer a small amount of information to the NFC reader. An NFC-enabled device is capable of reading four basic tag types based on ISO 14443 types A and B which corresponds to contactless smartcards, as well as Sony FeliCa smartcards. The different NFC tag type definitions are as follows (NFC Forum, 2011):

- **Tag 1 Type:** Based on the ISO14443A standard. They are read and re-write capable. Memory availability is 96 bytes and is expandable up to 2 kbyte. The communication speed of this NFC tag is 106 kbit/s.
- **Tag 2 Type:** Based on ISO14443A. They are read and re-write capable. The basic memory size is 48 bytes and can be expanded to 2 kbyte. The communication speed is 106 kbit/s.
- **Tag 3 Type:** Based on the Sony FeliCa system. Memory availability is variable, theoretical memory limit is 1MByte per service.
- **Tag 4 Type:** Defined to be compatible with ISO14443A and B standards. These tags are pre-configured at manufacture and they can be read, re-writable, or read-only. They have a memory capacity up to 32 kbytes. The communication speed is in the range of 106 kbit/s and 424 kbit/s.

In addition, the NFC specification also includes a common data format to exchange and store information using NFC-enabled devices and tags. This is the Data Exchange Format (NDEF). It can be used to store different types of objects encapsulated in several records. Each record contains information about the data or payload that it encloses, for this, it includes three parameters: the payload length, the payload type, and an optional payload identifier. NDEF can be used to encapsulate one or more message payloads of different applications, which may be of different sizes and types. Type identifiers may be URIs, MIME media types, or NFC-specific types. The payload length is an unsigned integer which indicates the number of bytes and cross-references between them. Figure 1 shows a NDEF message. It consists of one or more records, where the first record is marked with the Message Begin (MB) flag and the last one with the Message End (ME) flag (NFC Forum, 2006). The minimum length of a message is one record. In this case both flags, MB and ME, are placed in the same record. It takes at least two records to consider a segment payload. There is no limit to the maximum number of records.

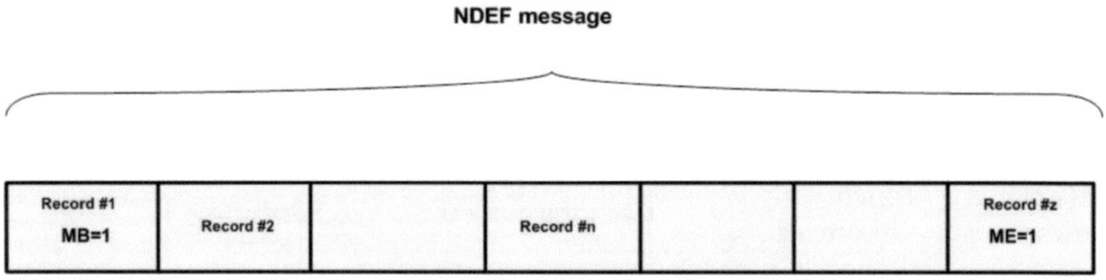

Fig. 1. NDEF message

2.2 Quick Response Code

Quick Response Code or QR Code is a two-dimensional (2D) bar code developed in 1994 by Denso Wave Corporation; QR Code got this name because it was developed to improve the reading speed of complex-structured 2D barcodes. This type of code was initially used for tracking inventory in vehicle parts manufacturing; now it is used in a diversity of industries and innovative applications. QR Code is established as an ISO standard, it has been defined in the *Information technology – Automatic identification and data capture techniques – QR code 2005 bar code symbology specification* (ISO/IEC18004). QR Code is free to use and the technology is open since its specification is disclosed and the patent right owned by *Denso Wave* is not exercised (Denso Wave Incorporated, n.d.).

The main characteristic of a QR Code compared with a traditional bar code is that it contains information in both the vertical and horizontal directions, while a bar code contains data in one direction only. For this reason QR code holds a considerably greater volume of information. In addition it can encode several types of data including symbols, control codes, binary data, and multimedia data. The typical barcode holds a maximum of 20 digits, while the maximum data capacities of a QR code are 7,089 characters for numeric data, 4,296 characters for alphanumeric data, 2,953 bytes for binary data, and 1,817 characters for Japanese Kanji and Kana data. Fig. 2 shows a QR Code compared with a traditional bar code.

Fig. 2. QR Code compared with a Bar Code [Source: http://www.qrcode.com/aboutqr-e.html]

QR Code is faster to read than other two-dimensional code, because it contains three large square patterns in the corners that are used for position detection. Additionally, the patterns are used to detect the size, the angle and the outer shape of the symbol. When a reader scans a symbol, it first detects these patterns. Once the position patterns have been detected the scanner can rapidly read the inside-code in all directions. The inside code consists of several small blocks where the information is encoded. The decoding speed of the QR Code can be 20 times faster than that of other 2D symbols (Soon, 2008). The structure of a QR code is shown in figure 3.

Fig. 3. Structure of a QR Code

The elements contained in a QR code are the following:

a. **Position Pattern**. Three big squares in the corners used for detecting the position, the size and the angle of the QR Code.
b. **Alignment Pattern.** A pattern used for correcting the distortion of the QR Code. These distortions could occur for example when attaching the codes onto a curved surface.
c. **Timing Pattern.** It consists in white and black modules arranged alternately and placed between two position patterns. It is used to determine the central coordinate of each cell in the QR Code.
d. **Quiet Zone.** A margin space that makes easier to detect the QR Code. At least four cells are required for the quiet zone.
e. **Data Area.** The area in the QR Code that contains the data (for example a URL) encoded in binary numbers. The data area also includes Reed-Solomon codes to provide error correction functionalities.

It can be observed that a QR includes information to provide error correction capability. Thanks to this capability it is possible to read the code even if it presents some distortions or damage. There are four different error correction levels, each one with an approximately percentage of the symbol area that can be restored at maximum: Level L (7%), M (15%), Q (25 %), and H (30%). This level can be configured by the user when he/she creates the symbol. If there is a high probability that the code will be distorted due to the usage environment, it is recommended to choose Level H for a 30% correction level.

There are 40 symbol versions of QR Code, each version has a different number of black squares that are called modules, more modules means that more information can be stored but also a bigger size of the QR Code. The minimum size is 21 x 21 modules (version 1) and the maximum size is 177 x 177 modules (version 40). Mobile applications use only versions 1 to 10 to take into account camera phone limitations (Kato & Tan, 2007).

QR code can be easily generated using free on-line generators. They can be printed on plain paper using an ordinary printer and attached to any object. Today we can see QR codes often in the media, like TV shows and newspapers. They are commonly used to store URLs or other small identifiers like e-mails and phone numbers that can be read using mobile devices. Once the information stored in the QR code is decoded the appropriate content is retrieved from a remote server, facilitating mobile navigation. Besides this, QR codes can have other several applications as explained in the following sections.

3. Using QR Code and RFID/NFC in mobile phones

The software and the application programming interfaces (APIs) required for providing the capability of reading QR Codes and RFID/NFC tags with a mobile phone depends on the operating system and the programming platform of the device. Currently there are several mobile operating systems and platforms available. The next sections explain the use of QR code and RFID/NFC in some of the most commonly used mobile platforms (e.g. Java ME, Android). Unfortunately at the moment (mid-2011), iPhone platform does not support RFID/NFC communication.

3.1 QR Code and mobile phones

QR codes can be decoded using mobile phones equipped with a camera and an appropriate scanner. In Java ME the mobile phone must support the Mobile Media API or MMAPI in order to take pictures. The MMAPI is documented as the JSR 135 in the Java Community Process (JCP); it extends the functionality of the Java ME platform by providing audio, video, and other time-based multimedia support to resource-constrained devices.

In Android platform the `Camera` class included in the `android.hardware` package is used to set image capture settings, start/stop preview, snap pictures, and retrieve frames for encoding video. The actual camera hardware is managed by the Camera service. The `Camera` class is a client of this service. To access the camera device, the CAMERA permission must be added to the Android Manifest. The manifest must include also the `<uses-feature>` element to declare camera features used by the application. To read QR-Codes the auto-focus feature must be included, as a result the manifest should include the following lines:

```
<uses-permission android:name="android.permission.CAMERA" />
<uses-feature android:name="android.hardware.camera" />
<uses-feature android:name="android.hardware.camera.autofocus" />
```

In the iPhone platform the `UIImagePickerController` class can be used for taking pictures and movies on supported devices.

Any Java ME based application requires taking a picture or snapshot, before any type of action can be performed. Others platforms like Android and iPhone can provide zero-click experience by using scanning type applications to read the code. In all cases an appropriate algorithm must be used to read and interpret the code.

Some recent mobile phones include pre-installed QR code readers, for example Nokia Barcode Reader is pre-installed on the N82, N93, N93i, N95, E66, E71 and E90 mobile phones (Nokia, 2008). Most Android mobile phones also include a preinstalled barcode reader. In addition there are several readers available for different mobile platforms like: *BeeTagg*, *QuickMark*, *Kaywa*, *Zxing*, among others. Once the appropriate QR code reader is installed on the mobile device, users only require taking a snapshot of the code to decode it. Additionally some readers are able to take the appropriate action depending on the code's content, for instance if the code contains an URL, the reader may launch a browser. Very few readers are open source providing the capability to developers to add more functionality to the reader besides the ones that it includes. Table 2 shows a comparison of the QR code readers that we consider the more popular at the moment.

Barcode-reader	Platform	Supported Codes	Features	Website
ZXing Reader	Android, iPhone, Java ME	UPC-A and UPC-E EAN-8 and EAN-13, QR Code, Data Matrix, and others.	Open source, developers can add new functionalities to the reader.	http://code.google.com/p/zxing/
i-Nigma	iPhone, Android, Windows Mobile, Symbian, Blacberry, Java Me	UPC-A and UPC-E EAN-8 and EAN-13, QR Code, Data Matrix, and others.	Provides a commercial SDK for developers to add barcode reading functionality to new mobile applications.	http://www.i-nigma.com
Scanlife Barcode Reader	Blackberry, Android, Symbian, iPhone, Brew, Windows Mobile, Java ME	UPC, EAN, QR Code, EZcode, Data Matrix	Commercial and personal use. Content can be interpreted as: Call, calendar, contacts, e-mail, web links, notes, MMS, SMS, or Twitter	http://web.scanlife.com/
QuickMark	Android, Symbian, iPhone, Windows mobile.	QR Code, Data Matriz, 1D Barcode	Content can be interpreted as: Call, contacts, e-mail, web links, MMS, SMS, or Location.	http://www.quickmark.com.tw/
Beetagg	Android, Symbian, Blackberry, Windows Mobile, Java ME.	BeeTagg Code, QR Code, Data Matrix, EAN-13 / UPC-A	Content can be interpreted as: Call, contacts, e-mail, web links, MMS, SMS, or Location	http://www.beetagg.com/
Kaywa	Symbian, Java ME	QR Code, Data Matrix,	Content can be interpreted as: URL, Text, phone-number, SMS.	http://reader.kaywa.com/
NeoReader	Symbian, Windows Mobile, Blackberry, Android, iPhone	Data Matrix, QR codes, Aztec Codes, EAN, UPC, and Code 128	Once content is read it tries to open it as URL, even if it is only text, it first redirects content to a proprietary server.	http://www.neoreader.com

Table 2. Comparison of QR Code readers

3.2 RFID/NFC in mobile phones

NFC technology is currently mainly intended to be used with mobile phones. As explained in section 2.1, this technology is based on a very short-range protocol that requires that the devices almost touch each other to establish communication or to read an RFID tag.

An NFC-enabled mobile device must have the appropriate hardware; it includes a Radio Frequency Unit, a baseband processor and a NFC Controller with an antenna. It also includes a secure smartcard chip known as the *secure element* that can be used for tag emulation mode allowing the mobile device to be used as a smart card. This means that the NFC-enabled mobile phone can operate in the following modes as depicted in figure 4:

a. Card emulation mode: Using the secure element the mobile device acts as a smart card following the ISO 14443 standard. Other devices and readers can use this mobile phone as a target to retrieve information.
b. Reader/Writer mode: The mobile device is used to read, edit or write information stored on a RFID tag or a smart card (it can be another mobile device).
c. Peer to peer mode: Two enabled-mobile devices are able to exchange information in a bidirectional connection.

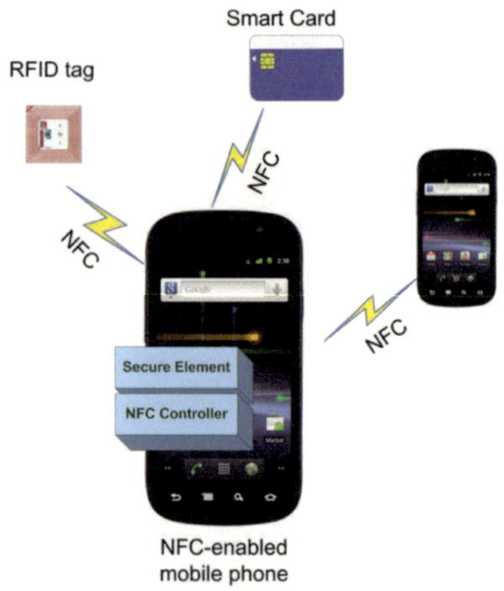

Fig. 4. NFC-enabled phone operating modes.

Besides the required hardware the mobile device must use appropriate software to establish an NFC connection. The next section describes the available APIs that can be used to implement NFC communication.

3.2.1 JSR-257

Nokia was the first one to introduce RFID/NFC enabled mobile phones. In 2007 the company launched the 6131 NFC phone, which was the first integrated NFC handset that was available to the public. Nokia Corporation also led the research group that developed the Contactless Communication API or JSR-257 (JSR 257 Expert Group, 2006), which is a Java ME optional package that allows applications to access information on contactless targets, such as RFID tags and bar codes, including QR-Codes. This API provides easy access to various targets, and provides mechanisms to discover and communicate with them transferring and receiving information. The API uses the NFC Data Packaging Format (NDEF) to exchange information between NFC devices and RFID tags. Using this data format the application developer can exchange NDEF formatted data with a target without knowing its physical type.

Figure 5 shows the structure of the Contactless Communication API.

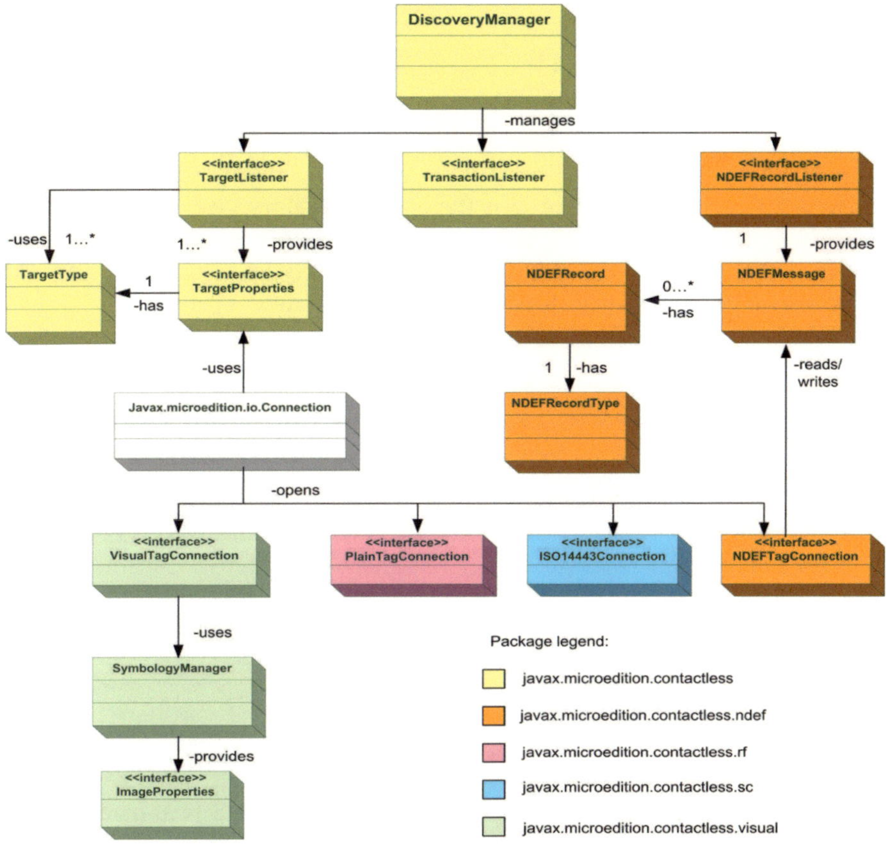

Fig. 5. JSR-257 API Overview

As it can be observed the API consists of five packages as follows:

- `javax.microedition.contactless`. The first step for a RFID/NFC application is to discover the available targets (tags or devices) in order to be able to receive later notifications about them. This package is then required to implement any NFC application since it provides target discovery using the `DiscoveryManager` class. It also provides other classes and interfaces common to all targets.
- `javax.microedition.contactless.ndef`. This package contains classes and interfaces needed to communicate with tags that have NDEF formatted data. In order to use this feature the application must register with an NDEF Record Listener to receive notifications about tags or devices.
- `javax.microedition.contactless.rf`. This package allows communication with RFID tags that do not have NDEF formatted data. It only contains the

PlainTagConnection interface that defines the basic mechanism to communicate with this type of RFID tags.

- javax.microedition.contactless.sc. This package enables communication with external smart cards. This is done using the ISO14443Connection interface.
- javax.microedition.contactless.visual. This package includes the required interfaces and methods to generate visual tags as well as for reading them. Tags can be generated using the interface ImageProperties. It can be observed that this package is built on top of the Generic Connection Framework (GCF). It extends the javax.microedition.io.Connection. This is done because tags connections may also be opened manually and in this case they do not require DiscoveryManager functionality.

javax.microedition.contactless is the only mandatory package in the specification, this means that the rest of the packages can be left unimplemented. A reference implementation is required to provide a list of the target types that it supports. This list of targets corresponds to the packages that must be implemented.

3.2.2 Android NFC API

Android platform includes the NFC API from version 2.3. In Version 2.3.3 an improved and extended support for this technology was added. From this version it allows mobile interaction with several types of tags, including the following (Android Developers, 2011):

- NFC-A (ISO 14443-3A)
- NFC-B (ISO 14443-3B)
- NFC-F (JIS 6319-4)
- NFC-V (ISO 15693)
- ISO-DEP (ISO 14443-4)
- MIFARE Classic
- MIFARE Ultralight
- NFC Forum NDEF tags

An Android device that includes NFC support, like the Nexus S, acts in reader/writer mode when the screen is on. In this mode the device looks for NFCs tags and starts activities to handle them. Android 2.3.3 also includes some limited Peer to Peer support. The NFC API is available in the android.nfc and android.nfc.tech packages.

The android.nfc package contains the high-level classes that allow interaction with the NFC adapter of the mobile device. It includes functionalities to represent discovered tags, and to use the NDEF data format. This package includes the following classes:

NfcManager: This class enumerates the NFC adapters on the Android device. Most Android devices include only one NFC adapter, in any case this manager is used to obtain the device's NfcAdapter.

NfcAdapter: This class represents the NFC hardware on the device. It allows direct interaction with tags using Android's *activities*. It also provides peer-to-peer support.

NdefMessage: This class represents an NDEF data message that is used to transmit data between devices and tags. One NdefMessage object may contain several NdefRecords.

`NdefRecord`: This class represents an NDEF record; it is delivered in a `NdefMessage`. Each record has a type that describes the type of data that is being carried in the record, such as text, URL, smart poster or MIME data.

`Tag`: Represents a tag that has been scanned by the device. When a tag is discovered, a `Tag` object is created and enfolded inside an Android's *intent*. The NFC dispatch system is then in charge of sending the *intent* to a compatible activity.

The `android.nfc.tech` package provides access to a specific tag technology once a tag has been read. Each type of tag contains different features and even a scanned tag can support multiple technologies (i.e. MifareClassic, NfcA and NDEF). This package contains one interface and nine classes as follows:

- `TagTechnology`. This interface provides access to tag properties according to the tag technology.
- The classes in the `android.nfc.tech` package correspond to the tag technologies implementations; the following are available to provide I/O operations for the corresponding tag: `IsoDep`, `MifareClassic`, `MifareUltralight`, `Ndef`, `NfcA`, `NfcB`, `NfcF` and `NfcV`. It is mandatory for all Android NFC devices to provide `TagTechnology` implementations for the following: NFC-A, NFC-B, NFC-F, NFC-V, IsoDep and NDEF.

Applications developed to use the NFC API, must also request permission from the user before establishing NFC communication. This is done in the manifest file where the following declaration has to be added:

<uses-permission android:name="android.permission.NFC">

In the same way, it is also recommendable to add another line in the manifest that allows filtering the application in the Android Market, so it is only discoverable by users with NFC-enabled devices. The manifest requires the following line :

<uses-feature android:name= "android.hardware.nfc" android:required = "true">

3.2.3 Open NFC

One of the main issues of mobile software development is heterogeneity. Today mobile phones range from several development platforms as well as operating systems and hardware. This is a challenge for both developers and final users. When talking of RFID/NFC for example, the APIs provided are commonly written to perform well under a determined type of hardware or mobile device. JSR-257 for example is intended for CLDC/MIDP devices, while Android NFC API works for NXP controller chips used in the first NFC Android phone, the Google Nexus S. However, allowing interoperability between various types of NFC hardware and software can help accelerating the adoption of NFC technology in the market. This is the idea of the Open NFC project. Open NFC™ is a NFC protocol stack developed by Inside Secure Company, and that is now available in an open source edition under the Apache™ License, Version 2.0. Open NFC acts as middleware for NFC-enabled phones, and the applications written for them. The platform is intended to be used by developers of different mobile platforms and operating systems, allowing them to create applications that will perform well between various types of NFC hardware and software, since it can operate with any NFC-compliant chip. Besides, the applications developed with this platform can also be utilized by any phone manufacturer. Software developers can take advantage of the open source platform to build on technology developed by others to create new applications.

At the moment the platform provides support for five platforms (Inside Secure, 2011):

- Open NFC for Android,
- WinCE/Mobile Edition,
- Linux Edition (for embedded Linux or Linux for PC),
- PC Edition (for Windows XP/Vista/7), and
- Core Edition for small OS (Nucleus, REX)

And includes 2 optional packages:

- J-Edition implementing the JSR257and extensions for J2ME, and
- JS-Edition implementing Java API on CDC or J2SE for Windows/Linux.

Open NFC can be used to developed different mobile applications since it includes several levels of functionality. The platform allows developing applications that involve peer-to-peer communications, Bluetooth and Wi-Fi, and interactions with single-wire protocol subscriber identity module (SIM) cards used in some mobile devices as well as in FeliCa, Mifare and ISO 14443 RFID tags.

In order to be hardware independent the Open NFC relies on a Hardware Abstraction Layer (HAL) to access NFC hardware. Each NFC hardware needs a specific implementation of the NFC HAL. Figure 6 shows the architecture of Open NFC platform.

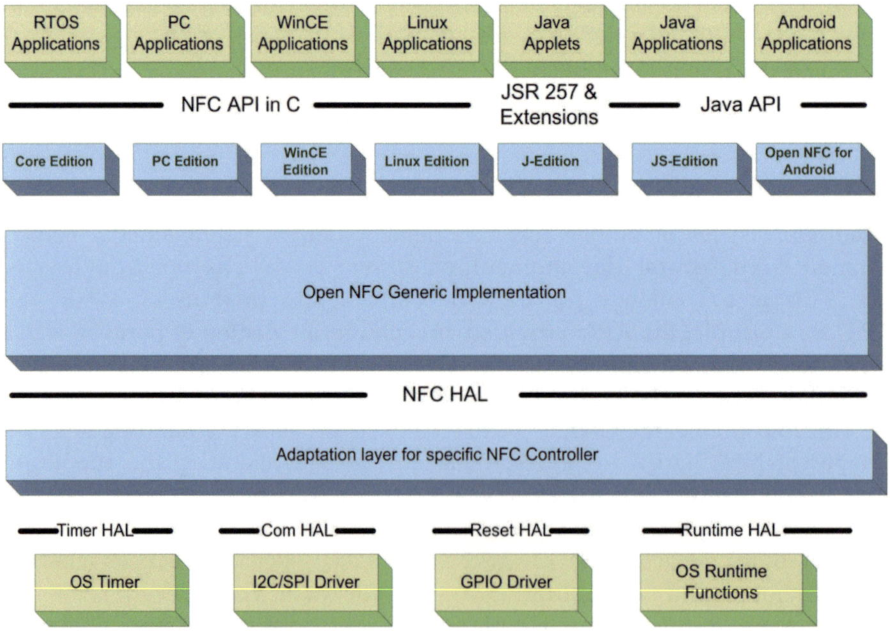

Fig. 6. Architecture of Open NFC

3.3 RFID/NFC and QR Code comparison

As explained before both technologies, RFID/NFC and QR Code, can be considered as AIDC techniques and used with mobile phones. In Table 3 we summarized the characteristics of both technologies and compared them.

	QR Code	NFC/RFID
Availability in mobile phones	High: Any camera-enabled mobile phone, several include preinstalled readers.	Low: Only NFC-enabled devices
Cost	Low: Tags can be printed in any printer, using common paper	Medium/High: Depends on the NFC/RFID tag or smartcard to be used.
Users Learning Curve	Low: Most users are already familiar with mobile cameras.	Medium: Users require learning NFC basis.
Security	Low: Information can be read easily by any camera-enabled device.	High: Devices must be very close to read information
Storage capacity	High	High
Damage resistance	Medium: QR Code includes error correction data that allows up to 30% recovery of a distorted or damaged tag.	Low: If wires are damaged tag cannot be read.
Visibility requirement	High: Code must be visible and well illuminated.	None: Tags can be hidden.

Table 3. QR-Code and NFC comparison

The main disadvantage of NFC is that at the moment the number of NFC-enabled mobile phones is still very limited, while QR Code can be read with any camera-enabled mobile phone. Another important aspect is that QR Code tags can be printed with any ordinary printer using common paper, while NFC and RFID tags or smartcards require special devices to write data on them. Some researchers and engineers consider that as the number of NFC-enabled mobile phones is increasing, QR Code will be replaced by this technology. We disagree with this assumption, and we consider that both technologies will coexist for a long time. QR code has the advantage of being almost free and easy to use, while NFC technology offers security and interoperability with different type of tags, besides both technologies are useful for several type of applications as will be seen in the following sections.

4. Related technologies

The use of mobile devices to link physical objects in the real world to the digital one using RFID, NFC and QR Code has impacted several technologies like Internet of Things, Object Hyper linking and Mixed Reality. These concepts are described in the following sections.

4.1 Internet of Things (IoT)

The IoT concept defines a new paradigm to identify and communicate with smart objects. The basic idea of this concept is the pervasive presence of different things or objects like tags, sensors, and mobile phones that can interact with each other and also with their neighbors through unique addressing schemes in order to reach common goals (Atzori et al., 2010). This concept relies in the possibility of implementing a global infrastructure of networked physical objects (Guinard & Trifa, 2009).

One of the basis of IoT is radio frequency identification (RFID), however the IoT concept allows communication between the physical world and the digital world also using other visual markers and embedded computers. In this way the information about everyday objects can be accessible in mobile devices. The IoT is still an emerging concept since several issues are still in progress like: addressing scheme, security, networking and standardization, however it promises to be a concept that will impact our everyday lives, just like the Internet itself has done. The U. S. National Intelligence Council lists the IoT among the six technologies that may impact U.S. national power by 2025 (Iera et al., 2010); similar results can be expected in many countries.

Although the IoT implementation is still in progress, several innovative applications already use this concept. Some of them require the use of NFC-enabled mobile devices as a key implementation element.

4.2 Object hyperlinking

Object hyperlinking is a new term that extends the current Internet to the real world. This is done attaching tags to real world objects, this tags contain URLs that can be read with a mobile device in order to retrieve and display information about the objects, like if we use a web browser and enter the object's URL. Besides this use, object hyperlinking may be useful for other applications like administering data objects in data bases or with text content management. The object hyperlinking concept allows using several tagging systems.

An object hyperlinking system requires the following components (Wikipedia, 2011):

1. An object marked with a visual tag containing an URL is mandatory. As mentioned before different tagging systems may be use, RFID and QR-Codes are two of them. In addition SMS tags, virtual tags and hardlinks have also been used. An SMS tag consists of an alphanumeric code that can be printed on a marker. In order to retrieve the information about the object, the user must send this code using the SMS service. Virtual tags as the name implies do not include any physical tag on the object. Instead a URL is associated with a set of geographical coordinates. These tags can only be read with a GPS-equipped mobile phone. A hardlink consists of an alphanumeric combination that is included in a URL. This URL targets a hardlink database containing information about the object.
2. An appropriate reader in order to retrieve information from the tag is also required; this may consist of a camera, a GPS or an RFID reader depending on the tagging system used.
3. The mobile device used to retrieve information must include the required software to read and display tags.
4. Since the information is retrieved from the Internet, a wireless network is also required, such as WiFi, WiMax or 3G networks.
5. Information on each linked object. This information could be in existing Web pages, existing databases of price information etc., or have been specially created.

6. Finally the mobile device must have an appropriate display to show the information on the linked object.

Object hyperlinking is being well accepted in several fields and new ones that have emerged as mixture of social and commercial applications.

4.3 Mixed and augmented reality

Milgram & Kishino (1994) defined mixed reality as "...anywhere between the extreme of the *virtuality continuum.*", where the Virtuality Continuum extends from the completely real through to the completely virtual environment with augmented reality and augmented virtuality ranging between, as depicted in figure 7. It can be said that Virtual Reality (VR) is when participants are completely immersed in a fictitious world that can take some properties of the real world but that replaces it with a simulated one. The road from the real world to a virtual one may include other environments where the participants are still connected with a real world while enhancing it with other contents, merging both worlds in some way. This concept can be referred as Mixed Reality (MR) and Augmented Reality. Augmented reality (AR) refers to augmenting the real-world with content generated with a computer or another device. This content can include sound, video, graphics, and other data.

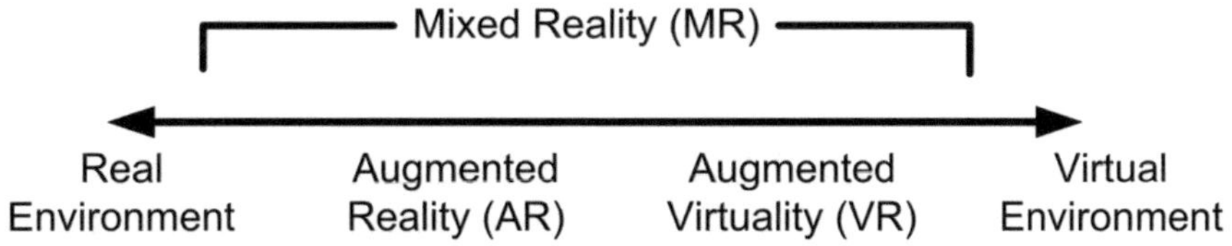

Fig. 7. Reality-Virtuality Continuum

Even though the MR concept was defined since 1994 it is until now that, thanks to the advances in the design of interactive technologies, it has been possible to start using mixed reality environments. Mobile mixed reality occurs when we use mobile technology, including wireless communication, mobile devices and mobile software to enhance or supplement the physical world with digital content. This can be done using several sensors available in mobile devices like GPS, camera, accelerometer, wireless sensitivity, compass direction, and sound and image recognition that can take properties and data from the real world in order to process it and provide enhanced content obtained from the digital world. Since not all mobile phones in the market have all these sensors capabilities, RFID and QR code can be used as a first step to implement mobile mixed reality systems. These technologies can be used to link the physical objects to the mobile device in order to provide enhanced visions to the user, allowing in some way the mixed reality content.

5. Applications and projects

In the next sections several projects found from the literature are presented. These projects illustrate how the use of mobile phones to link physical objects tagged with RFID/NFC tags or QR Codes can impact several important areas like education, health, culture and others.

5.1 Education

The study of QR codes and RFID tags in education can be placed in the context of mobile learning and ubiquitous learning. Mobile learning, also known as m-learning, can be described from different perspectives, considering that it allows people to learn without restriction of location (Lam et al., 2010) using wireless technologies and mobile applications. Though m-learning provides mobility, it is not context sensitive. A new mode of learning mechanism called u-learning is context aware and also provides anywhere, anytime learning using various mobile and sensor technologies. Several researches and institutions have found interesting ways to apply QR-codes and RFID tags for the m-learning and u-learning process.

The University of Bath is the predecessor of applying QR-codes in education (Law & So, 2010). They have incorporated this technology in several aspects related with the learning process. For instance, they use QR-Codes in the library to provide information about the books. They have also developed an enhancement for *Moodle* which automatically includes the QR code for the page that has been printed. The QR code contains the URL of the page on that particular *Moodle* course. They have also added QR codes on posters that can be found around the campus, on Websites and service blogs for bookmarking, in handbooks linking to activities, and in marketing materials from departments.

According to Susono & Shimomura (2006) in Japan almost 100% of college students have mobile phones, for this reason they are commonly used for education purposes. In their work they reported the use of mobile phones and QR-Codes to conduct surveys during class, this with the intention of providing feedback to the teacher at the middle of a long class (i.e. 90 minutes). With this project students answer a survey using their mobile devices and QR-Codes to choose from different options. They send the answer to a server and the teacher can have immediate feedback in order to improve his/her class if needed.

Another particular field in education where QR Code and RFID/NFC can be very useful is Outdoor learning; this is an education approach that can be very effective for multiple areas. For instance, Law & So (2010) propose using QR-Code in math and sciences trials. For this, QR-codes containing questions can be placed outdoors on different locations and students use their mobile phones to read the questions in order to answer them. Liu, et al. (2009) proposed the concept of Environment of Ubiquitous Learning with Educational Resources (EULER) using mobile devices and RFID tags for outdoor natural science learning. RFID tags are located on several learning objects, and can be used by the student to download context-aware content to the mobile device. The student can then immediately browse the provided content that can include audio, video and augmented reality content. In this work a PDA was used to read RFID tags, however similar works could be implemented using NFC-enabled mobile phones and the appropriate API.

Mandula et al. (2011) used mobile devices and RFID to implement a u-learning system, in this case for an indoor learning environment, like botanical gardens, smart museums or a smart lab. RFID tags are used to enable the learner to access the learning content of an object according to the surrounding context. This tags are placed on learning objects (e.g. smart posters), and when a student comes in proximity with her/his mobile phone, the mobile client application captures the object ID and sends it to the application server for processing. At a remote server, relevant content corresponding to object ID is fetched and presented to the learner's mobile device using WLAN or 3G networks.

Mobile and ubiquitous learning can be also very useful for language learning as it has been showed by Law & So (2010) who proposed using QR-Codes for an *English Listening Exercise* in the area of self-directed multimedia learning activities. In this case QR-Codes containing links to Websites for direct audio playback are placed onto worksheets. The QR codes link directly to the Web-based audio depository prepared by the teachers. Similar works can be implemented using RFID or NFC tags.

These projects are just a few examples of how QR code and NFC can be used on mobile phones to link physical objects, in this case, worksheets or objects existing in nature, labs or classrooms to implement m-learning and u-learning applications.

5.2 Health

The use of mobile technologies and applications for public health practice has led to the development of a new concept known as mobile health or mHealth. mHealth consists in using mobile communications—such as PDAs and mobile phones—for health services and information (Vital Wave Consulting, 2009). Recently several mHealth applications are beginning to incorporate RFID and QR-Codes. These technologies can be particularly useful for remote monitoring of health parameters. For instance, Gentag (Gentag, 2011) is developing a line of medical RFID patches that have patented as "smart" skin-patch technology to enable physicians and patients to monitor their health wirelessly. This line of patches include: A glucose-monitoring skin patch, a cardiac-monitoring skin patch, a UV-monitoring skin patch and a biomarker skin test patch. The first market application for the smart skin patch is a patient ID and fever onset bandage that integrates Gentag's proprietary sensor circuit in a disposable skin patch. Applications include using cell phones for monitoring the fever onset in a child, patient monitoring in hospitals, or remotely monitoring the well-being of elderly relatives via cell phones or the Internet (Sharma & Siddiqui, 2010). Another Gentag's health application is related with counterfeit drugs prevention. They have developed an RFID tag that is intended to be placed inside the caps of pharmaceutical bottles allowing consumers to check the authenticity of the product directly with their cell phones prior to purchase or use.

Other practical use of QR-code and RFID/NFC technologies for mHealth applications is patients' identification for retrieving or storing their information on electronic health records (EHR). For example Yu-Chi W. et al. (2009) propose using RFID enabled smartcards to allow patients accessing health data held in different systems, and share this information with their familiars and doctors. This smartcards could be also read using mobile phones allowing further uses of the proposed systems. Other works propose the use of this technology to identify patients in healthcare services implemented in developing countries, where maintaining accurate electronic health records can be a difficult task (Zalzala et al., 2011; Marcus et al., 2009). In the same way QR codes can also be used to retrieve health records or medical information. For instance people with some medical conditions can store medical information that can be quickly accessed in case of an emergency (Beck, 2011)

We have also proposed incorporating QR Codes to wellness applications (e.g. calorie and fitness trackers), as AIDC techniques that allow retrieving nutrimental information from food (Vazquez-Briseno, et al., 2010). We have developed a prototype called CalReader using Android platform and Zxing reader. We are also working in incorporating NFC tags to this application.

5.3 Entertainment and culture

Recently RFID/NFC and QR codes have been used to enhance visits to museums and art galleries, particularly for guided visits. Tags can be added to objects allowing visitors to retrieve more information about them using their mobile phones. Another interesting application has been proposed by Haberman O. et al. (2010). In this work tags are used to create an intelligent or augmented painting that delivers multimedia content to the audience using an NFC-enabled mobile device. The same artist that created the painting provides additional information about several aspects of it. This information has been stored on multimedia content as audio and video and placed on a server. In the original painting several hidden tags were placed. Visitors could intuitively find these tags and retrieve the content. They revealed that this was a pleasant experience that enhanced their appreciation and comprehension of the painting.

The *Tales of Things* project (Tales of Things, 2010), developed in collaboration among several universities in the United Kingdom, is a project that links digital content to physical objects using QR codes and mobile devices. This project has been developed with the idea of cataloguing physical objects with QR code and sharing their histories or information on line. The idea is to gather enough information about today's objects to provide this information to future generations and also to preserve social history. This project has already been implemented at the Scotland: A Changing Nation gallery, where Around 80 objects have been tagged with QR codes (National Museums Scotland, n.d.). People can add their memories or comments about the objects using the Tales of Things Website. The Tales of Things project is also open to people who desires to add new objects and their memories. People can upload an image of any object, they have to provide some information about it, as well as a hyperlink for extra content. The *Tales of Things* site generates the corresponding QR Code that links the provided content with the object.

QRator (QRator, 2011) is another interesting project powered by the Tales of Things. The project is intended to enhance museum interpretation by allowing members of the public to type in their own comments and interpretation of museum objects. Their interpretation becomes part of the objects history that can be shared with the community using QR-codes. Content currently covers two museums at University College London (UCL); The Grant Museum of Zoology and The Petrie Museum of Egyptology. At the Grant Museum ten iPads are attached to displays, each one holds a current question which visitors can respond to on the iPad itself, via Twitter or the Tales of Things app on their smart phones reading the QR-Code display along with the question.

5.4 Commerce

One of the main application areas of QR-Code and RFID/NFC technologies is mobile commerce or m-commerce, which involves any commerce activity such as ticketing, banking or purchasing goods and services, using mobile devices. With these AIDC methods m-commerce applications are being improved with new and effectives ways of reducing mobile inputs from the user.

There are diverse applications of 2D barcodes in m-commerce, according to Gao et al.(2007) these applications can be classified into: Wireless advertising and marketing, wireless trading (pre-sale/sale-and-buy/post-sale), product information tracking and checking, mobile security, mobile customer and product verification and wireless payment.

As mentioned before, Asia is at the moment the region where the fastest development of mobile 2D barcode industry and specifically QR-Code has occurred. In this area, and particularly in Japan and South Korea, QR Code can be found in many places to enable m-commerce activities, for instance: (Soon, 2008):

- On buildings for allowing users to retrieve information about the companies that are operating inside the buildings.
- On the packaging of fruits or vegetables to retrieve information about the name of the farm from which the fruits and vegetables are grown and harvested; also the fertilizers and insecticide used.
- On food packages to download information on cooking recipes.
- On maps in the Tokyo subway and central bus stations for location based services, for instance, passengers can find out the arrival time of the next bus.
- On bills for ePayment services of tickets for trains and airlines services.
- On TV programming guides to view information about programs.

In the same way, RFID/NFC technology is now being widely used in these countries for m-commerce applications. For instance, in Japan and South Korea people can now purchase food at McDonalds through their cell phones and also know when their order is ready (Shuman, 2007) in this restaurants. Customers must download a McDonalds application to their phone. There are RFID readers at the tables and RFID menus that have RFID built in chips. Customers then, with the reader plugged to their phones, can point at the item in the menu that they want to order. In Japan people can also pay through the cell phone number, or through an RFID chip, using the mobile e-wallet system developed by DoCoMo (Self-service world, 2008), which turns the smart phone into a type of credit card. This mobile payment tendency thru NFC is starting to be used worldwide. Spain realized a pre-commercial NFC trial showing that this technology can be used successfully in this country. The trial started by giving 1500 customers a Samsung S530 NFC, to make payments in taxis, markets and retail stores at the city of Sitges in Spain. The project "Mobile Shopping Sitges 2010" (Telefonica, 2010) was promoted by Telefonica Movistar a mobile phone network provider, together with La Caixa bank and Visa. Payments up to 20€ were automatic, but larger transactions required a PIN, introduced at the business terminal to approve purchase. The participants were trained with information on how to use their phones for the transactions, by Telefonica. The payment platform at that time was only trough La Caixa bank, but is expected to expand the service to other banks. The trial lasted six months and is now completed, but the phones were left in circulation so they can continue to be used. It is planned to extend this service to the city of Barcelona.

In the United States the Google Wallet application has recently been launched. This is an Android app that turns the mobile phone into a wallet using the user's registered credit cards (Google wallet, 2011). In this way, users are able to pay and make savings using their mobile phones and NFC technology. The application is being release with the Nexus S 4G mobile phone on Sprint operator. Merchants affiliated to the Google Wallet program are called SingleTap merchants. In these places users can pay using their mobile phone as well as redeem offers and earn loyalty points. Google is planning in a near future to add other functionalities like storing boarding passes, keys, ID and tickets. The Google Wallet now supports Citi MasterCard and Google Prepaid Card, and can be used in any Mastercard Pay Pass accepted business. Users can also be sync to Google offers, through NFC at SingleTap participating places. Other companies are joining to offer their savings and loyalty programs through Google Wallet.

Besides m-payments, there are also other interesting applications for QR-Code and NFC in commerce services. For instance, Fu, (2011) proposes the use of QR Code in a mall shopping guide service. In this work QR Codes are used to store information about products in a shopping mall, including latitude and longitude location of the product. Once the code is recognized, communication with a server is used to identify the customer's current position, as well as to provide different services like receiving the latest promotions of businesses and finding the best route from his current location to the destination. Chyi-Ren et al. (2011) propose using QR codes in a location-based mobile advertisement publishing system for vendors. This system is able to provide vendors a convenient way for creating and editing advertisements that may include the vendor's location as well as discount coupons stored on a QR code. Advertisement data desired by the consumers can be viewed when a QR code is scanned, thus providing information for the consumer to access. Linli et al.,(2010) implemented a universal mobile ticketing system where QR Codes are used as electronic receipts. This system can be used in several areas where receipts are required, for instance, for booking hotel rooms. The final receipt is generated with the client, instead of the server, in this case, the mobile phone, security is guaranteed by adding digital signatures thru the use of Message-Digest Algorithm (MD5).

5.5 Other applications

RFID and QR Code can be applied to a wide range of applications and areas, besides the ones described in the preceding sections. For instance Hsu, et al. (2010) implemented a Human-Building-Computer Interaction (HBCI) system using QR Codes to connect buildings to its occupants. The purpose of this system is to allow users to interact with the objects in a physical environment, namely rooms and appliances in a building, in order to maximize a users' comfort inside a building and minimize total energy usage via remote monitoring and control of devices. QR code tags are used as links to the remote server containing information about rooms or appliances that are considered objects in the HBCI system. Each object has a set of services that the user can monitor via QR codes, for instance: "Room Temperature", "Lighting" and "Energy consumption". When a user wants to retrieve information about and object, for instance a refrigerator, he/she needs to scan de QR code attached to the object to identify it and retrieve the web resources available for that object. Users could obtain a list of available services for electronic objects including the "Energy" service that could use to observe a graph about the energy usage history. The user could use another service in the same object to remotely turn on or off the HBCI object.

Cunha et al. (2010) used QR codes and NFC tags to implement a Viticulture Service-Oriented Framework (VSOF). The tags are used to connect remote parcels to a central server in order to retrieve and send useful information for the vineyard management. By pointing a mobile device to a tag, the viticulturalist may download data such as climatic data or upload information such as disease and pest incidence in a simple way, without having to provide coordinates or any other references, and without having to return to a central office. Both type of tags are used along with 1D Barcode and GPS to provide multi-tag capabilities to the system in order to be used in environments with different features (e.g. no nfc-enabled or GPS-enabled phone available)

As it can be seen from the examples presented in this section the use of QR Code and RFID/NFC for mobile services can be applied to many fields. In the near future we will see more applications since these technologies are still being incorporated to new and innovative services.

6. Conclusion

In this chapter we have explained the use of mobile phones for linking physical objects with the digital world using AIDC techniques. We have described QR Code and RFID/NFC technologies as well as the APIs required for implementing mobile applications with them. Several projects described in this chapter show the usefulness of this type of applications. These projects impact important fields in our lives such as education, health, commerce among others. There is no doubt that with the growing number of NFC and camera-enabled mobile phones available in the market these applications will become essential tools for everyday life.

7. References

Android Developers (October, 2011). Package android.nfc, In: *Android Developers,* 10-06-2011 Available from: http://developer.android.com/reference/android/nfc/package-summary.html

Atzori, L.; Iera, A. & and Morabito, G. (2010). The Internet of Things: A survey. *Computer Networks.* Vol. 54, No. 15, (October 2010), pp. 2787-2805 Available from: http://www.nfc-forum.org/specs/

Beck, S., (August, 2011). QR codes to be Used to Help Emergency Responders Find Medical Data on Patients, In: *QR-Code Press,* 9-30-2011 Available from: http://www.qrcodepress.com/qr-codes-to-be-used-to-help-emergency-responders-find-medical-data-on-patients/853379/]

Chyi-Ren D., Yu-Hong L., Liao, J., Hao-Wei Y. & Wei-Luen K. (2011). A Location-based Mobile Advertisement Publishing System for Vendors. *Proceedings of the Eighth International Conference on Information Technology: New Generations (ITNG), 2011,* pp.24-29, Las Vegas, Nevada, USA, 11-13 April 2011

Cunha C. R.; Peres, E.; Morais, R.; Oliveira, A.A; Matos, S. G.; Fernandes, M. A.: Ferreira, P. J. S. G. & Reis M. J. C. S. (2010). The Use of Mobile Devices with Multi-tag Technologies for an Overall Contextualized Vineyard Management. *Computers and Electronics in Agriculture* Vol. 73, No. 2 (August 2010), pp 154-164

Denso Wave Incorporated. (n.d.). *QR Code Features,* 9-20-2011, Available from: http://www.denso-wave.com/qrcode/qrstandard-e.html

Fu, L. (2011). Design of QR code-based Mall shopping guide system. *Proceedings of the International Conference on Information Science and Technology (ICIST),* Nanjing, Jiangsu, China 26-28 March 2011.

Gao, J.Z.; Prakash, L. & Jagatesan, R.(2007). Understanding 2D-BarCode Technology and Applications in M-Commerce - Design and Implementation of A 2D Barcode Processing Solution. *Proceedings of the the 31st Annual International Computer Software and Applications Conference, 2007. COMPSAC 2007,* pp.49-56, Beijing, China, 24-27 July 2007

Gentag (2011), Gentag applications, In: *Gentag Website,* 10-07-200, Available from: http://www.gentag.com/applications.html

Google (2011), Google Wallet, 10-10-2011, Available from: http://www.google.com/wallet/

Guinard, D. & Trifa V., (2009). Towards the Web of Things: Web mashups for embedded devices, *Proceedings of Workshop on Mashups, Enterprise Mashups and Lightweight Composition on the Web (MEM 2009),* Madrid, Spain, April 2009

Haberman O.; Damala A.; Pellerin R.; Haberman U. & Gressier-Soudan E. (2010). Exploring Contemporary Painting through Spatial Annotations Using RFID Tags. *Proceedings of the 11th International Symposium on Virtual Reality, Archaeology and Intelligent Cultural Heritage, VAST10.* ISBN 978-3-905673-76-0, Paris, France, September, 2010

Hsu, J.; Mohan, P.; Jiang, X., Ortiz, J. Shankar, S.; Dawson-Haggerty, S. & Culler, D. (2010), HBCI: Human-Building-Computer Interaction. *Proceedings of 2nd ACM Workshop On Embedded Sensing for Energy-Efficient Buildings, (Buildsys 2010).* New York, NY, USA, 2010.

Iera, A.; Floerkemeier, C.; Mitsugi, & J.; Morabito, G. (2010), The Internet of things [Guest Editorial]," *Wireless Communications, IEEE* , Vol.17, No.6, pp.8-9, December 2010

Inside Secure (2011), Open NFC Project, In: *Open NFC Developer Site,* 10-06-2011, Available from: http://www.open-nfc.org/

JSR 257 Expert Group (2006), JSR-257 Contactless Communication API, final release, Technical report, Sun Microsystems, Inc, 17 October 2006

Kato, H. & Tan, K.T. (2007). Pervasive 2D Barcodes for Camera Phone Applications, *Pervasive Computing, IEEE* , Vol.6, No.4, (October, 2007), pp.76-85

Lam, J., Yau, J. & Cheung, S. (2010). A Review of Mobile Learning in the Mobile Age. *Proceedings of the Third international conference on Hybrid learning* (ICHL'10), Philip Tsang, Simon K. S. Cheung, Victor S. K. Lee, and Ronghuai Huang (Eds.). Springer-Verlag, Berlin, Heidelberg, 306-315.

Law, C. & So, S. (2010). QR codes in education. *Journal of Educational Technology Development and Exchange,* Vol. 3, No. 1, pp 85-100

Linli H., Yuhao W., Dong L. & Jing L. (2010). A hybrid client/server and browser/server mode-based universal mobile ticketing system. *Proceedings of the 2nd IEEE International Conference on Information Management and Engineering (ICIME), 2010,* pp.691-695, Suntec, Singapore, 16-18 April 2010

Liu, T.-Y., Tan, T.-H., & Chu, Y.-L. (2009). Outdoor Natural Science Learning with an RFID-Supported Immersive Ubiquitous Learning Environment. *Educational Technology & Society,* Vol. *12* No. 4, pp 161–175.

Mandula, K.; Meda, S. R.; Jain, D. K. & Kambham, R. (2011). Implementation of Ubiquitous Learning System Using Sensor Technologies, *Proceedings of IEEE International Conference on Technology for Education (T4E),* ISBN 978-1-4577-1521-1, pp.142-148, Chennai, Tamil Nadu , 14-16 July 2011

Marcus, A.; Davidzon, G.; Law, D.; Verma, N.; Fletcher, R.; Khan, A. & Sarmenta, L. (2009) , Using NFC-Enabled Mobile Phones for Public Health in Developing Countries, Proceedings of *First International Workshop on Near Field Communication, 2009. NFC '09.,* ISBN 978-0-7695-3577-7, Hagenberg, Austria February 2009

Milgram P, & Kishino, A. F. (1994). Taxonomy of Mixed Reality Visual Displays *IEICE Transactions on Information and Systems,* E77-D (12), pp. 1321-1329, 1994.

National Museums Scotland (n.d.). Tales of a Changing Nation, In: *National Museums Scotland Website*, 11-10-2011, Available from: http://www.nms.ac.uk/our_museums/national_museum /explore_the_galleries/scotland_a_changing_nation/tales_of_a_changing_nation.aspx

NFC Forum (2006). NFC Data Exchange Format (NDEF) Technical Specification, 10-06-2011

NFC Forum (2011). NFC Forum Technical Specifications, 10-04-2011, Available from http://www.nfc-forum.org/specs/spec_list/

Nokia. (2008). Scan and Decode Mobile Codes, 27-09-2011, Available from: http://mobilecodes.nokia.com/scan.htm

Ortiz C. E., (2008). An Introduction to Near-Field Communication and the Contactless Communication API, 10-04-2011 Available from: http://java.sun.com/developer/technicalArticles/javame/nfc/

QRator. (2011). QRator about the Project, In: *QRator Website*, 06-10-2011, Available from: http://www.qrator.org/about-the-project

Self-service world (May, 2008), McDonalds, DoCoMo deal allows mobile payment for Happy Meals, In: *Self-Service World Website*, 10-08-2011, Available from: http://www.selfserviceworld.com/article/163674/McDonalds-DoCoMo-deal-allows-mobile-payment-for-Happy-Meals

Sharma, M. & Siddiqui, A. (2010). RFID Based Mobiles: Next generation applications, Proceedings of the *2nd IEEE International Conference on Information Management and Engineering (ICIME 2010)* Shengdu, China, 16-18 April 2010

Shuman, E. (September, 2007), McDonalds Starts RFID Ordering Trial in Korea. In: *eWeek Website*, 10-08-2011. Available from: http://www.eweek.com/c/a/Enterprise-pplications/McDonalds-Starts-RFID-

Soon, T., J.; (2008). QR Code. *Synthesis Journal 2008*, pp. 59-77, ISSN 0219-4767

Susono, H., & Shimomura, T. (2006). Using Mobile Phones and QR Codes for Formative Class Assessment, In A. Méndez-Vilas, A. Solano Martín, J.A. Mesa González and J. Mesa González (Eds), *Current Developments in Technology-Assisted Education (Vol. 2)* (pp 1006-1010). Badajoz, Spain: FORMATEX

Tales of Things (2010). Tales of Things press release, In: *Tales of Things Website*, 06-10-2011, Available from: http://talesofthings.com/totem_media/press/TalesofThingsPressRelease.pdf

Telefonica (December, 2010). "la Caixa", Telefónica y Visa finalizan con éxito la primera experiencia de pago por móvil en España. In: *Telefonica Website*, 10-08-2011 Available from: http://pressoffice.telefonica.com/jsp/base.jsp?contenido=/jsp/notasdeprensa/notadetalle.jsp&id=0&idm=es&pais=1&elem=15900

Vazquez-Briseno, M.; Nieto-Hipolito, J.I & Jimenez-Garcia, E. (2010), Using QR Codes to Improve Mobile Wellness Applications, *IJCSNS International Journal of Computer Science and Network Security*, Vol.10 No.12, December 2010

Vital Wave Consulting. (2009). mHealth for Development: The Opportunity of Mobile Technology for Healthcare in the Developing World. Washington, D.C. and Berkshire, UK: UN Foundation-Vodafone Foundation Partnership, 2009. 10-06-2011, Available from: http://www.vitalwaveconsulting.com/pdf/mHealth.pdf

Wikipedia (July, 2011). Object Hyperlinking, In: *Wikipedia* 9-24-2011, Available from: http://en.wikipedia.org/wiki/Object_hyperlinking

Yu-Chi W.; Pei-Fan C.; Zhi-Huang H.; Chao-Hsu C.; Gwo-Chuan L. & Wen-Ching Y. (2009), A Mobile Health Monitoring System Using RFID Ring-Type Pulse Sensor. Proceedings of *IEEE International Conference on Dependable, Autonomic and Secure Computing, DASC '09*. Chengdu, China, December, 2009

Zalzala, A.; Chia, S.; Zalzala, L. & Karimi, A. (2011). Healthcare Technologies in Developing Countries, Proceedings of *GCC Conference and Exhibition (GCC), 2011, Dubai,* United Arab Emirates, Feb. 2011

Part 4

Interactive TV, Film, Multimedia Production and Video Processing

13

Bringing All Users to the Television: A Platform Based on Java for Building Interactive Television Applications

João Benedito dos Santos Junior
Pontifical Catholic University of Minas Gerais, PUC Minas,
Computer Science Department,
Interactive Digital Television Laboratory, TVDILab,
Poços de Caldas, MG,
Brazil

1. Introduction

Evolving technologies for the treatment of audio and video along with the improvement of techniques for data communication systems for Digital Television (DTV) has provided, at first, the improvement in the quality of video and audio signals (images), enabling For example, experiments such as surround sound (surrounding) the resolution of images in high definition (HDTV). In a complementary way, tools that involve the viewer/user more actively with the access terminal cause that system to be characterized as interactive (iDTv). At this point, applications can be built to explore different forms of services, ranging from the popular Electronic Program Guides (EPG) via typical applications and voting polls, and reaching the portals of public services and/or e-commerce portals in the same way as in other interactive platforms, as is the case of the WWW (World Wide Web), accessible via the Internet infrastructure. Surely, the development of interactive applications and services for environments of Digital Television is a considerable challenge (Vrba & Sykora, 2006; Kyriazis et al, 2011), characterized by new standards that must be understood by application developers. As a complement, which are commonly used tools for developing applications in client/server and web does not fit (fully or partially) the development of applications/services for iDTv (Jianmin et al, 2011). The Interactive Digital TV systems are presented, truly, as a new paradigm for computer systems, imposing technological challenges to software companies and telecommunications. New areas of application such as electronic commerce (t-commerce), e-governance (t-gov), distance (t-learning), and others that can take advantage of potential resources of a system iTVD may benefit from technologies for building applications for this new model (Batista et al, 2003; Peng, 2002).

This chapter is organized with the following structure. In the next section, the main concepts, problems and motivations for this research are presented. The main assumptions and challenges in the context of the Brazilian Digital Television System are presented in the section three. The section four discuss on interactivity scenarios identified to develop applications in the Brazilian Digital Television System. The BluTV (Bringing All Users to the Television) Platform is presented in the section five, specially in terms of design and implementation. The section six presents the Interactive Television Application Guide for Citizenship, built with components of the BluTV Platform. The scenarios for testing and future directions of this research are presented in the section seven, and the final remarks and conclusions are discussed on last section.

2. Problems and motivations

As part of research in digital television and interactive digital television, there are efforts on the definition of development platforms for interactive applications, both with generic features and specifications covered in the middleware of SBTVD-T and for specific purposes and functions of equipment manufacturers and software industry and services (SBTVD Forum, 2010).

In the context of SBTVD-T, the middleware supports the development of interactive applications through its two environments: the first one, an imperative, called Ginga-J (Filho, 2007); the second, named Ginga-NCL (Soares, 2007), is declarative. This work focuses on the environment Ginga-J, especially in regard to the specification JavaDTV (JavaDTV, 2010), having the following basic assumptions: a) your TV as access terminal (screen) to the basic interactive applications, b) the remote control as main device (remote device) to the viewer/user interaction, c) the automatic identification of the characteristics of the access terminal (memory, disk and network interfaces) available for operating of the back channel (interactivity channel) (Meloni, 2007).

As a complement, whereas SBTVD-T is being implemented in its operations for transmission and reception of television content, people and organizations interested in developing applications and services for Digital TV, especially those need to work with interactivity, are exposed to five essential problems:

a. the Ginga (middleware of SBTVD-T) is a complex system and still needs a consistent regulation so as to be implemented fully, turning more difficult the development of iDTv applications compliant to it; the Ginga Common Core (Ginga-CC) is not available; Ginga Ready is the one Ginga implementation, powered by MOPA Embedded Systems (Clarasó et al, 2009);
b. since JavaDTV was specified, for developing iDTv applications the tendency concerns on Ginga-J instead Ginga-NCL;
c. limited availability of simplified platforms for prototyping iDTv applications and services;
d. services and platforms for Internet Video (like YouTube) and NetCast (GoogleTV, by example) are growing in Brazil, while the interactivity from Digital Television System is stopped;
e. limited availability of minimum hardware platforms for testing iDTv applications, including the infrastructure necessary to explore the back channel for testing the complete life cycle of iDTv applications and services (Santos Junior et al, 2010);
f. the Java Virtual Machine (JVM) is embedded as an *engine* into several TV (like Bravia model from Sony), allowing the execution of Java *bytecodes*, without to consider the presence of middleware Ginga; in addition, researches have been made in order to use Java Platform as a complete middleware to execute iDTv applications in the set-top boxes (Dong-Heon et al, 2010).

The research reported in this chapter is within the context of interactivity in a digital television system, including problems that occur in all stages of the life cycle of a program for interactive digital TV. The life cycle begins with the production and distribution of audio and video streams that are multiplexed to form structures in Transport Stream (TS), besides objects carousel (audio, video, images, text, graphics and executable/interpreted applications). These structures are received and presented at the access terminal of the viewer/user. The last stage is focused on the interaction of the viewer/user with resident applications without using the back channel; the interaction is completed using the back channel via any communication infrastructure. In this work, it also presented a proposal to implement a communication service that can be executed in the environment of the access terminal of the viewer/user, regardless of the middleware used/embedded in this terminal. The main function is the establishment of interfaces for data communication between the iDTv applications and the Interactive Service Provider (ISP), using the communication resources available for back channel.

3. Assumptions and challenges in the Brazilian digital television system

One of the most promising technologies of interactive video - the Interactive Digital Television - has as one of its objectives to provide new interaction ways to the viewer, like is the case of non-linear navigation as occurred on the Internet browsing. One of the main advantages of the advent of the Interactive Digital Television, especially in the brazilian context, is the possibility of the increase of the interaction between the viewer and the access terminal (like television) through services and applications, like games, video-on-demand, t-commerce, Internet browsing, among others. However, due to be a new technology, having few established standards and too many researches in progress, the building of applications for Digital Television still is challenge.

3.1 Channel of Citizenship

On March-25-2010, was published in the Brazilian Official Press an order of the Ministry of Communications with the guidelines for the operation of the Canal of Citizenship, provided in Presidential Decree on the deployment of SBTVD-T. The Channel of Citizenship is one of four channels that the Brazilian government could exploit the broadcasting service of sounds, images and data in digital technology. According to the decree, the channel will offer applications focused on citizenship (such as t-learning, t-gov and t-health) and the programming will be made by agreements signed by the Ministry of Communications and civil entities. The proposal is to make programming with local independent productions, giving visibility to the culture of each of the 5,564 municipalities in Brazil, according to the goals of the Ministry of Communications. The programming of Channel of Citizenship, in each municipality, will be prepared under the supervision of a media council, with the participation of diverse segments of the community. As already happens with community channels, the Channel of Citizenship cannot run commercial advertising or religious or political proselytizing. The content must disclose acts of government, and observe the social and cultural diversity, having artistic and educational purposes, among other principles. In this context, it is observed that the research reported here can contribute effectively to the Channel of Citizenship, serving as infrastructure for interactivity, allowing the viewer/user interaction with the television content and promoting digital inclusion actions.

3.2 National Survey by Household Sampling

Recently, the IBGE (Brazilian Institute of Geography and Statistics) released the results of the new National Survey by Household Sampling (PNAD) for the year 2009 (PNAD, 2009). The survey showed that in Brazil, 35% of households has computers and 27% has access to Internet. Some other results of the survey are worth mentioning in the context in which this research is inserted, namely:

a. in 58.6 million households surveyed in 2009, almost 35% (20.3 million) had computers (PC - Personal Computers), of which 16 million have access to Internet (27.4%);
b. the South-East region remained with the highest proportion of households with personal computer (43.7%) and computer with access to Internet (35.4%); the North region (13.2%) and North-East region (14, 4%) had the lowest proportion of households with personal computer with access to Internet; the Southern region had 32.8% and the Midwest region, 28.2%;
c. all age groups showed an increase in the proportion of people who used the Internet; the largest increases between 2005 and 2009, there were those who were in the younger age groups, the proportion of people 10 to 14 years of age increased 34.5%, reaching 58.8% in 2009;
d. for the age group 15 to 17 years the increase was 37.4%, and for 18 or 19 years was 35.9%, reaching so these groups 71.1% and 68.7% who used the Internet, respectively, during the reference period;
e. the national average of residents in a single household heads is 3.3%, with more than 26 million people consume TV programming by subscription;
f. an increase in the share of households with television, from 95.1% (in 2008) to 95.7%, reaching 56 million households;
g. the percentage of homes with DVD player skipped from 69.4% to 72%, totalling 42.1 millions of homes.

According to PNAD, it is observed that the TV and the television system elements are strongly present in the lives of Brazilian citizens, the most accurate and consistent than the computers and other electronic communications equipment (except mobile phones, but they are characterized as equipment for individual use). In this context, it is important to the citizens to use these elements for purposes of interactivity and access to information.

3.3 National broadband Plan

According to the National Plan which provides broadband, the digital cities and *telecentres* are much more than tools to access the Internet, since the digital divide is one of the axes of the formation of the Information Society. The "digital cities" can be developed into an important instrument of democratization of information, requiring investments of both public and private initiative.

The all levels (federal, state and city) of government should invest in the installation of infrastructure for communication networks that are available across a geographical area, exploiting the same infrastructure used by the *telecentres* for educational purposes, for example. *Telecentres* are rooms with computers, Internet and printer, where activities are developed for children and adults.

In the context of PNBL, entities such as the Telebras has a fundamental role in the task of inclusion, bringing the Internet to Brazilians who still do not have access to the network. But the outlook for next 5 to 10 years - until a possible connection to 100 Mbps - provides for preparing the country for the information economy based on the tripod of investment, efficiency and innovation. The issue of investment is obvious and this is to eliminate the bottlenecks that impede access in remote areas. On the efficiency side, the logic is to leverage the infrastructure work - such as new dams - as vectors of the expansion of telecommunication networks. Recently, the Telebras submitted the list of top 100 cities in the country - in addition to 15 state capitals and Federal District - which will rely on state provision of back haul and, therefore, Internet access within the ceiling price of US$15.00, as defined by the National Broadband Plan. The initial focus is in the North-East and South-East regions, but beyond that, there are also towns in the states of Goiás and Tocantins. Besides that, there is poorest cities, but some can be considered successful, like Campinas and São Carlos, both in the state of São Paulo. Apart from the capital, the affected population reaches 14 millions of people.

It is observed that actions such as PNBL pointing practical possibilities of using this communication infrastructure for services that require a back channel for interactivity in the actions of SBTVD-T, which reinforces the relevance of the theme explored in the context in which this research project is inserted.

3.4 Grand Challenges in Computing

As shown in the *Grand Challenges in Computing* document, prepared by the Brazilian Computer Society for the period 2006 to 2016, one of the six pillars of scientific research in computing to explore the theme of to provide participative and universal access to knowledge to the Brazilian citizen.

The Information Technology introduced a revolution in communication between people and their way of work. There are technological barriers, educational, cultural, social and economic structures that impede access and interaction. So the goal of this challenge is, therefore, to overcome those barriers, through the design of systems, tools, models, methods, procedures and theories able to address, so competent, the issue of access to knowledge of the Brazilian citizen. This access should be universal and participative, in that the citizen is not a passive user, which receives information, but also participates in the generation of knowledge. Only through the opportunity to participate in knowledge building is that access will be able to lead a full and conscious use of knowledge available.

The IBGE (Brazilian Institute of Geography and Statistics) recorded in 2003, 32.1 million functional illiterates, defined as the population over 15 years of age and less than 4 (four) years of schooling (26% of the population). Still, according to the same source, 24.5 million people have some type of disability (14.5% of the population). Government sectors, universities and the private sector can seek technological solutions that seek to reduce social impact such differences and salvage values of citizenship in our society.

Furthermore, it is also to produce computer-based technology that enables and motivates the participation of users in the process of knowledge production and decision on its use. Moreover, one should take into account legal, social and anthropological studies of Brazilian citizenship, precisely to reduce the risk of serious problems of this order, or even create new problems arising from their mere existence, exacerbating the "digital divide".

Concrete examples of target application/domain that would benefit from research in this challenge include, among others, electronic government systems, systems for lifelong learning, communities of practice related to work, community supported by network (networked communities) in several areas. In special case, *e-government* is understood here as not only the provision of services via the Internet, but also the possibility of citizen participation in the generation of knowledge to be shared in the discussion of matters that directly affect them.

Among the important research problems in computing this challenge are: a) creation of back-office systems - internal infrastructure needed to provide services to citizens, which may include long-term processes, involving several entities and interoperability issues; b) provision of an infrastructure necessary for direct interaction between the citizen and his communication with the process to be carried out in the back office.

4. Interactivity scenarios in the Brazilian digital television system

From the identification of the actors who could/should be involved in interactive scenarios, some instances of scenarios can be included in the scope of this work, as described in the following. From the perspective of broadcaster, the broadcast system for broadcasting is the only way for broadcaster to make with that data and interactive applications reach the viewer/user. Given the nature of the broadcasting system (the same information is sent to all receivers), it is not possible to customize information flow (Audio, Video and Data) for every viewer/user and/or groups of viewer/users.

From the perspective of the viewer/user, the Communication Providers are used exclusively to provide the resources necessaries to access the back channel (unidirectional), used to take information from viewer/users to broadcaster and/or interactive services providers, there is no possibility of transmission content streams (audio, video and data) from the broadcaster to the viewer/user (video on demand).

From the perspective of availability of communication resources in the viewer/users' access terminals, a viewer/user 1 (V1) has an access terminal without resources for communication with the communication providers. Thus, only resident applications may be implemented in the access terminal. In a complementary way, viewer/user depends solely on the broadcasting system, to send them data, applications and interactive services. A viewer/user 2 (V2) has an access terminal with intermittent access to communication networks (shared mode) to explore the back channel provided by a communication provider. Thus, both resident and broadcasted applications can be used in the access terminal. The intermittent access (shared) is characterized by the media that are not dedicated to a specific purpose, as in the case of the telephone (dial) network and cable to access the Internet over the broadband system. The viewer/user 3 (V3) has an access terminal with specific and dedicated resources to explore the back channel provided by a communication provider. Thus, all types of applications may be implemented in the access terminal. Dedicated access is characterized by the media dedicated to a specific purpose, as is the case of an ADSL network or PLC, offered by a communication provider, solely for interactivity in the context of SBTVD-T.

From the viewpoint of the relationship between the Communication Providers, Interactive Services Providers and Broadcasters, a communication provider ensure access (a public and free of charge and/or on payment of special taxes established in the contract of service) to the back channel for using by the viewer/user, and to maintain both hardware and software infrastructure necessary to ensure the delivery of information from viewer/users to the interactive services providers and/or directly to the broadcaster. It is for an interactive service provider to ensure the necessary infrastructure to collect information from the viewer/user (using the infrastructure provided by communication providers), organize it, store it (using a data center, by example) and to apply filters in this information to provide appropriated reports to the broadcaster.

From the viewpoint of the relationship between External Entities and Broadcasters, the external entities, such as government (at all levels - local, state and federal), commercial organizations (banks, by example), non-governmental organizations and other broadcaster can establish a partnership with a broadcaster to develop and provide iDTv applications and services to the viewer/user. In terms of classification, we can establish the following, regarding the nature of the external entity that wants to offer interactivity: a) t-gov (e-governance via interactive digital television): when an instance of government is the external entity that originated the interactive service; b) t-commerce (electronic commerce via interactive digital television): when a commercial organization (such as banks, shops, service businesses, among others) is the external entity that gave rise to the interactive service; c) t-learning (electronic education via interactive digital television): when an organization for educational purposes (schools, universities, research centers, among others) is the external entity that gave rise to the interactive service.

Finally, an advanced scenario can be defined based on another scenarios. The main change that occurs in this scenario is that the broadcasting system is not one and exclusive way to disseminate audiovisual content to the viewer/user; the channel of interactivity can be used for this purpose. However, at this phase of implantation and consolidation of SBTVD-T, the possibility of using the back channel (interactivity) to download data and applications is still undefined in its general form and specifications, without approval and publication of specific standards for this case.

5. The BluTV platform: Design and implementation

The research reported here is within the context of interactivity in a digital television system, including problems that occur in all stages of the life cycle of a program for interactive digital TV. The life cycle begins with the production and distribution of audio and video streams that are multiplexed to form structures in Transport Stream (TS), besides objects carousel (audio, video, images, text, graphics and executable/interpreted applications). These structures are received and presented at the access terminal of the viewer/user. The last stage is focused on the interaction of the viewer/user with resident applications without using the back channel; the interaction is completed using the back channel via any communication infrastructure (Meloni, 2007).

In this work, it also presented a proposal to implement a communication service that can be executed in the environment of the access terminal of the viewer/user, regardless of the middleware used/embedded in this terminal. The main function is the establishment of interfaces for data communication between the iDTv applications and the Interactive Service Provider (ISP), using the communication resources available for back channel.

In this context, this chapter intends to present the BluTV (Bringing All Users to the Television) Platform, developed in the Interactive Digital Television Laboratory at PUC Minas. This platform has been used to develop applications for the Brazilian Terrestrial Digital Television System (SBTVD-T). BluTV allows the development of interactive television applications using a set of tools and components. To the broadcaster (author), it is allowed to define the components of the television program (media objects, information elements and interaction controls).

This approach should be sufficient to allow the communication between viewer/user and broadcaster (content provider) (Carvalho et al, 2007). At this point, this work is adherent to JavaDTV specification, which is part of the standard Ginga-J of the Brazilian System of Digital Terrestrial Television (SBTVD-T).

The BluTV (*Bringing All Users to the Television*) Platform - developed since 2002 in the context in that work is inserted - is being used for both building and testing of iDTv applications (Santos Junior et al, 2008a, 2008b).

The BluTV Studio generates the data/object TV carousel with data information represented on XML schema. BluTV Streamer sends this carousel via communication infrastructure. In the TV viewer side (access terminal), the BluTV contains a set of tools, including a player, for receiving data carousel and to process/present data information contained into carousel.

The Figure 1 shows the Ginga Architecture and also highlights the Ginga-J Subsystem. It is observed in Figure 1 that there is space for specification and implementation of additional API, which allows increasing the functionality of the middleware and thus provide special and/or essential features to the applications that should be presented to viewer/user. In this sense, the Figure 2a shows the BluTV architecture inserted into Ginga architecture and also highlights the structural positioning of the JavaDTV API.

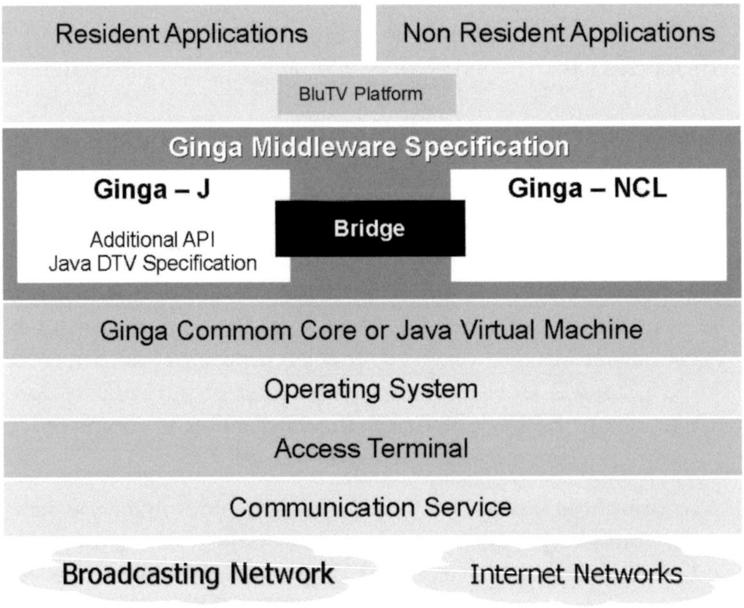

Fig. 1. JavaDTV on Ginga-J Context

The Figure 2b shows the layers of BluTV architecture, having main focus on the exploitation of the back channel for applications that make up an *Service Guide for Citizenship*.

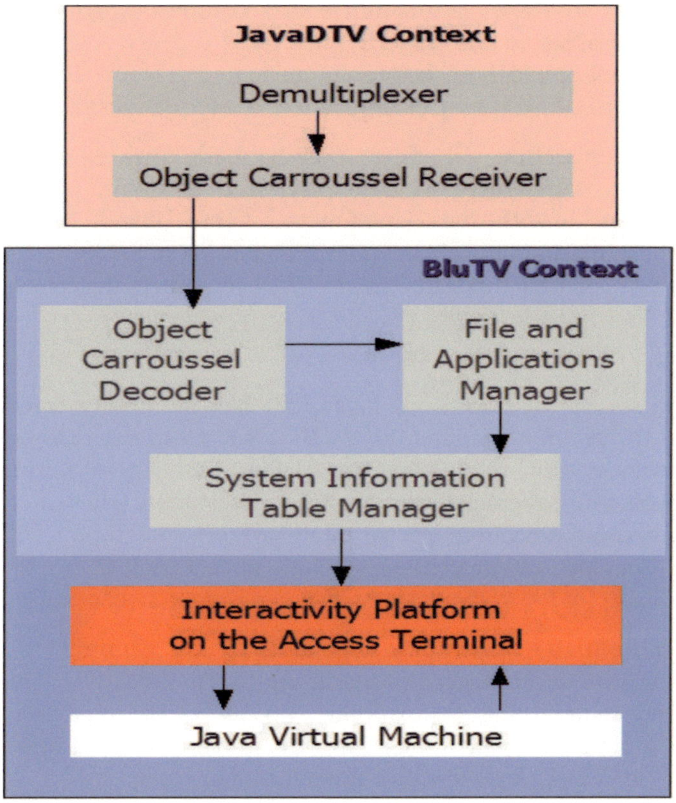

Fig. 2. The BluTV Architecture and its relations with Ginga Architecture

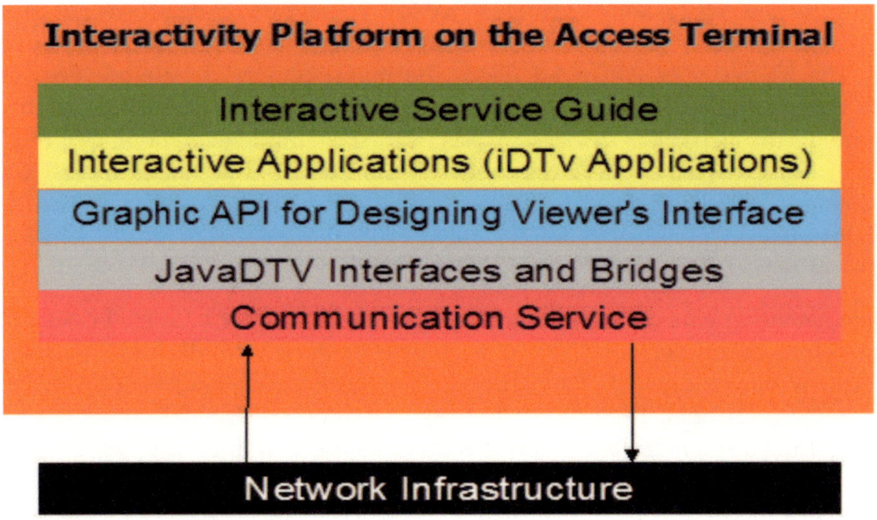

Fig. 3. Layers of the BluTV Architecture

5.1 Interactivity via back channel

Unlike what happens in other countries, where the back channel can be established using existing cable networks, in Brazil the situation is more complex (Meloni, 2007; Carvalho et al, 2007). Remote communities in the interior of a huge country like Brazil cannot attract operators of fixed or mobile telephony because of the high cost of installation and maintenance of equipment in comparison with the lack of prospect of back on investment in these regions.

Thus, in terms of infrastructure, yet efforts must be made towards the implementation of access means that do not deprive the less privileged economic classes open access to information. Experiences with the deployment of broadband networks with ADSL technology have been made in the same way that attempts to exploit the PLC (Power Line Communication) as a potential infrastructure for back channel in the context of SBTVD-T.

5.2 Implementing a communication service

A communication service is a software layer that has the ability to communicate with external servers to provide various interactive services, such as synchronous and asynchronous text messaging, download/upload files, exchange of information controlled by specific protocols and schemes based on XML description (Harren et al, 2004). In the context of iDTv, a communication service must provide integration with the interactive service provider, to enable tasks such as provision of feedback to the broadcaster and/or storage in the database (or file system using some persistence mechanism).

In the BluTV Platform, the software components of the communication service were implemented using Java technology, in accordance to the JavaDTV classes to explore the back channel, and maintaining compatibility (in terms of interfaces and integration mechanisms) with other components Ginga-J architecture, as indicated in the technical documents of the SBTVD-T. As a result of this work done from 2007 to 2010, we created a component called BluTVCommService, that was developed in order to suit any digital television system. Thus, it is possible use/adequate it to the specific frameworks, such as occurred with the specification JavaDTV in the context of Ginga-J (using the API of interactivity in the package br.org.sbtvd.net.rc) (Santos Junior et al, 2011), as illustrated in **Table 1**. The interactivity API must allow the manipulation of network devices of the receiver (access terminal). The **Table 1** shows, in summary, the main classes of the API for manipulation of network devices. Tests of the implementation of the classes BluTVCommService (which lists the network interfaces) and ConnectionRCController (which connects to an interface) have been made in the BluTV Platform. The classes to manipulate network devices were implemented using the concept of mocks, which simulate the behaviour of real objects in a controlled manner.

This implementation was done in a simulated process because the Ginga-J does not have a complete reference implementation. In a complementary way, the API of interactivity should control the deployment of synchronous and asynchronous messaging to the outside through the back channel. The class RCMessage for synchronous messaging is responsible for encapsulating a serializable object that represents the message being sent, and a locator, which contains the service of sending and destination address of the message. The constructor method of this class takes as parameters a RCMessage message to be sent as a serializable object from the Java language and a java.net.URL object, which is the locator.

Classes Ginga-J (JavaDTV)	Classes ReturnChannelCommService
br.org.sbtvd.net.rc.ReturnChannel	br.pucminas.jitv.net.rc.ReturnChannel
br.org.sbtvd.net.rc.ReturnChannelManager	br.pucminas.jitv.net.rc.ReturnChannelManager
br.org.sbtvd.net.rc.ConnectionReturnChannel	br.pucminas.jitv.net.rc.ConnectionReturnChannel
br.org.sbtvd.net.rc.ConnectionRCController	br.pucminas.jitv.net.rc.ConnectionRCController
br.org.sbtvd.net.rc.ConnectionParameters	br.pucminas.jitv.net.rc.ConnectionParameters
br.org.sbtvd.net.rc.ConnectionListener	br.pucminas.jitv.net.rc.ConnectionListener
br.org.sbtvd.net.rc.ConectionRCEvent	br.pucminas.jitv.net.rc.ConectionRCEvent
br.org.sbtvd.net.rc.ConnectionEstablishedEvent	br.pucminas.jitv.net.rc.ConnectionEstablishedEvent
br.org.sbtvd.net.rc.ConnectionFailedEvent	br.pucminas.jitv.net.rc.ConnectionFailedEvent
br.org.sbtvd.net.rc.ConnectionTerminatedEvent	br.pucminas.jitv.net.rc.ConnectionTerminatedEvent
br.org.sbtvd.net.rc.ReturnChannelException	br.pucminas.jitv.net.rc.ReturnChannelException
br.org.sbtvd.net.rc.IncompleteTargetException	br.pucminas.jitv.net.rc.IncompleteTargetException
br.org.sbtvd.net.rc.NoFreeInterfaceException	br.pucminas.jitv.net.rc.NoFreeInterfaceException
br.org.sbtvd.net.rc.NotOwnerException	br.pucminas.jitv.net.rc.NotOwnerException
br.org.sbtvd.net.rc.RCMessage	br.pucminas.jitv.net.rc.RCMessage
br.org.sbtvd.net.rc.RCAsynchronous	br.pucminas.jitv.net.rc.RCAsynchronous
br.org.sbtvd.net.rc.AsynchronousMessageTable	br.pucminas.jitv.net.rc.AsynchronousMessageTable

Table 1. Comparison between Ginga-J API (JavaDTV) and BluTVCommService

The intention in having a communication service is to ensure that each application has to implement its own form of negotiation with the interactive service provider. The layer of software has the ability to communicate with an external server to provide a wide variety of interaction services. As a complement, the HSQLDB database was incorporated into the implementation (HSQLDB, 2010), providing a persistence layer for information, both in situations of temporary lack of communication via the back channel and in situations where data persistence is necessary for logic operations provided in the application.

5.3 Main middleware aspects on interactive digital TV systems

Similar to what occurs in other technology segments, in the context of SBTVD-T we can find a good variety of digital television signal receivers, with different characteristics in terms of resources that support interactivity. This diversity of platforms suggests the existence of a layer of software, called middleware, responsible for isolating the interactive applications of the peculiarities and complexities of the hardware platform (equipment). The middleware provides a unique form of communication between applications and the operating system of the receiver, so that applications can easily use the resources of the devices. Each DTV system has its own middleware. As cited, a new system (Ginga) was built in Brazil, having implementations under development at both the industry and academy. However, the Ginga model is not well accepted and adopted by the broadcasters, specially. Thus, an interactive platform is lacking and there is space for implementing of new approaches.

The SBTVD-T middleware supports both applications with declarative languages (Ginga-NCL) and procedural languages (Ginga-J). Ginga-J incorporates many innovations and, as mentioned, became recently JavaDTV compatible with the specification developed by Sun. This work has strong links with JavaDTV.

Interactive services may require different levels of communication between the viewer/user and service provider (Soares, 2007). The, it is possible to classify a system according to the way they interact with the viewer/user. This interaction can be a local way, in which the back channel in the access terminal is not required in this case (pseudo-interactivity) (Soares, 2007). In this form of interaction, the viewer/user can interact with applications, but there is no back of information to a provider/server accessible over the communication infrastructure.

On the other hand, the full interactivity occurs when requiring the viewer/user to send information through a communication network. The information generated by applications can be transmitted freely or with restrictions (such as aspects of privacy) to the TV station (broadcaster), often having a service provider as an intermediary entity. This entity may be a component of the company itself or a broadcaster company it hired for this specific purpose.

In the context of the application, an answer / opinion of the viewer/user may be in the form of a simple command to vote or buy a product or in the form of media such as audio and video/image. Anyway, on the other end of the communication infrastructure, the interactive service provider, which may be associated with broadcaster from a business model, should be able to "hear" and react to information received by viewers, according to an interaction model defined by the broadcaster. According to Smity (Morris & Smity-Chaigneau, 2005), yet fully interactive system can be divided into unidirectional and bidirectional. The application allows only one way to send data to the viewer/user, while the application allows the bidirectional transmission of data.

5.4 Communication service interfaces and extensions to the middleware

The service BluTVCommService consists on software modules (components) and its architecture shown in **Figure 4**. These modules are: Communication Monitor Service (BluTVCommServiceMonitor); Send List Monitor (BluTVSendListMonitor); and Database Monitor (BluTVDataBaseMonitor).

The BluTVCommServiceMonitor has the aim to monitor a communication infrastructure in search of flows of serialized bytes in XML format, which represents messages being sent over the back channel. The service is materialized as a specific directory on the file system of the operating system embedded on access terminal.

The messages are collected, handled by a parser structural duly represented in accordance with the communication protocol and, finally, are placed on a waiting list to be sent. By definition, the monitor "wheel" every 30 seconds, but this time value is parametrized. Thus, a message added to the service of communication will lead up to the time stipulated by the parameter to be captured and forwarded to the sending subsystem.

The module BluTVSendListMonitor monitors the list of messages to be sent. The subsystem attempts to send each message on the list for back channel considering its parameters. Messages that are on the list are new messages or send messages whose previous attempts to have failed. If any of the messages cannot be sent, either by a failure in the back channel

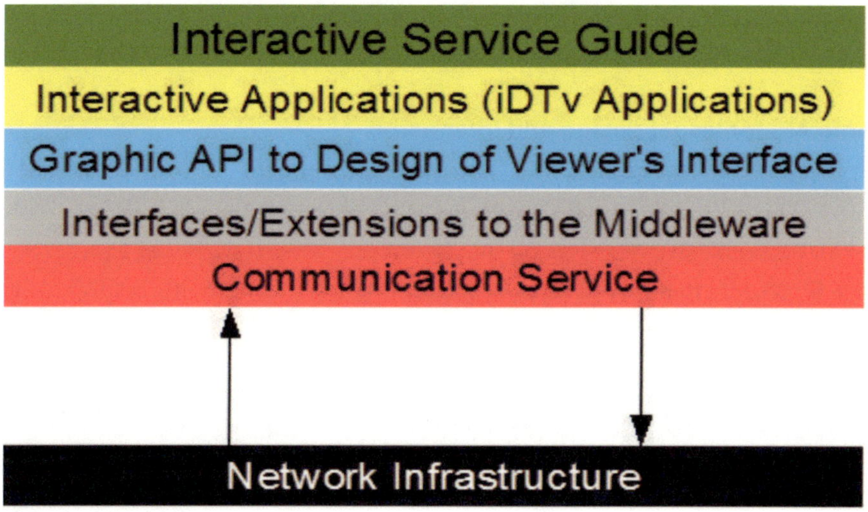

Fig. 4. BluTVCommService Components

for parametrization error message or a lack of communication service in the remote location (service provider), only the failed message will be stored in a database, to retry sending is performed when possible.

The module BluTVDataBaseMonitor is responsible for retrieving the messages that were stored in a database and put them on the list for sending. Messages that are stored in the database correspond to those which have failed to send at least once.

In terms of implementation, these monitors are threads (processes) that run independently on a recurring basis according to the time defined. So there is no problem of competition between the various threads on the mailing list, a timing system was implemented to control access to the list of messages. The various applications running on an access terminal can use the services BluTVCommService, simply by adding an XML file corresponding to the message being sent.

The first part, represented by the transport element corresponds to the configuration needed to send the message, as email addresses, socket server, web server, and others. The second part, represented by the bookmark element, is the content of the message being sent. The transport systems allowed are: email, socket, HTTP (posting on the form), FTP and web service.

5.5 Platform for prototyping

The BluTV Platform is a form to validate requirements of the interactivity in iDTv applications. This platform enables development of applications for Interactive Digital TV, with authoring tools, middleware, media distribution and media players for viewing and interaction with the viewer/user. On the viewer/user side, the BluTV Platform contains a set of tools and applications that encourage interaction. There is a multimedia player (implemented with JMF 2.1) based on multiple channels of programming, which allows control of the presentation of an audio channel and recorded video, one channel of live audio and video, an audio-only channel, a connection from a web browser, as well as areas for visualization of interacting objects and component interface such as menus, buttons, icons, among others. It is also possible to launch applications (Java bytecodes).

5.6 Graphic API for visual design and interaction

The BluTV Platform has a set of graphic widgets to design visual interfaces with the viewer/user. This API, called BluTViewer, is compatible with the LWUIT API, which is part of JavaDTV.

The **Figure 5** presents the BluTVPlayer application implemented with BluTViewer widgets, which, besides allowing interaction via remote control, also provides accessibility features for people with special needs (Santos Junior et al, 2009; CENELEC, 2003).

Fig. 5. Screenshot of the Main Application (Player) on Access Terminal (Set-top Box)

6. Interactive television application Guide for Citizenship

The Interactive Service Guide (*Citizen Portal*) is composed by nine applications. All applications are already in a state of functional prototype, with the first full version of the guide could be tested early in 2011. From the moment that all applications were properly developed and tested, the Interactive Service Guide can be embedded in equipment receptors (set-top boxes), reaching the homes of viewers/users. New features and applications can be developed and aggregated into the guide. The next sections present a summary for each one of the nine applications that make up the first version of the *Service Guide for Citizenship*. All applications are already in a state of functional prototype, with the first full version of the guide could be tested early in 2011 (Santos Junior et al, 2011).

6.1 Understanding Dengue

The application **Understanding Dengue** encourages the participation of the viewer/user through a survey of health factors to his residence in order to help identify impending risk of outbreaks of the *mosquito* that transmits the disease there. Using the remote control, the viewer/user answers a questionnaire with four questions, each one with three possible answers (Yes, Maybe and No). After collecting the responses from the viewer/user, the application takes one of two possible decisions: a) if there is no back channel available, the application reports the results on the TV screen and alert the viewer/user about these results, providing additional information about the disease; b) if there is a back channel available: the application asks for confirmation as to allow the viewer/user to send this information to relevant health authorities, particularly those at the municipal level.

6.2 Doctors in Your Home

The application **Doctors in Your Home** encourages the participation of the viewer/user by allowing the appointments through a table of medical specialities, in comparison with the needs of any patient. Using the remote control, the viewer/user needs to inform medical and query data on the availability of care in a given period, considering, including issues such as the proximity of his residence and office/clinic/hospital where exists the service. After gathering information from the viewer/user, the application takes one of two possible decisions: a) if there is no back channel available, the application displays a table with information about the availability of care, warning viewers about the fact that information may change over a period and that the request for an appointment should be made using other media such as telephone network, for example; b) if there is a back channel available: the application asks for confirmation of the viewer/user as permit the submission of information to an interactive service provider, which will provide the proper referral to the sectors responsible for scheduling the appointment.

6.3 Health Tests

The application **Health Tests** encourages the participation of the viewer/user to allow it to perform simple tests to identify risk factors for certain diseases affecting much of the population, namely: a) Hypertension; b) Obesity; c) Diabetes; d) Migraine; e) Stress. Using the remote control, the viewer/user selects the disease to which you want to perform the test and, in addition to obtaining information sheets about this disease, answered a questionnaire about their risk factors. After gathering information from the viewer/user, the application takes one of two possible decisions: a) if there is no back channel available, the application displays the test results and alert the viewer/user about these results; b) if there is a back channel available: the application displays the test results and inform viewers about the availability of health programs (at any level of government) for which the test results could be useful, where the viewer/user agrees with the submission of your test results, information will be sent to an interactive service provider, which will provide the proper referral to specific health programs.

6.4 In Case of Emergency

The application **In Case of Emergency** encourages the participation of the viewer/user by providing access to detailed information on situations of risk to health that can reach the population, namely: a) what to do in case of bites of poisonous insects; b) how to avoid domestic accidents; c) how to perform breast self-examination to identify breast nodules; d) how to perform first aid in cases of myocardial infarction and seizures; e) what to do in emergencies involving floods, fires and other natural phenomena. Using the remote control, the viewer/user selects the situation that interests you and, in addition to obtaining information on slides illustrative of this situation, also have access to telephone and contact with experts and specialized agencies in the treatment of each case.

6.5 Comprehending the Public Administration

The application **Inside Public Administration** encourages the participation of the viewer/user to allow access to information about activities, events and programs from any of the three levels of government: a) Municipal; b) State; c) Federal. Using the remote control, the viewer/user selects the level of government over which you want information. According to the selected level, information sheets are presented with details of: a) functional organizational chart of government; b) telephones and other forms of contact with government agencies and its officers; c) political and administrative agenda, especially in meetings, seminars and other events open to the public; d) job opportunities and to enter contests.

6.6 The Community Sends News

The application **The Community Sends News** is a complementary application to the **Inside Public Administration**, encouraging participation of the viewer/user by allowing the establishment of a communication channel between citizens and public administrations in any of three levels of government: a) municipal; b) state; c) federal. Using the remote control, the viewer/user selects the level of government with which to communicate. According to the selected level, the following contact options are allowed: a) claim; b) requests; c) advice; d) additional information. The viewer/user must select the type of contact and inform the data needed for each case. Fill in the contact data from the viewer/user, the application, considering the availability of a back channel and forward a copy of such data to an interactive service provider, which will provide the proper referral to the government authorities recipients. At any time, viewers/users can track the status of your contact.

6.7 Banking

The application **Banking** encourages participation of the viewer/user to allow access to basic information of the bank account, and allows the simulation of loans and financing. Using the remote control, the viewer/user selects the bank with which it has business relationships. To ensure the minimum security for access and requires the user ID by verifying data registered with the financial institution. Allowed access, the viewer/user has available a list of options for consultation and quote. It is worth noting that, at this moment, only query transactions can be made, not possible for now, operations are characterized as financial transactions.

6.8 Repository of News

The application *Repository of News* encourages participation of the viewer/user by providing access to news in real time, from the widely know brazilian portals, such as UOL, Terra, G1, among others. Using the remote control, the viewer/user selects the news class that wishes to view (**Figure 6**), namely: a) Lastest; b) News; c) Sports; d) Economy; e) Technology.

Fig. 6. Screenshot of the Repository of News Application Running on Access Terminal

According to PNAD (PNAD, 2010), this application could be used by 73% of brazilian population, that has no access to news by Internet. Using the remote control, after selecting a class of news, the viewer/user choose the news for viewing. Using the back channel, if it is available, comments about the news can be sent to an interactive service provider.

6.9 The School on TV

The application **The School on TV** encourages the participation of the viewer/user by providing access to data from the school life of a student, allowing parents and guardians may have a complementary form of monitoring of activities that are undertaken within the school. Using the remote control, the viewer/user selects the school and the series in which the student is enrolled. From that point, to inform the student's name, it is possible to get information about the transcript and also on the schedule of activities of the week. If desired, the viewer/user can communicate with the school, sending comments and questions through the back channel and an interactive service provider, which establishes the necessary communication with the provider responsible for maintaining the information the school wants to provide.

7. Scenarios for testing and future directions

As a cited, the BluTV is a platform for developing interactive digital television applications, specially in terms of context of the Brazilian Digital Television System Terrestrial (SBTVD-

T). The one of the most promising technologies of interactive video, the Interactive Digital Television has as one of its main objectives to allow high levels of interaction between the viewer and the interactive programs that are presented to him. From the point of view of the development technologies for interactive television, Java and XML blunt as good solutions contained into main international standards/systems for digital television (ATSC, DVB, ISDB). For testing BluTV Platform, several applications are being developed in the SBTVD-T scenarios, in partnership with the public brazilian broadcasters (*in portuguese* - TV Alterosa and Rede Minas de Televisão). In these tests, the both middleware requirements of SBTVD-T and BluTV functionalities are being validated. The usability heuristics are being used for usability tests.

According to Jacob Nielsen, there are ten general principles for user interface design, being used to test the usability of a system. For realizing tests with applications developed based on BluTV Platform, some these heuristics (five, more exactly) were both adapted and applied. In these tests, 500 (five hundreds) TV viewers are being used as subjects.

The *Visibility of Interactive Application Status* is the first heuristic on tests. The main objective is to identify if the interactive application always keeps the viewer informed on where in the application he is. In following, the *Match Between Interactive Application and the Real World* is the heuristic applied. The main objective is to identify whether the application has a language of communication appropriate to viewers, especially since Brazil has a large number of people with low education. The heuristic *TV Viewer Control and Freedom* is being used to identify whether the controls are clear enough for interaction, especially those selected to cancel operations wrong. Furthermore, the heuristic *Recognition Rather Than Recall* is being applied to identify whether the navigation in interactive applications cause the user to acknowledge the operations and actions, without having to memorize them, especially the fact that the remote control is the basic device to inputs and interaction. Finally, viewing aspects are being tested using the heuristic *Aesthetic and Minimalist Design of the Application Interface*. In this case, the main objective is to identify whether the information dialogue with the viewer is sufficiently clear and contains only the both essential and necessary elements.

Tests have been conducted both in laboratory and in specially created environments in broadcast television partner of the research projects in which this work is placed. Five hundreds subjects are being evaluated in these experiments. Results of these tests and developments in the implementation of the applications will be reported in further work.

8. Conclusions

This chapter has presented contributions related to the SBTVD-T, from the BluTV Platform, focusing on three main aspects: a) the architecture and implementation of the platform; b) the use of BluTV for building an Interactive Service Guide in the context of SBTVD-T, whose basic premise fundamental to building the infrastructure that supports the use of this guide on promotion of citizenship through digital inclusion via television; c) the scenarios for testing of this guide and validating of the platform components and tools.

This chapter also presents contribution related to the implementation of a *Service Guide for Citizenship* in the context of SBTVD-T, whose basic premise fundamental to building the infrastructure that supports the use of this guide on promotion of citizenship through digital inclusion via television. Besides the aspects of infrastructure and management, applications that make up the guide were presented, as well as the stage of their development. As cited, tests have been conducted both in laboratory and in broadcasting environments, using the infrastructure provided by broadcaster partners of this research. The results of these tests and developments will be reported in further works.

9. Acknowledgements

The authors are Granted to FAPEMIG (Research Support Foundation of Minas Gerais - *Programa Pesquisador Mineiro – Fase III*) and FIP PUC Minas (Research Incentive Fund).

10. References

Batista, C. E. C. F. et al. (2007). TVGgrid: A Grid Architecture to Use the Idle Resources on a Digital TV Network. In: IEEE International Symposium on Cluster Computing and the Grid: Vol. 0 (pp. 823-828). IEEE Computer Society, Los Alamitos, CA, USA.

Carvalho, E. R. de et al. (2007). The Brazilian Digital Television System Access Device Architecture. Journal of Brazilian Computer Society. I(2), Vol 13, 95-113. ISSN 0104-6500.

CENELEC (2003). Standardisation Requirements for Access to Digital TV and Interactive Services by Disabled People. European Committee for Electrotechnical Standardization-CENELEC. Retrieved January, 2011, from http://www.cenelec.org/NR/rdonlyres/8134-472D-BF06 009AEBA6A5B1/0/interimreportTVforAll.pdf

Claraső, J. et al (2009). Interactive Digital Terrestrial Television:The Interoperability Challenge in Brazil. International Journal of Digital Multimedia Broadcasting. I(2), Vol. 1, 17 p. Doi:10.1155/2009/579569.

Dong-Heon, J. et al (2010). Hybrid Java compilation and optimization for digital TV software platform. In: CGO'2010 Proceedings of the 8th annual IEEE/ACM International Symposium on Code Generation and Optimization (p.124). ACM New York, NY, USA.

Filho, G. L. S. et al. (2007). Ginga-J: The Procedural Middleware for the Brazilian Digital TV System. Journal of the Brazilian Computer Society. Special Issue on Digital TV. I(4), Vol. 12, 1-23. ISSN 0104-6500.

Harren, M.; Raghavachari, M.; Shmuele, O.; Burke, M.; Sarkar, V. & Bordawekar, R. (2004). Integration of XML Processing into Java. In: Proceedings of the 13th International World Wide Web Conference (p.214). New York, USA.

HSQLDB (2010). Joined Database System. Retrieved on June, 2010 from http://hsqldb.org.

Jianmin, J; Kohler, J.; MacWilliams, C.; Zaletelj, J.; Guntner, G.; Horstmann, H.; Ren, J.; Loffler, J.; Ying Weng (2011): LIVE: An Integrated Production and Feedback System for Intelligent and Interactive TV Broadcasting. IEEE Transactions on Broadcasting, Vol.57 , No. 3, pp. 646 - 661, 2011.

Kyriazis, D.; Kousiouris, G.; Menychtas, A.; Doulamis, A.; Varvarigou, T. (2011): Interactive Social TV on Service Oriented Environments: Challenges and Enablers. Games and Virtual Worlds for Serious Applications (VS-GAMES), 2011 Third International

Conference on Digital Object Identifier: 10.1109/VS-GAMES.2011.30. 2011, (p.152-155).

Meloni, L. G. P. (2007). Return Channel for the Brazilian Digital Television System-Terrestial. Journal of Brazilian Computer Society. I(1), Vol. 13, 83-94. ISSN 0104-6500.

Morris, S. & Smity-Chaigneau, A. (2005). Interactive TV Standards - A Guide to MHP, OCAP and JavaTV. ISBN-13 978-0-240-80666- 2. Elsevier, Focal Press.

Peng, C. (2002). Digital Television Applications. Ph.D. Thesis on Science of Information. Helsinki University of Technology, Espoo, Finland.

Santos Junior, J. B. dos et al (2010). Trends on Building Interactive Applications in the Brazilian Digital Television System. In: 7th Annual IEEE Consumer Communications and Networking Conference (p. 126). Las Vegas, CA, USA.

Santos Junior, J. B. dos et al (2011). Applications in the Brazilian Digital Television System. In: IMSA-IASTED 2011 Internet and Multimedia Systems and Applications (p. 95). Washington, D.C., USA.

Santos Junior, J. B. dos; Abrão, I. C.; Barrere, E. & Ávila, P. M. (2008b). Interactive Digital Television Programs: Formatting, Presentation and Interaction with the Viewer. In: Proceedings of EuroITV2008 (p.232). Salzburg, Austria.

Santos Junior, J. B. dos; Abrão, I. C.; Morselli, J.C.M.; Teixeira, F.C.; Prado, G. M. & Ávila, P. M. (2009). Back Channel in Interactive Digital Television Systems: Strategies for Prototyping Applications Using an Interactive Service Provider. In: 11th International Conference on Enterprise Information Systems (p.212). Milano, Italy.

Santos Junior, J. B. dos; Abrão, I.C.; Barrere, E; Avila, P.M.; Massote, G. & Santos, M. (2008a). A Platform for Difusion Interactive Multimedia Content: An Approach Focused on IPTV System and Broadcasting Digital Television System. In: Proceedings of EATIS 2008 - Euro American Conference on Telematics and Information Systems (p.156). Aracaju-SE, Brazil.

SBTVD-Forum (2010). The Brazilian Digital Television System Forum. SBTVD. ABNT/CEE-85. Retrieved on May, 2010 from http://tvdilab.inf.pucpcaldas.br/repositorioopenginga/SBTVD-T-Parte4-NormaGingaJ.pdf

Soares, L. F. G. (2007). Ginga-NCL: The Declarative Environment of the Brazilian Digital TV System. Journal of the Brazilian Computer Society. Special Issue on Digital TV. I(4), Vol. 12, 24-45. ISSN 0104-6500.

The JavaDTV Specification 1.0. (2010). On-line Documentation of Java Digital Television Specification. Oracle (Sun Microsystems) Inc. Retrieved June 30, 2010, from http://tvdilab.inf.pucpcaldas.br/openginga.htm.

Vrba, V.; Cvrk, L. & Sykora, M. (2006). Framework for Digital TV Applications. In: ICNICONSMCL '06: Proceedings of the International Conference on Networking, International Conference on Systems and International Conference on Mobile Communications and Learning Technologies (p.184). Washington, DC, USA: IEEE Computer Society. ISBN 0-7695-2552-0.

14

Molecular Model for Multimedia Screenwriting

Lamboux-Durand Alain
University Lille Nord de France, Lille,
UVHC, DeVisu, Valenciennes,
France

1. Introduction

From its inception, multimedia's documents have experienced many developments. These changes are often the result of technological advances, but economic pressures have also helped to change the form of documents produced and to change the methods of work to product the documents. In the euphoria of the 1990s many multimedia start-ups were created. The lack of good work practices and of risk assessment has led many of them to bankrupt (Viéville, 2003). This experience resulted in a restrictive streamlining of production. Today, most of multimedia documents are only a hierarchical and indexed form of an information website: the risks of financial excesses are limited by reproducing the same documents structures and by applying specific ergonomic rules. So there is a standardization of documents structures and of methods used to produce them (Cartier, 2003). Despite a specification of methods and tools for multimedia design documents – AUTHOR methodology (Huart, 2000) (see figure 1), web design in terms of effective

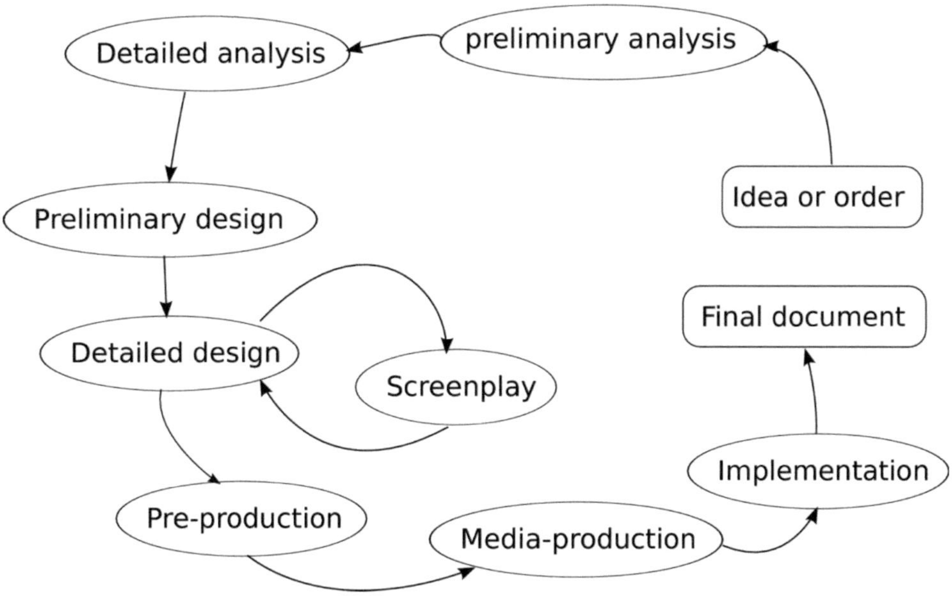

Fig. 1. AUTHOR methodology

communication (Rojas, 2007; Pignier & Drouillat, 2004) or specific tool (Bailey & al., 2001) – the writing process is often overlooked. Most often, creativity is only expressed only through the graphics and user interfaces.

The aim of the present work is to provide a writing formalism for multimedia usable by most authors (literary writer, artists). To quote Yves Jeanneret and Emmanuel Souchier the aim of this model is to define an "Architext" (Jeanneret & Souchier, 2005) writing tool.

Firstly, the functions of a multimedia screenplay will be presented. Secondly, molecular screenwriting, which has been adapted to the representation of multimedia documents, will be described in order to meet the criteria set out in the first part. The terminal goal is to provide a simple tool for textual representation of multimedia documents with autonomous entity able to interact with each other and the user – as an intelligent agent (Genesereth & Nilsson, 1987).

2. Screenwriting

Before describing the screenwriting problems in multimedia design, we will describe some characteristics of multimedia production.

2.1 Multimedia production

The multimedia development requires the production of various documents. These will be incorporated into the final document with functions for interaction between the document and the user.

For large documents, many specialists are involved in their implementation. Thus, the production of a multimedia document requires some flawless organization and planning. Indeed, the slightest malfunction involves problematic costs. So, it is necessary, before starting the production, to have the equivalent of high-performance "plan" for architects. From these we have to imagine what will be the document before completion. Television and motion picture production, for this point of view, are close to the multimedia (except the aspect of interactivity's development). The script is a centerpiece of the "plan". However, if the organization design and implementation models of the Audiovisual are partly adaptable to multimedia, the interactive specificities of multimedia and of associated supports are beyond the motion-pictures models capacities: shooting scripts and storyboards are too linear.

2.2 Screenwriting for which document

Today, there are several kinds of multimedia designers. The "lonely" designers and those who work in teams. The former tend to avoid the script writing and the latter must write a screenplay as revealed by Nicolas Viéville (Viéville, 2003).The script is based primarily on the graphic environment and on the model of interactivity, as the features to reach the different parts of the document – usually the definition of menus and buttons (Fournier, 2003).

However, the script models are ossified by the hyperlinks and documents are static (except in the virtual world of the games). Jean-Pierre Balpe already wrote on this fact in the 1990s about CD-ROMs (Balpe 1997). Today, despite the development of broadband networks and computer performance, link structure can be found in most websites. The capacity for self development of the document is thin.

So, the multimedia script, as a product of multimedia design (whether web design, game design or other types of documents) is similar to the description of a puppet wire show. Each wire (which is a link, a built-in function) enables a specific action controlled by the puppeteer (representing the user). Then, the author acts as a master of the world: nothing can be done, nothing can be predicted, unless it was clearly conceived by the designer. We are in a logic of "nothing-but": nothing is possible except what is expressly specified. To represent some living document (with the dimension of generativity, and scalability), you must sweep the hierarchical representation and adopt a different approach (as the droid approach which enable the logic of "all-except" described in part 2.2.2).

2.2.1 Diegesis as a multimedia script

In fact, more than screenplay, it would be wise to talk about potential screenplay : that's the diegesis - to borrow a film term. This concept, was introduced in France by Etienne Souriau (Souriau, 1953). The diegesis is the (fictional) world in which the situations and events narrated occur, and telling, recounting, as opposed to showing, enacting (Prince, 2003). It is a virtual world, with entities, and which is governed by laws. Entities are objects, things (real or imaginary), involved in the development and the description of the environment.

Contrary to a film scriptwriter - who represents a linear story - it is impossible for the multimedia author to know the structure, the order, of the information units which will be broadcast through the document. This fact hampers the design of live documents when the authors are artists.

The current software abilities may enable agent reasoning in the design documents. So the author defines each entity - spaces (concrete places,...), abstract objects (active, inactive...), people (real, imaginary...) and so on - of the document.

Each entity "knows" the actions or the changes it can cause. At the opposite of "wires puppets" thinking (the author observes the document as a world master), the droid reasoning enables the observation of the environment throughout each entity. It is then possible to imagine live entities. The authors could even use an "all-except" thinking: everything is possible except that which was prohibited by the author.

To adopt this reasoning, a radical change of mindset is needed. The representation of live entities has led to abandon the linear representations (the tree structure of the scripts) in favour of a structure that the computer scientists could name intelligent agents (Russell & Norvig, 2010).

2.2.2 Form of representation as an object of multimedia screenplay

This change in attitude causes serious ideological problems. Jean-Pierre Balpe would say that "The book is the problem..."(Balpe, 2001). Indeed, today, the author (or the designer) does not accept that the "scenation" (i.e. order of informations units broadcast) (Colin, 1992) is not strictly equivalent to what he expected. This fact limits inevitably the range of possibilities. Many authors consider that if they can't define all "scenation" of the document, part by part, they are deprived of their creation. This is a major problem for researchers who are working on generative and interactive storytelling: what is the author's status in an automatic generation of documents (texts, dialogues, computers graphics...) (Szilas & Axelrad, 2009)? Yet the author holds a prominent position in the autonomous documents. He instils his creative vision in the document - through the entity descriptions and their potential evolutions... If the designer has defined how the entities of the document work with sufficient creativity, the document will then be imbued with his creative power. The author will not be dispossessed of his creation, quite the contrary.

2.3 Features of the multimedia screenplay

The screenplay is the abstract representation of the document. It uses a specific formalism, appropriate to imagine the document. The multimedia script is a model of the document which will be made. It includes interactive features. With the screenplay, all stakeholders of the production and its preparation may imagine the future document.

First, the script used to evaluate the production costs - and thereby its financial feasibility. For a financed document, this could result in an increase or decrease in the scale of the multimedia document.

As in the audiovisual sector, the multimedia screenplay can help the author to find funds for the document production. Then, script - as any plan in architecture - is written and drawn, or at least separate of any process of production (unlike the "author software" which implements media or - at the best - simulates the "scenation" process).

2.3.1 Production process separated from screenplay

The screenplay is a document required for the pre-production staff - to prepare the media production and their implementation. It enables one to define technical solutions to produce the document. If the script clearly expresses the communicative choices of the product and its appearance, the staff can then best produce the document and approach more likely the original objectives. This is only possible if the screenplay is separated from any production process. Even if the specifications define some technical constraints, they should not impose an ossified mode of creation.

The author imagines a multimedia document. He designs an interactive creation. He is guided by his personal knowledge (or ignorance) about the possibilities of technical support. However, the script is not concerned with the media production and their implementation: he frees himself from describing the technical solutions.

A production process separated from screenplay means that the script is not a simulation of the document (unlike the script for software engineering) but a formalized representation of the creation (Colin, 1992). The screenplay is so far from any automation of the media implementation. It will be the preferred means of communication of the production and implementation team. Anybody can correctly imagine the document with a shared reference: the screenplay. It outlines the communication goals of the document and also the component objects.

This representation of the document is the reference for its production and its implementation process. It requires a formalism, a code, which enables it to be understood by the greatest number of stakeholders during the project process. This code becomes identified with formal model of design. It will become a tool for the author to express his ideas. So, the written screenplay highlights the coherence of the creation, before its production.

Consequently, with the formal model of design the designer can express:

- the functions of the document parts,
- the solutions (directly or indirectly perceived by the reader, the document user), to achieve the communication goals during the script writing.

This enables an audit by comparing the solutions (proposed by the designer through the screenplay) and the objectives (defined in the specifications). In addition, each stakeholder of the project can thus operate with defined goals. Everyone in the staff offers the optimum technical solutions within the framework of the document production, while enabling any creative (or aesthetic) "finds". This enables a calmer work during the production and this improves the creator's job. Bertrand Tavernier (a French film director) said about this idea: "When I make a movie, I spend a long time to polish the script. With Jean Cosmos, we wrote 17 versions of Conan... After I'm free, I know where I go, I can use the improvisation" (Raspiengas, 1997). So when the shooting starts, everything is perfectly defined: the film director can entirely focus on his artistic work.

To achieve these objectives, the formal model design should be suitable for the human processes of the creation and needs of the script reader.

2.3.2 Relevance to human processes: Creative process

Creation is a development, a series of continuous exchanges between ideas and their expression. The expression of an idea leads to its conceptualization. It then has to developed, broken down: a vague screenplay element become clearer. The product of this formalization generates new ideas that must respect the project coherence. Creativity changes constantly from a general specification to a detailed expression and vice versa. During all stages from script writing to production, the possibility of an overview as so as the precision of details is important.

Screenplay generic model could facilitate the breakdown of meaningful entities in several others smaller, the braking down of elements specifies the original entities. At the opposite, an author also writes the screenplay with detailed ideas. He then joins it to the general design model before it is completely structured. To some extent, this is a synthesis of elements of scriptwriting. This abstract is based on a composition of elements to introduce more general ones.

Furthermore, with some detailed elements the creator is able to write other script elements - particular or general - while maintaining the overall coherence of the future document. Often a particular point is the catalyst for a part of the creative process. Moreover, the details can be dramatic nodes (i.e. milestones which structure and justify the development of the way).

This is consistent with the thinking of John Locke. For him, all our ideas come from experience: "Our understandings derive all the materials of thinking from observations that we make of external objects that can be perceived through the senses, and of the internal operations of our minds, which we perceive by looking in at ourselves. These two are the fountains of knowledge, from which arise all the ideas we have or can naturally have." (Locke, 1690)

2.3.3 Relevance to human processes: Microscopic and macroscopic view

The different accuracy level of the document's representation is particularly important for the coherence study or for the understanding of the document objectives.

Also, some stakeholders only need to have a large point of view and to read the general properties of the document. Conversely others use only specific elements of the screenplay. However, they still want to soak up an overall feel to apprehend the subject, and have development issues that affect them specifically.

In short, a model of multimedia screenplay should enable

- to develop general facts of the script by making elemental components conversely
- to build general constituent by assembling simple elements.
  These possibilities are related both to the script itself and to its formal model. Indeed, the making up and the braking of microscopic and macroscopic components are as important for writing the script as for reading it afterwards.

2.3.4 Autonomous entities and reader model

In video games, some rules of operations, of games, define the live entities. It is commonly accepted that the games are not scripting (Alvarez & al., 2007). This is only a consequence of the lack of representation for live entities. So, the multimedia screenplay should define some entities with their operating rules. Thus, each entity can interact with any other entity (virtual entity in the document or the most important: the reader). The document is designed for readers. So, the human part of the receptor guides all the design process. It is therefore better if the script includes some imprint of relationships - cognitive and psychological - as intended by the author. This can go through a reader model.

The reader model is not the user model defined in artificial intelligence. In fact, it should provide the representation of the reader imagined by the author. It is an avatar. This is not to reify the reader but to specify some possible evolutions of entities based on a hypothetical user. Thus, changes in the document may be determined by the state of the imagined reader through his model.

It will also arbitrarily define a mental model of the reader toward the messages broadcast in order to facilitate:

- The assessment task,
- The objectives understanding by all stakeholders.

In addition, a reader's model takes into account the modes of action of the user. These action modes will enable the definition of a reader type (in conjunction with the hypothetical operating rules of the mental model) according to his responsiveness and the document itself. The document will then develop a strategy for development adapted to different types of readers. Few documents were based on a hypothetical nature of the reader (following his behaviour and his attitude during the broadcast).

The reader is part of a system in which the document takes place with its technical environment. The model of the reader enables one to imagine the reader with the data provide by the human-computer interface. The image of the reader within the document is not an exact representation. It can even be completely wrong, perhaps because the reader acts to deceive the live document, or simply because the model is not suitable to the reader's type.

In an artistic design, the model of the reader is often designed without specific reference. Then, the reader's representation - constructed by the document - is not likely to correspond to the reality. It reflects an artistic approach. This approach will provide the coherence between the document and the author's project.

2.4 Rule of the screenplay and its generic model

In short, the specifications for a generic multimedia script are classified under two headings.

The first defines the script and its model at a conceptual level and thus separates the script from its implementation in order to:

- provide a real creative process,
- help the designer to express and expand his ideas,
- enable the production of a script for improving the communication between stakeholders.

The second advises the integration of communication characteristics with humans through:

- a model of formalization of functions,
- a hypothetical model of the reader,
- a formalism that enables a representation of the document from a macroscopic to a microscopic point of view and vice versa.

These criteria, which may seem based on a common sense, are only partially used in multimedia design. The lack of writing tool, and before, the lack of formalization for an abstract representation of multimedia documents (from websites to virtual worlds through the video games) are one of the reasons for the paralyse of multimedia documents mentioned above. The rest of this chapter proposes a writing structure for multimedia authors based on the principles outlined above.

3. Molecular scriptwriting

The general way of molecular representation uses the document's diegesis. The representation with entities makes it possible to formalize evolutionary or generative elements. Thus, with a model of the reader, the author can imagine ways for reader-document interaction. This model can be defined by hypothesis.

3.1 Introduction to molecular screenwriting

The goal of the molecular model is to be able to write and to represent some live documents while forbidding an automatic implementation of the document with the script. This formalism designed for writers, artists (possibly hermetic to technical tools of production) to provide a way to write the screenplay of a multimedia document. This script will enable stakeholders to understand and to realize the multimedia document as the author imagined it.

This model, as its name implies, was designed by analogy with the concepts of chemistry. It is therefore based on atoms and molecules. The molecular model doesn't consider the script as a sequence of things, facts and actions any longer. It aims at representing entities, with their operating rules and their potential actions (based on the environment). Atoms and molecules describe the entities and their potential actions induced by special circumstances. They are necessary for the formal representation of the multimedia document. Atoms are simple elements. A single text entity describes a script atom. In contrast, the molecules are complex elements whose description requires several distinct components. Thus, a molecule can be composed of several atoms or molecules.

3.2 Atoms and molecules of a screenplay

There are three major families of atoms and molecules to build the model:

- The diegetics atoms and molecules describe the entities of the document;
- The circonstantials atoms and the cyclical molecules describe the different circumstances involved in the document;
- The atoms and the molecules of actions describe the actions by changing situations, the entities, the state of the document.

3.2.1 Diegetic atoms and diegetic molecules

Atoms and molecules diegetic represent the entities of the document.

Each one is a fragment of a screenplay and represents the element as an entity of the document.

A diegetic atom with an elementary representation (partial or total) is sufficient to define conceptually - at a particular stage of the design - the part of the entity.

Here, the diegetic atoms are represented here by oval elements.

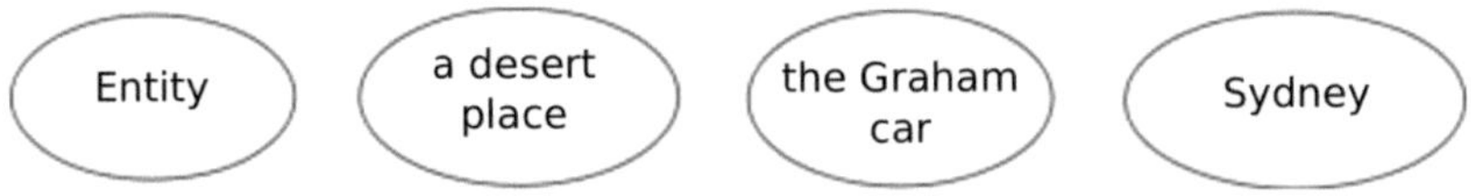

Fig. 2. Examples of diegetic atoms

A diegetic molecule is the complex conceptual representation of an autonomous entity of the document. The temporal dimension of those molecules is underlying (the entities have the ability to obey to rules of operation or behaviour, and thus are related to time).

A diegetic molecule is composed, in addition to the name that defines of:

- interlocking factors: they define the conditions of occurrence of the represented entity,
- perceptible descriptions: they describe the factors affecting the physiological perception of the entity by the reader,

- semantic descriptions: they describe all orders which aren't perceptible.

The name given to the entity can be identified. This identifier is usually an expression representative of the entity. The name can also be called an alias.

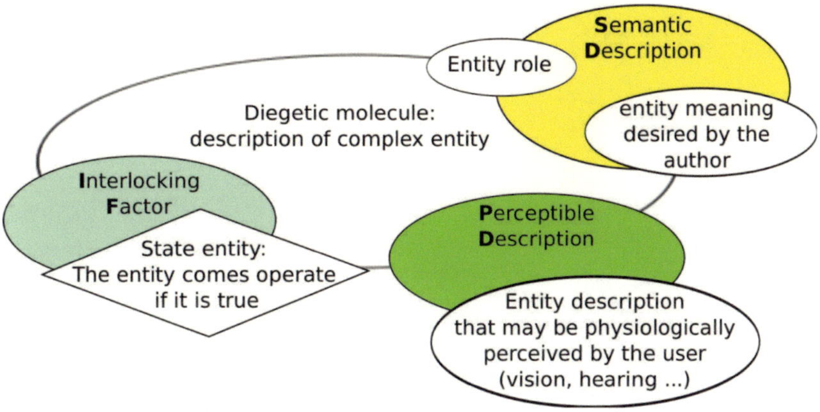

Fig. 3. Graphical representation of a diegetic molecule

Elements of Perceptible Descriptions describe the characteristics of the entity actually visible. This description may contain a set of atoms or molecules of sensible nature, that is to say related to events that will physiological affect our senses of perception (if the corresponding entities are shown). These can be compared to the description of expressions of a message in semiotics (Deely, 2005).

Thus, the apparent descriptions define what can be seen and heard of the entity during the reading of the document. These descriptions can be purely factual (definition of an established fact) or set of potential actions of the entity (travels, environmental changes...)

If - for example - a diegetic molecule represents a house, the size and the appearance of the building descriptions are visible.

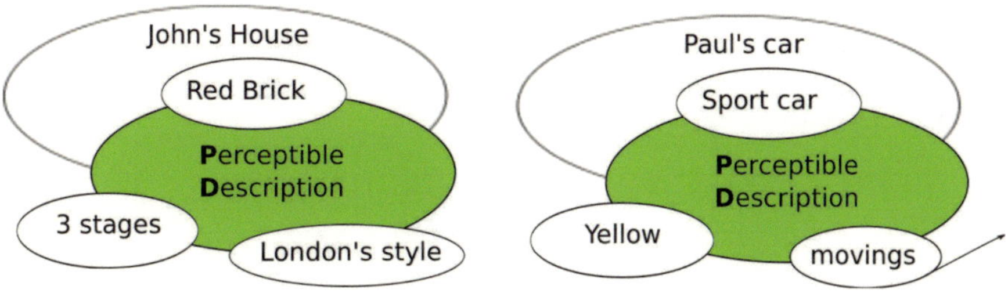

Fig. 4. Example of descriptions of two visible molecules

The elements of Semantic Descriptions specify the entity significance (intended by the author) and anything that can not be directly seen physiologically.

The communication's functions of the entity are also described in the semantic descriptions.

For example, if the author wishes to define a molecule representing a character who is afraid, the indication of the fear of the character is the semantic description. At this level of design, this fear is not directly observable. This is however not necessary. This description will be converted by visible facts (beads of sweat, eyes bulging, stillness, nervous tremors, screams, etc... falling within the perceptible description) much later, when one approaches the "scenic" and the manufacture of the document - the "scenic" is the process to translate the text into a concrete reality: it is the result of aesthetic choices, practical constraints or financial... (Leleu-Merviel, 2005) .

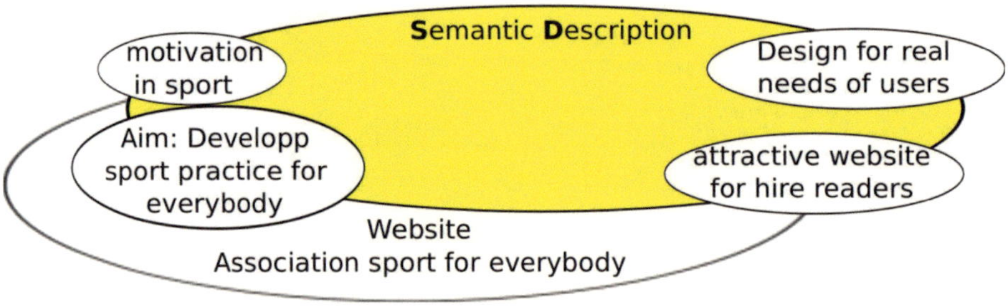

Fig. 5. Example of semantic descriptions related to the functions of the document

The semantic descriptions can also define some useful information for the staging of the document. Thus, the psychological description of a character occurs within this description.

In the early stages of writing the script, in the macro-molecules (molecules most general), the semantic descriptions are very important. They can indicate the function (particularly in terms of meaning) of the documents being written.

The direction indicated by these descriptors is potential. The semantic descriptions are a statement of intents. They contain the objective meaning of the information transmitted to the reader.

The interlocking factors are running the entity. They depend on the entity being described. If any of the circumstances (or conjunctures) specified (within the factors) is true the entity is showing it, putting it on the stage, making it active...

These interlocking factors are major players in the autonomy of the represented entities So the entities themselves contain the conditions of the necessary information (but not necessarily sufficient) for putting them into function (display, arrival in the area of a perception of the reader...).

Tetris	**Interlocking factor**	**Sémantic Descriptions**
	Lancement du jeu	Jeu
	Perceptible Descriptions	
	Partie Tétris	Fin de partie

Fig. 6. Example of switching factor of a molecule in a tabulo-graphic representation

It may be noted that an active entity is not necessarily perceived directly by the reader. For example, if a light bulb in a closed tightly box, it is not perceived as operating from outside.

3.2.2 Circumstantial atoms, cyclical molecules

A circumstantial atom, formalized in figure 7 with a diamond, is the representation of a screenplay circumstance.

Circumstance specifies an instance of state. The state of circumstances is evaluated by a logical variable. Thus, in binary logic, a circumstance is true or not true - It is also possible to adopt a fuzzy logic (Zadeh, 1965) to improve the evolution capacity of the document.

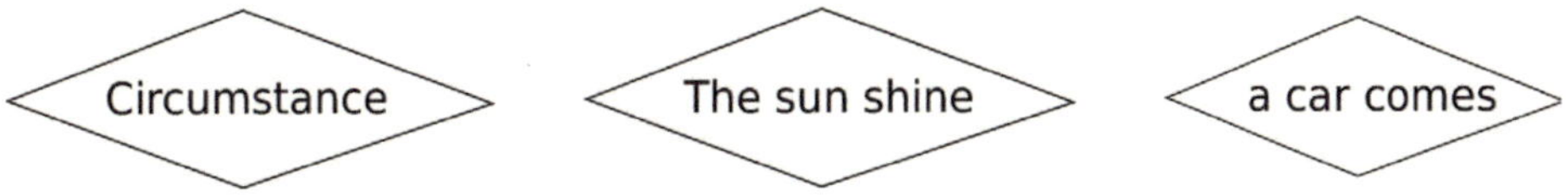

Fig. 7. Circumstantial atom and Examples

If a circumstance is insufficient to describe a state, it will be described by a combination of facts that is to say a conjuncture.

A cyclical molecule is the representation of a conjuncture within the script. (see figure 8).

A conjuncture is a set of circumstances (or of conjunctures). It is constituting a logical proposition. As a circumstance, a conjuncture is assessed in accordance with the logic used (binary, fuzzy...), even though the binary logic was chosen here in order to simplify the development.

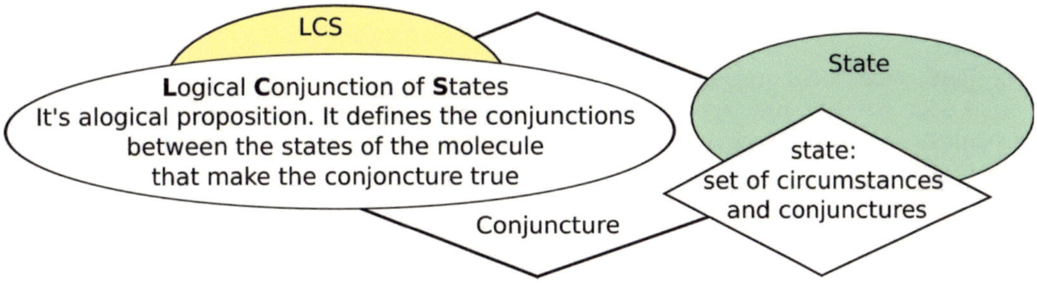

Fig. 8. Graphical representation of a cyclical molecule

A cyclical molecule is composed of:

- states (that correspond to conditions or circumstances which will be checked to make the situation true),
- logical conjunction of states (that define the logical links between all states of the molecule).

The states of a cyclical molecule are circumstances or conjunctures that the cyclical molecule contains. They represent conditions that contribute to real molecule.Cyclical molecule can be defined by a single state. In one screenplay, it can re-express a state. This enables one to define more precisely a fact without increasing the molecule which contains this state. The figure 9 is an example.

When a cyclical molecule contains several cyclical conditions or circumstances, rules are needed to prioritize their operation. It is the role of logical conjunction of the states.

Conjunctions of Logical States (LCS) define the logical links between all the states that define the molecule and contribute to its cyclical expression.

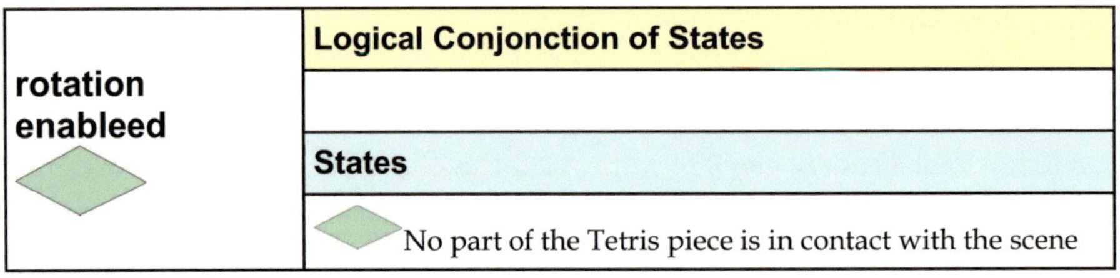

Fig. 9. Example of conditions defined by a single state

Indeed, a situation may be true if only one of the circumstances is true. Conversely, there may be an obligatory combination of a set of circumstances to asses it. So these conditions define relationships of the type "and", "or", "no" and other logical operators, among the elements in the circumstance.

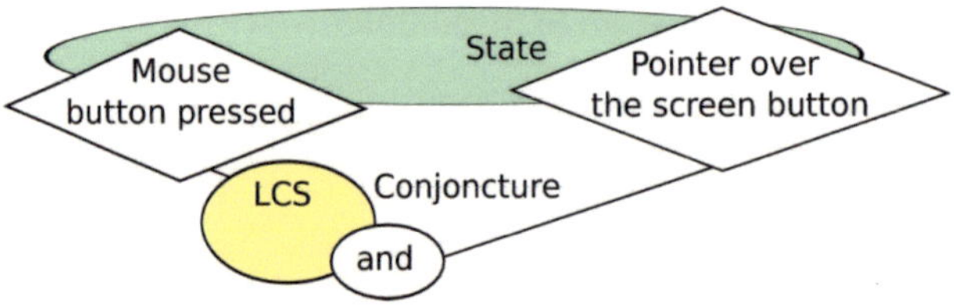

Fig. 10. Example of description of circumstances

At a given time, a circumstance or a situation is true or false. Depending on their value, entities can be put into operation (depending on the interlocking factors of diegetic molecules), or events can be triggered.

It is interesting to note that despite the binary logic used, it is possible for the author to introduce a form of fuzzy logic. For example, if a molecule is considered true if "the character is close to the trap" and if the author did not define absolute criteria of proximity, the programmer can adapt this concept in fuzzy logic.

3.3 Atoms and molecules of action

The last type of atom, the atom of action - that is, below in figure 11, the shape of an oval with an arrow - defines an event or a procedure of the screenplay.

An atom of action is an elementary event. An event is an action - or set of actions - aimed at changing the system.

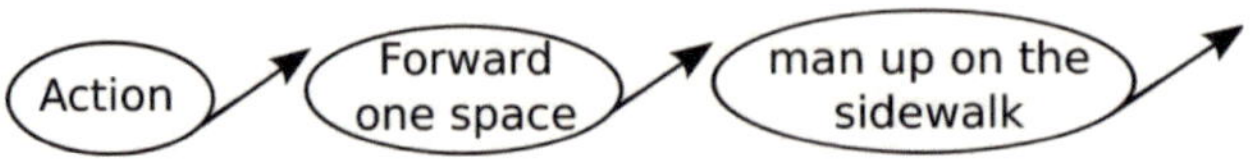

Fig. 11. Atom of action and examples

Induced actions may be limited to a change in the "scenation", that is to say display actions. However, if the molecules of action are elements of a script for a document with generative data, some of them define operations on entity contents. The events can then induce the modification or creation of entities. An event produces an action on the environment. The general situation of the system is modified.

A molecule of action (figure 12) is composed of:

- interlocking factors,
- actions, which are the different events making up the molecule,
- shares of logical conjunction that establish a logical link between the various actions.

The interlocking factors are all circumstances and / or conjunctures which (when they are checked) cause the event.

Interlocking factors have exactly the same role within the molecules of action and within the diegetic molecules. If the interlocking-factor is true, then the action runs.

Actions are events induced by the validation of the molecule.

The molecules of action can define the transformation or the creation of entities.

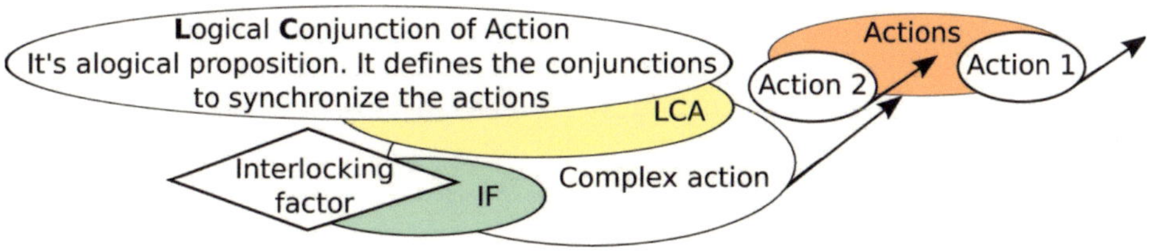

Fig. 12. Molecule of action

The Logical Conjunction of Action (LCA) defines the logical operators governing the actions contained in the event. Indeed, an event is characterized by any combination of several other events. This may be a chain, a simultaneous or even a choice of several actions. Logical Conjunctions of Actions are key rules for managing events contained. These include logical operators such as the algebra of Allen (Allen, 1986) (Allen & Ferguson, 1994).

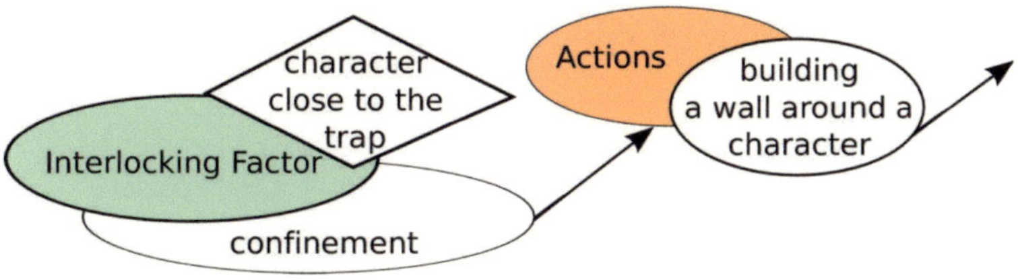

Fig. 13. Example of a molecule of Action

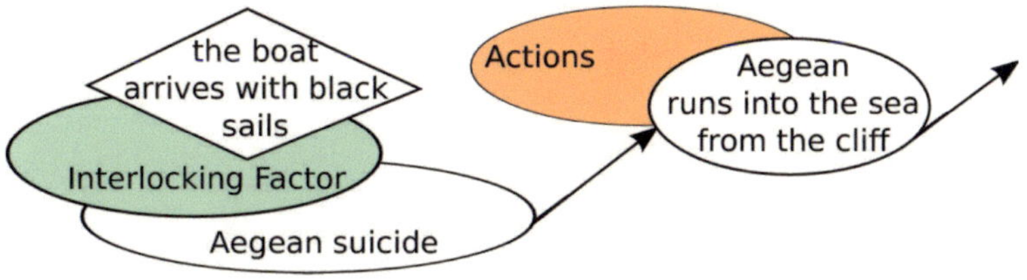

Fig. 14. Another example of molecule of action

The Algebra of temporality ALLEN defined between two entities A and B rigid reltionships:

- A equals B (perfect timing)
- A starts B (A and B start simultaneously)
- A finishes B (A and B ends simultaneously)
- A meets B (B starts when A has finished, what can be called sequential events if A and B are events)

and flexible relationships:

- A during (t) B (A starts t after B has started, with A ending before B)
- A before (t) B (B starts t after A is finished)
- A overlaps (t) B (B starts t after A has started, with B ending after A)

3.4 Representation of atoms and molecules

After defining the general structure of the molecular model (with its three types of components) this section discusses the diffrents shapes of molecules in the screenplay.

3.4.1 Forms of representations

Nowadays, multiple representation of atoms and molecules are possible.

- A graphical representation (mostly used in this document)
- A textual representation, (as in figure 9 or 17)
- A tabular representation,
- A graphico-tabular representation
- ...

Any of these representations can be used. It is even possible to use its own representation if the molecular structure is correct. In this text two representations are used: the graphical and graphico-tabular representation. The first because it is easy to differentiate the different types of atoms and molecules. However an author may find it difficult to use it in the absence of "script processor" (by analogy to word processor). The second is a compromise between usability and readability of scriptwriting: a simple template for word processing is used to write the screenplay.

3.4.2 Differentiation atom / molecule

In one screenplay, it is necessary to distinguish a molecule of an atom inside another molecule. In the graphic molecular representation is adopted, the molecules are "shaded", which distinguishes them from an atom. In the case of graphico-tabular representation it was decided to use the underline with a different colour (if colour display is possible) as a hyperlink symbol.

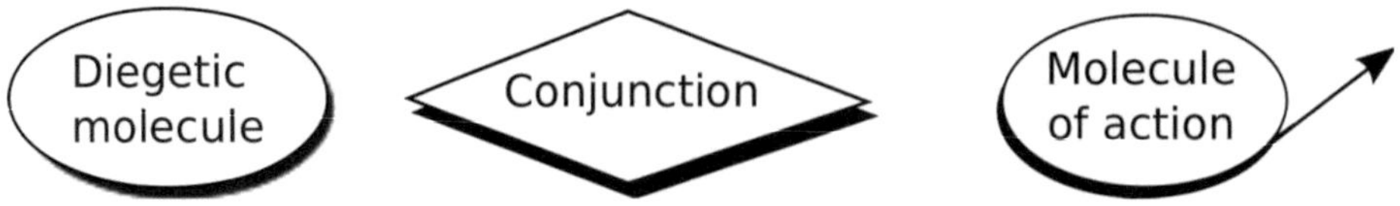

Fig. 15. Closed molecules

These modes of differentiation atoms / molecules are mainly features of links to some software used for general text editing or graphics. Indeed, when reading the version of the document, the selection of a molecule located in another molecule provides access to the detailed representation of the molecule in question.

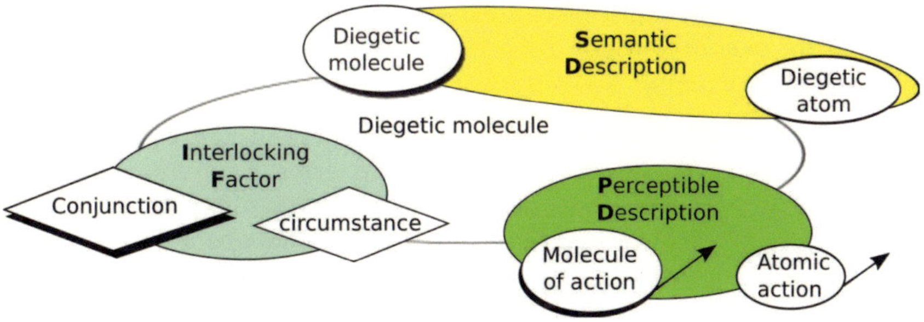

Fig. 16. Differentiation atoms / molecules in a graphical

	Name of diegetic molecule	Switch-factor
		Circumstance Conjunction
Descriptions Sémantiques		Descriptions Perceptibles
Diegetic atom Diegetic molecule		Atom of action Molecule of action

Fig. 17. Differentiation molecules/atoms in a graphico-tabular representation

4. Writing a script

The molecular model is based above all on a formalization of ideas (on the development of a text of the literal sense). This text (the script or the screenplay) represents the document throughout the eyes of the author.

Between the idea of document and the final script, many stages punctuate the work of the author.

In general, before setting out to write, the ideas of the author (or partner in an industrial context), are functions of the document.

4.1 Start writing

The functions of the document are usually expressed through the semantic descriptions and perceptible diegetic molecules. The document at this stage is in its "intent". The document itself is an entity. It will therefore be described by a molecule that can be described as parent compound or molecule aggregate.

In the initial state, the parent compound contains the different intentions of the author. Its semantic descriptions can then define the functions of the document. Thus, the author begins by setting out ideas, sometimes very descriptive - possibly by his own limited imagination. These ideas are not necessarily structured. It is only later that the author develops the script to provide solutions in terms of communication for the ideas presented which are functions of the document.

The parent molecule - or global molecule - is the whole document. If at the beginning of writing, the parent compound just contains the functions of the document, by the time the script is finished, the overall molecule contains all the molecules and atoms representing the paper (figure 6 show an example for the global molecule of Tetris).

Gradually, from the functions, the author defines entities that structure the screenplay. He has the ability to break down and identify (give solutions in terms of communication) functions. It also has the ability to assemble, integrate, molecules representing entities already written down. These functions of the molecular model are the structural operations of it

4.2 Writing and structural operations

Gradually, from the functions, the author defines the entities that shape the screenplay. To work out the script, develop ideas, organize them, the author uses structural operations. For example, an atom, previously defined, may prove too imprecise in writing. This screenplay atom can then be refined. Its decomposition will produce several elements (atoms or molecules). Conversely it is possible to form a "synthetic molecule". So, atoms or molecules can be combined to synthesize a new element of ideas...

The terms of these operations use particular properties of atomic fission and combinations.

The combination is to group multiple molecules or atoms to form a new molecule.

Thus, the combination creates a new molecule by "assembling" atoms and existing molecules. This method of design is useful when one has to build up entities to ensure the dramatic consistency of a document.

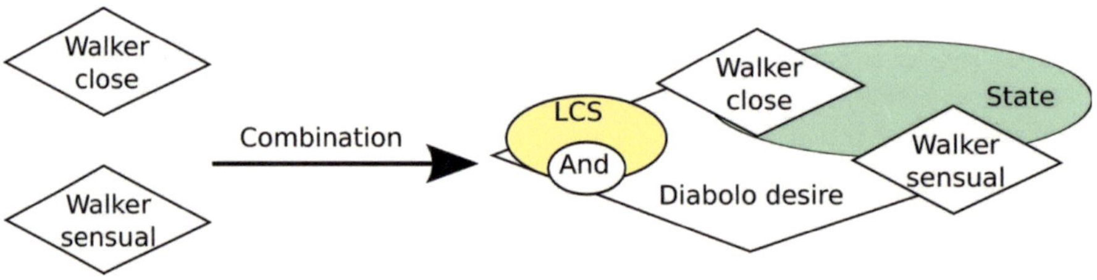

Fig. 18. Molecular combination

An atomic fission splits an atom into several others, as shown on of figure 19. A screenwriter uses rarely a fission alone but it is commonly used during a decomposition.

The author, with this function, must then clarify his ideas, his entities. This is the traditional process of creation. From the definition of a general idea, step by step, the creator define this idea precisely.

An atomic decomposition is the product of a fission followed by a combination. In figure 19, the fission of the atom "car" products two new atoms "body" and "wheel". The combination products the molecule "car" composed by next atoms. The splitting of the atom car leads to two atoms. The combination of these results in the synthesis of the molecule car.

At the end stage of writing (within "preproduction" phase) some decomposition can improve the understanding to reduce the gap between the entity representation (of the author) and its understood (by the achievement team). Indeed, if the creator has represented a "bird" entity by an atom, he may want, after some working time, to decompose the representation of this bird by characterizing its family, its colour of its feathers or its beak so that it perfectly represents the image that he has in mind.

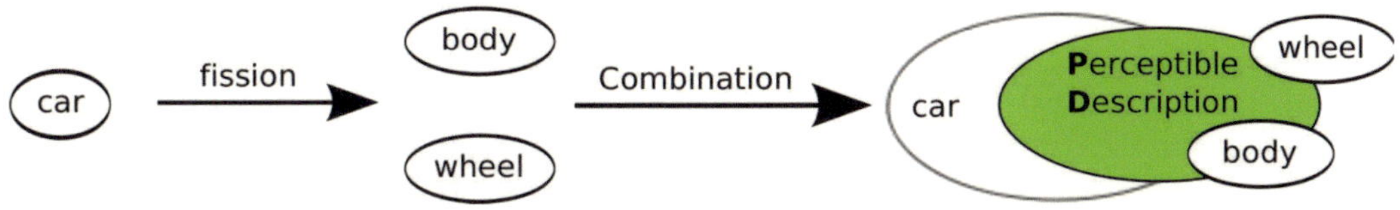

Fig. 19. Fission followed by a combination

Another example for the design of a document on the state of the world, leads to define a molecule "The earth" from several entities that are the continents (figure 20). Each of them can be cut into large geographic areas or independent states. One then has to perform a series of fission and combinations to achieve at the desired level of detailed screenplay.

It should be noted that during an operation of decomposition, the item is "shaded" or "outlined" (as has already been specified) to differentiate between atoms and molecules (figure 21).

The substitution operation is about replacing an atom or molecule with a new feature. They may be substituted by another atom of similar function, but it is possible to substitute an item whose function is different. Indeed, it is not uncommon, during the creation process, for some issues to be seriously altered. For example: "Light motor vehicle with four wheels for transporting several people with some luggage" substituted "car". "isolated castel" substituted "isolated mansion"

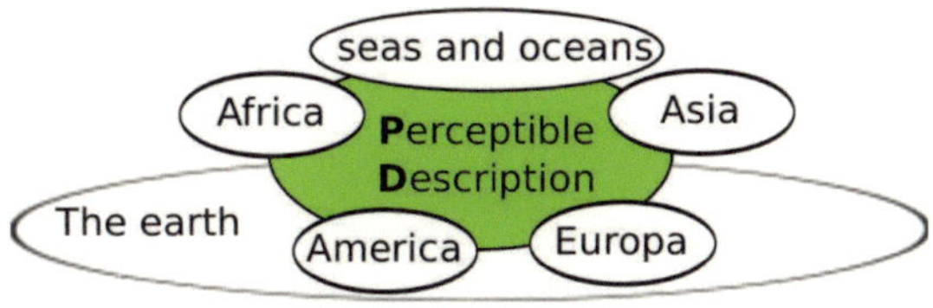

Fig. 20. Molecule composed only of atoms

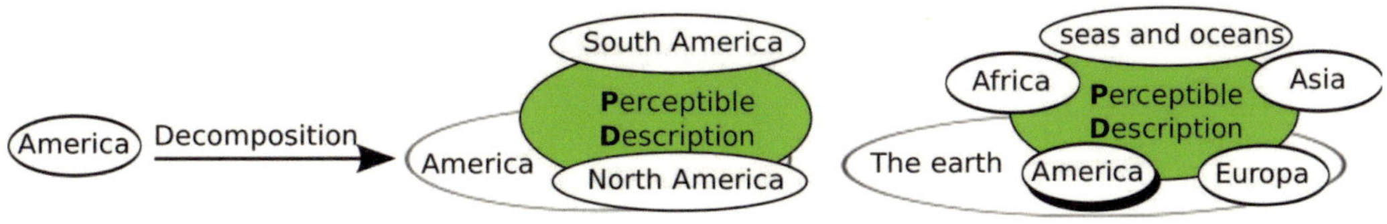

Fig. 21. Result of decomposition of the atom "America"

More simply, an author often re-expresses or reworks an idea. Rewriting a sentence of a script can be regarded as a substitution.

4.3 How to orient the "scenation"

The "scenation" of an interactive document is unpredictable. However, the designer can introduce guidelines or criteria "scenation" through the interlocking factors, logical conjunctions or perceptible descriptions.

So, the screenplay can specify the spatial position of some entities. This pieces of information are included in the descriptions or can be defined through specific events.

Interlocking factors are circumstances or conjuncture that define the conditions for which the corresponding entities and events will come into operation. If one of the factors identified in a molecule proves to be true, the entity is operated or the event is occured. If the validation - or the commissioning - of an entity is determined by the conjunction of ordered factors, the author will create an appropriate cyclical molecule.

If an entity is operating, it validates itself, and recursively, the entities that constitute it (provided that their interlocking factors are checked too): if the representation of the latter entities or events has no engagement, they are then validated by default. Thus, for the entity "documentary" to be enabled (see figure 22) the interlocking factor "session beginning" must be checked. The diegetic molecule "documentary" consists of two molecules covering "Life of tarantulas in South America" and "Bears in Europa". The first theme is treated with a documentary film "film 1". No constraint is specified for engagement "Life of tarantulas in South America". Therefore, this entity "film 1" is put into service as soon as the entity "documentary" is operated. This process could be described as "auto-switch". On the other hand regarding the entity "Bears Poldavia" it will be validated only when the documentary "film 1" is completed.

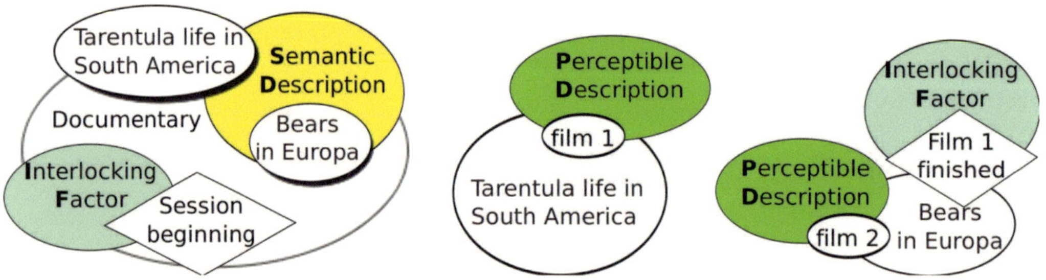

Fig. 22. Example of representation of validations "nested"

A lack of interlocking factors generates systematic validation of the entities or events, as soon as one part of the container is running.

Logical conjunctions of states and respectively cyclical molecules and molecules integrated actions are made up of shares of logical operators. These define the conjunctions between components. Some of these operators are presented in this text, but the list is not exhaustive. An author can define a new logical operator if the developed screenplay item requires it.

Thus, rules of engagement priorities can be defined on the basis of logical conjunctions of statements or actions. For example, if the designer decides that a part of the document will consist of a slide show with musical accompaniment (see figure 23), he may want to synchronize precisely audio and visual entities. In this case, the molecule of action "to play a slide show" is a script example of this documentary extract. This molecule indicates that the events "Play Music" and "show pictures" will be synchronous with the logical conjonction "equals" (which requires special attention when performing). On the other hand, the molecule "broadcast slide show 2", due to the use of the logical conjunction "starts" indicates that "view photos" and "play music" are operated simultaneously, but their perfect synchronisation is not required. The logical conjunction of actions "meets" of the molecule of action "photographs show" indicates that the three photos are displayed one after the other.

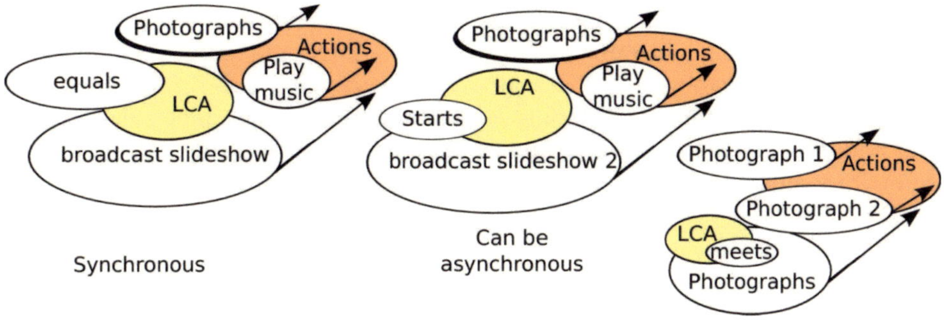

Fig. 23. Examples of parallel and sequential actions synchronous or not

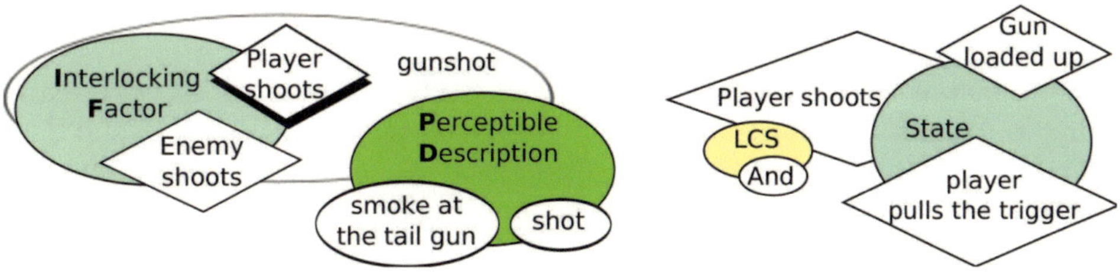

Fig. 24. Such entities simultaneously validated

The author can define the temporal position of the entities using interlocking factors of diegetic molecules. Thus, when two molecules have identical interlocking factors, the entities they represent are enabled simultaneously. Also - in the example in figure 24 - "shot" and "Smoke at the tail gun" entities are switched at the same time, or when "the enemy shoots", or when "the player shoots" (the latter screenplay occurs if the "player pulls the trigger" and the "Gun loaded up").

The definition of the circumstances - interlocking factors - and events induce a variable temporal "scenation". This enables the description of autonomous entities too. The live document involves the modification of the "scenation". The evolution of the document is modified by the actions of the user, but also by the combined actions of the user and the others entities in the document. Moreover events in the context of generative data documents can change the data. These documents are then dynamic documents.

5. Autonomy document

Entities in a document which generates data are "alive" (they can evolve with the progress of the document). They are dynamic. Moreover, a model of the reader extents the possibilities of the interaction and of the document's evolution.

An entity is dynamic if its characteristics are subject to change or modify something while the document is reading. This is particularly true in virtual reality where viewing the scene is drawn in real time, from a small database, or also when some states (such as the diagnosis of the presence of a visually impaired reader) can change the display of visual and auditory entities.

5.1 Documents and dynamic entities

The diegetic molecules are the representation of autonomous entities. By analogy with artificial intelligence, they set out the bases of declarative and procedural facts(diegetic atoms and molecules whithin the semantic and perceptible descriptions noticeable as declarative facts, molecules and atoms of actions within the molecules diegetic as procedural facts). Therefore, the molecules can describe dynamic entities. The entities can be operated with some the status of the document. It is the role of interlocking factors.

In summary, the entities contain their own operating procedures (interlocking factors and actions).

The evolution of an entity from the document results from the representation of its potential actions, the environment states or evolution or external events., For example, the visual space of Tetris is constantly changing until the gameover. Indeed, the forms that arrive alter the playing area. This one could be consider as a live entity.

It is possible that the user can not perceive an entity acting (if he is not seeing or earing it). (for example, if an entity represent the path of the reader through a document and if it is not displaying). The entity "path" is changing as soon as the reader travels through the document.

Moreover, the representation of dynamic entities, combined with the definition of a hypothetical sense produced by their display, enables an evolution by closing semantic.

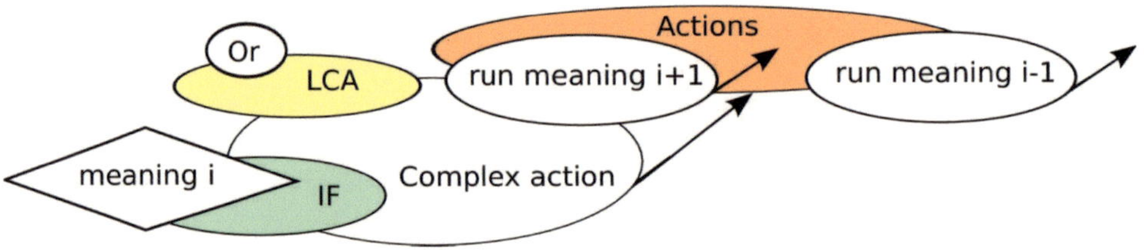

Fig. 25. Evolution by closing semantic

A meaning is defined by the creator from assumptions which are products of choices, possibly artistic ones and which often prove arbitrary. In the example in figure 25, if an entity means "meanings i" was displaying, the document will display an entity will mean "meanings i+1" or "meanings i-1". The document will be able to follow a coherent evolution towards the objectives of the creative elements. The document successively validates semantically close or at the opposite far away elements: some situations may indeed lead to strong semantic ruptures.

Such a conception leads to the realization of interactive documents without always a direct action of the reader.

5.2 Model of the reader

Most documents today have a relatively low level of interactivity. This appears through orders for direct action and reaction between the document and reader (the impact on the display of the player's action is instantaneous). Thus a mouse-click, a "drag and drop", a " rollover" causes an immediate reaction of the documentary system.

However, it is preferable to consider the behaviour of the reader to change the "scenation" of the multimedia document. Of course, the user, his relationship to document, his perception of the document are included in most multimedia designs, including through the design of interfaces (Pignier & Drouillat, 2008). The interfaces are increasingly based on metaphors designed primarily to facilitate the usability of navigation. The point of view is no longer restricted to specialists of "human-machine communication", but it integrates functions of esteem necessary for the reader to support the document.

However, an author, especially if he is an artist, will go beyond the functional aspect of the relationship between the reader and the document. He will want to innovate and have the means of expression needed to complete the document. The artist will dream a "game's situation" between the reader and the document.

The autonomy of the entities enables the representation of a model of the reader. It is not to reify the reader but to propose an "avatar" (an avatar is a representation - necessarily schematic - and approximate of the user within the system). These define a psychological state of the player according to their actions. This will often be in a totally arbitrary way, regardless of any psychological model scientifically established, as is the case in the examples in figures 26 and 27. The model serves only to establish a strategy of evolution. A novelist, a screenwriter or film-maker will write on the basis of the potential reactions of an imaginary reader. In the same vein, a model of the reader will enable the author to establish a strategy of interaction between the entities of the document and the reader.

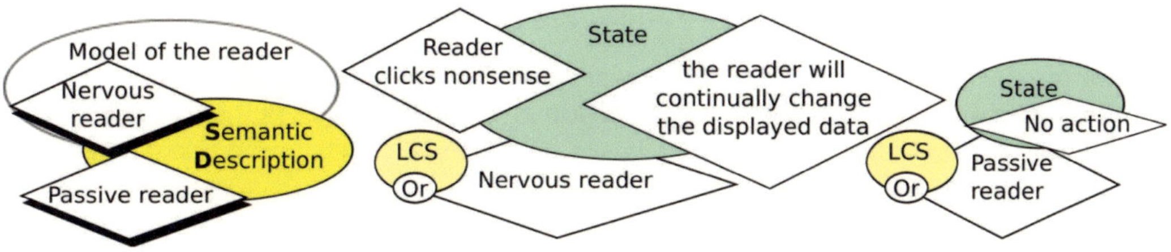

Fig. 26. Example of models of reader

Today, it is possible to determine few cognitive states and emotional states of an user (Labour & Kolski, 2010), but it is impossible to determine it directly, in real time and without complex interfaces.. This means, if you want to adapt the system to the reader, that one must go through models of representation of it. In fact, a model of the player is an entity that seeks to characterize the reader from facts which are objective and measurable by the document and its technical environment. The character deduced can also influence the evolution of the document. The author may delegate to specialists in artificial intelligence the design of a specific system of diagnosis of a cognitive, psychological state of the reader during the implementation of the document.

However, especially in a context of artistic creation, a designer may want to change the document according to the reader's behaviour with the document (regardless of any scientific model). He may be helped for this representation of a reader's model by some diegetic molecules he has built. The model of the reader that follows is primarily in this context. In addition, an imagined state of the reader can generate simple solutions for the diagnosis of one state of the reader. Thus, an author may decide that the document will consider a reader as nervous if he clicks continually. Conversely if the reader has no action, the document may consider him as a person in deep trouble or absent. This model of reader can be used to devise a strategy or mode of evolution of a document.

This type of model, from simple rule, has enabled student groups to script documents establishing strategies of evolution fwith the player behaviour (or his avatar). They were, for example, documents determining the presence (or absence) of visual impairment in the reader and in order to offer navigation features adapted to their handicap without special interface.

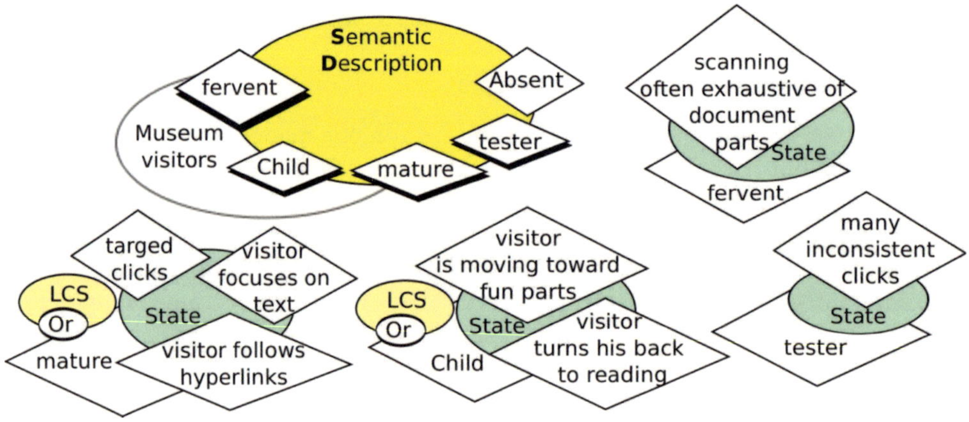

Fig. 27. Another example of models of reader: type of visitors

To sum up, the molecular model of the reader is not there to "manufacture" a reader, but to contain - in an arbitrary, possibly with the vision of an "artist" - a hypothetical mental state according to his reactions. This model is based on observable facts in the document and its technical environment.

6. Conclusion

The model in molecular scriptwriting which has just been introduced enables one to represent an imaginary world with its own laws, in the form of a screenplay. The latter defines the document with the representations of dynamic entities.

The creator no longer defines the connections between data. He characterizes entities (subject, location, character, real or imaginary, who participates in the development or description of the environment). The entities are defined by the criteria of state and characteristics of evolution. They are autonomous and may interact with each other. The reader participates in the evolution of the multimedia document through his avatar, "the model of the reader". This defines a hypothetical reader, imagined by the author, to enable artificial entities of the document to act on the alleged conduct of the imaginary reader. In this sense, the reader is an entity of the environment. Finally, the inclusion of a semantic description of the entities can be used to treat entities in terms of data but of possible meanings.

The basic principles outlined in this document may seem simplistic at first. However a study of several authors shows that the media idea of adaptive documents or autonomous entities do not come to the minds of designers. These principles are conceivable for any games, but definitely not for disclosure documents. Moreover, the method of collecting linear documents often prohibits the writing of autonomous entities. This was also revealed with students of audiovisual and multimedia sector positioned as authors (regardless of any subsequent effective implementation).

In summary, the imagination of entities that can be autonomous and the design of information units depending on different users cause problem. Today there is a lack of "witness's documents" with its screenplay to illustrate the model. Examples of scripts exist and the reader may consult published http://lambouxdurandrech.free.fr/ to illustrate better these concepts.

Another problem identified by the authors as "professionals" and by students (and any type of multimedia document produced), is the lack of suitable writing tool. This tool - which can be described as "multimedia screnplay processor" - must be developed.

7. References

Allen, J.F. (1986). Maintaining knowledge about temporal intervals. *Communication of the ACM*, vol. 26, n° 11, pp. 832-843, ISSN 0001-0782.

Allen, J.F. & Ferguson, G. F. (1994). Actions and Events in Interval Temporal Logic. *Journal of Logic and Computation*, vol. 4, n° 5, p. 531-579, ISSN 0955-792X, Retrieved from ftp://ftp.cs.rochester.edu/pub/papers/ai/94.tr521.Actions_and_events_in_interval_temporal_logic.ps.Z

Alvarez J. & al. (2007). Morphologie des jeux vidéo, In: *Hypertextes, hypermédias. Collaborer, échanger, inventer : expériences de réseaux*, Lavoisier/Hermès Science Publishing, pp. 277-294. ISBN 978-2-7462-1891-8

Bailey, B. P. Konstan, J. A. & Carlis, J. V. (2001) DEMAIS: Designing Multimedia Applications with Interactive Storyboards. In: *MM'01 ACM Multimedia*. ACM publications. ISBN: 1-58113-394-4. Retrieved from http://citeseerx.ist.psu.edu/viewdoc/download?doi=10.1.1.154.1699&rep=rep1&type=pdf

Balpe, J.P. (1997) Hypertexte et interactivité, *Hypertextes et Hypermédias*, Hermès, Vol 1, n°1/1997, pp. 11-22

Balpe, J.-P. (2001) Le livre est tout le problème... *Document numérique*. nouvelles écritures, Lavoisier/Hermès Science Publishing. vol. 5, n° 1-2/2001, pp. 9-15. ISSN 1279-5127 ISBN 2-7462-0454-1. Retrieved from http://www.auradigital.net/web/Escriptures-hipertextuals/Documents/ecriture-sans-manuscrit-brouillon-absent-jean-pierre-balpe.html

Cartier, M. (2003). *Un procédurier pour le nouveau Web*. Available from http://www.michelcartier.Com /pdf/Cartier_procedurier.pdf

Colin, Michel. (1992). *Cinéma, télévision et cognition*. Presses Universitaires de Nancy, 1992. ISBN 2-86480-555-3, Nancy, France

Deely, John. (2005). *Basics of Semiotics*. 4th ed, Tartu University Press, 2005. ISBN 9949-11-086-68. Tartu, Estonia.

Fournier, Josée. (2003). *Scénarisation multimédia : processus de scénarisation interactive.* Presses de l'Université de Laval, 2003. collection : laboratoire de communautique appliquée. ISBN 2-7637-7963-8. Quebec, Canada

Genesereth, M. R. & Nilsson, N. J. (1987). *Logical Foudations of Artificial Intelligence.* Morgan Kaufmann. ISBN : 0-934613-31-1. Los Altos, California, USA.

Huart, Julien. (2000) *Mieux concevoir pour mieux communiquer à l'ère des nouveaux médias : vers des méthodes de conduite de projets et d'évaluation qualité de documents multimédias.* Doct. th. : sciences de l'information et de la communication. Université de Valenciennes et du Hainaut Cambrésis.

Jeanneret, Y. & Souchier, E. (2005). L'énonciation éditoriale dans les écrits d'écran. *Communication et langages,* N°145, pp. 3-15, ISSN 0336-1500. Retrieved from http://www.persee.fr/web/revues/home/prescript/article/colan_0336-1500_2005_num_145_1_3351

Labour, M. Kolski, C. (2010). A Pedagogics Pattern Model of Blended e-Learning: A Step towards Designing Sustainable Simulation-Based Learning, in: *Affective, Interactive and Cognitive Methods for E-Learning Design: Creating an Optimal Education Experience,* pp. 114-137, IGI Global, ISBN 978-1-60566-940-3, PA (USA)

Leleu-Merviel, S. (2005). Structurer la conception des documents numériques grâce à la scénistique. In: *Création numérique ; écritures-expériences interactives.* Lavoisier/Hermès Science Publishing. pp. 151-181. ISBN 2-7462-1130-0. Paris/Londres, France/United Kingdom. Available from http://archivesic.ccsd.cnrs.fr/docs/00/46/64/34/PDF/Creation_numerique-Merviel.pdf

Locke, John. (1690). *An Essay Concerning Human Understanding. Book II ideas.* Pormona Press. ISBN 9781406790276. Available from http://www.earlymoderntexts.com/pdfbits/lo21.pdf

Pignier, N. & Drouillat, B. (2004). *Penser le Web design : modèles sémiotiques pour les projets multimédias,* L'Harmattan, ISBN 2-7475-7078-9, Paris, France

Pignier, N. & Drouillat B. (2008) *Le webdesign - Sociale expérience des interfaces web,* Lavoisier/Hermès Science Publishing, ISBN 978-2-7462-2102-4, Paris, France

Prince, G. (2003). *A Dictionary of Narratology.* University of Nebraska Press. ISBN 08-03287763, Nebraska, U.S.A.

Rojas, E. (2007) Internet, outil de médiation culturelle : vers un modèle de spécification basé sur les figures de médiation. *Hypertextes, hypermédias. Collaborer, échanger, inventer : expériences de réseaux.* Lavoisier/Hermès Science Publishing. pp.135-151. ISBN: 1-885636-32-0.

Szilas, N. & Axelrad, M. (2009) To Be or Not to Be: Towards Stateless Interactive Drama. In: Interactive Storytelling, pp. 290-291, 2009, Springer, Pages: 280-291, ISBN: 9783642106422, Berlin / Heidelberg, Germany

Raspiengas J.C. (1997). Bertrand Tavernier : L'ardent sommelier. *Télérama,* n° 2469, ISSN 00040-2699

Russell, S. & Norvig, P. (2010). *Artificial Intelligence: A Modern Approach.* 3rd Edition, Prentice Hall. ISBN 0-13-604259-7

Viéville, Nicolas. (2003). *écrire pour l'écran – vers un outil d'assistance à l'écriture multimédia.* Doct. th.: Sciences de l'Information et de la communication, Université de Valenciennes et du Hainaut Cambrésis, Valenciennes, France.

Zadeh, L.A. (1965). Fuzzi sets, *Informations and Control,* n° 8, pp. 338-353. Retrieved from http://www-bisc.cs.berkeley.edu/Zadeh-1965.pdf

15

Real-Time Multimedia Stream Data Processing in a Supercomputer Environment

Henryk Krawczyk and Jerzy Proficz
Gdansk University of Technology,
Poland

1. Introduction

The recent development of surveillance systems due to the threat of many attack sources, (including terrorists, organized and ordinary crime) has forced the municipal and state authorities to provide a wide range of security measures. The appropriate sensors are installed alongside the city streets and other public utilities providing a huge amount of incoming data, which needs to be processed and analyzed, either by a human or automatically by computer software.

The computer centers with high-performance computers seem to be a natural solution for automatic mass multimedia processing, for which the computational power is a crucial factor. Moreover, they are usually located near metropolises, which in conjunction with their usual high-speed network connection, or even their direct placement in the network hubs makes them well prepared to receive huge data streams gathered by all surveillance sensors.

A prototype of such an approach being a real proof-of-concept was built and deployed in the Academic Computational Center and ETI faculty of Gdansk University of Technology in Poland. The proposed solution is realized as a hardware-software platform: KASKADA (Polish abbreviation: Context Analysis of Camera Data Streams for Alert Defining Applications). Its development was performed as a part of the MAYDAY EURO 2012 project. Apart from the platform, three pilot applications were developed: suspicious object and dangerous events recognition; endoscopy examination and disease identification, and intellectual property analysis and protection.

Though the proposed platform is a new idea, it can be compare to a the typical distributed/parallel programming frameworks. In comparison to the typical grid computing solutions: Globus (Foster & Kesselman, 1997) or Unicore (Breuer et al., 2004), it provides built in mechanisms for quality of service in the developed services and integrated approach to data stream computation management. For the more classical high performance computation architectures, like MPI with some task queue (eg. PBS), the platform provides service-oriented and real-time features, enabling easy development of the live multimedia streams services and user applications.

The proposed platform can be also compared to the typical distributed/parallel programming frameworks, like J2EE or .NET, however they are general purpose solutions and have only limited support for massive multimedia stream processing. An interesting platform was proposed in (Yu et al., 2009), in general it is also dedicated for multimedia real-time processing, however the mechanisms used are different, where the computations are concentrated in the database layer, while the KASKADA platform is focused in the middleware.

2. Challenges of the distributed multimedia processing

The typical supercomputer system is designed for the scientific-based simulation-like computations. It usually works over a distributed operating system under supervision of a batch-based queuing system, collecting requests as a list of computational tasks. Their processing is executed off-line without direct communication with the user. The multimedia processing, related to the video and audio surveillance systems, requires a real-time environment, supporting the continuous processing of live data streams, which brings new challenges for system and middleware software.

The first recognized requirement for the computational platform is to provide a proper concept of service management. We assume a service is a piece of functionality performing computations on an input multimedia stream, exposed by a well-defined interface to a user application. Thus, the platform needs to provide support for development, tests, and execution of such services. The proper tools for stream algorithm implementations, service creation and composition, are needed. Moreover, the platform needs to provide a standard service repository for conversions, decoding, encoding, and distribution of video and audio streams. Another important aspect is runtime management of services, where the proper mechanisms of resource allocation and monitoring need to be considered, we proposed the set of algorithms enabling the proper resource management with the optimization of fragmentation of the cluster (Krawczyk & Proficz, 2010).

Apart from a proper computational model, the proposed solution needs to guarantee an appropriate level of usability. The applications using the designed platform should provide a simple and clear user interface; thus, the platform itself should have a set of features enabling easy service development and composition. The solution should unify the processing model and be properly tuned for video and audio streams analysis.

Another problem needing to be solved is event management. We assume any working service performing stream analysis can reach a set of conditions, when the special actions need to be performed by other services or even outside the platform. Such an event can be asynchronously delivered using the message-passing mechanisms provided by the platform. It's worth noticing that the number of recognized incidents can burst drastically, causing a high computational and communicational load, which should be properly handled preserving all required constraints related to event filtering, message distributing and delivering.

The above requirements demand the usage of high-performance systems, in both computational and communicational areas. With respect to other aspects, like security or safety, we decided to build the platform based on the computational cluster located in the academic computer center. It consists of 1132 computation nodes, each containing two multicore processors, with 10896 of available cores. The nodes are interconnected by a high speed 20-40GB/s Infiniband network. The above configuration gives solid capabilities for parallel processed services, based on the parallel computations, analyzing hundreds of multimedia streams.

The specific characteristics of the performed analysis - real-time, security-related services rely directly on the dependability of the underlying platform - the dedicated platform needs to provide the ability to replicate the same computations, thus more accurate results can be obtained. Moreover, the resource allocation algorithms must provide the minimal, guaranteed level of resources so that the executed analysis is performed smoothly without delays and data traffic jams. We assumed (the typical) three types of resources to be managed directly by the platform: CPU load, indicating the complexity of the performed computations, memory depending mainly on the size of the problem context, which needs to be maintained during the analysis, and network bandwidth used to provide the flowing multimedia stream.

The increasing number of the analyzed services, depending directly on the incoming data, requires the platform to provide a flexible way to extend its computational and communicational capabilities. Thus the scalability of the proposed solution is a crucial factor for the final outcome of the executed services. The management procedures need to comply with the constraints and limitations given by the underlying hardware according to capability for the extension of its resources. Moreover, even for a single node the increasing utilization of the resources (cores, memory) used by the executed services needs to conform with the speedup of their computations.

Finally, taking under consideration performance, dependability, and scalability of the proposed solution, the proper means for maintaining the required platform state have to be developed. The monitoring subsystem is responsible for measuring and control of the cluster nodes and executed services. In case of abuse, such a component needs to be properly handled, the service needs to be stopped and the node isolated from the cluster. Moreover the monitor provides the external API for tracing the above measurements by the utility applications, so as to be able to react flexibly to the occurring problems.

3. Multimedia processing model

Fig. 1 presents a layered processing model for multimedia processing. The whole platform is deployed in the cluster environment - system infrastructure including a Linux operating system, computation nodes and the network. On the other side, it serves as a middleware for user applications, which are directly responsible for the interactions with the users (Krawczyk & Proficz, 2010b).

Apart from the applications and the infrastructure, the model consists of the following four layers: (1) complex services, (2) simple services, (3) computational tasks, and (4) processes. The top layer manages the complex services exposed directly to the user applications, which are working according to defined scenarios of simple services included in the underlying layer.

Figure 2 presents an MSP-ML example of a complex service scenario being a part of a video-surveillance system supporting the monitoring of entrances, with automatic comparison of the amount of people passing the gates; generating an alert when any gate is overcrowded, version for 2 gates. Two cameras are used capturing video streams and implementations of the following algorithms: decoder - unpacking encoded video frames, background remover - the algorithm detecting moving objects in the video stream and removing the background, human detector - the algorithm detecting a human silhouette in the incoming images, event counter - comparing the number of messages with detected events describing incoming people and signaling large imbalance between them.

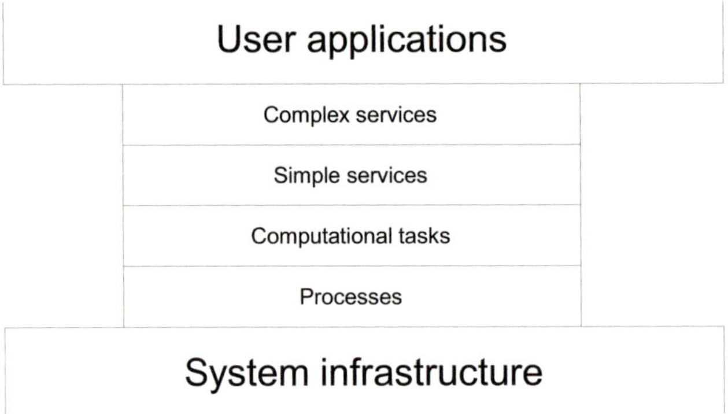

Fig. 1. KASKADA platform processing layers

- simple service (1) - decoding video stream from gate 1
- simple service (2) - background exclusion on the stream received from task #1
- simple service (3) - human detection on the stream received from task #2
- simple service (4) - decoding video stream from gate 2
- simple service (5) - background exclusion on the stream received from task #4
- simple service (6) - human detection on the stream received from task #5
- simple service (7) - counting and comparison of events from tasks: 4 and 6,with parameters indicating alert (event) if the number of passing people on any gate is 20% greater than average

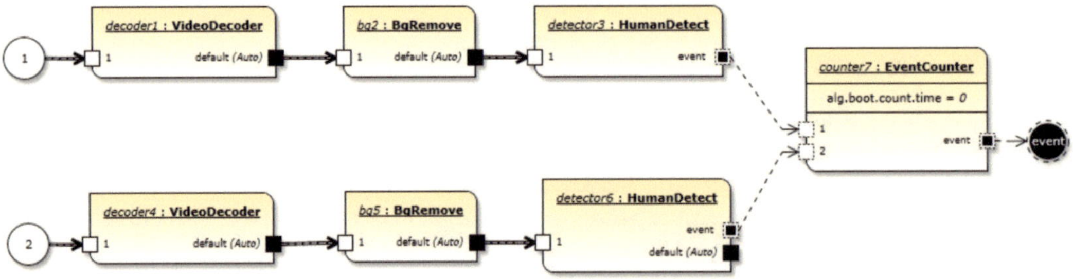

Fig. 2. An example of a complex service scenario in MSP-ML

The **complex services layer** is responsible for execution of scenarios consisting of complex and/or simple services according to the following steps:

1. *Creation and validation of a service scenario.* In the preliminary phase of service execution, the platform creates a sequence of simple services used by the particular steps of the scenario. It consists of the vertices representing the services and directed edges indicating data flow. We assume that such graphs are acyclic - no feedback is allowed.

The service descriptions are retrieved from the repository of scenarios and their input-output data types correctness id validated, see figure 3 (a).

2. *Algorithms' selection and required resource estimation.* In this step, the service scenario is converted into a new data flow graph including the computational tasks as vertices and directed edges representing data streams' flow, see figure 3 (b). This transformation is dependent on the requested quality parameters, which can have influence on the tasks algorithm selection as well as on the input data choice, e.g. camera resolution.

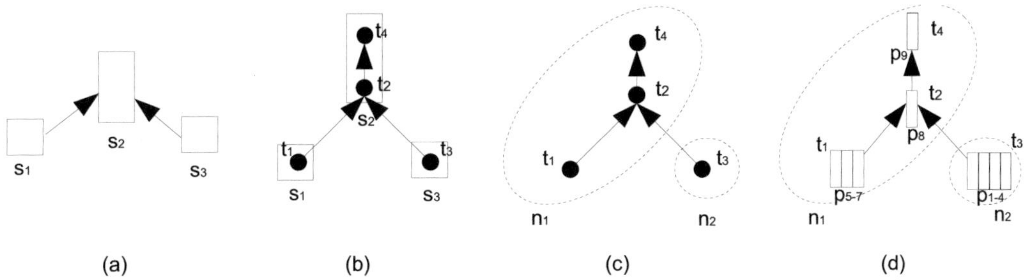

s_i – simple service, t_i – computation task, n_i – computation node, p_i – process/thread

Fig. 3. Phases of preparation to service scenario execution: (a) simple services; (b) task graph; (c) tasks' assignment to the computation nodes; (d) tasks running as processes and threads.

3. *Task assignment to the cluster nodes.* In this step, the vertices of the data flow graph, i.e. computational tasks (derived from the simple services) are assigned to the concrete cluster nodes, see figure 3 (c). We would like to emphasize that the tasks need to be executed parallel or concurrently, satisfying requirement for on-line processing and is more similar to a variable sized bin packing problem. The optimized criteria can be as follow: minimizing the number of partially used nodes (defragmentation), minimizing total network load, or the total delay of the scenario processing (Krawczyk & Proficz, 2010a).
4. *Scenario startup.* In this step, the computational tasks of the respective simple services are started up on the cluster nodes according to the given assignment. The task identifiers are generated and distributed. The proper data streams are assigned to the tasks and the communication is initialized. Each task after initiation consists of one or more processes/threads, whose execution is managed directly by the operating system installed on the cluster nodes, see figure 3 (d).
5. *Scenario monitoring.* During the scenario execution, the platform will monitor the running tasks and evaluate the following parameters: processor load, memory usage, multimedia, event and plain data streams' flow. The evaluation procedures are used for continuous collecting and verification of quality related meta-data describing the particular services.
6. *Scenario termination.* In the last step, the platform is responsible for the correct termination of all computational tasks executed with the scenario. This means that, all related processes and threads are finished, the associated resources are freed, the multimedia streams are closed, and the proper information messages are sent to the client.

The next layer of the proposed model, presented in figure 1 is involved in execution of the **simple services**, which are responsible for selection of the proper algorithm form alternative proposition according to the requested quality parameters. Moreover, the multimedia stream distribution to the computational tasks is established. For the sake of minimizing network load, the RTSP protocol with the multicast is used.

The next layer corresponds to the **computational tasks**, which are the implementation of the concrete stream analysis algorithms. They use the libraries of special functions such as cooperation with other components of the platform, including storage or an event server. It perceives the framework as a template, which already includes supporting objects used by the algorithm implementation, e.g. an image frame iterator for a video stream. This layer is responsible for task distribution, and requested resource allocation: nodes and processors. It also uses a typical launcher for these purposes, besides additional qualities of service policies, e.g. delays to the start of each task are considered.

The **process/thread layer** enables execution of the computational tasks. They can use typical mechanisms of concurrency and parallelism. The platform supports POSIX threads and other similar mechanisms provided by the underlying operating system.

The model described above was implemented in the KASKADA platform, all its layers are realized and their cooperation is managed by specialized servers. The description of the platform architecture is shown in section 6.

To create user application we build, we use a suitable application server cooperating with the KASKADA platform. The main part of the application is a specialized interface which allows to perform one or more of the possible user scenarios consisting of simple or complex services running on the KASKADA platform.

4. Development environment for multimedia stream processing

Fig. 4 presents the typical flow of activities leading to building of a complex service scenario. We start with an idea of multimedia stream processing, for instance identification of well-known objects or events. Then we can focus on the algorithm described in pseudo-code or other high level language, eg. flowchart. When that transition appears, we translate them to the real source code. It is compiled and linked into a computation task executable code. Having the executable algorithm program we enrich it with the quality and parameters metadata to obtain a simple service. The platform provides automatic generation of the WSLD description of this service, which in turn can be used to build more complex structures. The special language MSP-ML was designed to express the service composition keeping characteristic stream-processing constraints.

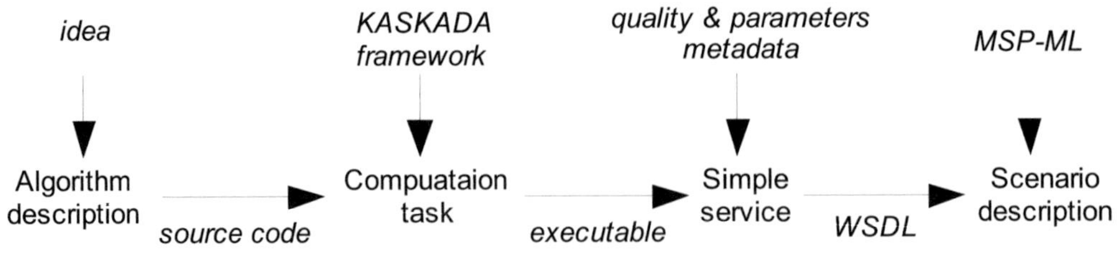

Fig. 4. A typical flow of activities of complex service creation

4.1 Algorithms to computation tasks

The KASKADA platform supports execution of multimedia stream analysis algorithms as computation tasks. They can be able to receive an input stream to detect objects and events, and finally to generate the output stream. Moreover, the tasks can be composed in pipelines or even more complex structures, so that the results of one task can be used as an input of the others. For instance we can distinguish a task detecting faces in the monitored video stream, and then one recognizing specific properties of the face, and a final task checking the database of persons wanted by the police.

The KASKADA platform provides a dedicated framework supporting implementation of the analysis algorithms. Every algorithm, embedded in the KASKADA framework, can use a special API providing the platform functionality: multimedia encoding and decoding, intermediate results interchange, signaling the events, processing the input parameters, and stream synchronization. The algorithms are implemented in C++ and together with the framework create computation tasks (see Fig. 5) under the Linux operating system in the cluster environment.

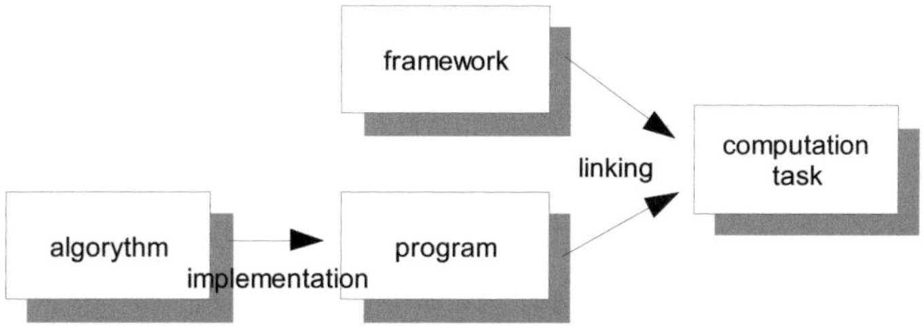

Fig. 5. Development of a computation task

Multimedia streams captured by the cameras or microphones are received under the RTSP protocol, the framework decodes the flowing video frames or audio probes and forwards them as input data to the task. Additionally, it can use the metadata related to the received stream, eg. the currently processed frame timestamp, resolution or video frame rate, or the audio probing frequency.

Another interesting feature provided by the KASKADA framework is a mechanism managing input parameters. They are formatted according to the convention used in GNU GPL license software. The framework recognizes the parameters related to the streams, filters and interprets them, in order to reconfigure the implemented algorithm. The platform provides the methods for parameters' propagation through the platform layers, so they don't need to be distributed manually to the destination services or tasks.

From an input data distribution point of view any task can be executed in three different modes: off-line streaming from a file, off-line streaming from a streaming server, and on-line directly from the stream source (see Fig. 6 a-c). The first mode enables direct usage of archived streams using a network file system, that the processing can be even faster than the recording, eg. for video streams the processing frame rate is limited only by the CPU speed.

The streams transmitted in the off-line streaming server mode are provided in a very similar fashion to the live streaming, with the exception of the data source, which is located in the off-line archive. This approach supports the tests using the archived content, but within the constraints of the live streaming. The later mode is based on the direct connection to the streaming device, ie. a camera or a microphone enabling their real-time processing.

From the point of view of output data distribution, the algorithm execution and tests can be performed using archiving or streaming modes (see Fig. 6 d-e). In the first case the processed output stream is stored into the archive file, and in the latter the results are transmitted by a streaming server to the client. There is also the possibility to use a hybrid approach where the data are simultaneously stored in the archive and transmitted after some transformations to the users (see Fig. 6 f).

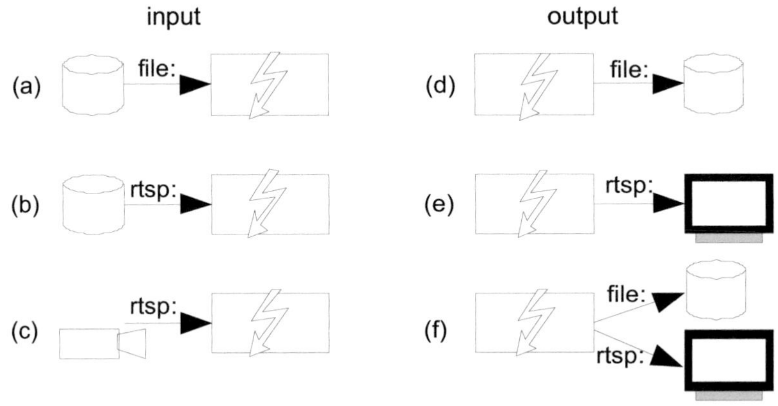

Fig. 6. Input/output algorithm modes, for input: (a) off-line from a file; (b) off-line through a streaming server; (c) on-line from a streaming device; for output: (d) archiving to a file; (e) transmitting through the streaming server; (f) hybrid.

The above algorithm input/output modes directly implies interaction modes with the services or even the whole platform. Thus we can distinguish the following interaction modes:

1. Real-time mode - when the multimedia streams are directly processed and the results are provided to the user.
2. Off-line mode - when the streams are read directly from the archive and the results are stored for the user.
3. Real-time simulator mode - when streams are read from the archive, but they are transmitted to the tasks just like from their original source, and the results are provided to the user - used for testing purposes.

Apart from the multimedia stream, any running algorithm can send the messages enclosing the detected objects or events it found during the processing. The KASKADA framework provides the message passing API, and the platform contains the mechanisms of their routing, delivering, and monitoring. Fig. 7 presents an example source code for sending the message, and the screenshot of the web browser with monitored messages containing the information about reported events.

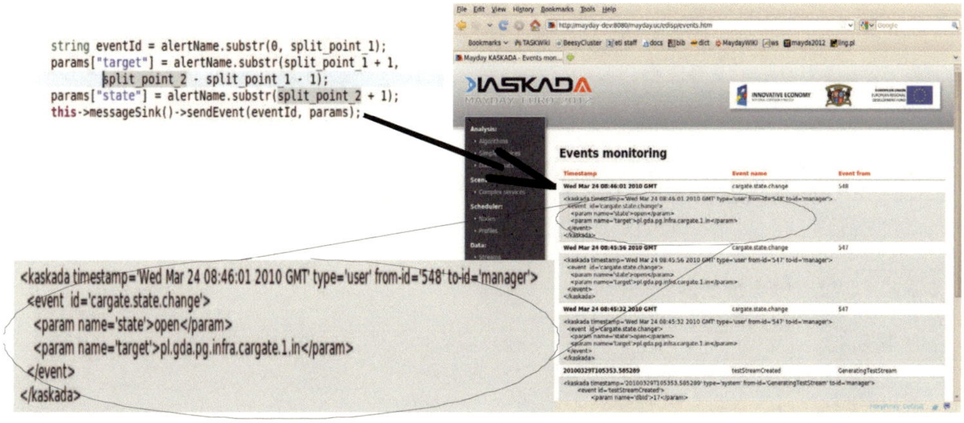

Fig. 7. Example of sending and monitoring the messages describing events

4.2 Algorithm to service transformation

The implemented algorithm, after linking with the KASKADA framework libraries and its preliminary tests, can be used as a base for creation of a simple service, which can be offered as its remote access. From the point of view of a programmer, the service is an interface backed up by the task and accessible through the platform.

It is possible to implement a few alternative algorithms realizing the same service, but providing different levels of processing quality, ie. dependability, performance. On the other hand, there can exist an algorithm matching two, or even more, services providing their functionalities. Fig. 8 presents an example of such multiple relations between algorithms' implementation and services.

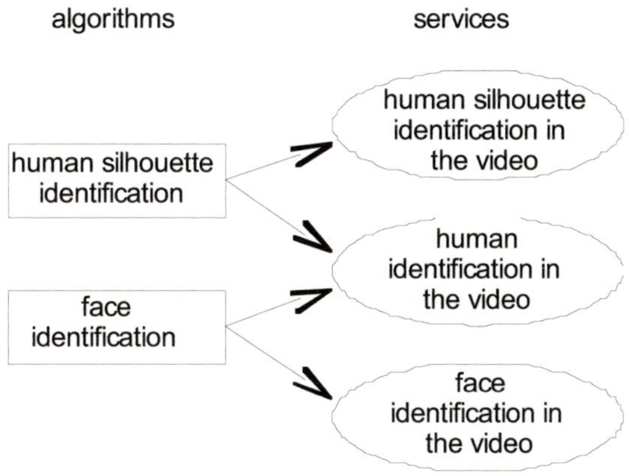

Fig. 8. An example of multiple relations between algorithms' implementation and services

The KASKADA platform stores algorithms' metadata, as well as providing the means to manage them. For this purpose an appropriate user interface was implemented including such functions as adding, removing and modification of the data: an algorithm's name, executable file path, input and quality parameters. An exemplary list of algorithms was presented in Fig. 9.

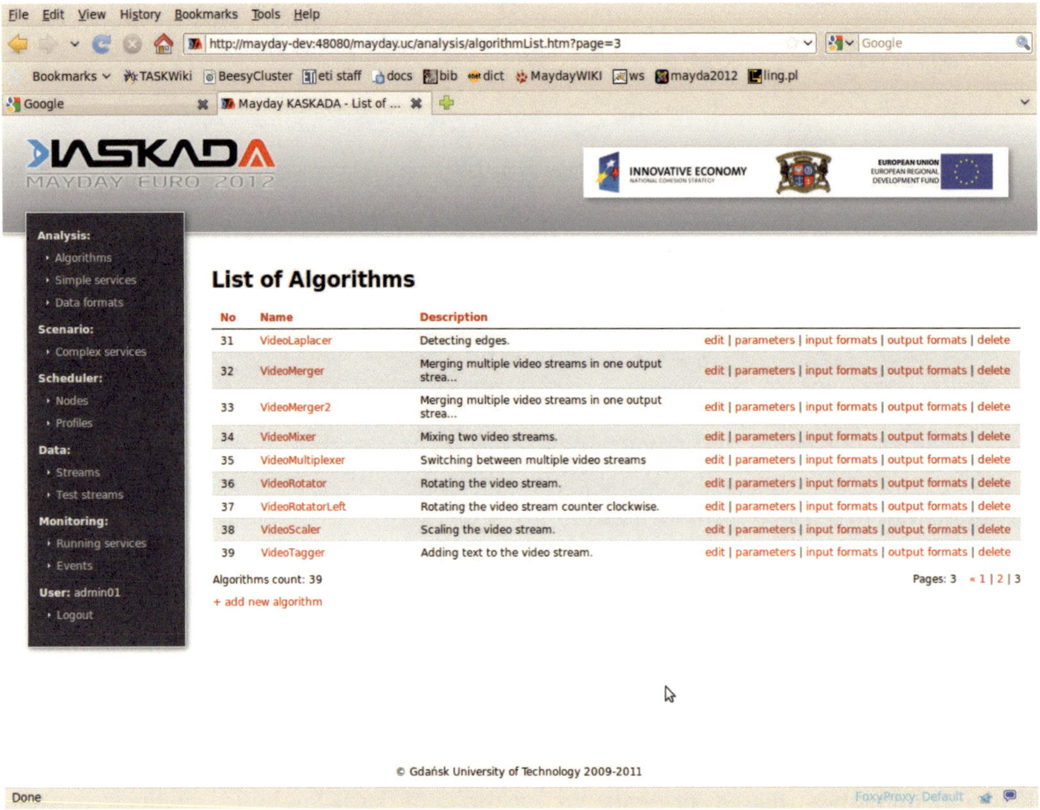

Fig. 9. An example of implemented algorithms in GUI of the KASAKDA platform

The algorithms, implemented in the KASKADA platform can be based on different processing paradigms. They vary from the typical high performance numeric computations, through different heuristics like different classifiers, Haar cascade, to more sophisticated artificial intelligence solutions like identification of objects by GHM (Gaussian Mixture Model), Kaman filter and codebook model, or even expert-systems for endoscopies disease recognition.

Similarly to algorithms, the simple services are described by their metadata, including: a service name, the description, input and quality parameters. Additionally, the implemented algorithms realizing the suitable service can be easily point out by simple name selection from the list. Every selected algorithm can use the service input parameters passed during its execution, however their handling is optional.

The developer can start the service in two modes: by remote call or using a web browser. For testing/debugging purposes the latter one is more feasible, when she/he just needs to introduce the parameter values and click the "start" button. Both modes are provided automatically by the platform, just after the service definition. Fig. 10 presents the steps for service definition and execution. After successful initiation, the developer can check the result data stream and the events in the messages generated by the algorithm and logged in the special logs.

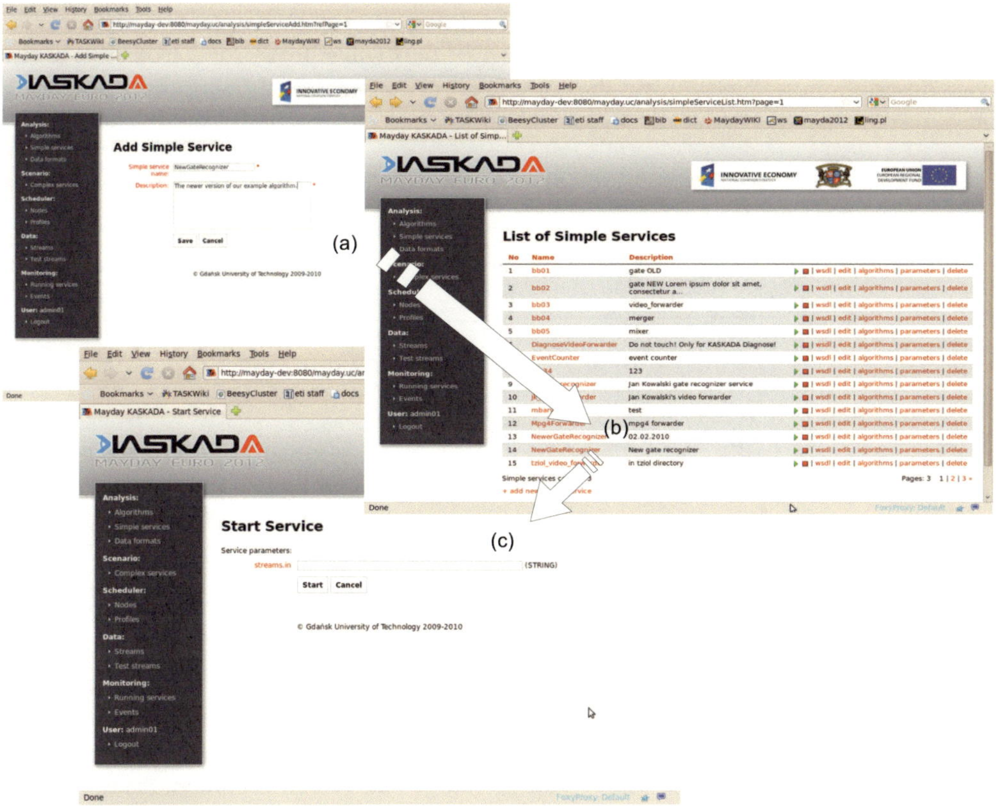

Fig. 10. Steps required to add and execute a simple service: (a) service definition, (b) service selection from the list, (c) entering input parameters

The remote call of a simple service can be realized using HTTP/SOAP protocols. In such a case the programmer is responsible for a proper implementation of client being part of user application. To simplify this process, the KASKADA platform provides its own UDDI registry, where the services are described using always-updated documents in WSDL format.

4.3 Simple to complex service transformation

Similarly to a simple service solution, the complex services are accessible by a web browser or through the external interface based on SOAP/HTTP protocol. The choice also depends on the input and quality parameters, and accept the multimedia streams as an input. They aggregate simple services within execution scenarios. ie. in more complex structures, which extends their functionality.

Fig. 11a presents an example of an execution scenario, discussed in section 3. The scenario can be described by XML language as a set of simple services and input/output data stream definitions, see Fig. 11b. The document is created by the developer using a typical text editor, or a specialized language: MSP-ML. Based on this we entered a GUI interface as the proper form as shown in Fig. 11c.

Every single service needs to have provided input and quality parameters, specific to its underlying algorithm. They can be introduced in two ways: forwarded from the complex service description, or fixed during the complex service definition. Using this approach, we achieve flexibility required for the service execution.

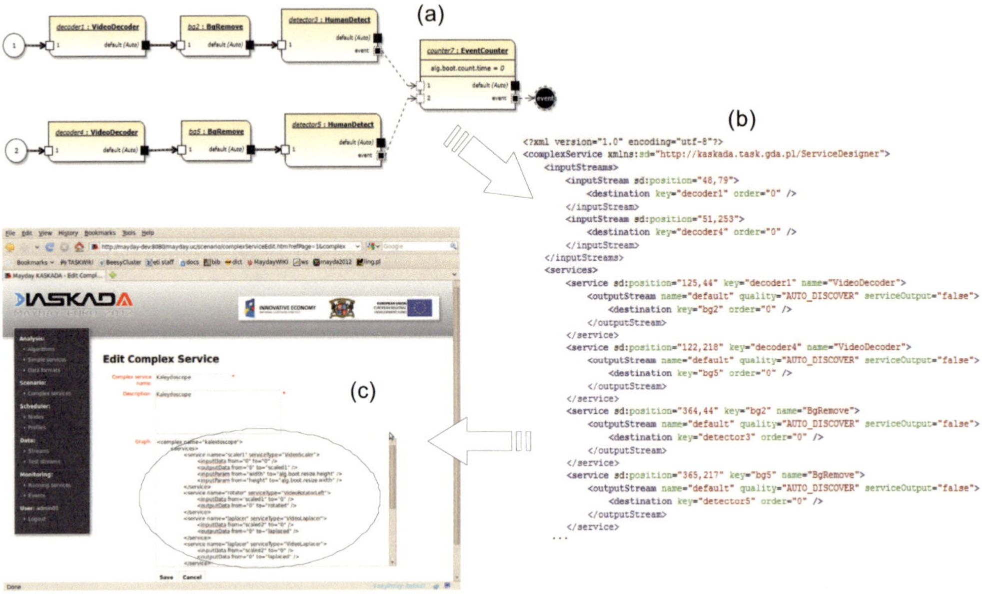

Fig. 11. From complex service scenario definition (a) trough XML document (b) to GUI service definition (c)

5. Execution environment for multimedia stream processing

We distinguish four domains of the platform management during service execution: (1) data, (2) computations, (3) communication, and (4) resources. Data as real-time streams of the incoming multimedia data either video or audio, need to be archived and distributed among computation tasks. Computation means the stream processing tasks, which are involved by instructions of program. Communication is understood as message exchange mechanisms enabling distribution of the events among service components and sending to the external client. Finally, the cluster resources are engaged in computations and constantly observed by the monitoring mechanisms, including checking and reacting on the inappropriate usage of the network, CPU and memory.

5.1 Data – Multimedia stream management

The multimedia data streams are generated by a geographically distributed set of video cameras and microphones. They need to be delivered to the computation center and preprocessed for further analysis. The number of streams, and their characteristics, demands the usage of a high bandwidth optic fiber network.

Fig. 12 shows the view of the multimedia streams in the considered platform regarding the users, as well as the external applications using the platform functionality. The arriving data needs to be received, validated, and archived, due to additional offline analysis and legal concerns. The above operations are performed by the tasks controlled by the management server. The server can also cooperate directly with the stream sources. Preprocessing is used to unpack the stream data from its native protocol, usually RTSP, and forward it to the proper analysis tasks located on the computational nodes using an Infiniband network. The higher platform efficiency can be achieved by allocation of tasks with streams to more cluster nodes. A special set of the cluster's computational nodes is assigned to perform such tasks using the high performance network file system LUSTRE. Physically, the data is stored on a specific data server with high performance 500TB hard drives.

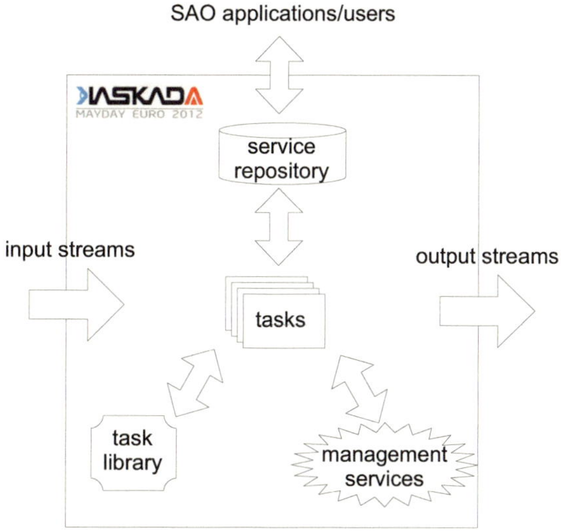

Fig. 12. Data and user interoperability of the KASKADA

The various algorithms exposed as services can consume incoming streams and produce messages (as events created during the analysis) as well as new output streams, which should be delivered to the user. See the next section for more details about the flow of events.

The information about produced output streams are sent back to the stream management server nodes and they are ready to be delivered to the selected users. It can be done by the user console module. The stream-related functionalities of the user console cover:

- registration and testing of new multimedia (audio or video) streams,
- configuring the meta-data of the stream, including codec, fps, width, height etc.,
- archive configuration with individual settings of each stream,
- creation (by upload or archive selection) of the test streams used for benchmarking and testing of the algorithms,
- playing and replaying of the live or archived streams.

5.2 Communication – Event management

An application controlling the processing of the started service can receive the results of the predicted analysis by means of event processing. An event, as specified in section 1, is information generated by a task belonging to the service, which is potentially important for external applications or their users. Such information is expressed by a message transported in XML document format. The type of the message and its content are determined by the particular algorithm implemented by the task. It is not compulsory for the task to finish its work after creating and issuing an event; the multimedia streams can be processed continuously causing generation of many events for different situations detected in the streams during their processing. Such series of the events can be conceived as the events stream or the data stream (Olken & Gruenwald, 2008). The processing of such a data stream can be focused on the selected events, treating them independently, or as the sequence of events, where state-aware operations analyze one event after another.

Fig. 13 shows the event processing idea in the KASKADA platform; starting from the event creation, through event handling and ending with the special message being passed to the specified destinations.

The tasks belonging to the service searching media streams, with respect to detection of special object and/or particular situations. The successful detection of such situations causes generation of an event containing information about its origin and processed media time, apart from data related to the particular event type. Then, each event is passed to an Event Handling Module through the message queue maintained by Apache ActiveMQ. The choice of ActiveMQ as the message queue provider is, among other things, determined by different technologies, C++ and JEE, being the runtime environments for the event processing flow elements. The Event Handling Module performs the operations during event processing, such as save, apply events, create and send message (see Fig. 13).

Operation: Saves the event in repository: each event incoming to the Event Handling Module is stored for administrative and safety purposes, using the Events Repository mechanisms. The storage structures associate the event with the data stream related to the service in order to enable later backtracking of the selected service results. Using the information about the service-starting details, preserved by the KASKADA platform, and the archive of media streams, it is possible for the particular event to reconstruct the conditions which led to such an event generation.

Operation: Applies filters to the event: the user console of the KASKADA platform supports a choice of filters applicable to the event processing. A filter can be applied to check if particular properties of the event fulfill criteria defined for that filter. The criteria for a filter can specify a service or XPath expression. If there is consistency between XML content of the event and the specified filter settings, the service and the expression, the event becomes active.

Operation: Sends the event message to the channels: the filter applied to the processed event contains one or more channels. A channel represents a final destination for the information about processed event. The XML message describing the active event is delivered to the recipients specified by details of each channel. The information contained in the channel details is determined by the channel type which represents the transport mechanism used by the particular channel. The currently-supported channel types are the e-mail type and the JMS compliant message queue system type. Nevertheless, the KASKADA platform is ready to support additional types, and also for implementing the transport mechanisms related to them.

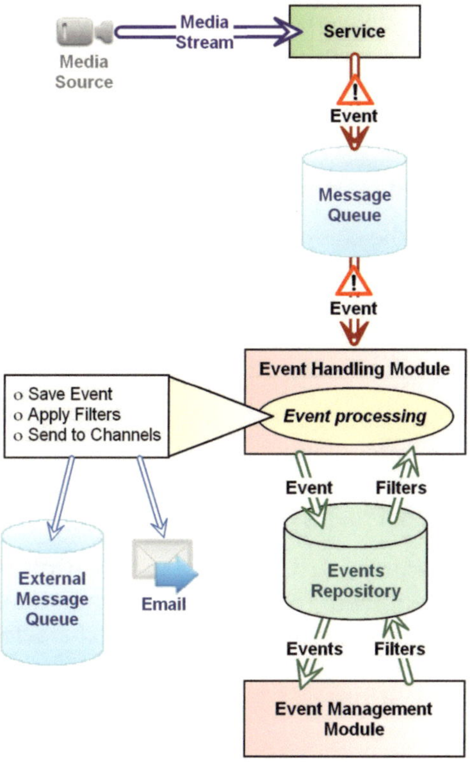

Fig. 13. Event processing idea in the KASKADA platform

An Event Management Module is a part of the user console of the KASKADA platform; and, as other modules of the console, is designed to work with an end-user in an interactive mode. There are a few functionalities supported by the module (apart from the described-above definition) and management of event filters. The module makes available a real-time monitoring of incoming events related to the particular service while it is still running. The console user can inspect the archived event streams, for example searching for particular circumstances. The module allows replaying the part of the archived media stream related to the selected event during its examination, adjusting the time frame of the played part if necessary.

Different types of destination channels open the KASKADA platform to the various technologies of implementation of the applications receiving the results of calculations of services. Apart from the technology, there are two typical scenarios of the interoperability of the user applications and the KASKADA platform. The scenarios can be described as follows:

- The operator of an external, interactive, application starts a service through the application monitoring mechanisms. Then, the application processes incoming events and stops the service; for example after receiving a particular event, presenting the operator with the processing results. The above sequence applies to the processing of a selected part of the stream, as a result of a more general, continuous, analysis.
- The advanced, distributed, application automatically starts a service with mechanisms contained in one of its components. The started service, without stopping its work,

generates events which are delivered to another component of the same application, or even to another application. The scenario separates the management of a service execution from the pure event processing, allowing the application to be more flexible and modularized on a high level.

5.3 Computation – Service and task management

As was described in section 1, the complex services are executed as a set of simple services according to the describing scenario. The simple services are realized by the computation tasks, which in turn are represented by the processes and threads in the cluster environment (see Fig. 1 for comparison). The tasks need to be placed in a suitable computation node, according to the appropriate task schedule achieving the required computation time.

The typical problem of task scheduling is defined as assignment of a set of tasks into the set of computational nodes in an order to execute them in minimal time. It is proved, the above problem is NP-hard for the general case, and there exists a polynomial solution for task scheduling on two computational nodes (El-Rewini & Lewis, 1994).

The proposed architecture assumes that tasks are executed continuously, consuming and producing data streams. Each of them requires concrete computational power to realize the provided functionality. We assume that due to the character of multimedia stream processing, the tasks require real-time execution, and they cannot be queued and started with delay in the sequence one by one.

We propose a specific a task-to-nodes assignment strategy regarding the above constraints. The tasks could be assigned to the computational nodes, which are able to execute them directly. Otherwise, if there no such nodes exist in the cluster, the service scenario (scheduled tasks) is not executed, its execution is refused and signalized to the user. To minimize the occurrences of such cases the platform should optimize its selection using the criteria of minimizing the fragmentation.

In such a way the assignment strategy is quite similar to the well-known bin packing problem (BPP) (Garey & Johnson, 1979), especially its version with the variable bin sizes (VBPP) (Haouari & Serairi, 2009). Typical BPP minimizes the number of baskets (computational nodes in our case) used for packing a set of objects (tasks). The version with the basket variable sizes introduces additionally a finite set of basket types with different sizes. An exact algorithm for (V)BPP is NP-hard (Garey & Johnson, 1979).

In the proposed assignment strategy we can use as many baskets of possible type (size) as we need, but the number of each type is finite. Moreover, the optimisation goals are different, VBPP minimizes the number of used baskets and our startegy considers the number of partially used nodes.

The fragmentation factor indicates the number of nodes partially engaged in task processing. Fig. 14 shows a situation where a new heavy task cannot be assigned to any node, because all nodes (c_1- c_4) offer less computation power than it is needed for the task t ($\Phi(t)=6$). In (Krawczyk & Proficz, 2010a), we proposed a few heuristic algorithms to minimize the fragmentation what in turn enables execution of more tasks with high load, ie. $\Phi(t)=6$ in the example.

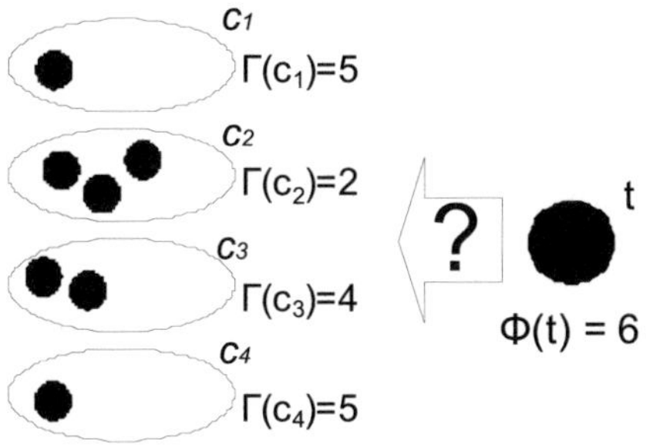

Fig. 14. Example of the cluster fragmentation preventing a new task assignment

5.4 Resources monitoring

In the case of the KASKADA platform we distinguish three kinds of resource characteristics: network bandwidth, memory size and CPU load. According to the assumptions described in the previous section, each computation task needs to have guaranteed the proper amount of the resources, and the tasks behaving incorrectly have to be deactivated and their service stopped. Moreover the monitoring information needs to be presented to the external client using either GUI or by the webservice interface.

The KASKADA platform monitor is responsible for the following functionality:

- managing the services and tasks,
- monitoring the current resources utilization,
- informing the user about the tasks' errors and exceptions,
- logging the information about the platform, services and tasks behavior,
- checking the computational node states related to network connection and file system behavior.

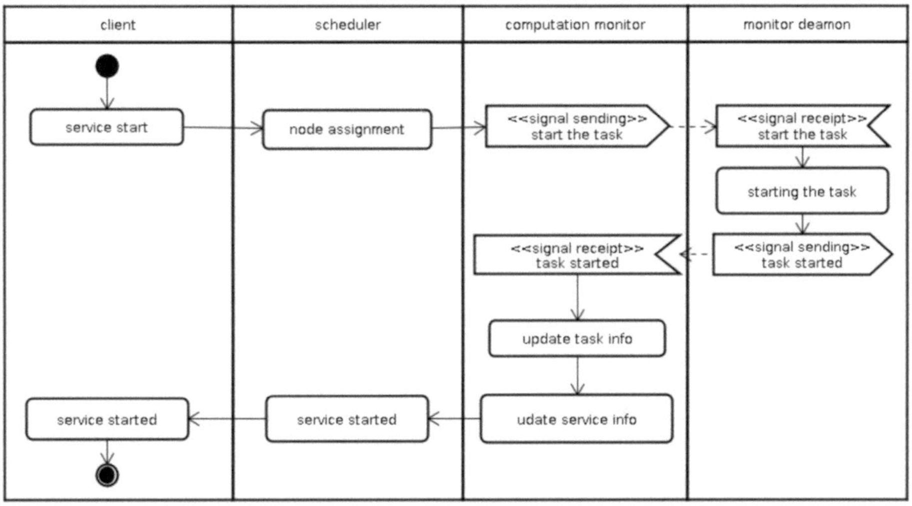

Fig. 15. The basic activities for starting a service in the KASKADA platform

The KASKADA monitor consists of two functional components: computation monitor - the central component keeping the states of the services and their tasks and monitor daemon, running on every single cluster node, which cooperates directly with the tasks, gathering the information and executing orders from the computation monitor. Fig. 15 shows an example diagram of the scheduler and both monitor components when the user starts a service.

6. KASKADA – Architectural design and realization

6.1 Software architecture

The proposed in section 3 processing model was implemented as the KASKADA platform. Fig. 16 presents the main classes to satisfy functional requirements. From the user's point of view the main goal of the platform is to provide the webservices based on SOA architecture. They will be responsible for execution of the complex service scenarios supported by simple services. The example sequential diagram of the scenario execution is presented in figure 17.

Both service types, i.e. simple and complex ones, are going to be deployed on the same JEE application server, we consider using a Tomcat web container for this purpose. They will utilize SOAP technologies over HTTP(S) protocol, in case of synchronous remote calls, and a queue system, i.e. ActiveMQ for asynchronous communication within JMS interface. The result return will be performed in separated objects (and components): Event Handler for messages and Dispatcher for multimedia streams.

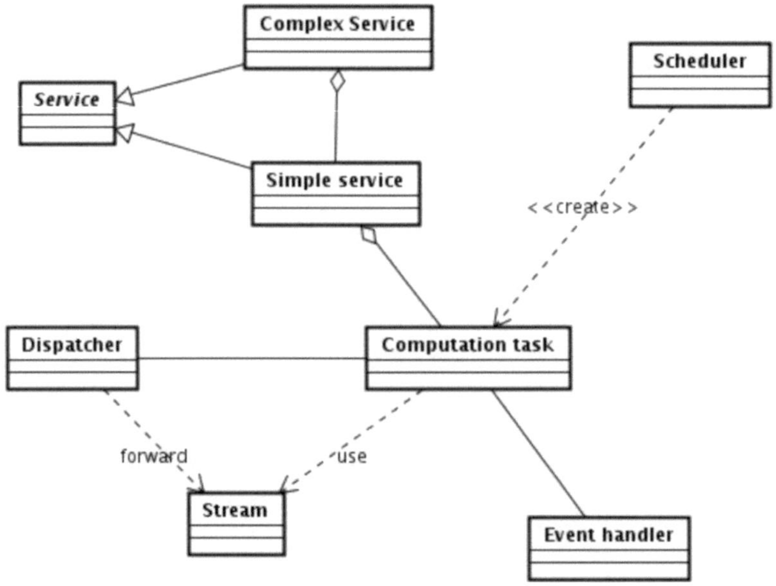

Fig. 16. Domain class diagram of the KASKADA platform

According to the assumed processing model, simple services manage the distribution of the input and output data streams among computational tasks. The object of classes Dispatcher and Scheduler support this functionality. Moreover, the responsibility of the Dispatcher object is the stream recording in the storage and sending them back to the client. The example sequential diagram of the simple service execution is presented in Fig. 18.

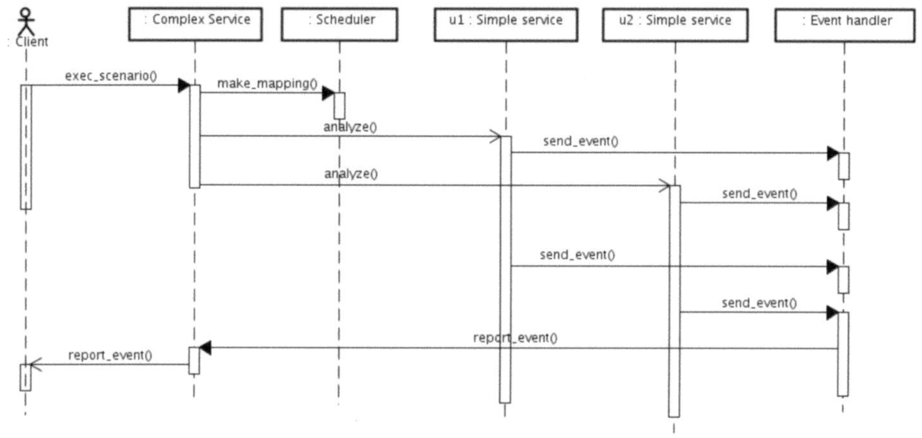

Fig. 17. A sequence diagram of the complex service execution within the domain model (see Fig. 16)

Computational tasks - the executable code of the multimedia stream analysis algorithms embedded in the framework accomplish the appropriate computations. They receive the multimedia streams generated by a camera, microphone, or other device (e.g. medical equipment), make the required analysis and transformation and send an output data stream including discovered events to the proper components, mainly to Event Handler and Dispatcher, forwarding them through the service layers to the clients - a users or an external applications (see Fig. 19).

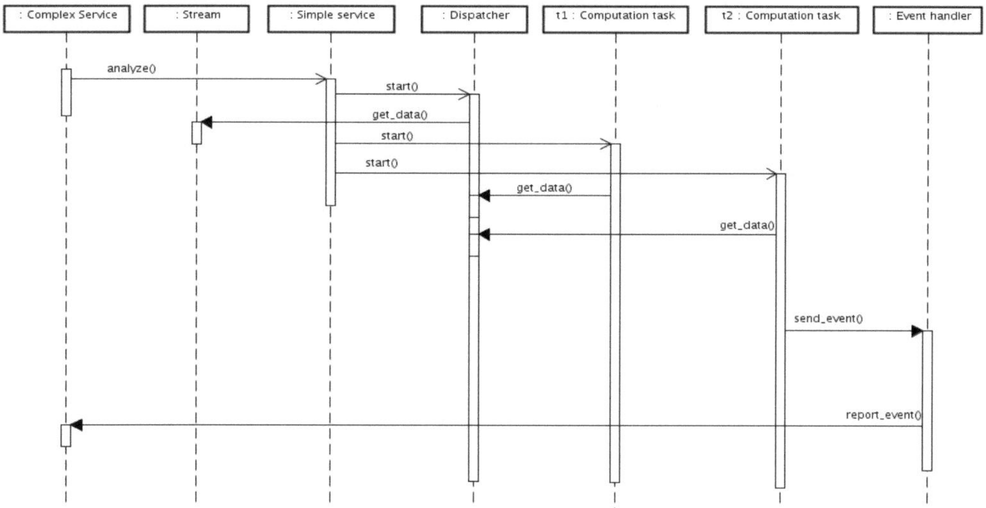

Fig. 18. A sequence diagram of the simple service execution within the domain model (see Fig. 16)

During the algorithm implementation, the programmer can use software components provided by the computation cluster environment: POSIX threads and openMP library for shared memory processing and object serialization (supported by boost library) for object data exchange between the computational tasks.

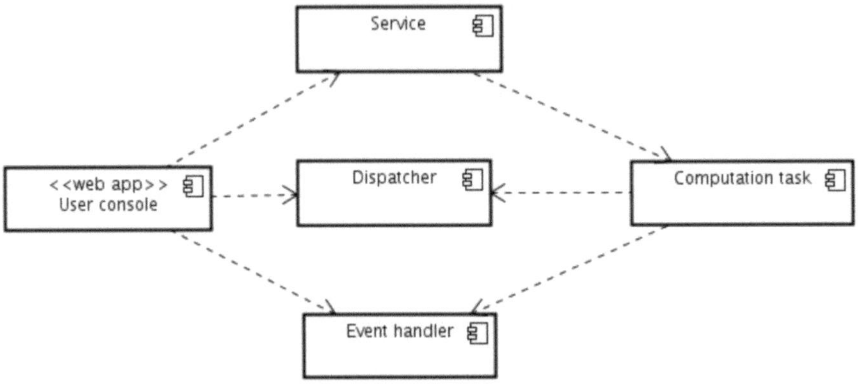

Fig. 19. Component diagram of the KASKADA platform

Almost all the above domain classes presented in Fig. 16 can be straightforwardly converted into the software components of the proposed platform. The only exception is the User Console component which aggregates Scheduler class as well as manages the other platform components including operations on the multimedia and other data streams (especially in off-line mode - using recorded data), security and service configuration and deployment (a service repository with the WSDL and UDDI support).

User console functionality is provided through a web interface and can be easily accessed with an Internet browser. For its development, we use JEE standard supported by an application server, i.e. a Tomcat web-container, including technologies: JSP and AJAX.

6.2 Hardware architecture

To execute computation tasks all software components should be deployed on the computer cluster. Fig. 20 presents the deployment diagram including hardware nodes with the assigned software components. The core of the platform is the cluster which consists of 672 two-processor (Intel) nodes connected by the fast Infiniband network, each processor has 8 cores, which gives in total 5376 cores.

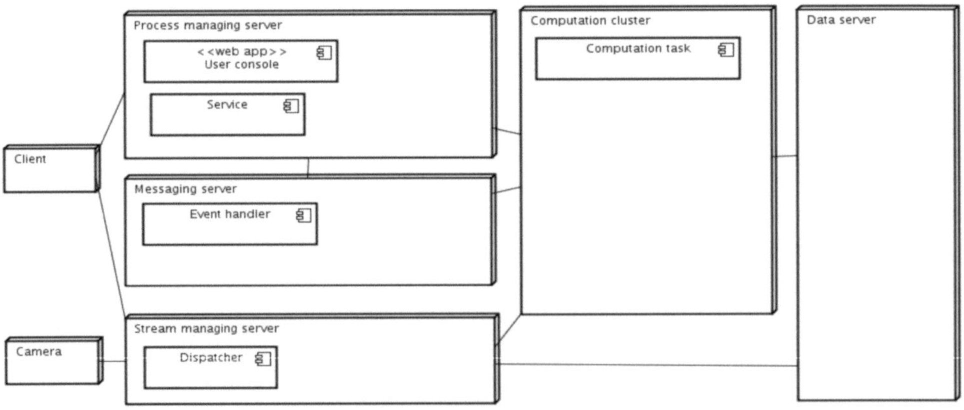

Fig. 20. Deployment diagram of KASKADA platform

The stream managing sever is responsible for multimedia stream format and communication protocol conversion, enabling its usage by the computational tasks and receiving by the clients. It is especially important due to the large number of streams, and network load minimizing strategy: some cameras or other devices, do not support multicast data transmission, so it needs to be provided by the platform. The Dispatcher component is responsible for this functionality, as well as stream recording and archiving.

The process managing server is responsible for direct cooperation with the client software. Here are deployed services and the User console component. It is prepared for serving a large number of webservices, the simple ones - which are easily mapped to the computational tasks - as well as the complex ones, executing the scenarios.

The messaging server supports the Event handler component. It enables receiving, analysis and former processing of the data (but not multimedia) streams containing discovered events. It cooperates with the process managing server where the event related services are deployed.

The data server is used for recorded data storage. We use high performance hard drives with 500TB capacity and the Lustre file system, the server is going to be connected to the cluster and other servers by the Infiniband network, for its low delay and high bandwidth.

7. Applications available in KASKADA platform

The KASKADA platform was heavily tested for two pilot applications, developed as a proof of concept of the proposed multimedia processing model: identification of dangerous objects and unusual situations (DOUS) occurring in multimedia streams coming from cameras located in different places, and medical recommender for endoscopy examinations (MREE) showing some disease changes in film taken during gastroscopy track. The former is used for automation of typical video and audio surveillance tasks, like dangerous person identification or left luggage detection. The latter helps medical staff to quickly find the possible lesions in the video recorded during endoscopy examinations. Table 1 presents the usage of the platform features by the applications.

Functional feature	DOUS	MREE
video processing	yes	yes
audio processing	yes	no
real-time analysis	yes	no
streaming server	yes	yes
simple services	yes	yes
complex services with scenarios	yes	yes
test streams	yes	yes

Table 1. The main KASKADA platform functional features available for the applications

Quality characteristics are one of the most important features evaluating the whole platform behavior. During the platform analysis and design, we found out we need to focus on four key factors: performance, scalability, dependability and security. Performance is crucial for real-time processing, both processor speed and network bandwidth need to be examined, for the platform to work in the real environment. The scalability is another important factor, especially when large numbers of the input streams need to be archived, processed, and transmitted back to the customer. Moreover, even the high performance solutions can't provide the satisfactory results until they are dependable (the designed algorithms are correct and acceptable for various conditions), and finally the character of the processed streams, including surveillance and medical data, requires high security protecting access from unauthorized persons. The above applications, especially DOUS, can achieve the appropriate public security level using strategy illustrated in Fig. 21.

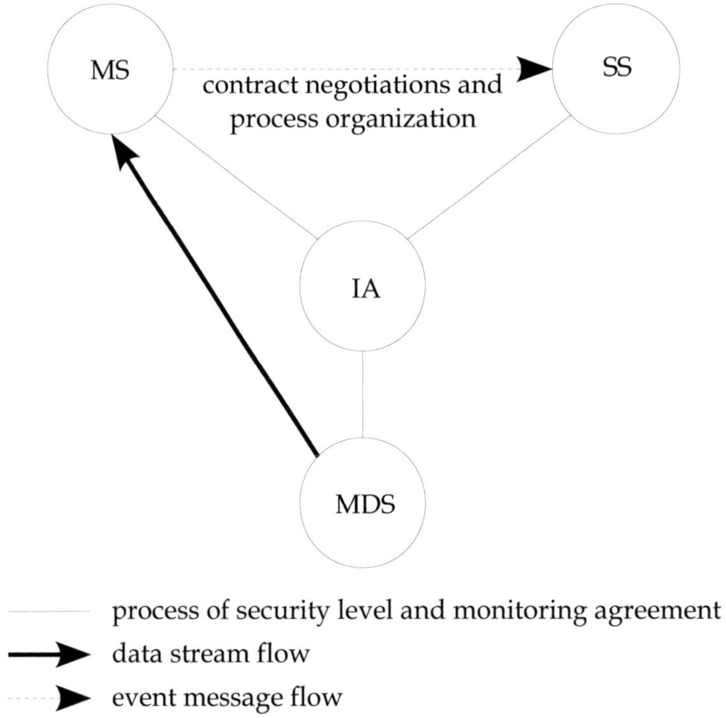

Fig. 21. Public security agreement strategy, MS - monitoring systems, SS - service services, IA - intermediary agency to provide SLA (service level agreement), MDS - multiple data sources

8. Conclusion

The KASKADA platform is designed to cooperate with external systems and applications. We decided to use a typical approach based on the SOA architecture with support for both synchronous and asynchronous communication, and implement a typical HTTP/SOAP protocol to start the exposed functionality, and message-passing queue system, supporting JMS and XMPP protocols to return the results of the long-lasting processing.

The platform is developed using agile development process principles, so the possible updates and new features can be added quite quickly, from one iteration to another, with release of a new version. The platform itself is flexible with easy and extensive configuration enabling quick adaptation to a new environment, or volume of the problem. With possible virtualization and cloud computing support.

The KASKADA platform is already developed and deployed in the Academic Computer Center of Gdansk University of Technology in Poland. The current development is focused on the quality tests related mostly to the performance and scalability characteristics. The whole project, including the proposed applications, is going to be finalized in 2012.

In the future we plan to continue development of new applications based on the currently available services, as well as new algorithms for the various multimedia processing problems, with a special focus on massive stream processing and various quality parameters, like dependability and security.

9. Acknowledgment

The work was realized as a part of MAYDAY EURO 2012 project, Operational Program Innovative Economy 2007-2013, Priority 2 "Infrastructure area R&D".

10. References

Breuer D., Erwin D., Mallmann D., Menday R., Romberg M., Sander V., Schuller B., Wieder P. (2004) Scientific Computing with UNICORE, NIC Symposium, ISBN: 3-00-012372-5, Forschungszentrum Jülich, February 2004

El-Rewini H., Lewis T. G., Ali H. H. (1994) Task Scheduling in Parallel and Distributed Systems, Prentice-Hall Series In Innovative Technology, ISBN: 978-013-0992-35-2

Foster I., Kesselman C. (1997) Globus: A metacomputing infrastructure toolkit, International Journal of Supercomputer Applications, Vol. 11, No. 2, (June 1997) pp. 115-128, ISSN: 1094-3420

Garey M. R., Johnson D. S. (1979) Computer and Intractability: A guide to the Theory of NP-Completeness, W. H. Freeman, ISBN: 978-071-6710-45-5

Haouari M., Serairi M. (2009) Heuristics for the variable sized bin-packing problem, Computers & Operational Research, Vol. 36, No. 10, (October 2009), pp. 2877-2884, ISSN: 0305-0548

Krawczyk H., Proficz J. (2010) The task graph assignment for KASKADA platform, Proceedings of International Conference on Software and Data Technologies, ISBN: 978-989-8425-22-5, Greece Athens, July 2010

Krawczyk H., Proficz J. (2010b) KASKADA - multimedia processing platform architecture, Proceedings of Signal Processing and Multimedia Applications, ISBN: 978-989-8425-19-5, Greece Athens, July 2010

Olken F., Gruenwald L. (2008) Data Stream Management: Aggregation, Classification, Modeling, and Operator Placement, IEEE Internet Computing, Vol. 12, No. 6, (November 2008), pp. 9-12, ISSN: 1089-7801

Yu T., Zhou B., Li Q., Liu R., Wang W., Chang Ch. (2009) The Design of Distributed Real-time Video Analytic System, Proceedings of CloudDB'09, ISBN: 978-160-5588-02-5, China, Hong Kong, November 2009